Peasants in Distress

Series in Political Economy and Economic Development in Latin America

Series Editor
Andrew Zimbalist
Smith College

Peasants in Distress: Poverty and Unemployment in the Dominican Republic, Rosemary Vargas-Lundius

Distorted Development: Mexico in the World Economy, David Barkin

State and Capital in Mexico: Development Policy Since 1940, James M. Cypher

Central America: The Future of Economic Integration, edited by George Irvin and Stuart Holland

Struggle Against Dependence: Nontraditional Export Growth in Central America and the Caribbean, edited by Eva Paus

The Peruvian Mining Industry: Growth, Stagnation, and Crisis, Elizabeth Dore

Cuban Political Economy: Controversies in Cubanology, edited by Andrew Zimbalist

† *Rural Women and State Policy: Feminist Perspectives on Latin American Agricultural Development*, edited by Carmen Diana Deere and Magdalena León

†Available in hardcover and paperback.

Peasants in Distress

Poverty and Unemployment in the Dominican Republic

Rosemary Vargas-Lundius

Westview Press
Boulder • San Francisco • Oxford

Series in Political Economy and Economic Development in Latin America

This Westview softcover edition is printed on acid-free paper and bound in library-quality, coated covers that carry the highest rating of the National Association of Textbook Administrators, in consultation with the Association of American Publishers and the Book Manufacturers' Institute.

Published in 1991 in the United States of America by Westview Press, Inc., 5500 Central Avenue, Boulder, Colorado 80301, and in the United Kingdom by Westview Press, Inc., 36 Lonsdale Road, Summertown, Oxford OX2 7EW

Library of Congress Cataloging-in-Publication Data
Vargas-Lundius, Rosemary.
  Peasants in Distress : poverty and unemployment in the Dominican
Republic / by Rosemary Vargas-Lundius.
     p. cm.—(Series in political economy and economic
development in Latin America)
  Includes bibliographical references and index.
  ISBN 0-8133-7972-5
  1. Peasantry—Dominican Republic. 2. Rural poor—Dominican
Republic. 3. Unemployment—Dominican Republic. 4. Labor supply—
Dominican Republic. I. Title. II. Series.
HD1531.D6V36   1991
331.13'797293—dc20   90-32923
                                                                      CIP

Printed and bound in the United States of America

The paper used in this publication meets the requirements
of the American National Standard for Permanence of Paper
for Printed Library Materials Z39.48-1984.

10   9   8   7   6   5   4   3   2   1

Contents

Tables and Figures

Figures

Preface

All writing, I believe, regardless of whether it deals with fact or fiction, is largely influenced by the author's life experience. This work is no exception. I was born and raised in a small Dominican village and many years of schooling in Europe have not changed that fact. I belonged to a family that by village standards was not so poor. But already as a child I was confronted with the harsh living conditions that prevail in the Dominican countryside. I had to walk for hours to the school of the nearest town but I was still privileged since many children of my village could not even afford the obligatory school uniform. From an early age I was troubled by the presence of poverty and injustice around me. Why was it so bad to be a *campesino*? Why should *campesinos* live such a wretched life? If, as I often heard, earth was a gift from God, why was not land enjoyed equally? Why did a few own a lot and others so little, or none? Why was it so bad to have kinky hair, dark skin, or to be a Haitian?

I sought the answers to these questions in school. Doña Diega, my first teacher, used to say that education is the answer to everything. I also saw it as a means to avoid the life of a peasant and to an opportunity to enjoy the "comfortable" city life. After finishing high school, I realized that I had not found adequate answers to all my questions. On the contrary, they had multiplied by then. I wanted to continue my education, something that was rather unusual in my village at that time. The common opinion was that it was no use to invest in higher education for a girl, since after marriage she would become a housewife anyway.

I went to Santo Domingo in 1969, entered the university and supported myself through various odd jobs. There was no question about which career to choose. Since I had to work during daytime, the only courses available at late hours were the ones at the Department of Social and Economic Sciences. After three years of studies in Business Administration, I was not really satisfied. Driven by my endless search, I decided to leave the Dominican Republic. Almost twenty years later, I am still at the university, now at the Department of Economics at the University of Lund.

My postgraduate studies began when, in 1979, Professor Mats Lundahl took interest in an undergraduate paper of mine concerning the Dominican economy. He encouraged me to continue with my research. The interest of Mats Lundahl was not only due to his professional obligations as supervisor. He also happened to have a profound knowledge of and interest in questions related to the island of Hispaniola, which the Dominican Republic shares with Haiti. He had already written an outstanding study on Haiti and probably saw me as the potential writer of a similar study on the other part of the island. He offered me constant encouragement and his engagement proved to be different and probably more extensive than could be expected from a supervisor. I am very grateful to him but I fear I have not been able to live up to his initial expectations.

When I embarked on the task of writing this work, I had a somewhat naïve dream of being a spokesperson for the Dominican peasants. Many years of studies have given me the opportunity to view the problems from a more distant perspective and analyze the situation of the peasantry in an objective way. Through the years, I have gained some insights into the reasons behind the different problems that afflict the peasantry and the Dominican economy in general. At the same time, however, I feel that the presence and voices of the peasants have been drowned in the writing process. I have therefore given the word to a peasant and present his views in the prologue to this work.

Julio's and Ana's names and the name of their village are fictitious. The visits there took place during the period 1980-85. I let them represent the hope and strivings of many other rural dwellers and before I offer my acknowledgements I would like to state that my greatest indebtedness is to the people who unlike myself still struggle to make a living in the Dominican countryside and to those who cherish the hope of a better life in the city slums.

My journey from the small village of El Mamey-Altamira to Lund took a long time and the path was both winding and toilsome. Many people helped me in the Dominican Republic, Santiago de Chile, Buenos Aires, Caracas, New York and Los Angeles where I spent some years before coming to Sweden in the mid-seventies. I would like to thank them all but space does not allow me to name every one of them. However, I would like to express my gratitude to Anders and Birgitta Lundin and their parents, who through their friendship and hospitality aided me in taking up my studies in Sweden. The unconditional help of Charlotte Holmén, foreign student adviser at the University of Lund, was of decisive importance for the accomplishment of my undergraduate studies.

At the Department of Economics, I benefited a lot from the exhaustive International Economics seminars under the chairmanship of my supervisor, Mats Lundahl. None of my emotionally colored arguments found mercy under his scrutinizing eye. His comments greatly improved the structure and content of my work and I am very grateful for that.

I am deeply indebted to the ex-Head of the Department, Göte Hansson, and to my colleague and friend Anders Danielson, who both took on not only the arduous task of reading the manuscript several times, but also served as my *paño de lagrimas* in my most difficult moments. Their help has been of great value for accomplishing this work.

My field work in the Dominican Republic was facilitated by small grants from SAREC, SIDA, and Alice and Knut Wallenbergs Minnesfond. I benefited a lot from the experience that I gained from working at the Department of Agricultural Economics in the Ministry of Agriculture in the Dominican Republic. The Head of the Department, Joaquín Nolasco, was kind enough to let me participate in the CENSERI project in spite of my limited experience. I am grateful to Garibaldi Pezzotti and his staff, as well as to the different peasants with whom I came in contact.

Special thanks are due to Don Luis Crouch, who was kind enough to give me his support in various ways. Frank Marino Hernández as well as Frank Moya Pons and his staff at the Fondo para el Avance de las Ciencias Sociales were also of great help by assisting me in obtaining valuable contacts and information from libraries and institutions.

I am also grateful to the Universidad Católica Madre y Maestra and its rector Monseñor Agripino Núñez who gave me the opportunity to participate in the program of Applied Economics at the Recinto Santo Tomás de Aquino, where I learned a lot from both my students and colleagues.

At IICA, Jerry LaGra was of great help and Michel Montoya became a good and generous friend. At USAID, Mr. Castro offered me valuable information and my dear friend Lisa Early did the same, as well as being a good companion in my spare time. I owe special thanks to Jeffrey Poyo and Hector Guilliani at the Banco Central, Miguel Ceara at INESPRE, Nelson Ramírez at IEPD, Maritza García at ONAPLAN, Orlando Sánchez at the Banco Agrícola, Darío Jiménez, Antonio Núñez and their fellow *camioneros* at the Mercado Nuevo, and to the library staff at UCMM in Santo Domingo, ONE and Casa de los Bibliófilos.

Last, but not least, I want to thank my dear friend Michiel Baud, who has taken great pains in reading the manuscript and contributed with countless and valuable suggestions to improve my work. I also want to thank Professor Kumaraswamy Velupillai for inspiration and enlightenment.

In spite of all the acknowledged help, the accomplishment of this book would not have been possible without the love and patience of my husband, Jan Lundius, and my daughter, Janna Natalia. The first has been my warmest supporter and my hardest critic, the latter, the best thing that happened in my life. Both have helped me to combine the invariably conflicting tasks of motherhood and work. The support and encouragement of all my relatives and friends have been invaluable.

***

This book is a new edition of the Ph.D. thesis I presented at the University of Lund in 1988. In preparing this edition I benefited from comments provided by Professor Claudio González-Vega, Claes Brundenius and Rolf Olsson. The assistance of José Alfredo Guerrero, Susana Sánchez and all my friends at the Fundación Economía y Desarrollo, Inc., is also highly appreciated.

Rosemary Vargas-Lundius
Lund, Sweden

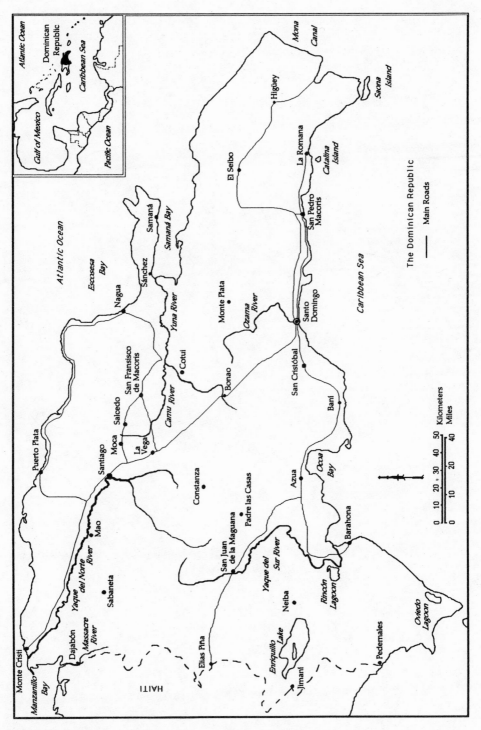

The Dominican Republic

—— Main Roads

Prologue:
The Voice That Was Never Heard

Monte Río is peasant country. You meet the peasants riding on their mules or on small, ragged horses. You see them sitting on the porches of their pastel-colored wooden houses, or working with machetes and hoes under the burning sun. A narrow and winding road cuts through a landscape dominated by undulating mountain ranges, with pastures and fields creeping up along the slopes. On the hillsides you may still see giant solitary trees with rich foliage, or even small subtropical forests. A long draught was recently followed by eagerly awaited rains and the countryside is now embellished with different shades of a fresh and lush greenness.

The town closest to Monte Río is called Altamira, a small place with only one street, since it is surrounded on each side by two deep ravines. Altamira is situated nearby the main road that connects Santiago with the busy port and tourist center of Puerto Plata. The small road that leads from Altamira to Monte Río was built by President Joaquín Balaguer not so many years ago. If you ask a peasant living in the Monte Río area what has been the most positive change during the last few decades, he would probably answer: "The road." The road has opened up his world and brought him closer to the urban areas, widened his outlook and made social services, such as medical care and education, more accessible than before. But it has also tied him closer to the market economy and put his own way of living in sharp contrast to the sort of life he might enjoy as a wage laborer in town. Monte Río is not a poor place, compared with the desolate places you may come across in, for example, the dry areas of the Southwest. In Monte Río you may still find the shade of large trees and you do not have to walk too far in order to find water. Nevertheless, most peasants' existence there means a constant struggle for life, against odds that sometimes seem impossible to overcome.

In Monte Río you do not find small villages with houses lying close to each other along a village road or around a small plaza. Here the houses are spread along the road, or lay a bit further away among the hills close to their owners' small plots. Julio lives by the road not far from a bridge that spans a deep ravine with a little creek, that once was a river. His house is up on a steep mountainside; a blue-painted wooden cabin, with red windowframes, neat and tidy like most Dominican peasant dwellings. He shares his home with his wife Ana and their nine children: seven girls and two boys. Like many other Dominicans Julio also has children from earlier relationships; one daughter of his lives nearby and another lives in New York. Both of them are grown-up and have good contact with their father's new family. The house is small but has a porch, a livingroom, a diningroom and three bedrooms. The family shares six beds. The blue-painted planks of the walls are decorated with the common rural adornments - a heavily retouched photograph of Julio and Ana, oleographs in bright colors, depicting saints or American landscapes with deer and pinetrees, thickly painted ceramics representing cherubs and Madonnas. The livingroom looks crowded with a vinyl-covered, three-piece suite, and four rockingchairs. The dining room is furnished with a rustic display cabinet, a plastic-coated table and six chairs. The entire interior decoration, the concrete floor and the zinc roof bear witness that Julio does not belong to the group of "poor" peasants. He is rather a "middle-size" cultivator, able to support his family with the fruits from his land and he can even sell some of his, and his neighbors', surplus in the market.

Julio's home is consequently also a production unit. At the side of his house he has a cement covered area for drying coffee beans and cocoa kernels. A mechanic peeler that separates the shells from the coffee beans is housed in the pigsty, which also lodges two big pigs. Hens and ducks are running around freely. On a small meadow, close to the creek below the house, two black-and-white cows are grazing. Julio is self-sufficient in milk for his family.

Julio is also the owner of a *pulpería*, a small store. The shelves behind the counter exhibit the stock you find in almost every *pulpería*, all over the Dominican Republic - bottles of rum and beer, tincans with sardines, condensed milk and tomato purée, spaghetti, soap, detergents, biscuits, salt, cooking oil, and rice. That is about all there is. Before you could also get dried fish like *bacalao* (dried cod-fish) and *arenque* (dried herring), but never meat or fresh vegetables. Behind the *pulpería* is a small storeroom where Julio keeps sacks with products harvested by himself - corn, pigeon peas, plantains, etc. You also find sacks with coffee and cocoa, bought from other peasants. They grow these crops on small plots and they have neither the time nor the means, to collect amounts that are large enough to interest the purchasers from the urban areas who during the harvest time pass along the road with their trucks. Thus, these small producers trust the owners of *pulperías* in order to obtain cash or credit. Most producers sell the coffee and cocoa fresh. Julio peels and dries it himself. He is able to offer credit from harvest to harvest and during the "deadseasons," poor peasants may subsist on the goods he has in store. Julio passes on the coffee and cocoa to other purchasers. He is a "small-scale middleman" since he lacks a truck of his own, and is accordingly unable to transport the goods directly into town.

Many small peasants do not have sufficient land in order to support their frequently large families, and they have to buy the bulk of their food in the *pulperías*. Between harvests and during bad seasons they are sometimes forced to sustain themselves on a diet made up of spaghetti and tomato sauce. On the whole, the peasants' food intake is meagre. They rarely eat meat, and even Julio seldom kills one of his hens - mainly when visitors come from town or on holidays. Plantains and beans are common ingredients in the peasant's food, but he rarely eats fresh vegetables, like lettuce and tomatoes. Earlier, dried fish was common on the table, but it has now become too expensive for him and you seldom see fish in the countryside anymore. The food Ana prepares for the fieldhands that are sometimes hired by Julio consists of *moro*, a dish with rice and beans, and spaghetti.

Julio works very hard in order to keep his head above the water. Every day, from early morning to late in the evening, he is busy in his fields. In spite of this, his own work is insufficient to generate an acceptable income. He has to hire workers in order to get the clearing of the fields, the planting and harvesting, done in time. The average number of workers he hires is twenty. He pays them 4 pesos (around US$ 2) per day, and offers them breakfast and lunch. Ana does all the cooking (for 30 persons) as well as cleaning the house and doing the family laundry. She also looks after the shop, together with her daughters, when they are not in school. Most of the time she works in the backyard where the cookhouse is situated, a wooden shack with a fireplace and a table. The diningroom in the house is used only when visitors come. She also has a gasstove, but the high prices of liquefied gas limits its use. As a matter of fact, the stove constitutes a kind of status symbol, since it is placed in the diningroom. It is always shining clean and, if gas is available, it is only used in order to prepare coffee for honored guests. For everyday cooking plain firewood is used.

Ana keeps her home nice and tidy. You find flowerpots all over the place. The soil around the house is no good for flowers, so she brings the earth from far away. Her children cannot be of much assistance since most of them are in school during the day.

The children's schooling constitutes a heavy expenditure for the family. Julio keeps two daughters in secondary school in a village far away. Their transportation, that does not always show up, costs him 1 peso per day, and he pays more than 10 pesos per month in school fees. He could send the girls to Altamira, where education is free of charge, but this would not pay off since the transportation costs would be higher than the fees he pays for the moment. The girls attend school in the afternoon, when teachers come out from Altamira in order to teach the 150 pupils who have assembled from surrounding villages and made arrangements to improvise a private rural secondary school. Julio now plans to send another daughter and his oldest son to the distant town of Villa González, to live with one of Ana's brothers, and attend secondary school there. This arrangement could turn out to be cheaper than having them living at home. He would avoid the high transportation costs and the school fees.

Julio is convinced that all his children have to get a proper education, enabling them to leave the countryside. He states that: "My boys will not touch a machete. There is no future in the country."

Those of his children who do not attend secondary school go to another, smaller school, free of charge, situated more than half an hour's walk from home. His oldest girl has already left for Santiago, where she works in the sewingworkshop of an aunt. Another girl is an educated nurse, but she is still living with her parents since she is unable to find a job. She is now planning to educate herself further so she may enter a university.

Julio tills the soil of different plots that are spread over a fairly wide area. Most of them are small and situated on the steep mountainsides. At the moment he is busy on 100 *tareas* (6.3 hectares). Around 50 of them are his own. The rest he leases from other peasants. For the 25 *tareas* that he hires from his father-in-law, he pays 750 pesos. This gives him the right to use the land for two years. When he began to rent this land, situated on a steep hillside, it was covered with a thick layer of vegetation and old, high and leafy trees. He cut all of them down, because "things do not grow under shadow." Then he cleared away the vegetation, and finally burned all that was left. In the ashes he planted various food crops, such as corn, pigeon peas, manioc, peanuts and calabashes. All crops were interplanted, with the exception of one field where he planted beans. All of these were later destroyed by lack of rain. He worked with machete and hoe. A small part, that was not too steep, he plowed with the help of a pair of oxen, hired for 75 pesos.

Julio is well aware of the fact that the agricultural technique he uses is destroying the land. He states:

Production decreases every year. The felling of the trees destroys the climate and makes it possible for the rainwater to carry the soil away.

Now it rains less than before and the water in the rivers disappears. In reality these mountains are only suitable for forests.

Still he persists in using the same traditional and harmful methods. He contends that he is totally unable to change techniques and production. The land is hired for only two years. Then it is no use to plant coffee and cocoa. These crops would be ideal since they protect the earth to a higher degree than the crops he grows at the present, but their great disadvantage is that they grow too slowly. He has to grow subsistence crops in order to support his large family, and he must have crops that he can sell as quickly as possible.

Julio is engaged in a persistent battle against time and insecurity. He must always have an emergency fund in order to raise cash if some unexpected expenditure would arise, for example, a short time ago his oldest son got *fiebre mala*, typhus, and he had to take him to hospital and spend 150 pesos on the drops alone. A few miles away from Julio's place is a rural clinic, but it is closed, since it was short of staff. The nearest medical services are in Altamira, where a doctor is in charge of a private clinic with a few beds. Cases he cannot treat has to be taken the long way to Santiago or Puerto Plata - a hard and costly route, since there is a lack of an adequate ambulance service. Living in the countryside means to be exposed to the deadly threat of diseases, that could be avoided or rendered as harmless in an urban setting. A constant reminder of this fact is the withered arm of one of Julio's daughters. It was affected by polio.

Julio is caught in a merry-go-round of uncertain incomes and recurrent expenditure. Money flows through his fingers, but he seldom acquire a real surplus. Compared with some of his neighbors, he is a wealthy man, but compared with any towndweller he is poor. His clothes are tidy but threadbare. He does not have access to electricity, has no car and no TV, and he does not nurse any hope of improving his meagre existence, at least not in the countryside. His dream is to live on flat land, to grow things on a soil that can be irrigated, something that is impossible to do on the slopes. Julio is a bit jealous of the peasants around Villa González where the land is flat and irrigation facilities are available. Like them he wants to possess soil that won't get tired after three years of use, land that can yield harvests year after year, not like the poor earth around him, where harvests start to decrease after a few years use and have to lie fallow at least twenty years in order to "restore their old strength." But since there is little hope for him to get such land, he thinks that the best thing for him to do would be to emigrate into a town, but not to a Dominican town, "because there is hardly any drinking water." Julio is referring to the easy access his family has to water from the little creek that crosses his grounds. He is well aware of the fact that he is running the risk of decreasing his standard of living if he moves to a town and gets stuck in a slum. In spite of all, he has his own land and business, and does not want to lose it all. He wants to be sure of gaining something if he leaves: "No one goes if he does not think he can get something better. You must be firmly resolved if you leave what you have."

What is looming in his mind is the prospect of making a living in the United States. In the Northern parts of the Dominican Republic, New York is very close. Often it feels closer than the capital of the Republic. Many have relatives and neighbors who have gone there. You can take a car that stops outside your house and takes you to the airport in Puerto Plata in an hour's time, catch a plane and be in New York after just three hours. But the obstacles are often impossible to overcome - visa, working permit, and above all money, are hard to get. Julio says: "Of course it is better to till the soil, than to work in the factories. But, here everything is getting worse with every year. You break your back for nothing."

Julio has relatives in USA. He knows the disadvantages - the cold, the longer hours of darkness in winter, the alienation, the hard and monotonous work, but he also talks about the positive things over there: "The people who come back are different, they are rich, more 'cultivated,' more 'white.'"

They bring with them all the symbols of "progress" and the "good life": TV sets, stereos, fancy suits, etc.; and they all have stories about a life that might seem hard and terrible, but these stories also carry attractions for a peasant who tortures himself on deteriorating lands, whose whole existence is threatened by a slight change of the weather:

> Over there you get a steady income. All is close at hand, medical care and education for your children. Of course you have to work, but when you return to your home you can rest, forget about debts and preoccupations. You go to the supermarket, that is filled with all kinds of goods, return home, relax with your family, eat and have a good time in front of the TV.

While Julio speaks in this manner he looks out over a landscape of a heartbreaking beauty. Veils of white mist linger over mountain ridges that succeed one another, until they turn blue by the horizon. They are covered by thick foliage, still wet from heavy rains:

> Everything was dying during the draught, but through the rain all is revived once more. The plantains started to grow immediately and the harvest of pigeon peas will be good this year.

Julio points to thin bushes that cover a field, rising from the furrow of a little stream, and the bushes are gleaming with small, flame-colored flowers. But the view is spoiled by the branches and trunks of enormous mango trees that are spread all around the clearing of the field, like parts of a giant skeleton. Julio knows that it is a crime to cut down a tree that needs decades in order to grow, and probably never will grow again on soils that are being demolished by a too-intensive agriculture. But, if you cannot implement soil conservation techniques, you have to clear new land all the time. Soon there will be no more land to clear:

> When a peasant does not have any more land to clear he has to go on tilling the soil he already has and try to squeeze some more out of the soil. But it yields less and less. In the end it will look like that.

Julio points to a piece of cracked, sterile and compact earth that hardly covers the bare rock under it. In fact, the soil is good on the mountainsides. It has a dark, yellow appearance and a consistence like clay. The crops that grow best on it are coffee and cocoa. Julio is renting land that is covered with cocoa. He pays a high price for the lease of that plot - 1,200 pesos a year. Cocoa is his most secure investment. It grows under the shade of large trees and its strong roots protect the soil. Coffee also binds and protects the soil, but during the last few years a disease has been killing the plants. Julio thinks that climatological changes have generated the plague. Poor peasants cannot afford to grow any coffee or cocoa. They need fast growing crops in order to survive.

Julio is subleasing a part of the land he hires from his father-in-law to another peasant. Their mutual arrangement is the most common one in such cases - *arriendo a medias*, i.e., Julio contributes the land, the other peasant contributes his labor. Then they split the profit. The peanut company, *La Manicera*, provides them with the seeds. After the harvest they have to return the same amount of peanuts that they were provided with and sell the surplus to the company. In the event of a bad harvest, if the planted peanuts get destroyed, they have to pay the company for the "free" seeds.

Julio is of the opinion that many of the poorest people do not like to work. The reason for this is that they are never able to get enough income to invest in land, or to educate their children. Their only concern is to survive the day, to get the money for a meal:

> Poor people have another kind of stomach than the one I got. It is much smaller than mine and when they have filled it up, they are content. I always have to plan for a distant future, seek solutions, make

arrangements in order to keep hunger away from my doorstep. I have to bring my kids to school and get them well when they fall ill. I have to buy, sell and lease land all the time. I am never free from all my debts and obligations. On the contrary, a poor peasant, or landless fellow, is so poor that his sole preoccupation is to get his next meal. When he gets it, he can relax for the time being, until emergency forces him to fill his stomach once more. He cannot plan for more than a few hours ahead, because he has no earth, and no job. When he is satisfied he sleeps. If he gets money left over after buying his meager food, he tries to get more by wasting them on gambling. What else can a poor fellow do?

Julio seldom goes to town, but he is still well informed of what goes on there. He has relatives in Santo Domingo, Santiago, Boston and New York. Now and then, small trucks and *carros públicos* pass by his house and people always drop by and chat in his *pulpería*, bringing with them news from the "big world." He meets friends at the cockfights in a nearby village. Nowadays there are cockfights every day, because there are always people who find time for that type of activity. The Dominican countryside is an incredible mixture of fervent activity and forced idleness. Julio does not rest during weekdays, but in the evenings he listens to the radio and talks politics with his neighbors over a game of pool, or dominos:

The peasants of this area have no hopes for changes in the future. Things only change for the worse. There is no hope, no land, hardly any water is left. The government is a disaster. They do not care about the countryside. Jorge Blanco was a good lawyer before he became president, but a lawyer who defended the rich and powerful that live in the towns. What does he know about peasants?

Like many other Dominicans Julio tends to focus political hopes and fears on individuals. They see politics as the results of the ability and goodwill of one person alone. "Balaguer cared. He built the road and gave peasants land on the plains. Furthermore, he was experienced and cultivated, he wrote his own speeches."

Balaguer was president under Trujillo, made a comeback in 1966 and held the presidency until 1978. The economic boom that the country experienced under a period of his regime still lingers in many peasants' minds. It is easily forgotten that things got worse during the end of his period in office and that most of the savings that originated from the rural zones were invested in the towns. Many peasants do not see things in the long run, they do not consider the fact that some of the problems of today may have been inherited from the old regime. Most important is that "more progress was made in the countryside under Balaguer than is happening today":

> Balaguer killed many persons, but for political reasons, in order to keep peace and order. Blanco says he is peaceful and democratic, but he killed a hundred poor persons in the towns in just three days, and he does not do anything for the peasants.

A month before our visit to Julio around 100 persons were shot to death in street riots that occurred in major cities. The unrest originated from drastic increases in medicine and basic foodstuffs prices.

"Everything is getting worse." Julio tells us how much cocoa he has to sell in order to buy a can of cooking oil:

> They are negotiating with the Fund [IMF], and they are too weak. The prices continue to rise every day. What can we expect from this government? Nothing. Maybe they could aid us to move away from here, to the fertile plains. Here we can do nothing. You cannot live here for any length of time, it is too hard, no land is left to clear and you cannot gain anything more.

We are on our way back home from the fields. We pass the bridge over the deep gorge, with the diminishing little stream. On our right is another little *pulpería*, and we can hear blows from a shack by its side; the poor play pool for money. Julio comments on the sounds: "Before you could see the men go with the machete to the fields in the morning, now you see them wander off to the pool table, or to the cockfighting arena."

We walk along the empty, steep and dusty road and reach Julio's house. Ana sits on the porch, surrounded by her many daughters, one of them tending her long, black hair. A dog sleeps in front of the house, a mule and a horse are tied to a tree. You sense the fragrance of tropical flowers in the air. Butterflies flutter by. All is serene and picturesque. An occasional tourist passing by on the road could return home and describe the lovely, peaceful Dominican countryside, and probably would find it difficult to understand why the peasants leave such an idyllic existence, in order to encounter the misery of overcrowded towns.

* * *

A few years have passed since we visited Julio. Things have changed, but not for the better. Julio moved to the town of Villa González with his entire family. His case is typical. It is often the industrious and rather well-off peasants that leave the countryside.

Staying behind are their poorer neighbors, who in the void after the migrants feel that their situation is even worse than before, nourishing even more desperate hopes to leave themselves. It can be argued that more space is left for the ones who stayed behind, that they can fill the gap of the ones who left, but considering the deteriorating state of the soils, the increasing poverty and lack of initiative, it is doubtful.

Balaguer, now blind and much older, is once more in power. Apparently much has not yet been done for the rural inhabitants. But once more, the hope for a better life was awakened among the peasantry. The president has renewed his image as defender of the peasants. Every week he fulfils an exhausting program, visiting impoverished villages, delivering land title deeds, promising electricity, roads, irrigation and justice for all. But when the presidential helicopter has left, doubts often stay with the peasants, or as one of them said after a presidential visit, broadcast directly over the national TV network: "If you do not help us, we will be left with just the title deeds, because the *latifundistas* will never give it [i.e. the land] to us."[1]

* * *

In the story told above many of the problems that harass the Dominican countryside have been exposed. However, one has to keep in mind that Julio lives in a particular part of the country. Other districts present other characteristics. The Dominican countryside is very varied, both in a topographical and in a sociological sense. For example, the state of isolation that still prevails in many Dominican villages, the conspicuous desolation of the border regions and the use of Haitian labor that abound in many parts of the country, are not so evident in Julio's neighborhood. Nevertheless, I think that Julio shares most of his worries with a majority of the peasants in the Dominican Republic and his story may serve as a background to the different issues related to the Dominican economy that will be systematically analyzed in the following study.

Throughout this study, it will become evident that the problems afflicting the Dominican peasantry largely constitute the core of the situation of poverty and unemployment which prevails in the Dominican Republic. As a matter of fact, for many Dominicans, in both rural and urban areas, everyday life consists of these problems. If asked where the origins of their present situation are to be found, the majority of them would probably answer like Julio: "in agriculture." Accordingly, this study will focus on problems related to the rural (agricultural) sector. Through such a procedure I hope to shed some light on the causes of the complex phenomenon of unemployment and poverty in the Dominican Republic.

Notes

1. Cited in Torres (1988), p. 46.

1

Introduction

Like most underdeveloped countries, the Dominican Republic faces a serious and growing problem of unemployment and underemployment. Open unemployment in urban areas affects more than 20 percent of the labor force while underemployment in urban and rural areas varies between 40 and 60 percent. Paradoxically, these high rates of unemployment and underemployment coexist with massive imports of foreign labor. The sugar industry, which for many years has been the principal productive activity of the country and the prime generator of employment, imports a substantial part of its labor force.

The employment problem in the Dominican Republic is much more complex than is revealed by the statistics on unemployment and underemployment. The concepts of unemployment and underemployment are very difficult to define and measure empirically in countries where a substantial proportion of the working population is not engaged in wage employment. Many are self employed in low productivity agriculture and services since very few can afford to be unemployed. In the Dominican Republic, most people work, although the income obtained from the work effort keeps them in absolute poverty. Hence, unemployment and underemployment rates do not adequately reflect a situation where low productivity and poverty affect the majority of the workers.

The rural sector is the main supplier of labor. However, this sector is unable to provide productive employment for a growing labor force. At the same time, since the employment situation in urban areas seems to be more attractive, there has been an intensive rural-urban migration. This peasant influx into the towns has had a tremendous effect on Dominican society. It has radically changed the structure of the labor force, increased the pressure on employment in the urban areas and created diverse problems related to rapid unplanned urban growth.

The employment issue is considered both by Dominican authorities and international observers as the main problem affecting the country. In 1973, following an official request from the Dominican government, the International Labor Office (ILO), carried out an exhaustive study of the employment problem in the country.[1] The ILO mission estimated the different levels of unemployment and underemployment and suggested different measures in order to generate productive employment and economic growth.

One and a half decades have passed since the ILO mission study but the problems of unemployment, underemployment, widespread poverty and rural-urban migration in the Dominican Republic persist and the available evidence suggests that the situation has been aggravated.

Despite its magnitude and importance, very few studies of the employment problem in the Dominican Republic have been undertaken. In most academic works concerning the country, the employment problem has not been a major subject, although its magnitude is generally stressed.

Scope of the Study

The central thesis of the present work is that labor resources are poorly utilized in the Dominican Republic and that the economic structures prevailing in the country and the economic policies pursued are not adapted to generate sufficient productive employment for the increasing labor force. It will be argued that the roots of the problems of low productivity, poverty and migration are not to be found in the operation of the labor market, but mainly in the factors that tend to undermine labor demand. Therefore, in this study, attention will be focused on the structure of landownership, the pricing policies of agricultural products, and the problems related to agricultural credit and the immigration of Haitians. Attention will also be given to policies that have tended to favor industry and concentrate social services in urban areas while agriculture in particular and the rural sector in general have been neglected. The argument presented in this work is that without considering these factors, the employment problem in the Dominican Republic cannot be fully understood and viable solutions will not be found.

The focus of the study will be the agricultural (rural) sector, since the high levels of poverty found today in rural and urban areas are intimately related to the performance of this sector. The development policies pursued in the Dominican Republic during recent decades have mainly been oriented towards modernization (urbanization) and industrialization. Most of the resources have been allocated within the urban sector, while the rural sector has in practice been neglected or disfavored. The result has been stagnation in agriculture, increasing rural poverty and unprecedented mass migration of peasants into the cities.

The industrialization policies implemented have not been adequate in the sense that employment opportunities have not been large enough to absorb the increasing supply of labor.

The main task of this study is to identify the forces that have led to such a poor utilization of labor and to mass migration of peasants into the cities. We shall study the push and pull factors behind the migration and the inability of the agricultural and the industrial sector to provide productive employment for the increasing labor force.

The study is divided into three major parts. The first part (Chapters 2 and 3) presents a general survey of the employment situation in the Dominican Republic, and how it is measured. Unemployment, underemployment and income levels in urban and rural areas are analyzed on the basis of information obtained from the available statistics. The reliability and accuracy of these statistics are explicitly discussed. Part two (Chapters 4 to 9), constitutes the main part of the study. It analyzes the performance of the agricultural sector, concentrating on the problems associated with the commercialization system, the land tenure system, credit availability, labor imports, land erosion, social services and other factors that can be considered as push factors of migration. The last part (Chapter 10) analyzes the performance of the industrial, urban, sector and discusses the industrialization policy pursued in the country. Different pull factors of migration are examined. The magnitude of the migration and the situation encountered by the majority of the rural migrants in the towns are also considered.

The study will devote considerable attention to the poverty problem since in a basically agrarian economy such as the Dominican one, the poverty concept is of greater relevance than unemployment and underemployment. It is argued that the employment problem consists of a range of related problems which basically have their origin in the development strategy followed in the country. This strategy has systematically neglected the agricultural sector in general and the peasantry in particular. By means of different policies, the Dominican state has tended to stimulate the concentration of land and credit in a few hands. The unequal distribution of resources has resulted in great inefficiencies and market imperfections, which in turn have given rise to an underutilization of agricultural resources, especially labor. This marked underutilization of human resources in the agricultural sector has led to a mass migration of peasants into the cities which has in turn generated a series of problems related to unplanned urban growth at the same time as it has placed great pressure on the urban labor market.

Summary of the Study

The Employment Problem in the Dominican Republic: An Empirical Overview

In Chapter 2 the employment problem in the Dominican Republic is discussed. The chapter starts by describing the population and labor force growth in a historical perspective. The Dominican Republic has one of the highest rates of population and labor force growth in the world (2.9 and 3.8 percent, respectively, 1970-81). The problem of unemployment, underemployment and income levels in both rural and urban areas is analyzed. Although the figures on unemployment and underemployment are highly unreliable, they provide a rough indicator of the extent of the problem. Open unemployment in urban areas is above the 20 percent level, while underemployment both in rural and urban areas ranges between 40 and 60 percent. These high levels of unemployment and underemployment coexist with massive imports of Haitian workers. Such workers are brought in to work on the sugar plantations but have increasingly been participating in other agricultural activities as well.

Poverty is widespread in both urban and rural areas. In 1980, 44 percent of the urban workers earned less than the established minimum salary of 125 pesos per month. However, the situation in rural areas is even worse. The average monthly income of a rural family is about half that of an urban family. Rural-urban income differences may be one of the reasons behind the tremendous outflow of labor from the agricultural sector. At present, 52 percent of the population of the Dominican Republic live in urban areas (the corresponding figure was 24 percent in 1950). At the same time, the urban labor force is growing three times as fast as the rural. Despite the high rates of urban unemployment and underemployment, the migration flow continues. The high rates of population growth and the low possibilities of new job creation assure that the Dominican Republic will continue to confront a serious employment problem during the next decades.

The Appendix to Chapter 2 analyzes the statistical information on unemployment and underemployment in the Dominican Republic.

Unemployment or Poverty?

Chapter 3 discusses some theories related to the employment problem in underdeveloped countries and presents a critical exposition of the way in which the employment problem is defined and measured in these countries. The deficiencies and limitations of this procedure are discussed with reference to the Dominican Republic.

The statistical data on which our discussion of the employment problem in the Dominican Republic is based have been collected by different institutions using the conventional approach to definition and measurement of the employment problem. This approach is the one generally used in developed countries. The practice has, however, been criticized strongly by many scholars. It is argued that the employment problem in underdeveloped countries consists of a range of related problems and therefore it cannot be fully understood by simply measuring unemployment and underemployment rates. These two concepts are very difficult to define and measure in an accurate way in countries where labor markets are not well organized and where a considerable portion of the working population is outside the wage sector.

It is also argued that underdeveloped countries may not have an employment problem *per se* but rather a poverty problem. In these countries, most of the people work, generally very hard. However the return from their work effort is so low that they can hardly earn a living. Thus, a more adequate approach to the employment problem and its possible solution is to put the emphasis on the poverty aspect of the problem.

The Dominican Peasantry

In Chapter 4 we set out to analyze different variables which may help to explain the underutilization of labor in the Dominican Republic. An attempt is made to trace the origin and development of the Dominican peasantry and identify the socioeconomic and historical factors which have led to the present situation of widespread rural poverty and accelerated out-migration of peasants. The chapter serves as a preliminary to Chapters 5, 6, and 7, but also shows how the present land tenure structure and land use pattern developed, and how the Dominican peasants have systematically been neglected by the ruling urban elites. Throughout Dominican history, the peasant sector has been highly discriminated against in relation to urban dwellers. The peasantry has held a marginal position, unable to enjoy the fruits of development and to influence important socio-political and economic decisions in the country. In the name of progress and development, the peasant family has been subject to heavy taxation but much of it has been for the benefit of urban areas. This is evident in any comparison between the availability and quality of services in rural and urban areas.

The peasants have not, however, remained totally passive. On different occasions they have manifested their dissatisfaction and unrest. These manifestations have taken different forms, common to peasant societies, such as social banditry, religious movements and regional caudillo fighting. Lately, protest has also taken the form of land occupations. The mass migration of the peasants into the cities, mainly a result of the rural-urban disequilibrium that prevails in the country, is one of the ways the peasants express their dissatisfaction with the *status quo*.

Produce Marketing and Price Policies

Chapter 5 deals with the Dominican produce market. In the Dominican Republic, rural poverty is usually blamed on exploitation of the peasants by intermediaries. This has been one of the major reasons behind the participation of the state in the marketing system. This chapter analyzes to what extent the peasants have actually been exploited by the intermediaries and whether the intervention of the state in the marketing system has been beneficial for the rural producer.

The Dominican peasant is highly integrated into the market economy. Most of what he produces is intended for the market. The performance of the market can therefore largely influence the level of income in the rural areas. The majority of food crops and a considerable amount of export crops are produced on small farms, while large farms are mainly dedicated to cattle breeding, sugar cane production and some other export crops. The commercialization processes confronted by large and small farm products are very different. While the former may reach the final consumer, or the international market, in one or two steps, the latter have to go through a long commercialization chain.

The commercialization system presents a series of deficiencies which directly affect the level of income of the small producers. The system is to a high degree oriented towards large urban wholesale markets, since most of the commercialization services are absent in rural areas. The state participates actively in the commercialization process, mainly through the Price Stabilization Institute (INESPRE). This is a leading institution in the commercialization of agricultural products. INESPRE regulates marketing and prices of more than a dozen agricultural commodities and controls the imports of food staples. At the same time, it actively participates in the commercialization of basic foodstuffs at the consumer level.

The increasing participation of the state in the marketing system has been justified as a means of supplying cheap food to the urban poor, to prevent indiscriminate exploitation of the peasants by the intermediaries and to guarantee stable prices for peasant products.

The first section of Chapter 5 describes the general characteristics of the produce market and the degree to which peasant products are sold in this market. Thereafter, an analysis is made of whether the peasants are subject to exploitation by monopsonists and monopolists in this market. The scarcity of data does not allow definite conclusions about the exploitation hypothesis. However, with the exception of the export firms, where oligopsonistic conditions prevail, the rest of the market seems to work under fairly competitive conditions, and oligopsony does not necessarily preclude competition. The deteriorating living standards of the peasantry cannot be blamed on the intermediaries. The intervention of the state in the marketing system cannot therefore be justified on grounds of exploitation. Although INESPRE has been successful in stabilizing food prices, its policies have in general been to the detriment of the rural producers. The policy of providing cheap food to the urban poor has tended to discourage agricultural production and to reduce income and employment in rural areas. Many peasants have been discouraged from staying on the land and migration has been encouraged.

Land Tenure Structure and Reform Attempts

In Chapter 6, the Dominican land tenure system is analyzed. We also discuss the extent to which the application of the agrarian reform program has affected the land tenure structure and the employment situation in the rural areas. It is shown how the land tenure system evolved during and after the colonial period and how the concentration of land became accentuated with the rise of the sugar industry. The *latifundios* have been growing in size while the land base of the peasantry has been shrinking. It will be argued that a major factor behind rural poverty is the limited access the peasants have to productive land.

The Dominican Republic ranks among the countries with the most unequal distribution of land: less than 2 percent of the landowners own 56 percent of the cultivable area. The majority of the peasants are relegated to small plots of marginal land while the best soils are concentrated in the hands of a few large landowners, including the state. It is argued that the land tenure structure found today in the Dominican Republic is mainly the outcome of a process where different government dispositions on land rights and agricultural development encouraged the concentration of land.

The application of the agrarian reform program which started in the early 1960s has had very little effect on the land tenure structure and rural employment. Very few families have benefited. Redistribution has been slow and unable to catch up with population growth. The Dominican land reform program has been marred by different institutional factors, but a major reason for its failure is the fact that the *latifundios* dedicated to pastures and sugar cane have been excluded from the program. The program was never meant to change the agrarian structure of the country. It was mainly set up as a political façade by the governing urban elite in order to secure a political clientele among the rural poor.

The concentration of land in a few hands generates imperfections in the land market. As a result, prices diverge from social opportunity costs. Land, although a scarce factor for the country as a whole, becomes an abundant factor for the *latifundista* and a scarce factor for the *minifundista*.

Agricultural Credit

Chapter 7 discusses the problem of credit in the Dominican agricultural sector. The possibilities of savings and the demand and supply of credit in the sector are analyzed. It is shown that there is a limited supply of funds for financing agricultural production and that the possibilities of financing capital formation by rural savings are very small. Despite the low level of income prevailing in the rural areas, most peasant families tend to save. However, very little investment to improve production techniques takes place. Instead, most peasants tend to hold assets in order to protect themselves in times of distress.

The low amount of financial funds in the sector is partly due to the fact that there is a lack of any institutional arrangements between savers and investors in agriculture, but also, and more important, to the fact that the group of large farmers, which is the group with the greatest opportunity to save, consists mainly of absentee landowners. The savings of this group, if ever invested productively, are generally allocated to non-agricultural activities.

The low availability of funds in the agricultural sector is deeply aggravated by the unequal distribution of institutional funds between different producers. Institutional credit mostly benefits large-scale farmers and, more recently, agrarian reform settlements. Hence, small producers have to procure their loans from alternative credit sources who generally charge high interest rates. The high rates prevailing in the informal credit markets are generally seen as a sign of usury or exploitation of the peasantry by the money lenders or intermediaries. Interest rates in this market are however, not determined solely by lender behavior. The behavior of the borrowers is also important.

Marketing and moneylending is generally carried out by the same agent. At the rural level, competition seems to prevail among these intermediaries. Thus, the high rate of interest charged cannot be a result of usury or exploitation. On the lender's side, the most important factor influencing the interest rate is his risk perception. In order to compensate for possible defaults, the lender tends to charge high interest rates. As for the borrower, the most important factor is the rate of time preference. The fact that most peasant families are barely able to meet subsistence requirements implies a high rate of time preference. Borrowers are willing to pay high interest rates since they are likely to attach a higher value to present than to future consumption.

In general, the peasants' demand for loans is not for production purposes, but mainly to finance consumption while waiting for the coming harvest. Credit is usually not employed for improvements in production techniques and the introduction of modern inputs in the peasant sector. The high rate of interest charged by informal credit sources together with the low availability and unequal distribution of loanable funds in formal credit sources may be important factors behind the low level of capitalization found in Dominican agriculture. In the absence of capital formation, the possibilities for generating productive employment in the sector are very limited.

The Use of Haitian Labor

Chapter 8 deals with the migration of Haitians to the Dominican Republic and its effect on the Dominican labor market.

The employment problem in the Dominican Republic cannot be fully understood without taking into consideration the participation of Haitian workers in the labor market. Ever since the rise of the Dominican sugar industry, the participation of foreign workers has been significant, and the number of Haitian workers has been increasing throughout the years. Different factors, such as those related to the Haitian occupation of the Dominican Republic (1822-44) and the simultaneous occupation of Haiti and the Dominican Republic by the US Marines (1915-34 and 1916-24, respectively) are important. Another important factor is that at the time of the rise of the sugar industry, the Dominican Republic had a very small population. Sugar cane production is an activity that requires a large amount of labor. The domestic supply of labor was, however, not large enough and in order to satisfy the demand from the sugar plantations, labor was imported from Haiti where it was relatively abundant.

In spite of various interruptions, the imports of Haitian *braceros*, sugar cane cutters, have continued until the present day. In the meantime, the Dominican Republic has experienced an unprecedented population explosion and a tremendous increase in its labor force. However, in spite of the high rates of unemployment and underemployment, as much as 90 percent of the workers in the sugar plantations are Haitian nationals. The participation of Haitian workers in other agricultural activities, such as coffee-picking and certain urban activities, is also increasing in importance. The major importer of Haitian labor is the Dominican state-owned sugar council (CEA). The traffic of *braceros* is legally regulated by a recruitment treaty between the Dominican and the Haitian government. However, a considerable number of Haitian workers are also brought illegally into the country.

The heavy dependence of the sugar industry on the Haitian braceros became evident when, in the mid-1980s, due to the political unrest prevailing in Haiti, it proved extremely difficult to recruit Haitian workers and activities in the sugar fields almost came to a standstill.

Chapter 8 analyzes the different factors determining the high participation of Haitian workers in Dominican agricultural activities. It is shown that the presence of these workers tends to depress agricultural wages and to discourage Dominican workers from participating in certain agricultural activities.

The Effects of Market Distortions

In Chapters 6 and 7, different imperfections prevailing in the land and capital market, respectively, are illustrated. In Chapter 9, the consequences of these imperfections for rural employment and income are analyzed. It is shown that the unequal distribution of land and credit depresses the demand for labor in the agricultural sector. Market imperfections in the credit and land markets prevent an efficient allocation of agricultural resources with the result that production and employment in the sector are lower than what would otherwise have been the case if competitive conditions had prevailed in these markets. Agricultural production per capita has been stagnant and a food deficit has arisen.

As a result of distortions in the land market, increasing amounts of land have been devoted to export crops and livestock production. The problem of rural employment has been aggravated since the activities that have been growing in importance in the sector, namely livestock production, are the least labor-intensive. Thus, monopoly power in the land market has influenced the land use pattern in agriculture and this in turn has affected the demand for rural labor. As less land is put into labor-intensive crops the total demand for labor falls. Rural wages will also tend to fall since the absence of alternative employment forces all members of the peasant family to remain on the small family farm.

This implies that the marginal productivity of labor in the *minifundio* subsector will fall. At the same time, there will be less work opportunities for the landless workers who usually depend on the large farms for employment. There is still the possibility of working on the sugar cane plantations and to a lesser extent, on the coffee farms. These activities require large amounts of labor inputs. However, producers in these two branches largely rely on Haitian workers who are prepared to accept low wages and thereby outcompete Dominicans.

In general, Dominican agriculture presents a low level of capitalization. Labor tends to have the largest factor share, followed by land. Very little modern machinery and other inputs are used in the production process. The introduction of modern technology seems to have very little impact on the employment situation of the sector and consequently cannot be responsible for the high levels of rural underemployment. The relatively easier access of large farmers to financial resources implies that the introduction of modern inputs is concentrated in the hands of these producers. Imperfections in the capital market have hindered the peasants from using modern technology.

Traditional land use and cultivation patterns in combination with population growth have increased the problems of deforestation and erosion, thereby reducing further the land base of both the peasantry and the country in general. The growth of population has led to increased erosion in two ways. First, the increased demand for charcoal and firewood for cooking purposes has led to an increase in the deforestation of mountainous areas. Second, in the absence of alternative employment, an increasing agricultural labor force has to be absorbed by the *minifundio* subsector since most of the land is concentrated in the hands of the *latifundistas*. At constant relative commodity prices, the peasants will increase the production of food crops (the labor-intensive crops). This will in turn increase the rate of erosion since this type of crop tends to expose the soil more to erosion than for example export crops such as coffee and cocoa. Hence, the supply of available land will shrink and the process of erosion becomes self-sustaining and increases with time.

The shift into more labor-intensive cultivation of the soil could in principle be counteracted by a fall in the price of food crops in terms of export crops. In recent decades, due to the food price policies pursued in the country and to upward trends in the world market price of the peasants' export crops, the relative price of food crops has fallen. In spite of this, there seems to be no evidence of peasants having shifted away from food crops and into export production. Probably, the low short-run elasticity of supply of export crops and the difficulty of obtaining credit have prevented the peasants from making this shift. Thus, the erosion process has continued to accelerate.

The shrinking land base of the peasantry, due on one hand to the land tenure system of the country and, on the other hand, to population growth in combination with unchanged technology, undoubtedly constitutes an important push factor behind the rural-urban migration.

Rural Out-Migration and the Allurement of the Modern Sector

Chapter 10 analyzes the different factors (pull factors) attracting the peasants into the cities. The migration flow and the consequences of migration for employment are also analyzed. It is shown that rural-urban migration has put tremendous pressure on the urban labor market, as well as on the physical urban environment. Urban unemployment and poverty has been growing and the majority of the urban population is concentrated in slum areas.

The industrialization policies pursued in the country in the early 1950s and 1960s constituted a major reason why the peasants migrated to the cities. The newly created industries generated employment opportunities, but these were insufficient to absorb the huge amount of workers who, with the expectation of obtaining higher incomes and better living conditions, moved into the cities. A major factor hampering the creation of employment was the industrial structure generated by the industrialization policies pursued by the government. Due to various forms of government intervention, capital was priced below its opportunity cost and as a result, most industries tended to use highly capital-intensive production methods.

Unable to find employment in the urban, formal (industrial) sector, many workers have turned to the informal sector. The latter sector is characterized by small-scale operations, with low productivity, easy entry and low, flexible wages - in contrast to the formal sector where wages are generally above the institutionally determined minimum. The importance of the informal sector has been steadily growing. It is in this sector that most of the migrants manage to gain a livelihood in the cities. Nevertheless, most migrants are satisfied with their decision to migrate. It is shown that the income maximization objective is but one of the components of the expected value of migration. Other factors, such as risk aversion, chances of social advancement, etc., also enter into the migrants' calculations. Many of the self-employed workers (*chiriperos*) in the urban informal sector have higher current incomes, better life time prospects and greater access to a range of social services than many hard working peasants in the countryside.

Migration abroad also represents an attractive alternative for many Dominican workers. Such migration has tended to alleviate the pressure on employment. Moreover it has represented an important source of foreign exchange. As in the case of internal migration, the migration of Dominicans abroad has been highly selective. It is the better educated and more enterprising individuals that have tended to leave. Migration abroad tends to improve the economic situation of the migrants and their relatives at home. This constitutes another incentive for others to migrate.

Rural-urban migration is likely to continue not only as long as the rural-urban wage differential exists, but also as long as most social services, such as education, health, minimum-wage legislation, etc., are limited to urban areas.

Notes

1. See OIT (1975).

2

The Employment Problem in the Dominican Republic: An Empirical Overview

This chapter provides an empirical overview of the employment problem in the Dominican Republic. It starts out by describing the growth of the population and the labor force. Then it goes on to discuss the problems of unemployment and underemployment and the level of income in urban and rural areas. (The accuracy of unemployment and underemployment data for the Dominican Republic is discussed in the Appendix to the chapter). Finally, the chapter describes the use of Haitian laborers in Dominican agricultural activities.

Population and Labor-Force Growth

During the 1960s and 1970s, the Dominican population increased at a rate of 3.0 percent per annum. This is estimated to be the net result of a natural rate of increase of approximately 3.5 percent minus a strong migration movement, mostly to the United States.[1] During the 1960s, the urban population expanded at a rate of 5.8 percent and the rural population at a rate of 1.2 percent per annum (see Table 2.1). In the rural areas about two-thirds of the annual population increase was offset by emigration to the cities or to other countries. This migration has been so significant that around half of the yearly urban population increase may be attributed to rural migrants. The Dominican Republic is thus experiencing an intensive rural-urban migration process which creates very serious strain in the labor market, both by changing the composition of the labor supply and by placing a burden on the capacity of the economy to absorb the flow of an increasing number of people into the cities.

TABLE 2.1   Total Population, Population by Urban and Rural Areas and Rate of Growth of Population*

	Total Population	Urban Population		Rural Population	
		Total	% of Total Population	Total	% of Total Population
1920	894,665	148,894	16.6	745,771	83.4
	(3.4)	(3.8)		(3.3)	
1935	1,479,417	266,565	18.0	1,212,852	82.0
	(2.4)	(4.3)		(2.0)	
1950	2,135,872	508,408	23.8	1,627,464	76.2
	(3.6)	(6.1)		(2.7)	
1960	3,047,070	922,090	30.3	2,124,980	69.7
	(2.9)	(5.8)		(1.2)	
1970	4,009,458	1,595,764	39.8	2,413,694	60.2
	(2.9)	(5.2)		(0.98)	
1981	5,647,977	2,935,860	52.0	2,712,117	48.0

*Population growth rates (compound annual rate of increase) within parenthesis, i.e.:

$$P_n = P_o e^{rt}$$

where r = annual growth rate; t = intercensual period; P_n = population at year n; P_o = population at year o. t = 15; 15; 10; 9.4; 11.9 years for the period 1920-35, 1935-50, 1950-60, 1960-70 and 1970-81, respectively.

Sources: 1920 to 1970: ONE (1971), Table 3, p. XV. 1981: ONE (1982:1), p. 3.

Due to the migration to other countries and because of the lower growth rate of the population in the 1940s, the Dominican labor force[2] increased between 1960 and 1970 at a lower rate than the population, i.e. at 2.7 percent per annum. As Table 2.2 indicates, the rural labor force increased at a rate of 0.7 percent per annum while the urban labor force expanded at a rate of 6.0 percent. In the capital, the corresponding rate was 6.3 percent.[3] The male and female labor forces increased at the same rate in the rural areas but not in the cities, where the former increased at the rate of 5.1 percent per annum and the latter at 8.5 percent per annum.[4] The situation during the 1970-81 period appears to be more or less the same. However, the rate of growth of the labor force has increased from 2.7 to 3.8 percent. Even if this discrepancy could be partly due to statistical inconsistencies, it may also be explained by the increased growth rate of the population in the 1950s which was 3.6 percent per annum.

The higher rate of increase for women is partly due to their increasing participation in the labor force, especially in the urban labor market. Most women who migrate to the cities leave in search for work - especially as domestic servants. There is also a significant number of women employed in the industrial free zones. Another reason could be the strong emigration abroad of men of working age.[5]

TABLE 2.2   Rate of Growth of the Labor Force, 1960-1981

	Rural Areas		Urban Areas		Total	
	1960-70	1970-81	1960-70	1970-81	1960-70	1970-81
Men	0.7	1.1	5.1	5.8	2.1	3.1
Women	0.7	2.3	8.5	7.6	6.7	5.2
Total labor force	0.7	1.4	6.0	5.9	2.7	3.8

Source: 1960-70: OIT (1975), p. 6. The growth rate for 1970-81 was calculated with data from the respective censuses, using the same methodology as in Table 2.1.

If no measures are taken to slow down birth rates and incentives are not provided to make people stay in the countryside, population growth and rural-urban migration are likely to continue at the same pace. According to World Bank projections, the Dominican population will be 12.3 million in the year 2000, provided that the fertility rate is kept constant. With a moderately rapid decline in fertility, the size of the population will be 8.8 million.[6] Assuming a slow rural-urban migration, 64 percent of the population will be located in urban areas, while with rapid rural-urban migration, the proportion of the population located in urban areas will be 70 percent.[7]

The growth rate of the population during the next two decades has no impact on the labor force before the year 2000. The potential work force entrants for the next two decades are already born. It is estimated that about 1.4 million persons will enter the Dominican labor force during the period 1981-2000 (see Table 2.3). About 72 percent of the new job seekers will be located in urban areas. Table 2.3 shows the distribution of the labor force by urban and rural areas for the period 1960-2000.

TABLE 2.3   Economically Active Population by Rural and Urban Areas, 1960 - 1981 and Projections for 1990 and 2000
(thousands)

	Total Labor Force	Urban Labor Force		Rural Labor Force	
		Total	% of Total Labor Force	Total	% of Total Labor Force
1960	820.7	264.5	32.2	556.2	67.8
1970	1,072.5	477.6	44.5	594.9	55.5
1981	1,800.8	966.3	53.7	834.5	46.3
1990	2,462.0	1,493.0	60.6	969.0	39.4
2000	3,166.9	1,945.6	61.4	1,221.2	38.6

Sources: 1960: census data excluding population aged 10-14 years of age, in IEPD (1983:3), p. 40. 1970: census data recalculated by OIT (1975), Table 40, p. 95. 1981: preliminary census data, excluding population aged 10-14 years of age, in Secretariado Técnico (1984:1), pp. 6-7. 1990: IEPD (1983:3), p. 24. 2000: Graber (1978), p. 73. Estimation based on slow rural-urban migration.

Urban Unemployment

In the Dominican Republic, the employment problem is considered to be the most serious political and social problem of recent decades.[8] The evidence suggests that the problem is most likely to remain serious long into the next century, if drastic measures are not taken in order to provide employment for the increasing number of new entrants to the work force. Until now, the tendency has been towards job shortage and failure of the traditional measures to cope with unemployment. In a survey made in 1973,[9] it was found that one in every five persons belonging to the labor force of Santo Domingo was unemployed and was actively looking for a job in the week of the survey. This means that the rate of unemployment in that city was 20 percent. Another survey, made in 1980, shows a rate of 20 percent unemployment for the city of Santo Domingo while the population census of 1981 and the Central Bank survey of 1987 show a similar unemployment rate for the country as a whole. Although, as noted in the Appendix, these figures are not comparable and may not reveal the real dimension of the unemployment problem, they give some hint of the persistence and extent of unemployment.

TABLE 2.4   Rates of Unemployment and Underemployment (1966-1990)

Year	Reference Area	Unemployment Rate (%)	Underemployment Rate (%)	Source
1966	Whole country	17.1	-	ONAPLAN estimates (in ONAPLAN (1980), p. 24.)
1968	Santo Domingo	22.0	-	ONAPLAN (1968), p. 101.
1969	Santo Domingo	13.2	-	Banco Central in Del Rosario (1982), Table 1, p. 19.
1970	Whole country	24.1	-	ONE (1971).
1973	Santo Domingo	20.0	60.0	OIT (1975), pp. 2-3, 31-44.
1973	Rural areas	-	between 40 and 50	Ibid., pp. 46 and 133.
1975-1976	Rural areas	-	63.6	SEA (1977), Table 4.4, p. 40.
1976-1977	Santo Domingo	11.5	-	Banco Central in Del Rosario (1982), Table 1, p. 19.
1977-1978	Santo Domingo	24.2	-	ONE in ibid.
1979	Santo Domingo	19.3	-	ONAPLAN (1981:1).
1979	Santiago	18.5	-	Ibid.
1980	Urban areas	19.0	43.4	ONAPLAN (1982).
1980	Santo Domingo	20.7	39.0	ONAPLAN in Sec. Téc. (1983), p. 3.
1980	Rural areas	26.1	-	ONAPLAN in IEPD (1985), Table 1, p. 8.
1981	Whole country	20.7	-	ONAPLAN in ibid., Table 7, p. 18.
1981	Rural areas	22.8	-	Ibid.
1981	Urban areas	18.8	-	Ibid.
1983	Santo Domingo	21.4	-	Ibid., Table 6, p. 17.

(continues)

TABLE 2.4 *(continued)*

Year	Reference Area	Unemployment Rate (%)	Underemployment Rate (%)	Source
1983	Whole country	24.6	-	World Bank estimates (in World Bank (1985), Table VIII, p. 71).
1985	Whole country	28.3	-	Ibid.
1986	Whole country	25.1	-	Banco Central in Ceara (1989), p. 6.
1987	Whole country	19.5	-	Ibid.
1987	Santo Domingo	22.7	-	Ibid.
1988	Santo Domingo	18.2	-	Ibid.
1990	Whole country	32.4	-	World Bank estimates (in World Bank (1985), Table VIII, p. 71).

In table 2.4, we have gathered the total available information on unemployment and underemployment covering the period 1966-1990, but given the variety of sources, the different methodology and nature of the surveys, these figures should not be interpreted as a homogeneous historical series (see Appendix). In what follows, we will discuss the results of the most relevant surveys.

The surveys of 1973 and 1980 reveal that the level of unemployment was not uniform among different population groups. It seemed to depend on the relative necessity of employment of each group. The rate of unemployment among family heads (men between 25 and 54 years) was 6 and 9 percent in 1973 and 1980 respectively, while among the rest of the population (persons over 15 years of age integrated in the labor force), the rate of unemployment, reached 26 and 24 percent, respectively, during these years.

The reason for these differences is that the character of the labor supply among male heads of family is different from that of other members of the labor force. The need for gainful employment in the first group is so acute that its members are forced to accept any job they may come across, irrespective of wages and working conditions. In other words, their reservation wage is very low. For this reason, as Table 2.5 shows, this group exhibits the highest rate of participation in the labor force and the lowest unemployment rate. On the other hand, since the members of the second group are not heads of family, and since they have the opportunity to carry out alternative activities outside the labor market (such as studies or house-work), their attitude towards job hunting is more selective and their reservation wage higher than that of the first group. Their participation in the labor force is very low, while their unemployment rate is higher than average. The highest unemployment rates are found among family members, such as wives and youngsters. In 1980, the unemployment rates for these groups were 20.3 and 31.7 percent respectively.[10] The figures for 1973 and 1980 presented in Table 2.5 are not really comparable. The first refer to Santo Domingo while the latter refer to total urban areas.

TABLE 2.5   The Employment Situation in 1973 and 1980
(Percent)

Rates	Group I (Male heads of family within the ages of 25 to 54 years)		Group II (Population over 15 years of age excl. Group I)		Population aged 15 years and above	
	1973	1980	1973	1980	1973	1980
Rate of participation*	92	94	44	43	53	52
Rate of employment**	94	91	73	76	80	81
Rate of unemployment**	6	9	26	24	20	19

*Share of the economically active population in the total population of the respective age category.
**Share of employed or unemployed persons in the economic active population.

Sources: 1973: OIT (1975), p. 47. (Refers to the city of Santo Domingo.) 1980: ONAPLAN (1982), p. 27 and Table 11, p. 29. (Refers to total urban areas.)

Unemployment varies also between the different regions of the country. The highest unemployment rate is found in the Southwest (see Figure 2.1) with 24.3 percent of the urban work force unemployed. For the Southeast and the Cibao, unemployment in 1980 was 20.5 and 14.5 percent, respectively. As in the total urban sector, the category of workers in Group II (population over 15 years of age excluding male heads of family within the ages of 25 to 54 years) presents the highest regional unemployment, being 30.8, 25.5 and 17.9 percent for the Southwest, Southeast and Cibao regions, respectively.[11]

FIGURE 2.1   Regions of the Dominican Republic

1. The *Southeast* region includes the Distrito Nacional and the provinces of El Seibo, Hato Mayor, La Romana, La Altagracia, Monte Plata, Peravia, San Cristóbal and San Pedro de Macorís.

2. The *Cibao* region includes the provinces of Dajabón, Duarte, Espaillat, La Vega, María Trinidad Sánchez, Monseñor Noel, Monte Cristi, Puerto Plata, Salcedo, Samaná, Sánchez Ramírez, Santiago, Santiago Rodríguez and Valverde.

3. The *Southwest* region includes the provinces of Azua, Bahoruco, Barahona, Elías Piña, Independencia, Pedernales and San Juan.

The unemployment rates in the different regions of the country vary directly with the distribution of resources between regions. As will be seen further on in this study, the Southwest region is the poorest region of the country. As shown in Table 2.6 below, in 1980 the workers of this region received an average monthly income of 159 pesos, while 51.3 percent of the workers earned incomes below the minimum wage of 125 pesos per month. The corresponding average monthly wage for the Southeast and the Cibao areas was 224 and 183 pesos respectively.

Although the Dominican labor force on average has very low levels of schooling, unemployment seems to affect both educated and non-educated workers. In 1980, 16 percent of the urban population above 15 years of age was illiterate and 45 percent had less than a complete primary education.[12] The illiterate had unemployment rates of between 17.5 and 22.5 percent. Unemployment among persons with higher educational levels, 13 and more years of schooling, was 17 percent.[13]

Level of Income in Urban Areas

The income distribution in the Dominican Republic is very unequal. In 1977, 78 percent of the families received only 45 percent of the total income in the country while 22 percent received 55 percent of the total income. The poorest 10 percent received 1.3 percent of the income while the richest 10 percent received 38.5 percent. 23 percent of the Dominican families received incomes below the poverty line[14] of 94.9 pesos a month. 77 percent of these families were located in rural areas and 23 percent in urban areas. Thus, the level of poverty is relatively lower in urban areas. During the same year, the average monthly income of an urban family was 331 pesos while the corresponding figure for a rural family was 177 pesos.[15]

TABLE 2.6   Income from Main Job in Urban Areas, 1980

	All Urban Areas	Region Southwest	Southeast	Cibao
Average monthly income (DR$)	206	159	224	183
Percentage of workers earning less than the minimum salary of DR$125 per month	43.7	51.3	40.2	49.0

Source: ONAPLAN (1982), Table 40, p. 77.

The ILO survey of 1973 reveals that the level of family income depends on the combined employment situation for the members of the family. In Santo Domingo, families with income below 20 pesos a week

(35 percent of the families) had a level of employment of less than one person per family. In half of the families belonging to this income category, the entire household was unemployed. Frequently, the only means of subsistence available to some families, were the money orders which they received from relatives working in the United States. Families earning incomes between 20 and 60 pesos a week (43 percent of the families) had an average of 1.5 family member employed while families earning more than 60 pesos a week (22 percent of the families) had a level of employment of two persons per family.[16]

The income situation among workers had not improved by 1980. The survey of that year reveals that 44 percent of the workers in urban areas earned less than the established minimum salary of 125 pesos per month[17] (see Table 2.6). 27 percent of the workers in Group I (male heads of family between 25 and 54 years of age) and 53 percent of the workers in Group II (population over 15 years of age excluding Group I) earned incomes below the established minimum.[18]

Urban Underemployment

The figures presented so far reveal the magnitude of the problem of open unemployment, especially among members of Group II. Although the level of unemployment is relatively lower among members of Group I, this in no way implies that their employment situation is less serious. As heads of families, the members of this group are more inclined to accept whatever kind of job they may be offered. Many of these workers fall within the category of underemployed.

In the 1973 ILO survey, employed workers were divided into different categories according to the nature of their work (workers with fixed salary, workers with variable income and occasional workers). Within each category, workers could be considered to be underemployed due to the occasional character of their work, the magnitude of fluctuations in their activities and income, the limited number of hours worked per week or because they were earning less than they did in previous jobs. According to these criteria, the ILO mission estimated that about 60 percent of the employed workers of Santo Domingo were underemployed although it is unclear how the mission actually arrived at this figure. Apparently, the average degree of underemployment was estimated by calculating for each category the proportion of workers working less than 40 hours a week and the proportion of workers using less than their potential working capacity.[19] The extent of underemployment was then estimated by multiplying average degrees of underemployment by the proportion of the employed labor force in each category and summing the total.

The highest degree of underemployment was found among occasional workers, i.e. workers who did not hold a fixed job but only a temporary one during the week of the survey. The most common type of job for this group was all-round chores that only lasted for a few days. The income of these workers was less than 15 pesos per week.[20]

According to the ONAPLAN survey, underemployment continued to be high in the 1980s. The urban survey carried out by ONAPLAN in 1980 covers all urban areas and defines categories of workers that differ from those included in the ILO survey of 1973. The criteria used to estimate underemployment were the same as in the ILO survey. However, the reference norm was the number of hours worked (35 hours a week) and the level of income (the officially established minimum wage). Table 2.7 shows the percentage of each category of workers who were thus estimated to be underemployed. Accordingly, underemployment affected 43.4 percent of employed urban workers in 1980.[21]

TABLE 2.7   Urban Underemployment by Regions and Category of Workers, 1980

Category	Distribution of employed workers by category of workers (percent)	Underemployment Rates*			
		All Urban Areas	Southwest	Southeast	Cibao
Total	100.0	43.4	50.1	40.9	46.6
1) Employers	5.5	29.4	n.a.	30.6	25.7
2) Independent workers	18.7	56.1	55.4	52.4	61.7
3) Workers with fixed salary	57.2	34.4	38.5	32.8	37.5
4) Workers with variable wages	10.6	62.6	76.5	60.5	63.0
5) Occasional workers	5.7	79.0	n.a.	79.4	77.1
6) Non-remunerated family workers	2.3	29.5	n.a.	31.8	23.4

*Share of underemployed workers to employed workers in the respective category.

Source: ONAPLAN (1982), Tables 21, 66, and 68; pp. 44, 122 and 126.

As in the 1973 survey, the 1980 survey shows that the highest rates of underemployment are found among the category of occasional workers, i.e. workers who did not hold a fixed job. Underemployment among these workers was nearly 80 percent. In general, when interviewed, the occasional workers considered themselves as unemployed,[22] since they held very sporadic jobs and earned insignificant incomes. This group constitutes 5.7 percent of "employed" workers.

Other categories of workers who have high underemployment rates are those classified as "independent workers" and "workers with variable wages." These two categories constitute 29 percent of total "employed" workers and have underemployment rates of 56 and 63 percent respectively. These workers receive fluctuating incomes and work less than 35 hours a week. The majority of workers in these categories, when interviewed, expressed their willingness to work additional hours and earn a fixed wage.[23]

Workers who receive fixed wages constitute 57 percent of employed workers. The majority of these workers belong to the "modern" sector of the economy. This sector is expected to utilize labor resources in a more efficient way. However, the category of workers who have fixed wages have underemployment rates of 34.4 percent. This category includes domestic workers. The latter group consists mainly of women working as maids and, although working more than 35 hours a week, they generally earn less than the minimum wage. Underemployment among domestic workers was estimated to be 83 percent. If domestic workers are excluded, underemployment among workers in the modern sector falls to 27.3 percent.[24] This rate is much lower than the rates of underemployment among the above mentioned categories, but it is still very high considering that these workers belong to the most efficient sector of the economy.

As in the case of unemployment, the level of underemployment varies among the different groups of the working population and among the different regions of the country. The highest rate of underemployment, 70 percent, was found among the members of Group II, while the rate for the members of Group I was 40 percent.[25] Among the regions, the Southwest presents the highest underemployment level, affecting 50 percent of the employed workers (see Table 2.7).

The above figures on unemployment and underemployment roughly indicate the magnitude of underutilization of labor in the Dominican Republic and the challenge that the employment problem poses to Dominican authorities. Based on the results of the survey of 1980, the Planning Office calculated the "equivalent" rate of open unemployment to be 36 percent.[26] This is obtained by assuming that any increase in the demand for labor is mainly absorbed by the underemployed.[27] The number of jobs that must be created in order to fully employ the underemployed is then equivalent to 17.1 percent of the total urban active labor force. In order to provide employment for the 19 percent of the urban labor force that are openly unemployed and for the 43.4 percent that are underemployed (equivalent to 17 percent open unemployment) the Dominican economy would have had to generate about 347,900 new jobs in 1981.

Underemployment in the Agricultural Sector

Despite rural-urban migration and the relative growth of employment in other sectors of the economy, the agricultural sector continues to be a major employer in the Dominican economy. However, in the last few decades, there has been a substantial decrease in the importance of the agricultural sector as an employer. As shown in Table 2.8 below, in 1960, the sector employed over 60 percent of the total labor force, while in 1981 it employed less than 35 percent.

The relatively low growth rate of the rural labor force seems to have had very little impact on the employment situation in the agricultural sector. Rural employment statistics are very scarce. The most recent survey on rural employment was carried out in 1980. A preliminary estimate indicates that the rural labor force was around one million workers. This includes two categories: agricultural workers (56%), and non-agricultural workers (services, commerce, etc.) (44%). The majority of the agricultural workers had access to land, either by owning land (26%) or by working in family-, state-, and/or collectively owned land or by leasing land (26%). Another important category among agricultural workers is the landless workers and the occasional workers representing 29 and 18 percent of the agricultural workers, respectively. Rural unemployment was estimated to 26.1 percent.[28]

However, the concept of open unemployment is difficult to apply in rural areas. Since the majority of the production units are family owned and the production method is labor intensive, most family members take part in the production process. In this sense, it is considered as more adequate to measure the level of underemployment by determining the total labor requirement of the sector in a year and compare it with the total labor supply in that same year. This method, however, presents certain difficulties, mainly because of the seasonality of agriculture. The incidence of unemployment or underemployment tends to vary quite substantially between different seasons in an agricultural economy. It is, therefore, possible to overestimate labor supply and labor requirements at peak seasons and to underestimate it at slack seasons.

TABLE 2.8   Economically Active Population by Sector of Economic Activity, 1960, 1970, 1981*

(Percent)

Sector of Economic Activity	1960 (1)	1970 (2)	1970 (3)	1981 (4)
Agriculture, forestry, hunting and fishing	61.4	45.3	55.5	34.1
Mining and quarrying	0.3	0.1	0.1	0.3
Manufacturing industry	8.2	8.8	7.6	15.0
Electricity, gas and water	0.4	0.2	0.2	1.0
Construction	2.5	2.5	2.8	5.6
Commerce	6.7	6.7		13.2
Transport, storage and communication	2.6	3.8	33.8	2.7
Services	11.1	15.1		26.6
Activities not adequately described	6.8	17.5		1.4
Total	100.0	100.0		100.0

*Columns (1), (2) and (4) are based on census data. Column (3) is based on census data recalculated by the ILO mission.

Sources: Column (1), (2) and (3): World Bank (1978:1), p. 113. Column (4): Secretariado Técnico (1984:1), p. 7.

In order to gain a better insight on the rural employment situation, we shall analyze some of the results of two previous surveys, the ILO survey of 1973 and the SEA survey of 1976. These surveys provide an estimate of the level of rural underemployment by comparing average labor supply and labor requirements in agriculture. As noted in the Appendix, the results of these surveys are not accurate, they should therefore be considered as rough estimates.

In 1973, the agricultural labor force was estimated to 595,000 workers occupied throughout the year, plus 114,000 temporary workers, mainly women and children. Of the total number of workers occupied throughout the year, 500,000 owned their farms or worked on farms owned by relatives while approximately 100,000 were landless workers.[29] Assuming that non-temporary workers worked 255 days of the year and temporary workers 127 days, the ILO mission estimated the total labor supply in 1970-71 to be 166 million man-days, while labor requirements in the sector amounted to 83 million man-days for the same year. Accordingly, the level of underemployment in the sector was 50 percent.[30] This figure would, however, be misleading. In order to tackle the problem of seasonality, the mission compared the monthly supply of labor with monthly requirements. However, the labor supply was assumed to be constant throughout the year. This is a strong assumption since during the busy season not only does agricultural employment increase, but also the size of the labor force itself, since many workers who otherwise would be inactive may take employment. Such is the case, for example, of women and children. The opposite happens at the slack season.

Agricultural workers were divided in four categories according to the size of the farms they cultivate: workers cultivating farms of less than 5 hectares, workers cultivating farms of 5 to 10 hectares, workers cultivating farms above 10 hectares and landless workers. The workers who cultivated farms of less than 5 hectares present the highest rate of underemployment. About 365,000 workers (61 percent of total agricultural workers) belong to this category. According to the census of 1970, 72 percent of the farms are of a size of less than 5 hectares. However, these tiny plots provide employment to an average of 6.5 family members. These small production units can hardly provide productive employment to all family members. However, from the *income* and *recognition* aspect[31] they are "employed," they all share the fruits of the farm as well as any additional income obtained from the surplus sold in the market, and they all participate in farm activities. From the *production* aspect, they are almost unemployed since the concentration of the entire family on a small piece of land necessarily implies that part of the employed labor is effectively non-productive. It is estimated that workers cultivating farms of less than 5 hectares (*minifundistas*) occupy less than half of their working capacity on their farm and devote part of their time to work as wage laborers on nearby farms. In total, these workers are effectively occupied only six months of the year.[32]

Underemployment among the *minifundistas* is greater than among the landless laborers. The latter are occupied about two-thirds or three-quarters of the year. The reason for this difference seems to be that the *minifundistas* have less freedom of movement because they must take care of their fields; this would be impossible if they were to work at any greater distance from their farms.[33]

Workers cultivating farms of a size of between 5 and 10 hectares are occupied only half their time. Although having the time, the members of this group do not work as wage laborers in other farms since they consider that this would lower their social status. This group constitutes 10 percent of the total agricultural workers. The rest of the workers, 13 percent of non-temporary agricultural workers, cultivate farms of a size over 10 hectares. These workers are subject to the lowest rate of underemployment. Workers cultivating farms of a size of between 10 and 20 hectares present an underemployment rate of 10 percent, while those workers with farms of a size over 20 hectares occupied all the members of their family and hired additional workers.[34]

When the level of underutilization of the different categories of agricultural workers is added, a total rate of underemployment of 41 percent is obtained (see Table 2.9). Comparing the total supply of and demand for labor in the sector, a rate of 50 percent underemployment is found. Thus, the ILO mission concludes that total underemployment in the agricultural sector may be between 40 and 50 percent.

TABLE 2.9   Underemployment in Agriculture, 1973

		Workers (in Thousands) with Access to Land by Farm Size						
				(Hectares)				
Workers	Landless Workers	Less than 2	2-5	5-10	10-62	62-182	Total	%
Total	100,000	300	63	60	64	8	595,000	100.0
Employed*	70,000	150	38	30	58	7	353,000	59.3
Under-employed	30,000	150	25	30	6	1	242,000	40.7

*equivalents of man-years of work.

Source: OIT (1975), p. 55.

The figures on underemployment in Table 2.9 were estimated by the ILO mission.[35] In 1976, the Secretariat of Agriculture (SEA) carried out an extensive survey on rural employment. According to this survey, underemployment in agriculture affects 64 percent of the total agricultural labor force. The supply of labor in the sector was estimated to an average of 575 man-days per farm while the demand was estimated to be an average of 209 man-days per farm.[36] Demand estimates are much lower than the estimates made by the ILO mission in 1973. Since the surveys are not comparable, we cannot say anything about changes in the employment situation in the agricultural sector. Besides, the SEA survey did not consider the problem of seasonality and therefore, as discussed above, their figures could be misleading.

Like the ILO survey, the SEA survey shows that the underemployment rate among the *minifundistas* is the highest. Underemployment in this group is 69 percent, while among medium and large farms underemployment rates are 62 and 43 percent respectively.[37] These figures seem very high, especially that on underemployment among large farms, since these farms usually demand labor in addition to family members.

The SEA and ONAPLAN surveys do not show any significant difference in the underemployment and unemployment rates prevailing in the different regions of the country. As Table 2.10 shows, the highest rates are found in the Southeast region, being 65.4 and 28.9 percent respectively.

TABLE 2.10   Rural Underemployment and Unemployment by Region, 1976 and 1980

	Underemployment Rate (1976)	Unemployment Rate (1980)
Country, total	63.6	26.1
Cibao	63.4	24.7
Southwest	62.6	24.6
Southeast	65.4	28.9

Sources: For 1976, SEA (1977), Table 4.4, p. 40. For 1980, ONAPLAN in IEPD (1985), Table 1, p. 8.

Considering the high rates of underemployment prevailing in the agricultural sector and the slow changes in land tenure and land-use structures experienced in the last decades,[38] the sector is not expected to generate sufficient employment opportunities to the increasing labor force. It is estimated that in 1990 employment in agriculture will not exceed 750,000. The sector's active labor force in the same year is estimated to exceed one million workers.[39]

Level of Income in the Rural Sector

According to the estimates of the ILO mission, in 1973 there were 495,000 workers cultivating their own land and 100,000 landless peasants working as wage laborers on medium and large size farms.[40] The mission estimated that a landless laborer could receive higher incomes than a *minifundista*, assuming that the latter did not work outside his farm. Thus, some *minifundistas* would earn less per month than the 33 pesos that, in 1973, was the average income of the landless workers.[41]

In general, rural incomes are very low. In 1973, 64 percent of the rural families received cash incomes equivalent to 37 pesos a month. In this same year, it was calculated that the per capita income in the sector represented one-fourth of the per capita income in urban areas.[42] In 1977, the average wage in the agricultural sector was 95.44 pesos per month. This was equivalent to the absolute poverty line which at the time was 94.90 pesos a month. In this year, the average monthly income of a rural family was 177 pesos. This is about half the corresponding figure of an urban family.[43]

The present income situation in the agricultural sector is probably worse. During the last few years, the factors affecting income levels and income distribution between the two sectors have not undergone any improvement. On the contrary, the situation may have worsened since the terms of exchange between rural producers and urban consumers have been biased against the former. (See Chapter 5.)

As a rule, small producers cultivate products such as rice, beans, roots, plantains, etc., which constitute the major components in the diet of the poorest group of the population. Products such as meat and milk for which there is a high demand among high income groups, are generally produced by large landowners.[44] The governmental policies implemented for keeping prices of basic food staples low and protecting poor urban consumers have had a negative effect on the income level of the small producers and widened the gap between rural and urban incomes. (See Chapter 5.)

Underemployment, Labor Shortage and Labor Imports

In spite of the high measured underemployment rates, many agricultural activities suffer from labor shortage and the participation of imported Haitian workers in the different activities of the sector is rapidly increasing.

Labor demand in the agricultural sector fluctuates throughout the year. The month of greatest activity is December. During this month, part of the sugar cane *zafra*, the coffee harvest and part of the rice, tobacco, peanuts and cocoa harvests all coincide. According to the ILO mission, even in December and the following months when the sector's activities are at a maximum, underemployment remains while in the harvesting areas a tremendous labor shortage exists. It is reported that in some areas, it is impossible to pick the entire coffee yield because of labor scarcity, while in the areas outside the hills where coffee is cultivated, labor exists in abundance.[45]

It is difficult to grasp that people should acquiesce to underemployment and poverty knowing that their labor is in demand some miles away from their homes. It is even harder to understand that in a country as poor as the Dominican Republic, with an extraordinarily high level of unemployment and underemployment, part of the product of the most important sector of the economy is actually lost because of labor shortage and that a considerable amount of the required labor is actually imported. In effect, about 90 percent of the sugar cane cutters and 29 percent of the coffee pickers are Haitian nationals. In the southwest region, these proportions are even higher; 98 percent of the cane cutters and 85 percent of the coffee pickers are Haitians.[46] Paradoxically, as noticed above, this region has the highest degree of urban underemployment and poverty among Dominicans (see Tables 2.6 and 2.7).

Referring to this problem, the ILO mission argues that the coexistence of underemployment and labor shortage in such a small country, with a relatively good network of path and roads, shows that the Dominican labor force has very little mobility. The low mobility is said to be a consequence of the composition of the rural labor force; at least four of every five rural workers are *minifundistas*, who have no desire to move from their small land plots to far away places for any greater length of time. This immobility of the rural labor force is also put forward by the mission as the explanation of the necessity to bring in Haitian laborers every year to the sugar cane plantations.[47]

However, the tremendous rural migration which has taken place in the Dominican Republic, provides a strong reason for doubting the validity of this argument. Why should rural workers take the paths and roads to the cities venturing the risk of becoming unemployed or underemployed instead of choosing the roads leading to those areas where a demand for labor exists? It is true that the *minifundistas* refuse to leave their *fundos*, but it is also true that the working conditions and the salaries paid in most agricultural activities are anything but attractive.

Obviously, if a person is to choose to work and live on subsistence land plots, or to migrate to a city risking unemployment and misery in the slums, the other alternatives before him must be even worse. Thus, if the rural worker prefers to continue to be underemployed on his small farm instead of moving to areas where labor is scarce, it must be because he is aware of the fact that moving will not award him any income increase. Although he may very well secure employment, he judges the wages paid in those areas to be too meager to justify the move. The opposite situation occurs when he decides to move to the city, i.e., although employment is far from being secured, he judges the wages paid and the living conditions prevailing in the urban areas as being worth the move.

There exists a direct relation between labor scarcity and the wage level paid in agricultural activities. The largest labor shortage is found in sugar cane cutting. However, this activity pays the lowest wages in the sector. In 1981, a worker could earn an average of 2.50 pesos a day in cane cutting and less than 2.00 pesos in weeding cane, while the average day wage in coffee plantations was 3.50 to 4.00 pesos.[48] These wage differentials attract the Haitian workers who originally were imported to work in the sugar cane plantations, but not the Dominican peasants who, on average, earn less than that by cultivating their small land plots.

For the latter, this wage differential is not sufficiently attractive to compensate for the cost of moving away from their families and farms and submitting to the difficult conditions of seasonal workers. Besides, as we will see in Chapter 8, sugar cane cutting has traditionally been an activity carried out by Haitian immigrants. Living and working conditions in the sugar plantations have never been good and Dominicans have generally considered cane cutting to be a job for Haitians. Coffee picking has traditionally been an activity carried out by Dominican landless laborers or small peasants, especially women. However, the increasing participation of Haitian workers has tended to outcompete the Dominicans. Haitians are generally preferred by the employers since, given the difficult economic situation in their home country, they are prepared to work for lower wages and endure working and living conditions that Dominicans reject. (The migration issue will be discussed in details in Chapters 8 and 10.)

Conclusions

The data presented in this chapter support the hypothesis that there is widespread underutilization of labor in the Dominican Republic. Although the figures should be taken with some care, the persistence of the problem during the last two decades emphasizes its magnitude.

Another indicator of the magnitude of the employment problem is the persistence of poverty, especially in rural areas. More than 60 percent of rural families live in absolute poverty. There is a considerable gap between rural and urban incomes. The average income of a rural family is about half the average income of an urban family. Rural-urban income differences may be one of the factors attracting the peasants into the cities.

Although there has been an intensive rural-urban migration movement, the rural sector continues to be the major supplier of labor. This sector, however, is unable to provide productive employment for the labor force. At the same time, since the employment situation in urban areas seems to be more attractive, many peasants prefer migrating to the towns rather than working in the sugar cane plantations or the coffee farms where labor is scarce. This labor shortage is filled with imported Haitian workers who, unlike the Dominicans, are prepared to accept the low wages paid in agricultural activities.

In the remaining parts of this work, we shall analyze the main factors behind the high levels of poverty and rural-urban migration prevailing in the Dominican Republic. The emphasis will be on the poverty aspect since, as will be discussed in Chapter 3, unemployment and underemployment measurements are highly unreliable and of limited relevance for understanding the complexity and dimension of the employment problem.

Notes

1. See OIT (1975), pp. 83-84.

2. The *labor force* consists of employed and unemployed persons. *Employed* are those persons who have a job. *Unemployed* are those who do not have a job and are currently looking for one. *Inactive* are those persons who do not have a job and are not looking for one. The sum of the labor force plus the inactive constitute the total population. (OIT (1975), p. 31. See also ONAPLAN (1982), pp. 11-12.)

3. OIT (1975), p.6.

4. It should be pointed out that, due to inconsistencies in the censuses of 1960 and 1970, the figures for the period 1960-1970 presented in Table 2.2 have been adjusted by the ILO mission (see OIT (1975), pp. 89-90). The figures for the period 1970-1981 are based on data from the respective censuses. The censuses of 1970 and 1981 allow some comparison. (See Appendix to the present chapter.) However, when interpreting the figures in Table 2.2, one has to keep in mind that they are somewhat shaky.

5. Internal migration and migration abroad will be discussed in Chapter 10.

6. World Bank (1978:1), p. 116. According to Graber (1978), p. 69, by the year 2000 the Dominican population will be 10.2 million, assuming that family planning programs will be moderately successful. If the birth rate is maintained unchanged, the total population will exceed 12 million persons by the year 2000. ("Moderately rapid decline" in fertility is not explicitly defined by these sources.)

7. Graber (1978), p. 70.

8. Del Rosario (1982), p. 11.

9. OIT (1975), pp. 31-34.

10. ONAPLAN (1982), Table 12, p. 31.

11. Ibid., Table 11, p. 29.

12. Ibid., p. 53.

13. Ibid., 31, p. 61.

14. The poverty line is, somewhat cryptically, defined as the "observed expenditure of a basic population group adjusted to compensate for the caloric deficit of this particular group." (Del Rosario (1982), p. 13.)

15. This includes on-farm consumption which constitutes 28 percent of rural family income. See Del Rosario (1982), pp. 14-15 and Tables 10, 10-A and 10-B, pp. 26-27.

16. OIT (1975), p. 34 and Table 4, p. 48. The minimum established wage in 1973 was 60 pesos per month. The minimum wage was unchanged throughout the period 1966-73. It was increased to 95 pesos a month in 1974, to 125 in 1978, to 175 in 1984 and to 250 in 1985. These wage increases, however, did not imply any increase in real terms since the inflation rate has been steadily increasing. Prices increased from an index of 100 in 1966 to 379.5 in 1983. (Dauhajre (1984), p. 45.)

17. The survey on the employment situation in the cities of Santo Domingo and Santiago in 1979 reveals that in those cities, 41.4 and 50.2 percent of the workers in the respective city earned less than 125 pesos a month. ONAPLAN (1981:1), p. 20 and p. 81.

18. ONAPLAN (1982), Table 47, p. 91.

19. OIT (1975), pp. 3, 35 and appendix 4, pp. 287-95. The definition of underemployment according to the norm of potential working capacity was very ambiguous. This included, for example, employed workers with few possibilities of promotion or earning low wages. The mission, however, acknowledged the deficiency of this measurement (ibid., p. 293).

20. Ibid., pp. 35-42. As will be discussed in Chapter 3, the concept of underemployment is difficult to define and measure. The figures on underemployment should thus be considered as rough indicators.

21. ONAPLAN (1982), pp. 120-21.

22. Ibid., p. 123.

23. Ibid.

24. Ibid., Table 67, p. 126.

25. Ibid., p. 125.

26. Ibid., p. 131. "Equivalent unemployment" among the underemployed is given by the following two equations: a) For the "visible" underemployed, i.e.,

those workers who involuntary work less than 35 hours per week, the "equivalent" rate of open unemployment is given by:

$$EU = \frac{S_v\,(J\text{-}H)}{J}$$

where S_v = number of workers visibly unemployed; J = number of hours worked by fully employed persons (35 hours); H = number of hours actually worked by the visibly underemployed. b) For the "invisibly underemployed," i.e., those workers earning less than the established minimum of 125 pesos per month and working more than 35 hours a week, the "equivalent rate of unemployment" is given by:

$$EU = \frac{S_i\,(Y_m - Y)}{Y_m}$$

where S_i = total number of workers invisibly underemployed; Y_m = the established minimum wage; and Y = total income earned by the invisibly underemployed. (See ibid., pp. 139-140.)

27. This assumption does not take into consideration the problem of indivisibility of labor. A man that is "invisibly" underemployed may not be able to take a new job to complement his income and thereby become "fully" employed, in that case, he will be confronted with a time constrain. This is however not the case of the "visibly" underemployed. There seems to exist some evidence of a rise in labor demand during the period of 1967-1973 been absorbed by underemployed. (See OIT (1975), pp. 112-113.)

28. Secretariado Técnico (1984:2), Table 6, p. 5 and Table 7, p. 6. The figure on rural unemployment seems to be an overestimation. (See Appendix to the present chapter.)

29. OIT (1975), p. 45. According to the 1980 SEA survey, the number of landless workers was 173,000 (see Rodríguez 1987), p. 30.)

30. Ibid., pp. 132-134. The level of underemployment varies throughout the year. The month with the highest rate of underemployment is October (67.3%) while December presents the lowest rate, 22.1% (Ibid., Table 58, p. 148.)

31. Amartya Sen distinguishes three aspects of employment: i) the *income aspect*, employment gives an income to the employed; ii) the *recognition aspect*, employment gives a person the recognition of being engaged in something worth his while; and iii) the *production aspect*, employment yields an output. (Sen (1975), p. 5.) We will come back to this in Chapter 3.

32. OIT (1975), pp. 45 and 131.

33. Ibid.

34. Ibid., pp. 45-46.

35. Estimates were based on interviews and data obtained from the agricultural census of 1971. (Ibid., p. 45.)

36. SEA (1977), Table 4.1, p. 38. Assuming the number of farms is the same as in 1971, i.e., 305,000 (see Table 6.4, Chapter 6) then the equivalent total labor supply and demand for 1975-76 are 175 and 64 million man-days, respectively.

37. Ibid. The SEA survey classified farms as follows: small farms (*minifundios*) = less than 5 hectares; medium-seized farms = 5 to 30 hectares; large farms = above 30 hectares.

38. In the last decade the group of *minifundistas* has been growing. The number of farms in this group has risen from 305,000 in 1971 to 385,000 in 1981. (See Chapter 6.)

39. IEPD (1983:3), Table 2.9, pp. 25 and p. 29. See also IEPD (1983:1), p. 21.

40. These figures differ from the preliminary results of the rural employment survey of 1980. According to the latter, there are 304,000 workers with access to land (50% own land and 50 % have access to it by leasing land, working on agrarian reform land, etc.) and 174,000 landless workers. (See ONAPLAN (1984).) It is difficult to say whether these differences are due to statistical deficiencies (the two surveys are not really comparable) or if in fact the number of workers with access to land has been decreasing and the number of landless workers has been increasing.

41. The figures refer to *minifundistas* owning less than 2 hectares and working part of their time on other farms. The information was obtained from a sample of 12,000 farms in the Cibao. (OIT (1975), p. 135.

42. See ONAPLAN (1983:1), p. 92.

43. A rural family has an average of 6 members, the corresponding figure for urban families is 5.5 members. (See Del Rosario (1982), pp. 14-15 and Tables 10-A and 10-B, p. 27.)

44. ONAPLAN (1983:1), pp. 92-93.

45. OIT (1975), p. 133.

46. ONAPLAN (1981:2), p.8. The number of Haitian workers participating in coffee picking seems to have increased over the years. According to a 1984 survey, 54 percent of the coffee farm workers were Haitian nationals (IEPD (1988), p.8).

47. OIT (1975), p. 134.

48. ONAPLAN (1981:2), p. 33. Wage differentials exist between the different agricultural activities as well as between the different regions of the country. The best paid activities in agriculture are the application of fertilizers and pesticides and the watering of different crops, while land preparation before planting and sowing is the lowest paid activity. In 1976, the wages paid in the former activities were 12 percent higher than in the latter. The same year, the lowest wages paid in agricultural activities were found in the Southwest region. The average wage in this region was 1.95 pesos per day, while the Cibao and the Southeast regions paid 2.22 and 2.69 pesos respectively. (SEA (1977), p. 47.)

Appendix to Chapter 2: Employment Statistics in the Dominican Republic

Any study of the employment problem of an underdeveloped country (in this case, the Dominican Republic) has to be based on statistical information. However, the available data on this subject are very scarce and of dubious quality. To use these data directly, without careful consideration of the procedures and methodological approaches with which the information was collected and recorded, will lower the quality of the study and thereby lead to highly questionable conclusions and misleading policy recommendations. The main purpose of this appendix is to analyze the available data on unemployment and underemployment in the Dominican Republic. The different sources of information, the procedures and methodology followed, the accuracy of the information and the degree of comparability between the different data will be considered.

Measurement Approach to the Employment Problem

One of the most important sources of information on the employment problem of the Dominican Republic is the national census of population and housing. This survey is carried out every ten years and it has the whole country as its reference population. The first national census with some information on employment was carried out in 1950 and the latest was accomplished in December 1981. However, the quality of the information on unemployment provided by these surveys is very low.

The definitions and measurement schemes used since 1950 in the unemployment surveys seem to have been uniform, but the methods used in the recollection and tabulation of the information have been very diffuse, varying from one census to the other.[1] As a result, the information obtained in the different surveys is not comparable and the construction of historical series on unemployment is almost impossible. Of the four censuses carried out until now, the one from 1950 seems to be the least accurate one. In this census, the population was not questioned about the type of working activity performed and it is not possible even to differentiate between the employed and the unemployed population.[2] Although the censuses of 1960 and 1970 are less diffuse, their information on unemployment is not comparable. While the reference period in 1960 was an unspecified week within a period of 7 months (January 1 to August 7), the reference period in 1970 was the week immediately before the survey (1st to 9th of January).[3] Another problem presented by these surveys is the reference age. The reference age for the economically active population of 1950 was seven years and above, whereas for 1960 and 1970 the reference age was ten years and above.[4]

Judging from the questionnaire designed, the recent 1981 population census seems to be fairly complete. Although it is constructed within the traditional approach, it would seem to be a potentially useful source of data provided that the information is processed in a thorough manner.[5] The reference period was the week immediately before the survey (7 to 12 of December) and the reference age, ten years and above. In this respect, the 1981 census is similar to the 1970 census and this may allow comparison of the employment situation of these periods.

An amazing fact is that in the 1981 census, as well as in the previous ones, the problem of seasonality in work availability is totally ignored. The period of the year in which the week of the survey is chosen is of great importance, but it seems that this is arbitrary. The 1981 census was first set for the 19th and the 20th of September. It was then postponed until November 14th and 15th and finally, by government intervention, the date was arbitrarily changed to the 12th and the 13th of December. This incident provoked a protest from a group of technicians, working in the statistical service, who considered the date to be very inadequate and culminated with the resignation of the director of the National Office of Statistics. A new director took office and the survey was carried out. December is the month of greatest activity in the country not only in commerce, but also in agriculture. According to the ILO mission, labor demand in the agricultural sector reaches its maximum in December as compared to the months of August, September and October where labor demand diminishes by 60 percent. During this month, part of the sugar cane *zafra*, the coffee and part of the rice, tobacco, peanuts and cacao harvests all coincide.[6] Obviously the information collected by the 1981 census may give a very misleading impression about the levels of urban and rural employment and unemployment.

Apart from the national census on population there are other complementary sources of information related to the employment problem. Different surveys have been carried out by government institutions such as the Central Bank, the National Planning Office (ONAPLAN), the National Office of Statistics (ONE) and the Secretariat of Agriculture (SEA). In 1973, the International Labor Office (ILO) carried out a survey on the employment situation. This survey seems to be the most complete one. Although it applied the traditional approach to the measurement of unemployment rates, it measured underemployment rates in urban and rural areas by using a combination of the income and the surplus labor approaches.[7] The Central Bank followed the income approach, while the SEA used the surplus labor approach.

The surveys carried out by ONAPLAN are fairly complete and uniform. Both unemployment and underemployment rates are measured, following the procedure of the ILO mission.

In this study, we make use of all available data on employment or any other data that may complement the information on the employment problem. Of course, we shall take into consideration the limitations and deficiencies of the data and the implications of the different methods with which they have been recorded. The next section discusses the accuracy and comparability of the available information on the employment problem in the Dominican Republic.

Statistical Data Available in the Country

The present available data on the employment problem, as reflected in unemployment and underemployment, were presented in Table 2.4. As discussed above, it is difficult to analyze the employment problem in a historical perspective. Unfortunately, the national censuses of 1950 and 1960 did not provide any valid information on unemployment.[8]

The data on unemployment rates presented in Table 2.4 were elaborated from different sources using different reference populations. Consequently, comparison of the unemployment rates of those periods is not possible. The only surveys that are at least partially comparable are those carried out by the Central Bank in 1969 and by the ILO mission in 1973. The Central Bank data were obtained from a survey on family budgets where the size and sources of income, as well as the expenditure pattern, of 552 families were studied. The ILO mission data were obtained from a survey on the employment situation in Santo Domingo using the same sample as the Central Bank survey. However, there were differences in certain definitions and question formulations in the surveys. Consequently their results are not comparable without previous adjustments.

According to the ILO mission, the sharp increase in the unemployment rate shown by these surveys (from 13.2% in 1969 to 20.0%

in 1973) is a result of differences in question formulation and definitions. Accordingly, after adjustment to the results of both surveys, the mission concludes that the rate of unemployment did not change during the 1969-1973 period but was maintained at a level of 14 percent in both 1969 and 1973. The sharp difference in unemployment rates shown by the two surveys, according to the mission, is due to the fact that in 1969, the unemployment rate was determined by asking those persons that did not work during the reference week if they did look for a job during that same week, whereas in 1973, the unemployment rate was determined by asking the unemployed persons if they were looking for a job without specifying the date.[9]

The surveys carried out by ONAPLAN in 1979, 1980 and 1983 allow some comparison of unemployment rates in Santo Domingo. These surveys use the same methodology and the same reference population. Accordingly, unemployment in the city of Santo Domingo increased from 19.3 percent in 1979 to 21.4 percent in 1983. According to the latest Central Bank surveys, total unemployment decreased from 25.1 percent in 1986 to 19.5 percent in 1987. The corresponding figures for the city of Santo Domingo were 22.7 and 18.2 percent for 1987 and 1988, respectively.

The results of the population census of 1970 and 1981 on unemployment rates, also allow some comparisons as the week of the surveys is relatively close (1st to 7th of January in 1970 and 7th to 12th of December in 1981). Accordingly, unemployment rates in the country have decreased from a level of 24.1 percent in 1970 to 20.7 percent in 1981. The unemployment rates for 1983, 1985 and 1990 presented in Table 2.4, are not the result of a formal survey but are estimates made by the World Bank mission. The shortcomings of these estimates are acknowledged by the mission.

The data on underemployment rates presented in Table 2.4 are not comparable. The only data available on urban underemployment are those elaborated by the ILO mission in 1973 and by ONAPLAN in 1980. No comparison can be made as the samples and reference populations are different. The data on rural unemployment and underemployment present the same difficulties.

In 1973, the level of underemployment in the city of Santo Domingo was measured by the ILO mission by studying the magnitude of fluctuations in the activities and income of employed persons, the number of hours worked per week and the difference in their earnings in previous and actual jobs.[10] The level of urban underemployment was then estimated to be 60 percent. The same year, the mission carried out a survey in rural areas and measured the level of rural underemployment by determining how small producers and rural workers expended their time during that year. With this procedure, underemployment was found to affect 41 percent of the agricultural labor force.[11]

However, the rural survey only covered a very limited number of workers and the sample was not really representative.[12] Using a surplus labor approach, where the traditional technology used and the productivity of labor were assumed to be unchanged, the mission related the labor requirements for different agricultural activities during the year 1970-1971 to the rural labor supply in 1970 and determined that the underemployment of labor in the agricultural sector was at a level of 50 percent.[13]

The SEA survey of 1976, although it followed a surplus labor approach, differs from the ILO calculations both in the reference sample and the procedure used to determine the labor surplus. While the mission measured the level of rural underemployment by first determining labor requirement per agricultural activity during a year, then relating it to the total rural labor supply during that same year, the SEA determined the level of rural underemployment by relating labor requirement for each farm size during the period of a year to the total labor supply of that same year. Thus, in 1973, the ILO mission estimated the rate of rural underemployment to be 50 percent, while three years later, the SEA estimated it to 63.6 percent. Given the differences in methodology, it is difficult to say which of these estimates is closest to reality. However, it has been argued that the SEA estimate is more reliable because it was calculated with information obtained from a formal survey,[14] while the ILO mission estimate is based on the mission's own calculations. However, as discussed in the main text, due to the problem of seasonality in agriculture, the results of both surveys are not really accurate.

The most complete survey on rural employment seems to be the one carried out by ONAPLAN and ONE in 1980. A preliminary rate of 26.1 percent rural unemployment has been presented. In this survey, the unemployed were defined as those who did not work during the reference period (the agricultural year before the survey) but tried to find a job or would have done so if they considered that they would be able to find one.[15] This definition includes the "discouraged" rural workers of which 73 percent are women. This may explain the high rate of 26.1 percent rural unemployment. Unemployment among rural women was as high as 53.2 percent, while among men it was 14 percent.[16] The 1980 survey takes the agricultural year as the reference period and not the week before the survey, as is usually the case.

Of the surveys mentioned in Table 2.4, detailed information on the employment problem can mainly be obtained from the Central Bank

survey on family budgets, from the ILO mission survey on employment
and from the ONAPLAN surveys of 1979 and 1980. Unfortunately,
despite the urgent need for information on the magnitude and evolution
of the employment problem, very little has been done to improve the
amount and quality of the statistical data.[17]

Conclusions

After analyzing the available statistical data on unemployment
and underemployment in the Dominican Republic, the following
conclusions can be drawn. First, given the variety of sources and the
differences in methodology, samples, reference periods and nature of
the surveys, it is difficult to analyze the evolution of the employment
problem in a historical perspective. Secondly, the only comparable
statistical data, albeit with certain reservations, are those concerning
unemployment rates for 1970 and 1981 obtained from the population
census for these years, those that refer to unemployment rates in the
city of Santo Domingo elaborated by ONAPLAN in 1979, 1980 and 1983
and those obtained by the Central Bank in 1986, 1987 and 1988. Finally,
(a) if the adjustments made by the ILO mission in the survey of 1973 and
on the Central Bank survey of 1969 are correct, the rate of open
unemployment in the city of Santo Domingo did not change during the
period of 1969-1973, (b) according to the data obtained from the
population censuses, the rate of unemployment in the country decreased
by 3.4 percentage points from 1970 to 1981, (c) according to the
ONAPLAN surveys, the rate of unemployment in Santo Domingo
increased with 2.1 percentage points between 1979 and 1983 and (d)
according to the Central Bank survey the rate of unemployment in the
country decreased with 5.6 percentage points between 1986 and 1987,
while in the city of Santo Domingo it decreased with 4.5 percentage
points between 1987 and 1988.

Considering the different sources, one could say that during recent
decades, the level of open unemployment, at least in the urban areas
has been around 20 percent. In the case of underemployment, the figures
seem to be less accurate which creates uncertainty regarding the real
rate. The figures however give some indication as to the dimension of
the problem.

Notes

1. See De Moya Espinal (1980), p. 15.
2. Ibid.
3. Ibid., pp. 15-16.

4. Ibid., p. 16.

5. See "Ahora" (1981), no. 938, p. 47. In 1989, the final results of the 1981 census were not yet available.

6. OIT (1975), p. 133.

7. For a description of these approaches see Chapter 3.

8. ONAPLAN (1968), p. 34.

9. For a comparison and readjustment of the 1969 and the 1973 surveys see OIT (1975), pp. 69 and 297-302.

10. Ibid., p. 35.

11. Ibid., p. 46.

12. Ibid., pp. 45 and 131.

13. Ibid., pp. 132-133.

14. See De Moya Espinal (1980), p. 30.

15. Secretariado Técnico (1984:2), p. 9.

16. Ibid., Table 14, p. 9.

17. In 1973, considering the strong need for information on the evolution of employment, unemployment, underemployment and income of the workers, the ILO mission recommended the realization of periodical surveys in the country. It suggested that at least two surveys per year should be carried out in the cities and rural areas. Accordingly, skilled personnel to carry out these surveys was already available in the country and the cost of carrying out the type of survey designed was relatively low. (OIT (1975), pp. 25 and 251-56.)

3

Unemployment or Poverty?

In the preceding chapter, we described the problem of underutilization of labor in the Dominican Republic. The description was based on the available statistics on employment, unemployment and underemployment as well as the level of income in rural and urban areas. It was pointed out that due to definition and measurement inconsistencies, the available information may not reveal the real dimension of the employment problem. In the present chapter, we will provide a critical exposition of the way in which the employment problem has been defined and measured in underdeveloped countries. The deficiencies and limitations of this procedure will be discussed with reference to the Dominican reality.

We will first briefly discuss some of the theories of employment in underdeveloped countries, as treated in the literature of development economics. This will provide a background to an explicit discussion of some of the concepts related to the subject which will in turn suggest the analytical framework underlying our study.

It will be argued that in the discussion of the employment problem of underdeveloped countries, too much emphasis has been put on the unemployment aspect. Although important, the group affected by open unemployment only represents the tip of an iceberg. A more widespread and serious problem is constituted by underproductive workers.

Approaches in terms of unemployment and underemployment could be very misleading when trying to grasp the magnitude of the employment problem, to identify its causes and find possible solutions. These concepts are very difficult to define and measure empirically, especially in countries where wage employment is relatively small and the majority of the workers are engaged in low productivity agriculture and services. A more adequate approach is to emphasize the poverty problem and identify the circumstances under which this arises.

The Employment Problem in Development Economics

Development economics is a relatively new field within economic science. In the 1950s, various development theories appeared. With few exceptions, these theories were of a very general nature.[1] The underutilization of human resources was often identified as one of the major factors constraining development[2] in the so-called Third World countries. Accordingly, the employment problem has received a great deal of attention in the economics of development but it has been one of the least successfully studied subjects within this discipline.[3]

Models of the labor market were essentially concerned with the transfer of workers from the rural or traditional sector, where they were considered to be underutilized, to the urban or modern sector where they would be efficiently employed. The dualistic model of Arthur Lewis[4] is the most well known model of employment. In spite of the severe criticism it has undergone,[5] it is perhaps the one that has had most impact on employment research and employment policies concerning underdeveloped countries. The Lewis model, refined and formalized by John Fei and Gustav Ranis,[6] identifies the presence of a modern industrial sector and a traditional subsistence sector as one of the outstanding characteristics of underdeveloped countries. The two sectors are assumed to function in totally different ways. The modern sector is dynamic and market oriented, the traditional sector produces for subsistence and does not necessarily follow profit-maximizing norms. In the former sector, output is a function of capital and labor while in the latter, output is a function of land and labor. The coexistence of these dissimilar sectors is what defines the dual structure of the economy.

Three key features that underlie the Lewis-Fei-Ranis model are: a) there is a surplus of labor in the rural traditional sector, b) capitalists in the modern sector invest most of their profits, and c) real wages are kept constant until the rural surplus labor is absorbed by the modern sector. These assumptions sharply differ from actual realities in underdeveloped economies. Firstly, the implicit assumptions that there is full employment in the modern sector and that, as the capitalists reinvest profits there will be a demand for labor that will absorb the rural labor surplus, seem to have little basis in reality. Often, the opposite has been the case: high rates of open unemployment and underemployment characterize the urban modern and informal sectors and so do low savings and investments by the capitalists. Secondly, the assumption of constant real wages is also defied by reality. In many underdeveloped countries, urban industrial wages have risen considerably in spite of high rates of urban unemployment while rural wages have lagged behind in spite of the outflow of labor to urban areas.

Nevertheless, the dualistic model has provided two major contributions to the understanding of the employment problem in underdeveloped countries. On the one hand it has emphasized the differences between the rural and urban sectors. On the other, it called the attention to the enormous transfer of labor that has taken place between the two sectors through the flow of rural-urban migration.

However, whatever positive insights the model has provided for the understanding of the employment problem of underdeveloped countries have been outweighed by its negative impacts on the policy designed for the solution of the problem. Firstly, the model has emphasized the general idea of a vertical development process and strengthened the belief that urbanization, industrialization and modernization are the ultimate solutions to the problem of underutilization of labor in these countries. Secondly, it has helped to perpetuate the erroneous belief that today's underdeveloped countries ought to follow the same development pattern as the industrialized countries, ignoring thus the historical and institutional factors that to a large extent influence development variables such as capital accumulation, technological changes and human capital.

The modernization and urbanization syndrome in underdeveloped countries has led to an unprecedented mass migration of peasants into the cities. It has widened the gap between urban and rural areas as most development policies have been biased in favor of the urban sector. The rural sector, which is the one which these economies rely upon for food production and the necessary surplus to stimulate the rest of the economy, has thereby been neglected.

The Employment Problem in Underdeveloped Countries

In the development literature it is very common to find expressions such as the following: "Unemployment is our most important problem"[7] or "One of the most perplexing - and serious problems now confronting many LDCs is their growing level of urban unemployment,"[8] or "Unemployment is increasingly emerging as the most striking symptom of inadequate development in most countries of the Third World."[9] This preoccupation is not only shared by large numbers of scholars dealing with development problems, but it is also one of the main topics among planners and policy makers within the underdeveloped countries. No doubt, an employment problem exists in these countries. The problem seems to be more serious than is revealed by actual statistics. The concepts of unemployment and underemployment are very complex and their measurement is difficult.

The employment problem is also present in the developed countries and the difficulties of definition and measurement are also apparent in these societies. However, in these countries, there exists a well structured labor market which to some extent facilitates accurate statistical quantification of the problem.

The employment problem in underdeveloped countries is highly complex. The group of persons confronting open unemployment may represent just a small fraction of the number of people affected by the employment problem. The concept of open unemployment is closely related to wage employment and, in many countries, only a small percent of the labor force is in wage employment,[10] while self-employment and family labor are common.

The Definition Problem

The concept of unemployment is, in its statistical measurement, generally identified by the Keynesian category of "involuntary unemployment." This refers to a person who is actively looking for work, who is prepared to accept the going wage and who is unable to find a job. Involuntary unemployment, as defined by Keynes, covers every unemployed man or woman willing to sell his or her labor at the going wage:

> ... there is involuntary unemployment to the extent that, at the current money-wage and with the current price-level, the number of men desiring to work exceeds the number of men for whose labour there is a demand.[11]

This definition clearly refers to a well structured labor market where the forces of demand and supply work in an efficient way. It implicitly assumes that information is available to the different agents of the market and that the unemployed person is qualified to do the type of work he or she is looking for. However, labor markets in underdeveloped countries are far from being well structured and efficient. In most of these countries, only a small fraction of the economy presents some of these characteristics.

In poor countries like the Dominican Republic, where only a very small section of the economy can be identified as "modern" and where largely backward agriculture is the main economic activity, the labor market presents characteristics which are totally different from those prevailing in more developed economies. It is extremely difficult to find a meaningful definition of unemployment and it is very misleading to limit the problem to the concept of "involuntary unemployment."[12]

If we look at the employment situation in the rural Dominican Republic, it is almost impossible to determine who is really employed or unemployed. First of all, for a peasant, work and leisure are not particularly clearly differentiated. The production process is a circular one. He may work very intensively during a given period or less intensively in another period, depending on the character of the crop. However he does not actively look for extra work. Others may work very hard but the income generated by their work is often below the subsistence level. Still, these workers are classified as "employed."

Another problem concerning the rural labor market is that of woman and child labor. These two categories of workers are usually involved in family or domestic activities. They participate intensively in harvest activities at peak seasons and are a very important factor providing services which, in the case of developed communities, would otherwise be purchased. Periodic entry and withdrawal from the labor force is also a very common phenomenon among rural women. This makes it very difficult to define the employment situation of these workers. The situation in urban areas is not less complicated, but here it is somewhat easier to identify at least those persons who are totally unemployed.

Given the limitation of the definition, in the sense that it may only apply to the wage sector of the economy, different efforts have been made towards defining the employment problem of the majority of the population in underdeveloped countries.

Those persons who, although working long hours, earn a very meager income, have been identified as the "working poor." There are also the "willing" and "idle" categories, respectively (see Figure 3.1 below). The "willing" group is composed of discouraged workers who are not actively looking for jobs but who would be willing to work if market opportunities were favorable. This group is outside the labor force but may enter it if the wage they require equals the wage rate prevailing in the market. The "idle" group is composed of people who work less hours than they may be willing to work. The "willing" people constitute the *hidden unemployed*, while the "idle" and the "working poor" constitute the *underemployed*.[13]

Within the category of the underemployed, a distinction may be made between the visible and the invisible. The visible underemployed are the employed persons who are seeking more work at going wages but are unable to find it.[14] Invisible or disguised underemployment covers those persons who are "technically at work but virtually idle."[15] However, these phenomena are also difficult to conceptualize and measure empirically. Very little has been done to develop appropriate techniques to measure their magnitude.

FIGURE 3.1   Classification of the Unemployed and Underemployed

1) Open unemployed

The "willing"   =   2) Hidden unemployed

The "working poor"⎫   ⎧Invisible

⎬   =   3) Underemployed   ⎨

The "idle"   ⎭   ⎩Visible

To determine whether a person is unemployed or underemployed, four criteria have been suggested: time, income, willingness, and the productivity criteria.[16] Thus, a person is considered to be underemployed if: (1) according to the time criterion, he works less than a determined number of hours or days a week; (2) according to the income criterion, his return from work per year is less than a determined minimum; (3) according to the willingness criterion, he is willing to work more hours than he is actually working, (4) according to the productivity criterion, his removal from work does not bring about any fall in output once the productivity of the remaining workers is improved by changes in technique and organization. However, these criteria may not exclude one another and may be difficult to apply since a person could be underemployed in more than one sense.

The use of these criteria is not sufficient for estimating the total underutilization of labor in the underdeveloped countries. In this respect, referring to the employment situation in South Asian countries, Gunnar Myrdal argues that it is not possible to acquire an accurate estimation of the size of the labor reserve in an objective way without considering the problem as a function of the policy measures to be applied in order to absorb the labor reserve at higher levels of labor efficiency and productivity.[17]

Given the complexity and the various aspects related to the employment problem, it may be very difficult to find an acceptable general definition of the problem. We cannot speak of an employment problem but of a range of related problems. According to Amartya Sen, in order to obtain an adequate understanding of the phenomenon, we have to consider both objective and subjective factors. Accordingly, the concept of employment includes an "income aspect," a "production aspect" and a "recognition aspect."[18] According to his view, the theoretical discussion around the employment problem of underdeveloped countries has mainly emphasized the production aspect.

In the surplus labor approach, it is assumed that people could be removed from the traditional sector without affecting production levels. This theory has failed to include the other aspects related to the problem. Labor is one of the most complex resources of production, it is a faculty or capacity inherent to human beings:

> By labor-power or capacity for labor is to be understood the aggregate of those mental and physical capabilities existing in a human being, which he exercises whenever he produces a use-value of any description. ... [The laborer is] obliged to offer for sale as a commodity that very labour-power, which exists only in his living self.[19]

Therefore, a theory of employment must take into consideration not only the perception of the theoretician, but also that of the people who are the object of the theories: "... the concept of employment has to be related to some notion of 'value' of the work. And the 'value' would vary depending on the persons from whose point of view the work is evaluated."[20]

From the production point of view, the man removed from the family farm may have belonged to the "disguised unemployed." However, from the income and the individual (recognition aspect) point of view, he was employed. He was sharing whatever income that was obtained from the farm and he was producing something. He was accomplishing a physical effort.

The production, income and recognition aspects may, in many cases, be independent from one another. The peasant working on a marginal plot may be disguised unemployed both in the production and in the income sense. However, he survives economically by means of borrowing or by relying on better-off relatives. Nevertheless, he may not view himself as unemployed and, in many cases, may not be ready to take up wage employment on other farms or in places away from his own farm.

In many cases, people engaged in work programs, promoted by the government as part of its political programs, may be just included in the payroll of a public institution. They may not be adding anything to production but, from the income and recognition aspect, they are employed. Furthermore, there are cases of the wealthy people who, although having plenty of income, are neither engaged in production nor in wage or self employment.

Given the many aspects related to the employment problem, it has proved to be very difficult to find an adequate definition of the problem, let alone its conceptualization and empirical measurement.

The Measurement Problem

When measuring underutilization of labor in underdeveloped countries, two major approaches are generally followed: a traditional approach, which consists of unemployment rate measurements, and a complementary approach which includes surplus labor and income measurements.

The Traditional Approach

The approach to the measurement of unemployment in underdeveloped countries is similar to the one used to measure periodical fluctuations of unemployment in developed economies. According to David Turnham:

> Of the few countries which undertake regular surveys, definitions are similar to those used by the developed countries, especially the United States, which in turn are very close to those recommended by the ILO ... the reference period is usually one week, part time workers are usually included in the total of employed ... and the unemployed comprises those actively seeking work who did no work during the reference period.[21]

This approach tends to ignore the reality of the labor market in most underdeveloped countries. The division of the economically active population into employed and unemployed does not allow us to measure low productivity and poverty which are two of the most important problems afflicting these countries. The measurement of unemployment rates may be of little relevance for countries where the majority of the workers are self employed in low productivity agriculture or services while the number of workers engaged in wage employment are relatively few.

This measurement scheme limits the employment problem to mere unemployment, thus reducing its magnitude to a fraction of the problem. Although this is important, it fails to reveal the complex range of questions related to the employment situation in underdeveloped countries. This procedure does not only underestimate the overall size of the employment problem but may also underestimate or overestimate the rate of open unemployment. By considering one week as the reference period, the problem of seasonality of work availability may be ignored. The approach further underestimates the magnitude of the employment problem by excluding from the economically active population those persons who, knowing the characteristics of the market, do not look for jobs because they know that, under prevailing conditions, they will be unable to find one.[22]

The limitations of the procedure place a heavy burden on any scholar trying to study, with some accuracy, the employment problem of an underdeveloped country. He is not only confronted with a scarcity of data but also with the low statistical quality of whatever data that is available. Generally, the economist dealing with the employment situation of an underdeveloped country washes his hands by means of a warning phrase at the beginning of his work on the accuracy of the data. With the help of these data, he then goes on to analyze the situation, presents general conclusions and makes policy recommendations.

The validity of these conclusions is seldom questioned. When it is, the economist may blame the quality of the data. He may blame the authorities for not providing financial means and qualified personnel to carry out the research. Authorities may argue that those means are not available. Hence, the practice of producing and misusing inadequate statistics continues. I am not suggesting that economists should not engage in studying the employment problem in underdeveloped countries because of the inferior quality of available data. However they must be more careful when dealing with these data and try to do whatever they can to improve their quality. The economists' indifference towards the quality of statistical data on underdeveloped countries has been pointed out by Myrdal:

> In regard to their dealing with figures, economists have never shown the same urge for clear and realistic concepts and the same concern for estimating uncertainty of measurements as, for instance, has been standard in demographic research. In studying underdeveloped countries, their carelessness with figures reached a climax, and this is still largely true about much of the economic literature on these problems.[23]

According to Myrdal, the accuracy of statistical data in underdeveloped countries is not only affected by deficiencies in the statistical service of those countries but to an even greater extent by the inadequate categories and misleading concepts under which reality is observed. In view of the deficiencies of statistics on unemployment in those countries, he asserts:

Unemployment is properly defined as involuntary worklessness within a fluid labour market with standardized requirements, and where the unemployed are fully aware of work opportunities and are skilled for the type of work they are seeking. In underdeveloped countries there are only minor sections of the economy where such conditions exist, and even there only with important reservations. Labor utilization has to be studied in terms of: who works at all, for how long a time during the day, the week, the month and the year, and with what effectiveness. On that there exist no overall statistics, and the trust in the carelessly assembled false statistics on unemployment and underemployment actually discourages the undertaking of more realistic and relevant research on worklessness.[24]

The Complementary Approach

General censuses and other major surveys on the employment situation in underdeveloped countries are carried out using the traditional approach and are limited to measuring unemployment rates. In order to compensate for some of the limitations of this procedure, complementary approaches such as "the surplus labor approach" and the "income approach" have been developed.[25] These two methods are designed to measure the phenomenon of underemployment and permit the study of those groups of persons who, although employed, have such low productivity levels that, in relation to their income and consumption, their situation is not much different from that of the unemployed.

The "surplus labor approach" is usually applied to the measurement of underemployment in the agricultural sector of underdeveloped countries. This method relates the amount of man-days available to the labor required to produce a given output or to carry out a given production activity. The excess of man-days available over labor requirement constitutes the labor surplus. This method also presents great limitations.[26] It is extremely difficult to determine how much work is required to carry out different agricultural activities since this is very much dependent on the type of technique used and the level of productivity expected. Thus, the proportion of man-days available, to man-days required to cultivate X hectares of rice varies directly with the techniques of production and labor productivity. If production techniques and productivity are assumed to be similar, or close, to that of a developed country, very few man-days will be required in rice production and the labor surplus will appear to be very high. Furthermore, as E. M. Godfrey has pointed out, the measurement of the labor surplus and its possible reallocation rely on three questionable assumptions:[27]

1) Divisibility. The surplus emerging from a labor-utilization calculation consists of a collection of fractions (expressed in man-days) of the working year of different workers. If the surplus is to be removed, it is assumed that a worker can do certain man-hours at the farm and the "surplus" man-hours in other activities. However, this would be possible only within a limited geographical area. Otherwise, only man-hours adding up to whole human units can be considered removable and the divisibility assumption would not hold.

2) Homogeneity. The nature of the man-days or hours worked by one individual does not differ from that of those worked by any other individual and, the nature of the work done at one time does not differ from that of the work done at any other time.

3) Involuntary unemployment. Anyone who works fewer than the stipulated number of hours does so involuntarily.

Despite its limitations, this method has been widely used to measure underemployment rates in agricultural activities. However, after discussing different attempts to measure surplus labor, Godfrey concludes that these estimates are "unlikely to be accurate enough to be usable as a basis for a policy of mobilizing that potential."[28]

The "income approach" to measurement focuses on the welfare of the population in order to determine the size and degree of the employment problem. The method is designed to measure the degree of poverty and the circumstances in which poverty arises mainly by collecting information on variables such as income, expenditure and sources of income. This approach allows measurement of the problem in a wider perspective. The poverty measurement covers both the unemployed and the low productivity workers.[29]

According to David Turnham, a poverty approach to the employment problem may help to correct the tendency to put too much emphasis on the unemployment aspect of the problem. At the same time, an emphasis on poverty offers "a somewhat more hopeful approach in the long term to measuring the size of the employment problem and degree of progress towards its solution."[30]

The employment problem is thus identified as a problem of inadequate income or, more specifically, as poverty that results from low levels of return from the effort of work. However, as Amartya Sen has suggested, although the concepts of poverty and unemployment are obviously related to one another, it may be wise to treat them as different categories as all those who are unemployed are not poor and all of the poor are not unemployed.[31] In the following, we will discuss the concept of poverty, in order to determine its relation to unemployment.

The Concept of Poverty

Poverty is a very controversial concept. Identifying its causes and finding a generally valid definition is very difficult. In many cases, the concept of poverty is related to subjective considerations. Some consider it to be a culturally conditioned phenomenon, or a voluntary state of individual cases. Others consider poverty as the result of "a downward process of circular cumulative causation"[32] or, as "an equilibrium state sustained by the people it generates."[33] But, however controversial the concept of poverty may be, very few would deny the existence of mass poverty. Most people in today's underdeveloped countries are very poor. Moreover they are also confronting increasingly deteriorating living standards.[34]

The characteristics and causes of poverty present a wide variation between the different underdeveloped countries. There has been a tendency to generalize on the causes of poverty. According to John Kenneth Galbraith, the causes of poverty have hardly been investigated, they have been simply assumed. Accordingly, these "assumed" causes of poverty became international macro level explanations such as lack of natural resources, lack of capital, the nature of government and the economic system, lack of education, intrinsic ethnic tendencies, climate, population pressure, colonialism and the specialization of underdeveloped countries as producers of raw materials and agricultural products. These arguments could be turned the other way around. Instead of explaining poverty, these arguments reflect the consequences of poverty.[35]

In general, the explanations provided for poverty are not the result of research on each individual country afflicted by poverty, but a diagnosis based on ethnocentric conceptions of poverty strengthened by the belief that poor countries, once cured from the disease of poverty, would reach development in the same fashion as the industrialized countries. Thus, what the underdeveloped countries need is what the developed countries have. In this respect, Galbraith asserts: "In the great explosion of concern over poverty, we did not ... move from cause to remedy; we moved from the only available line of remedial action to the cause that called for that action."[36]

Galbraith explains poverty as a state of equilibrium which is always restored by the acculturation or accommodation of people to the culture of poverty.[37] Accordingly, while in the rich countries people have accommodated to the idea of increasing incomes, in the poor countries, people have accommodated to persistent poverty. This absence of aspiration among the poor is what reinforces the equilibrium of poverty.[38] Galbraith argues that the efforts taken against poverty, have been made within the equilibrium of poverty. An example of these efforts is the case of improving agricultural methods in poor countries. Such a measure, it is argued, does not break the equilibrium of poverty. Industrialization and urbanization, which Galbraith calls "the escape to urban employment," have been neglected.[39] The myth of industrialization as the ultimate solution to poverty and as the road to development, is thus revived in about the same terms as the surplus labor theory:

> [The primary task of industrialization] ... is to employ those motivated to escape [the equilibrium of poverty]. The escape ensures their availability, and the motivation ensures, in the main, that they will seek to prepare themselves for the various kinds of industrial employment.[40]

There is vast evidence on the willingness of the rural poor of underdeveloped countries to escape poverty. An example of this is the tremendous rural-urban migration that has taken place in most of these countries during the last decades. However, in most of the cases, the escape has not been to industrial employment, but to urban self-employment and poverty.

Galbraith acknowledges that industrialization is not a firm promise for escaping poverty and thereby suggests migration of the poor to the industrial countries as the ultimate solution to escape the equilibrium of poverty. Taking Sweden as an example, he points to how successful the nineteenth century European migration flow to the United States has been, both for the countries of origin and the receiving country. He suggests that the story should be repeated in the case of the poor people of underdeveloped countries.[41] However, considering the strict immigration policies practiced today in the developed countries, this putative solution to mass poverty seems to be too optimistic. In order to understand the problem of poverty and find realistic and adequate solutions, we have to study each country afflicted by poverty as a special case and, without ignoring the responsibility of the industrialized countries, try to find solutions within the reality of the country in question.

Poverty and Unemployment

Poverty in underdeveloped countries manifests itself in a wide variety of aspects, ranging from malnutrition and diseases to illiteracy, inadequate production methods and inadequate income levels. Therefore, it may be inadequate to identify isolated factors as the causes of poverty. Low income levels are however one of the main factors maintaining the high level of poverty found in most underdeveloped countries. Poverty may not be the direct result of unemployment, but of the low level of return from work. In the poor countries, most people work very hard; many of them are not engaged in wage employment, nor are they unemployed or actively searching for jobs. In most cases, they are self-employed but the incomes obtained from the work effort keep them in absolute poverty.

An overwhelming majority of the poor are the "working poor." Open unemployment is largely concentrated among the young and better-educated in the urban areas. Waiting for better jobs, this group is generally supported by better-off relatives. "While not conspicuously poor, these young unemployed are often politically influential. Open unemployment is thus a political rather than an economic problem for governments. In these circumstances, there is little if any correlation between unemployment and poverty."[42]

Although intimately related, we cannot identify unemployment with poverty. Poverty is a wider concept and, in order to understand its dimensions, we have to consider the society afflicted by poverty in all its components:

> Poverty is a function of technology and productivity, of ownership of the means of production, and of exploitation and social arrangements for production and distribution. To identify unemployment with poverty seems to impoverish both notions since they relate to somewhat different categories of thought.[43]

Although belonging to different categories of thought and addressing two different problems, the concepts of poverty and unemployment are very much related. Using the concept of "exchange entitlements," i.e., the set of alternative bundles of commodities that a person can acquire in exchange of what he owns, Sen has argued that what prevents widespread starvation and poverty in countries like Great Britain or the United States is the guaranteed minimum values of exchange entitlements provided by the social security system. However, in the absence of social security, which is the case in most underdeveloped countries, the entitlement of a person's labor power will be zero if he cannot obtain employment.[44] In the absence of a well organized labor market, higher levels of productivity and social security system, general poverty or regular starvation will be inevitable since the exchange entitlement of most of the people will in consequence be very low.

Concluding Remarks

The employment problem in underdeveloped countries is intimately related to the development strategy followed by these countries. In the main, this strategy has focused on the implementation of development patterns experienced by the industrialized countries. Industrialization and modernization policies have been pursued without paying much attention to the resource endowments, and to the institutional and socioeconomic structures of the country in question. This has resulted in a major underutilization of human resources and in the marginalization of the rural (agricultural) sector.

The definition and measurement of the employment problem of the underdeveloped countries has been very much attached to the experience of the developed countries. Generally too much emphasis has been put on the unemployment aspect of the problem. There have been attempts to measure underemployment through different criteria, but both concepts have proved to be very difficult to define and measure adequately. A more adequate approach to measuring and finding solutions to the employment problem is to put the emphasis on the poverty aspect. Attention should be directed towards low productivity work since, unlike open unemployment, this affects nearly all workers and sectors of the economy.

In order to contribute to the understanding of the employment problem of the LDCs, the concept of employment must be broadened so as to include the aspects of income distribution and poverty, underutilization of labor, shortage of work opportunities, aptitude and attitudes to work. Limiting the employment problem to unemployment and underemployment may have very negative consequences for finding solutions to the problem. As Paul Streeten has emphasized:

> Approaches in terms of "employment," "unemployment" and "underemployment" are misleading because they suggest that an increase in effective demand and the provision of equipment are all that is needed to absorb labour and raise production while all other conditions are adapted or easily and quickly adaptable to full labor utilization.[45]

In most underdeveloped countries, these "other conditions" are far from being easily adaptable. A study of the employment problem of a country ought to be multi-faceted and interdisciplinary. The interplay of historical, economic, social and cultural factors must be taken into account if we are to tackle efficiently the wide range of different issues which ultimately constitutes the employment problem.

The Dominican Republic with its particular socioeconomic setting has an employment problem which is much more complex than may be suggested by unemployment or underemployment rates. Although it has many characteristics in common with other underdeveloped countries, the Dominican Republic exhibits certain features that make it, more or less, unique. It is, for example, one of the countries within the Western Hemisphere with the highest degree of state ownership. The state is the largest employer in the country but, at the same time, it patronizes labor imports to its sugar plantations. The state plays a decisive role in the performance of the country's economy. These, and many other factors, suggest that in order to get a broad understanding of the employment problem one has to study a range of related problems affecting the economy in question. Such an analysis may help us to identify different factors which are important in order to explain the persistence of unemployment and poverty.

In this study, much emphasis is put on the analysis of the socioeconomic structures of the Dominican Republic and the different policies that may have prevented an efficient use of labor resources in the country. The study focuses mainly on the poverty problem and the rural-urban dichotomy that has arisen due to the development strategy followed in the country. In other words, we shall identify the different mechanisms by which underutilization of labor and poverty are created and maintained.

The roots of the problem of rural poverty and migration are not to be found in the operation of the labor market itself, but in the factors determining labor demand and supply. They are to be sought in the pricing policy for agricultural products, in the distribution of land-ownership, in policies that bring about capital market imperfection, imports of foreign labor, high protection of industry and neglect of agriculture and the concentration of free or subsidized social services to urban areas.

The Dominican economy is predominantly agricultural. Thus, in any analysis of its employment problem, the presence of the agricultural sector will weigh heavily. A large part of this study is therefore concentrated on the analysis of this sector. Agriculture is a multi-faceted activity where different factors intervene in the process of production and marketing of the products. Production activities are in turn largely influenced by the performance of the factor markets, namely, land, credit and labor. An analysis of, on the one hand, the structure of and the interaction between these markets and, on the other hand, the different policies that have influenced their performance, will help us to identify the different factors that have given rise to an underutilization of labor resources in the agricultural sector and to mass migration of peasants into the cities.

The decision of the Dominican peasants to migrate is not only determined by the situation they face in the rural areas but also by the situation prevailing in the urban areas. Thus, it is also important to analyze the different urban factors attracting the rural migrants and the policies behind the urbanization and industrialization process.

However, contrary to some of the theories outlined above, migration will not be viewed as an equilibrating factor where "the Invisible Feet of faceless homogeneous workers"[46] tend to equalize wages and eliminate dualism between the modern and the traditional sectors, but as a process that tends to widen inequalities and dualism between and within these sectors.

Since the peasants are the main actors in the scenario we intend to analyze, we start by identifying them as a social group: who are they, how did they come about, how have they been affected by the development strategy followed in the country, etc. These issues will form the subject of the next chapter.

Notes

1. Rostow's stages of development is an example of this, see Rostow (1960). For a critical exposition of these theories see for instance Meier (1976), Chapter 2 and Lundahl (1981).

2. The meaning of economic development does not meet with general agreement. In the early years of the discipline, economic development was synonymous with economic growth and modernization. More recently, it has also been identified with the accomplishment of social objectives such as employment, equity, poverty eradication and basic needs. (For an extensive analysis of economic development as a policy objective for the underdeveloped countries and the different changes and divergence of opinion about this topic, see Arndt (1987) and Little (1982), Chapters 1 and 2.)

3. Yotopoulos and Nugent (1976), p. 198. Berry and Sabot (1984), present similar criticism in their account of the evolution of thought about labor markets in underdeveloped countries.

4. See Lewis, (1954) and (1958).

5. For a critical exposition of the dualistic theory, see e.g. Griffin (1969), pp. 19-31, Frank (1967), p. 6, Yotopoulos and Nugent (1976), pp. 205-233, Jolly et al. (1973), pp. 9-19.

6. Fei and Ranis (1964).

7. Lewis (1972), p. 9.

8. Meier (1976), p. 170.

9. Jolly et al. (1973), p. 9.

10. See Squire (1981), Table 17, p. 58.

11. Kahn (1976), p. 21. This is a reformulation of Keynes formal definition of involuntary unemployment (see Keynes (1973), p. 15).

12. For a detailed exposition of the limitation of this approach see Turnham (1971), pp. 41-71. See also Bruton (1978).

13. Yotopoulos and Nugent (1976), p. 201.

14. Turnham (1971), p. 57.

15. Ibid., p. 17.

16. Krishna (1973), p. 475.

17. Myrdal (1971), pp. 226-27, 229-30.

18. Sen (1975), p. 5.

19. Marx (1977:1), Vol. I, pp. 164-65.

20. Sen (1975), pp. 3-4.

21. Turnham (1971), p. 44.

22. An alternative measure of rural unemployment which considers the problem of involuntary withdrawal from the labor force by potential job seekers has been suggested by Bardhan (1978).

23. Myrdal (1981), p. 504.

24. Ibid.

25. See Turnham (1971), p. 17-21. In order to overcome the shortcomings of the traditional approach, a variety of alternative approaches to measuring underutilization of labor have been suggested by different authors. However, these approaches also present the shortcomings and difficulties related to their practical application (see Standing (1981), pp. 25-54). Here we shall only consider the surplus labor approach and the income approach which are the most frequently used.

26. Ibid., p. 18.

27. Godfrey (1967), pp. 61-63.

28. Ibid., p. 66.

29. Turnham (1971), p. 19. This approach has been used in the ILO country reports where an important component of underemployment is measured by an income criterion. Workers earning below some reference level, generally given by the officially established minimum wage, are classified as "invisible" underemployment. (Cf. Squire (1981), pp. 65-66 and ILO (1975), p. 37.)

30. Turnham (1971), pp. 18-19.

31. Sen (1975), p. 38.

32. Lundahl (1979).

33. Galbraith (1979).

34. In 1969, 47.9 percent of the population of the LDCs was receiving annual per capita income below the poverty line of US$75.00 (in 1971 prices). (See Ahluwalia (1979), p. 10 and Table 1.2, p. 12.)

35. Galbraith (1979), pp. 16-26.

36. Ibid., p. 40.

37. The "culture of poverty" concept has been in vogue during the last decades among sociologists and anthropologists. Sociologist Walter Miller (1968, p. 27) argues that poverty is a way of life supported by its own set of self-perpetuating values and attitudes. By the same token, Oscar Lewis (1966, 1968), considers the culture of poverty as an adaptation and reaction of the poor to their marginal position. Anthropologist Marvin Harris (1975, p. 475), strongly opposes these views and argues that they imply that poverty is largely the

responsibility of the poor, relieving thus any guilt from the ruling and middle classes.

38. Galbraith (1979), p. 56.
39. Ibid., p. 82.
40. Ibid., p. 96.
41. Ibid., pp. 97-101.
42. Arndt and Sundrum (1980), p. 65.
43. Sen (1975), p. 38.
44. Sen (1981), pp. 4, 8 and 212.
45. Streeten (1970), p. 55.
46. Nugent and Yotopoulos (1979), pp. 544. In contrast to the equilibrating mechanism inherent in the orthodox approach these authors suggest that migration should be viewed in a disequilibrium perspective.

4

The Dominican Peasantry

Until recently, the majority of the Dominican population lived in the rural areas and worked in agricultural activities. During the last decades, however, the country has experienced deep structural changes and an unprecedented mass migration of peasants into the urban areas. The migration flow has been accompanied by increasing urban unemployment and social distress.

In order to get a good grasp of the push factors behind this migration, it is important to analyze the performance of the agricultural sector. A study of the historical processes that have shaped the Dominican peasantry is important for understanding the actual realities. The subjects discussed in this chapter will serve as a background to the subsequent analysis.

The chapter contains four main parts. The first presents some characteristics of the peasantry as a social group. The second part analyzes the development of the Dominican peasantry in a historical perspective. Emphasis will be given to the relation between the peasantry and the different rulers of the country. The third part discusses the social situation of the peasantry. It will be shown that throughout Dominican history, the peasant sector has been highly neglected in relation to the urban dwellers. It has remained in a marginal position, unable to enjoy the fruits of development and unable to influence the socio-political and economic setting of the country.

The extent to which the Dominican peasantry has taken part in the political life of the country will be discussed in the fourth and last part of the chapter. It will be argued that mass migration is mainly a result of the rural-urban inequalities that prevail in the country and one of the ways the peasants expose their dissatisfaction with the *status quo*.

Definition of the Peasantry

Throughout this work, we refer to the Dominican rural population as peasants.[1] It could therefore be wise to state explicitly how we define a peasant and why we include the Dominican rural dwellers in this category. Teodor Shanin summarizes the most salient characteristics of the peasantry as a social group in four facets:[2]

1) The peasant family farm is the basic unit of a multidimensional social organization. The family provides most of the labor on the farm. The farm provides for most of the consumption needs of the family and the payment of the latter's duties to the holder of political and economic power.
2) Land husbandry is the main means of livelihood and provides directly the major part of consumption needs. Traditional farming includes a specific combination of tasks on a relatively low level of specialization. The mainly agricultural economy with low capital investment accounts for the crucial importance of landholding and makes it a decisive factor of social stratification in terms of wealth, power and prestige.
3) A specific traditional culture is related to the way of life of small communities. The predominance of traditional and conventional attitudes, i.e. the justification of individual action in terms of past experience and the will of the community, may be an example.
4) The "underdog" position, i.e., the domination of the peasantry by outsiders. Peasants, as a rule, have been kept at arm's length from the social sources of power. Political organization, educational superiority, and mastery of the means of suppression and communication give powerful outsiders an almost unchallenged hold over the village communities. Political subjection interlinks with economic exploitation and cultural subordination. Land tenure, political power and market cartelization operate here as the major mechanisms of exploitation.

Many of these characteristics are present in the Dominican countryside. However, due to migration and increasing contacts with the urban world, in some communities the "predominance of traditional and conventional attitudes" may not be so strong. In fact, many communities are going through a gradual disintegration.

The Dominican peasant is highly integrated into the market economy. Most of the peasants produce with the urban market in mind and many of them almost reach specialization. Besides, many peasants are totally or nearly landless and have to work as wage laborers on larger farms. Still, the Dominican peasant lives in relative isolation and in a subordinate position. He lives far away from the country's decision makers. Outsiders put the price on his products and make decrees that affect his life.

> The outsider sees the peasant primarily as a source of labor and goods with which to increase his fund of power. But the peasant is at once an economic agent and the head of a household. His holding is both an economic unit and a home.[3]

Unlike a farmer, a peasant does not run an agricultural business enterprise, he runs a household. His production unit is a small family farm where inputs are mainly family labor and rudimentary tools. Investment in terms of improved seeds and modern machinery is very limited or non-existent.

The peasant produces a surplus not only in order to obtain urban goods or complementary foods that he does not produce. Furthermore he sustains that group of outsiders that do not cultivate the soil. The peasant's surplus is appropriated by this group of urban rulers who in their turn use this surplus to develop the non-peasant sectors. The subordinate relationship of the peasants to an external power is what ultimately defines a peasantry.[4]

Of the four characteristics described above, we shall concentrate on the fourth, i.e. the "underdog position of the peasantry." We shall analyze the relation between the Dominican peasants and their different rulers and determine how the former have traditionally been neglected in relation to urban dwellers. But before, we must consider some of the stereotypes that have tended to reinforce the urban bias that today predominates in many underdeveloped countries.

The Urban Conception of the Peasantry

The alleged superiority of urban life is an old phenomenon.[5] Urban people tend to be more sensitive to changes. The town dweller normally does not see himself as a member of a close-knit community. His world is wide; cosmopolitan and new ways of thinking have a tendency to appear in urban settings.[6] Thus, urban people often have a tendency to look at the rural population with some sort of disdain. The awkward peasant is a stock-figure in literature and popular humor. One looks with amazement on his "conservatism" and "backward manners."

Notions related to this view, i.e. that the peasant is a person who stubbornly resists innovations and prefers to cling to his antiquated customs, have found their way into different ideologies. Marx, for instance, had some difficulties in accepting the peasants as a class. He was opposed to the private ownership of land and thought the peasants were an obstacle for the welfare of the rural proletariat. He however acknowledged the peasant's dependency on the outsiders:

> The small holding of the peasant is now only the pretext that allows the capitalist to draw profits, interest and rent from the soil, while leaving it to the tiller of the soil himself to see how he can extract his wages.[7]

However, this understanding did not hinder Marx from depicting the French peasants' support to Napoleon III as a symbol that "bore the unmistakable physiognomy of the class that represents barbarism within civilization."[8] In other works Marx further states that "peasants cannot represent themselves, they must be represented," since their way of life and economic interests means that one finds "no community, no national bound and no political organization among them."[9]

However, it is not only within Marxist ideologies that there exists a tendency to view peasants from the outside and consider them to belong to a class that has to disappear in the name of progress.[10] Some authors, using arguments resembling some of the postulates of the theory of the "culture of poverty," also uphold conceptions of the peasantry as a backward group of people characterized by apathy, resistance to innovations, suspiciousness, submissiveness and ignorance.[11]

These views are very common in today's underdeveloped countries. Peasants are generally absent from the political life there, are without representation and are subject to discrimination from the ruling urban elite. There also exists in these countries a socially important gap between the majority of the rural population and the urban population. This situation has, unfortunately, led writers like Michael Lipton to view the urban and rural areas of underdeveloped countries as opposite poles where the latter are discriminated and exploited by the former. This simplistic view has led Lipton to claim that "conflict and polarization between urban and rural classes is the 'leading contradiction' in most poor countries."[12] This geographical polarization tends, however, to ignore the existing inequalities and class conflicts within both rural and urban areas. Although an overwhelming majority of the poor of these countries are located in the rural areas, we cannot view inequality merely in geographical terms. One of the major conflicts found today in, for instance, the Dominican Republic and many other Latin American countries is that between the large landowners and the peasantry.

Origin and Development of the Dominican Peasantry

As will be shown in Chapter 6, the land tenure system that presently predominates in the Dominican Republic is the *latifundio-minifundio* system. This system implies that the overwhelming majority of the cultivable land (55 percent) is in the hands of a few large landowners or *latifundistas* (less than 2 percent of the landowners). On the other extreme we have the *minifundistas* (82 percent of the owners) cramped together on about 12 percent of the cultivable land (see Table 6.4). The members of the latter group belong to the category we refer to as peasants in the present study.

The Dominican peasantry is, however, of recent origin. Although during the colonial era there were some independent small producers - mainly Canarians in the Cibao area - it was not until after the abolishment of slavery in 1822 that the peasantry emerged as a social group. In the following we shall summarize how this process took place.

The Colonial Period

By the time Columbus sighted Hispaniola, the island was inhabited by around 250,000 to 400,000 Taíno Indians. In less than 40 years the Spaniards succeeded in exterminating the entire native population.[13] Many Taínos died from measles and other diseases but many others lost their lives owing to the labor the Spaniards forced them to execute, particularly in mining precious metals. Mining was the main economic activity of the island in the first decades of colonization, leaving agriculture as a marginal occupation. Most of the silver and gold was transferred to Spain. Thus, just a minor part of it was used for investment and accumulation. In the course of time, the supply of precious metals decreased and the cultivation of sugar cane came to play a more important role.[14] Cattle breeding also became an important part of the island's economy. The cattle the Spaniards had introduced multiplied rapidly and big herds of *reses cimarrones* (maroon cattle) roamed all over the island.

The vanishing Indian labor force was replaced by slaves imported from West Africa. At the close of the sixteenth century, a certain type of pattern had evolved in the agricultural production: on the one hand an agroindustry directed to the export market, i.e. sugar cultivation, and on the other hand small-scale farming of traditional, basic foodstuffs. Sugar was cultivated on *latifundios* owned by a few wealthy families.[15] Small-scale farming was directed only to internal production and the techniques used were rudimentary.[16]

During the seventeenth century, the Spanish colony suffered a period of decline. The English maritime dominance isolated Hispaniola from Spain and exposed its ports to raids from different hostile powers. The Western part of the island was penetrated by the French and in 1697 Spain, in the treaty of Ryswick, acknowledged French possession of this part. While the sugar industry flourished in the French colony, it deteriorated in the Spanish colony and an exodus of plantation owners and commoners alike led to a drastic reduction of its population - in 1509, 12,000 free Spaniards lived in the colony, but by 1730 their number was reduced to 6,000.[17] In those days cattle-breeding had replaced sugar as the main economic activity of the Spanish colony.

One can trace the rise of the Dominican peasant society back to the colonial period. In theory, the Spanish king was the sole owner of all land in Hispaniola, and theoretically speaking, the cultivators of the land did not own it. It was given them as a royal *merced*, i.e., a right to cultivate it, legalized in the form of an *amparo real*, a written evidence of the cultivator's occupation of the land.[18] From 1558 a wealthy settler who could support a large farming or cattle-raising establishment was given a larger, initial grant (*merced*) than a poor settler. He also had the right to establish tenants on his property.[19] Besides the *mercedes* there existed the so-called *ejido* system, i.e. land that was administered by the *cabildo*, the town council. The *ejido* land was mainly constituted by pastures and forests intended for common use, but it could also be leased to individual settlers.[20]

From the middle of the sixteenth century, the predominant system of landholding was that of *terrenos comuneros*. Under this system, there was collective possession of land so that several owners had shares called *pesos* , or *acciones*, in the same land. When the original owner of an *amparo real* died, the land was divided among his wife and children. One half belonged to the widow and the other half was divided among the children in equal parts, but the land was never surveyed. When they married and had children, their shares were further subdivided. However, these divisions were only theoretical. For centuries, land was neither surveyed nor partitioned. Landownership came to be defined as the ownership of *pesos* or *acciones de tierra*, which gave rights to use the land. A major reason that prevented the partition of the land was the high cost for surveying, the small value of the lands and the nature of the property itself:

As it would be impossible to give pasture, wood, arable land, and water to each of the owners, or to deprive them of a single one of these elements without causing them irreparable damage, the necessity arises for harmonizing their interests through community of possession under a common title. When any of the proprietors wishes to sell his share, after having offered it to his co-owners and been refused, he can sell it to a stranger, who enters not into the community of the family, but into that of the proprietorship as co-owner. ... Thus a person buying for $50 the right to enter a communero tract, that may comprise several leagues, can take any part or all of it that is not occupied, no matter how much it may be, provided he does not interfere with the improved land of any one else, or the land from which is drawn their supplies of timber. To secure his title he must, however, occupy and use it.[21]

This type of landholding had been reinforced by the low population density, by the abundance of land, and by a pattern of extensive exploitation associated with cattle-raising and woodcutting.

With the passage of time, thousands of sales, inheritances, donations, transfers, and turnovers of land took place. Everybody seemed to know what his rights were and nobody seemed uncomfortable with the system, since the main economic occupation of the population was cattle-raising, done by using the land extensively and letting the herds roam around as freely as possible.[22]

The *terrenos comuneros* were, however, often a source of dispute. Already by the late 1850s Pedro F. Bonó advocated the division of the land. He considered the system of *terrenos comuneros* to be negative for agricultural production since the uncertainty of property and the risk of usurpation discouraged many producers.[23]

The Consolidation of the Dominican Peasantry

The nineteenth century was dominated by extreme political unrest. In 1804 the western half of the island, occupied by France since 1697, freed itself and emerged as the independent Republic of Haiti. Some of the inhabitants in the Spanish part of the island lived in constant fear of being conquered by the Haitians, and annexation took place in 1822. This lasted until 1844 when the Spanish colony became the independent Dominican Republic.

At the beginning of the nineteenth century, Dominican agriculture was limited to the cultivation of some subsistence crops. The production of export crops was concentrated to the Cibao area, and a few *ingenios*, sugar mills with surrounding plantations, in the South. The most important economic activities were cattle-breeding and the felling and exportation of precious wood.[24]

The most important product of the Cibao was tobacco. The cultivation of this product had gained importance during the eighteenth century, particularly after 1770 when exports of tobacco leaves to factories in Sevilla began.[25] Tobacco growing in the Cibao was an activity for "free," small cultivators.[26] The *ingenios* in the South produced rum and sugar. They were operated by slaves who also produced subsistence crops for themselves on small plots, *conucos*, in the vicinity of the mills.[27] The political instability that characterized the end of the eighteenth century and the first half of the nineteenth led to a decline of the plantation economy. Many plantation owners left the country, while the slaves stayed on "their" *conucos* and with time became small peasants.

For a long time the most important production system in the Spanish part of the island had been the so-called *hatos*. A typical *hato* consisted of *la sabana*, pastures where 400-500 animals were tended and *la montería*, bushy backwoods where *reses cimarrones* roamed.[28] The *hatos* were operated by an average of five slaves. The slaves cared for themselves, tended the livestock on the pastures and hunted the wild cattle and pigs in the *monterías*, which together with the crops on their small *conucos* provided them with food.[29] The abolishment of slavery which took place with the Haitian invasion in 1822 did not change much of the *hato* slaves' existence.[30] They stayed on their *conucos* and many continued to work for the *hateros*, who in the course of the century drew more and more attention to the *monterías* where the felling of precious trees became an important source of extra income.

When the Haitians took possession of the Spanish part of the island they did not meet any resistance. As a matter of fact, their arrival was awaited with high expectations by some Dominican groups. The slaves wanted their freedom and also expected to be given land, as land had already been divided between the former slaves in Haiti. Some producers of export goods, like tobacco, wood and hides, hoped for better times through the opening up of new markets.[31]

In a way, expectations were fulfilled. From 1822 to 1842 the production of tobacco increased from 589,000 to 2,622,000 pounds per year. During the same period the exports of precious wood were doubled.[32] The Haitians started to distribute land to former slaves and Haitian officers. The settlers were given the land on the condition that they had to devote part of it to the production of export crops like cocoa, sugar cane, cotton and indigo.[33] The Haitians tried to limit the extensive cattle breeding that occupied fertile lands and damaged agriculture, since free-roaming cattle and pigs from the *monterías* did not leave the crops in peace. The Haitians aimed at eliminating the system of *terrenos comuneros* under which it was not possible for the state to control the landed property in the country. But this effort proved to be in vain.[34]

The *hateros* were upset about the measures taken by the Haitian government, and their indignation was soon to be shared with the majority of the Spanish speaking population of the island. The former *hatero* slaves were reluctant to change their customs and turn themselves into full-time agriculturalists. The tobacco growers in the Cibao area were unwilling to extend their production and cultivate other export crops as well. But the most important reason for the common discontent was a sudden change in Haitian agricultural policies.[35]

In an attempt to increase the agricultural production of the country, the Haitian president Jean Pierre Boyer abandoned the model based on small cultivators and tried to introduce large-scale production and forced labor. The *Code Rural* of 1826 stated that all men who were not state functionaries, or who did not have an occupation sanctioned by the state, had to work as agriculturalists and they were not allowed to leave their fields without permission. The distribution of land was stopped and landless laborers were not allowed to leave the land of their employers. If they did so they were to suffer severe punishments. The enforcement of the law failed, partly due to the fact that the military was reluctant to force people to obey the law. (The majority of the soldiers had been either slaves or small proprietors.)[36] The *Code Rural* increased the Spanish population's discontent with their Haitian rulers and became an important incentive to the revolt that in 1844 led to the formation of the independent Dominican Republic.

Considering that the severe Haitian laws were an important reason for the Dominican rebellion it may seem strange that the rural laws of the newborn republic were a faithful reflection of the despised Haitian ones. The Dominican law that was going to have the most profound influence on the treatment of the Dominican peasantry was the so-called *Ley de Policía Urbana y Rural* from 1848.

This law regulated rural life in detail. It stated that it was the duty of every agriculturalist to keep his land in good order and use its cultivable ability to the utmost. If he failed to do that he got a warning from the *comisario rural*. If the land was not put in good condition within a month's time from the issuing of the first warning, the cultivator could be arrested and deprived of the right to the land. The cultivator was obliged to dedicate an important part of the land to the production of export crops. All persons older than seven years of age who were unable to prove that they attended school or exercised a state sanctioned occupation would be forced to work as agriculturalists. All hunters of undomesticated animals, as well as tree-cutters, had to show a certificate from the *alcalde*, town mayor, that proved that they were acting on the behalf of the owner of the land. All peasants were obliged to work during weekdays. Cockfights and horse races were only allowed on Sundays and all bars had to be closed at nine o'clock in the evening. Peasants had to work on public works without compensation. They could only liberate themselves from this duty if they paid a fixed sum of money or a corresponding amount of foodstuffs.[37] It should, however, be kept in mind that these laws were enforced in a rather capricious and arbitrary way.

The peasants were subjected to a set of laws imposed on them by outsiders. "With the intention of increasing the production, our countryside became militarized, its inhabitants became submitted to severe restrictions in their mobility and innumerable fastidious permits."[38] One of the few exemptions the peasants enjoyed was liberation from the compulsory military service, but this privilege did not have much importance since they had to serve in the army in case of "national danger." Such "dangers" occurred quite often throughout the nineteenth century which was characterized by constant military tension created by the threat from Haiti and fierce civil wars. For instance, in 1862, during the annexation to Spain (1861-65), a decree was issued whereby the peasants were forced by law to carry from one district to another the equipment of any troops that passed a peasant community. The peasants were thus forced to abandon their homes for many days without any compensation whatsoever.[39]

In the nineteenth century, the Dominican Republic was characterized by a high degree of regionalization. Communications were extremely bad and it was hard for a central government to control the whole country. Different *caudillos* held political and military influence within the different regions. At times, some of these *caudillos* tried to grab the central power, and this in turn led to social unrest and civil wars. It was not until Ulises Heureaux took power (1882-99) that the country was pacified and the state could gain a firmer control of the different regions. A common characteristic among the majority of the regimes that followed Heureaux's dictatorial reign was the phenomenon of *clientelismo político*. This meant that the head of the state exercised his power in a personal way and became the center in a net of loyalties, controlled through a personal use of state resources. The origin of the Dominican *clientelismo* may be found in the regionalization that prevailed a good bit into the twentieth century. The possibilities of economic and social advancement within the traditional activities were very limited. Hence, the obtainment of political posts and favors through contacts with powerful leaders could be a means to advance socially and obtain a secure income.[40] This way of using politics for personal ends is still present in Dominican politics, which has led some authors to characterize the Dominican state as a "predatory" one.[41]

State interference in peasant life continued into the twentieth century and reached its culmination under the American occupation and the Trujillo regime. As we shall see below, Trujillo ruled the country with an iron hand and under his dictatorship (1930-61), severe laws circumscribed the mobility of the rural population and "vagabondism" was punished.[42] After the fall of Trujillo, the rigid rural laws that formerly regulated the peasants' life have disappeared, but a more than two-hundred-year tradition has left a durable stamp on the peasant's social position.

The Rise of the Sugar Industry and the Marginalization of the Peasantry

Before the 1880s the agricultural production of the Dominican Republic was comparatively small. The recurring warfare with Haiti took a heavy toll in lives and expenditure. Furthermore, constant power struggles, revolutions and civil wars hindered the development of a stable economy. The peasant was in reality without legal protection, devoid of education and health service, and the object of heavy taxation and military drafts. Agricultural production was mostly directed to self-sustenance which amounted to nearly 75 percent of the total output of the peasants.[43]

In the 1880s, the Dominican peasantry gained a higher degree of involvement with the non-agricultural sectors of the Dominican economy and with the international economic system. Vast rural regions were incorporated into commercial production. Railways and roads were constructed. These changes, among other things, were due to the introduction of external capital, mainly from Cuban immigrants who concentrated their efforts in the production of export crops, notably sugar.

As will be seen in Chapter 6, the Dominican state supported this development by legal protection of and cooperation with the new wealthy groups. The state ceded public land to the big cultivators of export crops. Thereby it accentuated the concentration of land in a few hands.[44] Land values rose and the fear of dispossession was growing among small producers. Many of them lived on *terrenos comuneros*. The majority of the country's peasants lacked titles to their land and those who had titles did not have any confidence in them. The notaries who kept the records of land transactions and titles were easily bribed and most of their files were in disorder. "A notary who kept accurate records was a rarity."[45] The manufacturing of false papers increased and many peasants were reluctant to improve their land since they feared to lose it any day. Many peasants had *pesos* or *acciones de tierra* and it was nearly impossible to determine what these titles really meant.[46] The government tried to make land surveys and force cultivators to inscribe their titles.[47] However, it was not until the US military occupation (1916-24) that topographic and cadastral surveys for land registration purposes were carried out, together with an organized program for inscription of land titles.[48]

The Land Registration Law of 1920 by and large benefited the sugar producers. The legal process for land registration was inefficient and in many cases the sugar companies obtained land by force. Villages were burned and hundreds of peasants were dispossessed of their land.[49] In the period 1915-23, the land areas under sugar cane production increased their size three times.[50] At the same time, land availability for food production was significantly reduced.

The development of the sugar industry increased the demand for labor and many peasants became wage laborers, permanently or temporarily.[51] This led to a greater geographical mobility and a major flow of money within the rural population. Thus, a number of small shops and ambulatory salesmen made their appearance in rural areas.[52]

The companies cultivating sugar increased their power and importance steadily, but other agricultural activities also benefited from the contact with the world market, such as tobacco, cocoa, coffee and bananas. The traditional sectors, like cattle-breeding and timber-cutting, also acquired increased importance. These sectors of the Dominican economy had been long dominated by the oligarchy.[53] On the other hand, the traditional peasant products, such as vegetables and fruits, experienced a notable decrease.[54]

The events of the last decades of the nineteenth century and the first decades of the twentieth strongly encouraged foreign investments in the Dominican Republic. Some 85 percent of the sugar industry was dominated by foreign capital. However other sectors also experienced a strong foreign presence. Particularly the United States enjoyed great advantages. Besides owning an important part of the sugar industry, American monopolies had direct or indirect control over banana plantations, cattle-breeding pastures and timber forests, banks, transportation and trade. In 1917, 80 percent of the country's exports were directed to the US market and the imports from this country reached 86 percent of the total.[55]

In short, at the turn of the century, the Dominican peasantry was hurled into the modern world, and came to experience the monetary economy, the world market demand and the unlocking of their traditional, isolated societies. But still the Dominican peasants were only marginal participants in a development process imposed by the urban rulers, and during the twentieth century they went on living as second-class citizens in comparison with the urban population. Victims of a socio-political exclusion, living at the margin of the economic and technological changes that washed over their country, they were doomed to obtain just a distracted attention from the authorities, while they at the same time generated the wealth of the country and provided cheap labor for the modern sector.

Trujillo's Authoritarian Rule and the Peasantry

The Americans left the country in 1924 and left behind General Rafael Leonidas Trujillo as commander of the *Guardia Nacional* they had created. In 1930, Trujillo managed to obtain the presidency by means of different maneuvers and manipulations.

For three decades, the Dominican Republic lived in the shadow of Trujillo, who used his power to exploit the resources of the country in order to enrich himself and his family. During his regime, the peasantry was heavily taxed. Especially penalized were the coffee growers who, besides being forced to pay high taxes, had to face lower prices because of the dictator's monopoly on the commercialization of this crop.[56] At the end of his life Trujillo's economic empire controlled around 80 percent of the industrial production and two-thirds of the total sugar production.

By means of intimidation and force, many peasants were evicted from their land in order to enlarge the dictator's sugar estates. Between 50 and 60 percent of the arable land ended up in the hands of Trujillo and his family.[57] His private companies employed 45 percent of the active labor force, and if one includes the 15 percent who worked for the state and takes into consideration Trujillo's absolute control of the government, the result will be that 60 percent of the Dominican families depended, one way or the other, on the dictator's benevolence. Trujillo's regime affected every imaginable sector of the economy. In 1938, when the economy started to recover after the worldwide crisis, an extensive program was launched in order to activate the economy. Roads, irrigation systems, and bridges were constructed and thousands of hectares were put under the plow. Agricultural production increased rapidly and the country became self-sufficient in rice, corn, beans and other primary products.[58] However, much of this production was concentrated to *latifundios*, mostly Trujillo properties, and this accelerated the proletarianization of the peasants who to an increasing degree started to work on the big farms.[59]

In the late 1940s, the interest of the dictator was concentrated in the sugar industry and most resources were allocated to this sector.[60] The production of food declined and agricultural production per capita fell.[61] The population experienced a spectacular growth. In 1935, the country had 1,479,000 inhabitants. In 1960 the number had increased to 3,047,000.[62] The Dominican Republic had always been underpopulated and this fact was one of the principal concerns of its different rulers. The Trujillo regime stimulated immigration, patronized big families and improved the health program initiated during the American occupation. The demographic growth that was the result of these different measures had immediate effects. Improvements of communications, modernization of the towns and the creation of some work opportunities drew many peasants to urban areas. This urbanization process accelerated during the 1950s.[63]

During World War II, Trujillo started to invest the capital accumulated through his agricultural activities in the establishment of new industries in Santo Domingo.[64] The industrialization process was carried out at the expense of the agricultural sector which to a large extent was neglected. The unequal distribution of resources between the two sectors attracted many peasants to the urban centers. In 1960, 30 percent of the population lived in urban areas in comparison with 18 percent in 1935.[65] This migration took place in spite of Trujillo's restrictive rural migration policy.

Trujillo changed the agrarian structure of the country. At his fall, the concentration of the land was amazing. In 1960, 1 percent of the farms were over 50 hectares in size and occupied 54 percent of the total farmland, while 50 percent of the farms were less than 1 hectare and occupied less than 5 percent of the total farmland.[66] At the same time, 45 percent of the small cultivators did not have sufficient income from their land but had to take temporal work on the bigger farms, or saw themselves forced to migrate to the growing cities. The industrial sector, commerce and construction started to replace agriculture as the principal sector of the economy. However, the contribution of agriculture to GNP in 1960 was 41 percent, and 90 percent of the export incomes were generated from agricultural products.[67] Thus, the agricultural activity was the principal source for the financing of the rapid expansion of the urban sector and the establishment of new industries. The peasants were integrated in an economic net where they became increasingly dependent on the urban markets.

The Trujillo regime brought some wealth and stability to the Dominican economy, but many of its measures have proved to be fatal.

The country underwent a fundamental change and many of the problems afflicting the Dominican Republic today have their roots in the Trujillo period. Nowadays, the power is distributed among many individuals and institutions, but the past is still weighing heavily and it will take a long time before a heritage based on thirty years of totalitarian government can be overcome.

The Post -Trujillo Period

The period after Trujillo's death was characterized by a high degree of political, social and economic instability. The peasants demanded their rights loudly. They created organizations and showed their dissatisfaction by, for example, occupying state land. The first two years of the period also witnessed a significant intensification in the migration movements from the countryside into the towns.[68]

The state increased its direct influence in the economy via the expropriation of the possessions of the Trujillo family. Through the fall of the dictatorship and the introduction of democracy the peasantry was converted into an important political force, something that is evident in the new constitution of December 1961.[69] In 1962, Juan Bosch was elected president. A new constitution issued under his regime sought to protect the interests of the peasantry. The *latifundios* were forbidden and the *minifundios* were declared to be against the social interest. A thorough agrarian reform was planned. Many of the reforms initiated under the Bosch regime threatened the interests of the *latifundistas* and other powerful groups. After seven months, Bosch was overthrown.[70]

The chaos and social unrest that followed the fall of Bosch culminated with civil war in 1965 and the subsequent occupation of the country by US military forces. A provisional government followed the withdrawal of the Americans. In 1966, Joaquín Balaguer was elected president. Balaguer, although representing the interests of the wealthy groups of the country, showed interest in the agrarian problem. In 1966, he proclaimed the necessity to carry out an agrarian reform and to increase the welfare of the peasantry in order to reduce social tensions and prevent rural migrations. He proposed to eliminate all peasant taxes, to increase peasant access to credit and to guarantee minimum prices for peasant products.

In 1972, an agrarian reform program was laid down. The *latifundios* were to be limited. This included pastures and rice land but excluded the sugar cane plantations. Soon the large landowners reacted against the proposed laws. By 1975, the emphasis on the agrarian reform program waned and the process of land redistribution slowed down.[71]

Nevertheless, during the Balaguer regime, many peasant families benefited from the agrarian reform and the expectations of the peasantry for better living conditions increased. Since these expectations could not be satisfied, discontent among the peasantry grew, however. This factor, plus the resentment of the landed elite contributed to the increased popularity of the PRD (*Partido Revolucionario Dominicano*), the opposition party which won the elections in 1978.[72]

During the Balaguer regime, the state concentrated its efforts on the modernization and reorganization of the former Trujillo-owned companies. It tried to stimulate the export sector, clear up the financial system and revise investment and savings mechanisms. Private domestic and foreign investments were particularly encouraged, and the government launched an industrialization process based on import substitution. The improved economic and political conditions of the country attracted foreign investors. However, 75 percent of the total savings of the 1966-78 period were of internal origin, and most of them were generated in the agricultural sector. Nevertheless, 60 percent of these savings went to the construction sector, 30 percent to the industrial sector and less than 5 percent were invested in the agricultural sector.[73] Several irrigation channels and dams were constructed. The neglect of the agricultural sector is, however, illustrated by the fact that during the 12 years of the Balaguer regime, the average yearly government spending on agriculture was 15.9 million pesos while the corresponding amount allocated to the armed force was 45.5 million.[74] During this period, the gap between the rural and urban sectors grew widely and the migratory movements from the rural areas into the towns continued with accelerated speed.

As mentioned above, many peasants contributed to the victory of the PRD (Partido Revolucionario Dominicano) in the 1978 elections, but it was still the votes from the urban masses that weighed the most. The PRD has mainly stood out as an urban party. A striking feature of the party's politics has for example been the policy of selling cheap agricultural products to the urban poor. As will be shown in Chapter 5, this policy has had a very negative effect on the welfare of the rural producers. In spite of its urban bias, the PRD government also tried to reach the peasantry through some reform attempts. The pace of land distribution within the agrarian reform program was slowed down and the government concentrated its efforts on the consolidation of the reform settlements. Likewise, attempts have been made to improve health services in both urban and rural areas.

A conspicuous feature of the PRD regime was the recruitment of employees to the public sector. In the first four years, the number of government employees nearly doubled. In 1977, there were 120,000 government employees. By 1982, this figure had increased to 210,000. Different reasons for this situation has been given,[75] but some speak of it as a kind of *clientelismo político*, i.e. as the government's way of repaying for services rendered to the party. In the early 1980s, the Dominican Republic found itself in a deep economic crisis. The country was facing falling prices for its major exports and a growing balance-of-payments deficit. The current account deficit combined with the requirements of serving the foreign debt (the total foreign debt was above US\$ 3 billion in 1983) compelled the government to appeal to the International Monetary Fund. In order to fulfil the agreement with the IMF, the government was forced to implement unpopular economic measures.[76] These factors plus fierce internal power struggles within the PRD led to decreasing popularity of the PRD government both in urban and rural areas. In the 1986 elections, Balaguer came to power for the fifth time. In much of his presidential campaign the improvement of the peasant's situation was a major issue. However, once in power the new government's major issue came to be urban construction activities.

In spite of some efforts from recent governments, the Dominican peasant continues to be neglected. He is still very important in election campaigns but very much forgotten once a party is in power. This underdog position of the peasantry becomes more evident if we analyze its access to different social services.

The Social Situation of the Peasantry

The visitor to the Dominican countryside will soon find that the rural areas present a rather similar picture all over the country. The houses may lie alone on the fields or clustered together in small villages. As a rule, the Dominican peasant dwelling is rather small and of simple construction. It usually contains one or two bedrooms and a sort of living room, where visitors are received. The cooking shed lies in the backyard and is the real center of the family life. Most rural households lack electricity, and cooking is generally done with the help of firewood. The basic food consists of beans, rice, bananas, plantains, cassava and sweet potatoes. Once a week meat may be served, mostly poultry. Hens run freely and the family often owns a donkey or a horse. The houses often lie in connection to the small plots where food crops are produced. Those that have larger plots also produce perennial crops like cocoa and coffee. Villages generally lie close to the roads, centered around local *pulperías*, grocery stores, where additional foodstuffs are bought - often on a credit basis.

Every Dominican village shows a division in social groups, each group with different possibilities of making a living. We find landless day laborers, smallholders and middle sized farmers, but also larger landholders. However, generally speaking, almost all villagers suffer from a system that has tended to favor the urban sector. Rural poverty is widespread. About 31 percent of the rural families live on income levels below the *poverty line*, while the corresponding figure for urban families is 13 percent.[77]

The rural inhabitants find themselves at different stages on the scale of poverty, depending on the size of their land, the quality of the soil, the location of the plots, etc., but the fact that rural areas are worse off than urban ones is apparent in nearly any comparison done between the availability and quality of the social services offered to the Dominican urban and rural areas respectively.

Education

Up to recent years rural education in the Dominican Republic has been inadequate, to say the least. The progress has been slow, the efforts to correct past deficiencies have been insufficient and it has been very hard to meet the needs of an expanding population.

During the nineteenth century, rural schools hardly existed. In 1867, the country had eleven primary schools outside of Santo Domingo. All of them were situated in towns. In 1871, a US commission estimated rural illiteracy to be 98 percent. During the last decade of the nineteenth century, probably less than one-eighth of the population had received enough education to be able to read and write.[78] During its occupation of the country, the US military government launched a vast educational program. By 1919, 50,000 children were enrolled in 647 simply constructed rural schools.[79] However, all this came to nothing since all public schools were closed down in 1921.[80]

After the withdrawal of the US forces in 1924, the school system "limped along barely alive,"[81] suffering from a lack of financial support. Nothing happened until Trujillo in 1934 established a Secretary of State for Education and Fine Arts and a vast educational program was launched. In 1951, educational laws were sharpened even more - parents were fined up to 50 pesos if they withheld their children from school, anyone who employed children that were not excused from school was fined up to 200 pesos. Ten years before the appearance of this law, Trujillo had ordered the foundation of a net of rural "emergency schools." The objective was to make rural youngsters literate and two years of schooling was considered to be sufficient in order to reach this aim.[82]

The results of Trujillo's educative efforts were somewhat dubious. They were clearly insufficient. He wanted to build an attractive façade of progress for the world to see, as soon as possible. Instead of training more and better teachers and improving the existing rural primary school system, too much effort and money were wasted on the emergency schools. In 1945, only 58 teachers were graduated. Most of them turned to teaching in the urban areas where wages were fifty percent higher than in the rural ones. This trend continued during the whole Trujillo regime and rural schools were equipped with teachers with only a very basic education.[83]

The surveys of 1945, 1956 and 1960 show an amazing progress in the educational field, but the figures are somewhat dubious since they were mainly intended to show this progress. This is something that probably can be said about some later censuses too. In the survey of 1968 the informants were only *asked* if they could read and if they could write their own names, if they said yes they qualified as literates.[84]

Considerable efforts have been made in the field of education, but during the last years, they have been hindered by restrictive governmental policies to decrease public spending.[85] The constant demographic growth is also a major constraint on the build-up of an efficient educational system.[86] In 1981, 31 percent of the population was illiterate. Of the literate, about 50 percent had only primary education. Illiteracy in rural areas was as high as 43 percent. The corresponding figure for urban areas was 21 percent.[87]

Not all rural schools offer the complete primary cycle. In 1970, most of them rarely offered education above the third grade, and only 5.5 percent continued to sixth.[88] The quality of the teaching staff differs between urban and rural areas. In 1980, 55 percent of the teachers on the primary level were fully educated. Of these only 25 percent worked in the rural areas.[89]

School attendance in the countryside is affected by long distances and an inadequate transport system. It is not uncommon that schoolchildren have to walk for more than an hour in order to get to school. If transportation exists, it often proves to be too costly for the parents. The children are often needed in order to help their parents with the daily work that is carried out at home and in the fields. Sending children to school can mean a considerable loss of labor for some families. The fact that children are needed in the fields is acknowledged by the school authorities that have adapted the school year in the coffee districts to the harvest seasons.[90]

Still, much of the education is not adapted to the rural pupils' environment. Many textbooks reveal an urban outlook, alluring in the sense that the urban way of life appears as the natural way. Rural life is seen from the outside, or totally ignored.

The lack of higher education in rural areas forces many youngsters to move into the towns, where they often live with relatives, something that tends to lighten the burden of maintenance for their parents. Few of these students return, partly because urban life may seem more attractive, partly because the chances of getting employment and fairly good wages in the countryside are very limited.

Traditionally, education aimed at agricultural activities has been neglected, especially in rural areas. However, recent decades have witnessed certain changes. Agricultural training institutions have been founded, and the universities offer academic careers in the field of agriculture. But there is still a lack of an organizing mechanism able to coordinate the educational activities by designating areas that ought to be given priority. There is also a need for rural centers for vocational training in the field of agriculture.[91]

Health

Until the beginning of the twentieth century, health services in the Dominican Republic were limited and practically non-existent in rural areas. Death rates were high and the rate of population growth was low. Health care was carried out by urban privately financed hospitals and some small public dispensaries. Infectious diseases were widespread all over the country and the cities lacked elementary sanitation. The supply of educated medical personnel was limited. In 1917, there were 95 doctors in the country - approximately one doctor per 8,500 inhabitants.[92]

During the American occupation, the health service was improved. In 1920, a sanitation law was issued and a vast campaign against infectious diseases was carried out as well as a program to improve sanitation.[93] Two new public hospitals were built and the services of the 5 existing hospitals were improved. The number of charity hospital beds was increased from about 100 to 450 and two nursing schools were created. A plan to extend health services to rural areas proved impossible since the few Dominican doctors did not want to participate. Some military medical personnel was put on duty in the countryside but this effort came to an end with the US withdrawal in 1924.[94]

The American health program was ambitious but its results were very limited. Nevertheless, infectious diseases, such as malaria and yaws, were said to be eradicated and a Ministry of Sanitation and Beneficence was created. With the withdrawal of the US forces, the health service practically collapsed. In 1923, under the Dominican provisional government, the ministry budget was reduced to one-seventh of the amount received in 1920.[95]

During the Trujillo era, some of the American efforts in the health care sector were continued. Public hospitals were built and the number of physicians were increased. The improvements in health services and communications[96] resulted in an unprecedented population boom. In twenty-five years (1935-60) the Dominican population doubled (see Table 2.1).

Today, most health facilities are concentrated in urban areas. Health service facilities are still very limited and mortality rates are high, especially in rural areas. In 1974, the infant death rate was 50 per thousand newborns in urban areas. In the rural areas the proportion was 128 per thousand.[97]

Most statistics concerning health and medical attention in the Dominican Republic do not account for differences between rural and urban sectors. They generally apply to a division of the country in six different areas. Differences between rural and urban areas can however be discerned from some official publications. Thus, in 1982, the so-called Sector 0, i.e., the sector that includes the capital, had 8.7 medical doctors per 10,000 inhabitants; Sector II, which includes Santiago, offered 3.8 doctors for the same number of persons; and the other important urban districts of the country, i.e., Sector V, with San Pedro de Macorís and La Romana, had 4.6. The other districts are predominantly rural and here the figures varied from 2.2 to 2.5.[98] The capital offered 2.5 dentists per 10,000 inhabitants. In the rest of the country the corresponding figure is below 1 dentist.[99] In 1982, 40 percent of the country's hospital beds were concentrated to the capital. Sector II, with Santiago, had 23 percent of the beds, and other districts had only between 2.9 and 7.3 percent of the hospital beds.[100]

In 1982, the Dominican Republic had 8 specialized hospitals, and 38 general ones, all located in urban areas, and 337 rural clinics.[101] Compared with figures from 1977, the increase of the number of rural clinics is considerable. In 1977, only 70 rural clinics existed in the whole country.[102] According to official sources, a rural clinic is intended to serve 1,500 to 8,000 inhabitants within a radius of 15 to 25 kilometers. Their main activity is preventive health care. They are supposed to control the health situation within the district, execute education and vaccination programs, give maternity attention, offer family planning, check hygiene and nutrition, etc. They also offer medical assistance, mainly through itinerant doctors.[103]

It is difficult to get qualified personnel to the rural clinics. Most doctors prefer to stay in the towns and work within the better paid private sector. This sector covers 5-15 percent of the country's health service.[104] The location of the rural clinics makes it hard to get severe cases to the hospitals in the towns. There is a lack of ambulances and many roads are in very bad condition. Many rural clinics lack potable water[105] and have a very limited supply of medicine. Virtually all of them do not have any beds at all, since the activity of the rural clinics is intended to be of an emergency and information character.[106]

Despite the significant improvements carried out in the health sector during the last decades, most services are still biased to urban areas, and it will probably take a long time before sickness and accidents will less often be a mortal threat to the peasantry than they are today.

Nutrition

When analyzing the health and nutritional situation in Haiti, Mats Lundahl concludes:

A situation where public health care improves at the same time as nutrition remains constant or deteriorates may have very undesirable consequences in the long run. Improvements in medicine and health care may lead to lowered mortality and increased population. When the population increases, so does the labor force. If the non-agricultural sectors of the economy cannot absorb this increase, the addition to labor force goes to agriculture, and the marginal productivity of labor falls in the absence of capital formation, increasing land resources and technical progress. Agricultural production per capita falls and this leads to a fall in nutritional standards ...[107]

Improved health services plus a persistent neglect of the food producing sector has put the Dominican Republic into a similar situation. The actual nutritional deficits of the country are alarming. Fourteen inquiries made between 1962 and 1980 indicate that malnutrition afflicts 30 to 75 percent of the population.[108] In 1973, it was found that 75 percent of the population did not consume the amount of calories required (2,400 calories), and 50 percent hardly consumed half of the recommended intake of proteins (55 grams).[109]

The situation is relatively worse in rural areas. This fact is reflected by the level of child mortality. In 1974, the total mortality of children less than one year old was 104 per thousand but the corresponding figure for rural areas was 128 per thousand.[110]

As will be shown in Chapter 9, agricultural production has not increased at the same pace as the population. Production of several food crops has fallen and the country has been forced to increase food imports.

Peasants and Politics

As pointed out above, the peasant's opinions are marked by his particular environment. He lives close to nature, depends on its changes and the rhythm of the seasons. He is surrounded by individuals who are well known to him and, furthermore, share most of his opinions. Their relatively isolated communities often lack contact with the centralized political power of the country, and their ability to act as a united political power is therefore limited. They are sometimes victims of authority and coercion. "Their roots are in the land and the homestead ... Once a man is married and on his holding, he is tied,"[111] unless he ventures into the unknown and migrates to the towns.

Still, the peasants constitute an important and relatively united group of a country's population. They are far from being uninteresting for the governing elite, or for persons aspiring to political power. Many ideologists have hinted that peasants are inclined to submit to strong, authoritarian leadership. Thus, Marx states: "Their representative must at the same time appear as their master, as an authority over them, as an unlimited power that protects them against the other classes and sends them rain and sunshine from above."[112]

The peasant's world is characterized by a recurrent cycle adapted to the preparation of the soil, planting and harvest. He is circumscribed by his daily work. Leaders are to be found among persons that are liberated from this routine.[113] Tough and self-reliant men with strong personalities and military talents have often appeared throughout the Dominican history, and some of them have succeeded in mobilizing the peasantry. Especially in times of political and social unrest, the Dominican *caudillos* have turned up and whipped up support in the countryside or in small towns in order to conquer the political power of the country. Many of these *caudillos* have been activists without elaborate political programs. Still, peasants who suffered under bureaucratic abuse and recurrent wars were willing to follow them.[114] Even today it is possible to hear peasants talk about the "old times" when "Concho Primo" stood up and defended the rights of the peasants.[115]

Also, leaders like Trujillo have tried to gather the peasants around them, giving the impression that they were God-sent protectors of the peasants. Trujillo staged great shows where thousands of peasants were gathered, receiving rewards and favors from the hands of the *Benefactor*.[116] His successors have also striven for an image as the defenders of the peasants. Particularly Balaguer liked to stand out as a representative for the peasants and the poor. During his presidency the delivery of land within the land reform program was characterized by much "showing-off."[117]

Some peasant societies tend to generate gangs of unbound persons who do not belong to the society, but have their roots within the peasant's environment. These persons are the so-called social bandits who live and act in small groups as presumptive peasant leaders, i.e. persons who live at the margin of the peasant society because they, for one reason or another, are not bound to a piece of land.[118]

Bandits seem to exist in connection with most peasant societies, but they multiply in times of crisis. The gangs grow by absorbing crowds of disillusioned peasants who turn to banditry as the only solution that seems to exist for them. In the Dominican Republic, bands of *gavilleros* multiplied at the beginning of this century in the country's eastern regions when landless peasants, dispossessed by the big sugar companies, joined the bandit gangs.[119] During the US occupation, the *gavilleros* constituted the only organized armed resistance against the US Marine Corps who often defended the interests of the US owned sugar companies. Their resistance continued during the entire occupation. When the Marines left the island, the *gavilleros* lost their role as defenders of peasant rights against the foreign oppressors and became common bandits once more, until they were suppressed by the Trujillo regime in the 1930s.[120]

Another feature of some peasant societies are the so-called religious revitalization movements.[121] The peasantry may be ready to follow the call of some local prophet who urges the peasants to leave their present wretched life behind them and follow him into the promised land. As late as the twentieth century the Dominican Republic has experienced two "messianic" movements. Both occurred in the poor western part of the country. The first Dominican Messiah of this century appeared in 1909 in a mountainous region close to San Juan de la Maguana. He was an illiterate day-laborer called Olivorio Mateo. Thousands of peasants followed him and organized a community. There, all work was carried out by united efforts and its fruits were divided equally among the members of the community. An ecstatic cult flourished around Olivorio, who was venerated as the new Messiah. The sectarians dressed in a particular way and Olivorio surrounded himself with a bodyguard consisting of armed peasants. In 1917, the US forces that had occupied the country the year before decided that the Olivoristas were a threat to the public safety. They were hunted for many years, until Olivorio was killed in an ambush in 1922.

In the chaotic times that followed after the death of Trujillo, the cult of Olivorio was revived in 1961. A place called Palma Sola was turned into a sanctuary and a "holy city" started to develop around it. The sick claimed to be cured and the spirit of Olivorio was said to be present. Local authorities wrote to the central government and complained about the growing community in Palma Sola. The government acted, the army moved in and burned down the place, killing dozens of peasants. [122] Palma Sola can be seen as a sign of the peasants' increasing urge to put demands on the government and organize themselves politically. Even if the Palma Sola movement was a religious one, it also had political aspirations.[123]

The fall of Trujillo triggered a tide of suppressed activity in the countryside, and it has been argued that the intranquility and recurrent land occupations in the countryside forced the new government in 1962 to rewrite the constitution in favor of the rural masses and urgently initiate redistribution of some state-owned land within the frames of the newly founded Agrarian Institute. It is symptomatic that every change in government and politics awakens the peasants' hopes for immediate changes of their situation, and makes them organize themselves. When Balaguer returned to power in 1966, rural tension forced the government to speed up the land reform program and create new, radical rural laws. At the same time, the number of peasant organizations increased and continued to increase in the beginning of the seventies.[124] When signs of economic stagnation and reduced political strength appeared during the presidency of Balaguer, the activity in the countryside also slowed down, while it gained new force with the coming of PRD in 1978, and a new wave of land occupations and rural migration started.

Conclusions

The pattern that evolves from an analysis of the development of the Dominican peasantry is one of discrimination and neglect. For centuries the peasants have been kept living in isolation, subject to restrictive laws and taxation, unable to enjoy social services and secluded from the political establishment. Recent governments have recognized that improvement of the peasants' economic and social situation is important for the development of the country. However, in spite of various political measures taken in that direction, the situation of the peasants has not changed much. Today, rural dwellers earn lower average incomes and receive lower quality education and health services than their urban counterparts. Higher mortality rates and deficient nutrition levels in the countryside further underline this social gap.

Improvements in communication have made rural areas geographically more integrated. The peasants, however, continue to play a relatively passive role in the political process of the country. Nevertheless, the Dominican peasantry has been able to demonstrate its dissatisfaction and unrest. Some have done this by joining religious movements, others by joining armed resistance groups and, more recently, by claiming their right to the land through illegal land occupations and by moving into the urban areas: "... the headlong avalanche of rural migrants ... have voted against the *status quo* with their feet by moving into the city slums."[125]

The influx of peasants into the towns has affected the pattern of political votes. Today, 52 percent of the population live in urban areas. An overwhelming majority are peasant migrants. Migration may have diminished the explosive potential of the countryside but has in its turn increased the explosive potential in the cities as the urbanization and industrialization process has proved incapable of providing employment opportunities and improved social conditions to all the migrants.[126]

As will be seen in the next chapter, the urban poor constitute an important political target. During the last decades, the agricultural price policies implemented by the government have mainly benefited the urban consumer while the effects of these policies on the welfare of the peasantry and the agricultural production have been neglected.

The description of the development and present situation of the Dominican peasantry that we have presented in this chapter should be kept in mind and serve as a background for the different issues that will be discussed in the remaining parts of this work. The picture that has evolved in this chapter serves as a point of departure for an understanding of the functioning of the produce market and the price polices implemented by the state (Chapter 5). It is also important for the analysis of the actual structure of landownership presented in Chapter 6, and the functioning of the agricultural credit market discussed in Chapter 7. The participation of Haitian workers in the Dominican labor market (Chapter 8) has also to be seen in relation to the situation of the Dominican peasantry and its participation in the labor market. Likewise, the historical picture is essential when discussing how traditional land use and cultivation patterns in combination with population and labor-force growth have resulted in an increasing deforestation and erosion process, thus diminishing the land base of the peasantry (Chapter 9). Finally, a certain knowledge of the situation of the peasantry is necessary in order to analyze the different factors attracting the peasants into the cities (Chapter 10).

Notes

1. In a Latin American context, the term *peasant* generally corresponds to the Spanish term *campesino*. The latter term is often interchangeable with phrases such as "the rural poor," "the mass of the rural population" or "the rural underclass" (Grindle (1986), p. XII). Cf. Landsberger (1969), pp. 1-5.

2. For details see Shanin (1971), pp. 294-96.

3. Wolf (1966), p. 13.

4. Wolf gives the following distinctions between primitive societies and peasants: "In primitive society, surpluses are exchanged directly among groups or members of groups; peasants, however, are rural cultivators whose surpluses are transferred to a dominant group of rulers that uses the surpluses both to underwrite its own standard of living and to distribute the remainder to groups in the society that do not farm but must be fed for their specific goods and services in turn."(Wolf (1966), p. 3-4.)

5. As an example; the word "pagan" means literally "one who lives in the country," this is a remnant of the times when Christianity was the religion of the progressing towns, while the "backward" rural dwellers clung to their old beliefs. (See Weber (1963), pp. 80-84.)

6. Particularly Robert Redfield (1955) has stressed the dichotomy between the "little" tradition of rural "folk societies" and "the great tradition" of the city.

7. Marx (1977:2), p. 481. Marx refers particularly to the situation of the French peasants under the rule of Napoleon III.

8 . Marx (1977:3), pp. 236-37.

9. Ibid., p. 481. As a result, today many Marxist ideologists tend to treat the peasantry as a group that has to be guided from outside. (See Wolf (1966), p. 92.)

10. For an exposition of different Marxist ideologists' views related to this issue see De Janvry (1981), Chapter 3. The disappearance of the peasantry as a distinct class is also implicit in some development models. See for instance Lewis' dualistic model where the rural sector is mainly considered as a reservoir of labor to be transferred to the modern sector of the economy (Lewis (1954)).

11. The existence of these traits as cultural characteristics of peasants has been highly questioned. Some authors argue that these traits may be rational behavioral responses to difficult situations. For references see Landsberger (1974:1), pp. 55-56.

12. Lipton (1977), p. 234. See also p. 13. Lipton's "urban bias" thesis has been questioned by many writers. See for instance Seers (1977), Byres (1979) and Currie (1979).

13. The figure of 250,000 is from Cassá (1977), p. 71. The estimations vary considerably. The first chroniclers of the island mention figures between 600,000 and 3,000,000. These figures seem to be overestimations and modern authors tend to diminish them to a great extent. (See Cassá (1974), pp. 190-98.) One recent and highly controversial estimation was made in 1971, when Cook and Borah through sophisticated methods reached an approximation of 8,000,000 native inhabitants in 1494 (Cook and Borah (1971), p. 408). This view was severely criticized by Henige, who stated that it is futile to offer any

numerical estimates at all on the basis of existing evidence (Henige (1978), p. 237). The methods of Cook and Borah are also criticized by Moya Pons, who offers an estimation of 377,559 inhabitants in 1494 (Moya Pons (1986), p. 187).

14. Moya Pons (1980), p. 32.

15. See Deive (1980), pp. 56, 89 and 92.

16. ONAPLAN (1983:1), p. 46.

17. Clausner (1970), p. 100.

18. Ibid., pp. 148, 109.

19. Ibid., p. 152.

20. Ibid., p. 93.

21. Hazard (1873), pp. 482-83. Later on, when woodcutting became a lucrative occupation, the landowners differentiated the *acciones de tierra* and assigned to them different values according to the use of the land. Woodcutting rights were limited only to those who owned at least two hundred *pesos* or *acciones de tierra* (Moya Pons (1985), p. 188). Cf. Clausner (1970), p. 253 and Boin and Serulle (1979), pp. 120-25.

22. Moya Pons (1985), p. 187.

23. Bonó (1980:4), p. 82.

24. Moya Pons (1980), p. 215.

25. Tobacco was first exported to the neighboring French colony. Later, in 1763, the creation of a *Factoría de Tabacos* in Santo Domingo (a royal institution intended to promote production and exports of Dominican tobacco) provided incentives for exports towards Spain (ibid. pp. 156-157). See also Lluberes (1977), pp. 13-14 and Cassá (1977), p. 150.

26. During the eighteenth century, 4,000 Canarians came to the colony. Many of them established themselves as small cultivators in the Cibao area (Cassá (1977), p. 148). Tobacco was cultivated on relatively small plots with fertile soil.

27. Deive (1980), p. 341.

28. Ibid., p. 344.

29. They had a hard life but few of them ran away. They got their means of subsistence from "their" *conucos* and few of them wanted to change their life for an insecure existence where they always ran the risk to be caught and severely punished (Deive (1980), p. 349).

30. Contrary to the events that followed the liberation war in the neighboring Haiti, where a drastic land reform was pursued, the Dominican land tenure system was left practically unchanged. (For details concerning the land reform in Haiti, see Lundahl (1979), Chapter 6.) For a comparison of the land question in Haiti and the Dominican Republic see Lundahl and Vedovato (1988:1).

31. Cassá (1977), pp. 214-15.

32. Ibid., p. 226.

33. Moya Pons (1980), p. 232.

34. Bosch (1979), p. 215. See also Moya Pons (1985), p. 193.

35. Moya Pons (1980), p. 233. In 1825, Boyer, Haiti's president, signed a treaty with France that meant that this country recognized the independence of Haiti, on condition that Haiti's government paid 150 million francs. This sum was intended to be a compensation for damages done to French property and lives

during the Haitian war for independence (1791-1804). France was the archenemy of Haiti and Boyer saw a chance to alleviate the constant military alertness that characterized the Haitian society and thus decrease the high military expenditures. The treaty proved to be costly for Haiti (ibid., p. 253). Cf. Lundahl (1979), Chapter 8.

36. Moya Pons (1980), pp. 235 and 237.

37. Vega (1977), pp. 18-21.

38. Ibid., p. 21.

39. Welles (1975), Tomo I, p. 238.

40. González (1985), p. 34.

41. See Mañón (1985), Vedovato (1986), and Lundahl and Vedovato (1988:2).

42. Cf. Cassá (1983), pp. 259-60. Law No. 9563 of December 1953 prohibited the peasants, or other rural residents, from moving to urban centers without permission from the central government, and any peasant that had moved to town after 1951 was compelled to return to his previous rural residence or any similar place (see Maríñez (1984), note 19, pp. 86-87). Weekly military drill was organized for the unemployed rural laborers and many peasants were enrolled in the rural police force.

43. Hoetink (1971), pp. 14-15.

44. ONAPLAN (1983:1), p. 52.

45. Clausner (1970), p. 251.

46. Ibid., pp. 274 and 263.

47. In 1911 an Agricultural Concession Law was promulgated. Vast land areas were expropriated and infrastructural facilities were built in favor of the sugar industry (Knight (1928), p. 48).

48. Clausner (1970), p. 236.

49. Knight (1928), p. 118 and Spitzer (1972), p. 351.

50. The land area under sugar cane production increased from 350,000 *tareas* in 1915 to 1 million in 1923 (1 *tarea* = 0.063 hectares; Muto (1976), p. 36).

51. Hoetink (1971), p. 33. However, a considerable amount of the work force in the sugar industry was imported from neighboring countries. (See below, Chapter 8.)

52. Hoetink (1971), p. 37.

53. Ibid., p. 40.

54. ONAPLAN (1983:1), p. 53.

55. Ibid., pp. 53-54. Cf. Cassá (1983), pp. 156-57.

56. ISA (1979), p. 131. Between 1952 and 1961, taxes on coffee exports varied from 18 percent ad valorem up to 50 percent on the price increase above 40 pesos per 100 lbs. It is calculated that in 3 years, coffee export taxes and permits generated 22 million pesos for Trujillo (Cordero et al. (1975), pp. 74-76). Cocoa and tobacco were also highly taxed. (See Chapter 9 below.)

57. Wiarda (1968), p. 83 and Cassá (1982), pp. 127-28.

58. Moya Pons (1980), pp. 518 and 516.

59. ONAPLAN (1983:1), p. 55.

60. The land area under sugar production increased from 92,000 hectares in 1948 to 183,000 in 1960 (Cassá (1982), Table III- 8, Chapter 3).

61. ONAPLAN (1968), p. 142.

62. ONE (1983), p. 12.

63. ONAPLAN (1983:4), pp. 6-7.

64. Industries for the manufacturing of cement, paper, processed milk, glass, bottles, nails, paints, medicines, different sorts of liquors, etc., were created within a short time span. The economic and political totalitarianism of Trujillo affected the foreign enterprises in the country. At the end of the 1940s and beginning of the 1950s he bought or confiscated foreign property such as sugar mills, the National City Bank, and the Electricity Company, both formerly US firms. He also seized domestic companies, mostly by harassing and threatening the former owners. Thus, he obtained, among others, a big insurance company and a tobacco manufacturing industry, Compañía Anónima Tabacalera. He also got hold of vast land properties, using the same ruthless methods. Furthermore Trujillo's monopolistic policy left little space for private enterprise, since no one was sure if he could keep his business from the greedy hands of the dictator. On all levels, a tradition of personal insecurity and reliance on powerful allies was created. (See Moya Pons (1980), pp. 515-18 and Clausner (1970), p. 491.)

65. See Chapter 2, Table 2.1. The pole of attraction was Santo Domingo. In 1960, 45 percent of the population living in this city was born in other provinces. (See ONE (1966), pp. 20-21.)

66. Clausner (1970), pp. 455-56.

67. ONAPLAN (1983:1), p. 56.

68. Ibid., p. 57.

69. Clausner (1970), p. 446.

70. For details on the seven months of the Bosch administration see Martin (1975), pp. 325-518. See also Cassá (1986), pp. 69-102.

71. For an analysis of Balaguer's agrarian laws see Cassá (1986), pp. 486-510. The Dominican agrarian reform will be discussed below in Chapter 6.

72. See Del Castillo (1981), pp. 31-32.

73. Public investments were also concentrated to urban areas. About 60 percent of total public investment was used in the modernization of towns, mainly Santo Domingo (ONAPLAN (1983:1), p. 63).

74. Alemany et al. (1981), Table 11, p. 68. The largest share of the national budget was, however, allocated to the presidency, which increased its share from 15 million (7.3 percent of the budget) in 1966 to 300 million (43.4 percent of the budget) in 1978 (ibid., Table 10, p. 67).

75. Dauhajre (1984), pp. 15-16, argues this was a result of the policy of "induced demand" implemented by the PRD administration. However, it seems that internal party politics was very important. This became evident when large disagreements arose between various fractions within the PRD. The leaders of these fractions complained that their supporters had been excluded from government jobs. (Cf. Espinal (1987), pp. 160-65.)

76. The peso was de facto devalued and prices of imported goods were to increase by 200 percent. Prices of many foodstuffs also increased due to the lifting of government subsidies. (For an account of the PRD administrations see Dauhajre (1984), pp. 15-32, Black (1986), pp. 129-146 and Ceara (1988)).

77. Del Rosario (1982), p. 13 and Tables 10-A and 10-B, pp. 26-27. The figures on rural and urban income and services should be interpreted as rough indicators since rural and urban districts are generally not strictly demarcated in official statistics.

78. Clausner (1970), pp. 212, 220 and 230. Cf. Bonó (1980:3), p. 291.

79. Clausner (1970), p. 336. The education program was financed through a land tax. Before the arrival of the US military government an official tax program had not existed in the country. The peasants paid a lot of different taxes, intended for special purposes, such as road and bridge taxes, etc. The new tax law was based on land surveys and landowners paid taxes related to the value of their land. After the depression in 1921 (in the international market sugar prices dropped from 22 cents/pound in 1920 to 2 cents/pound in 1921), the system collapsed and practically no one paid taxes. In 1935 the land tax law was swept away completely (ibid., pp. 344-51 and 356).

80. Ibid., p. 353. The reason given was that the worldwide economic crisis had hit the Dominican Republic particularly hard.

81. Ibid., p. 358.

82. Ibid., pp. 412 and 414.

83. Ibid., p. 416.

84. Hendricks (1978), p. 51. Many persons apparently said they could read and write in order to avoid attending classes.

85. ONAPLAN (1983:2), p. 149.

86. Ibid., p. 99. In 1983, 250,000 children aged 7-14 years lacked education, this figure does not account for children who left school without completing their grades (ibid., p. 101).

87. Ibid., p. 91 and Secretariado Técnico (1984:1), p. 5. The Dominican school is free and obligatory for children from seven to fourteen years of age. Due to the inefficiency of the public school system, the number of private schools have been steadily growing. By 1982, the private school system covered 15 percent of the educational service at the primary and intermediate levels. The private schools are limited to urban areas (namely large cities) and are generally attended by middle- and upper-class pupils (ONAPLAN (1983:2), p. 126 and Table 30, p. 129).

88. Hendricks (1978), p. 46.

89. ONAPLAN (1983:2), p. 157. Cf. Bell (1981), pp. 168-69.

90. ONAPLAN (1983:2), p. 106.

91. The number of professionals in agronomy and veterinary sciences has increased considerably. In 1972, 144 technicians and 200 professionals graduated. According to the ILO there is a risk that the supply of highly qualified agricultural professionals exceeds demand. (OIT (1975), p. 237.)

92. Calder (1984), pp. 40-43. Between 1880 and 1900, 52 certificates to practice medicine were extended (Hoetink (1971), p. 241).

93. Calder (1984), pp. 42 and 44. A sanitation law requiring 10 to 15 percent of municipal incomes to be dedicated to public health and sanitation was issued.

94. Ibid., pp. 43-45.

95. In 1916, the government dedicated DR$ 30,000 to public health, while private lotteries generated twice that amount for the support of five hospitals

and orphanages. The Americans reorganized the system and all public health came under the supervision of a Ministry of Sanitation and Beneficence. In 1920, the government's financial support to the newly founded ministry amounted to DR$ 657,000, and DR$ 125,000 came from the lottery funds. With the economic depression in 1923, the government's support was reduced to DR$ 62,976 and by 1923, when the Dominicans took over, the budget was further reduced to DR$ 35,820 (Calder (1984), p. 44 and pp. 47-48).

96. The Americans carried out a vast public works program based on previous Dominican plans and efforts. The road between Santo Domingo and Santiago was completed and extended to Monte Cristi. Secondary paved roads connecting Santo Domingo with the eastern and western parts of the country were constructed, as well as roads connecting the capital with the major towns in the Cibao. Highway bridges were constructed, port facilities were improved, the country's topography and resources were surveyed and a national penitentiary and a leprosarium were constructed (ibid., p. 50).

97. ONAPLAN (1983:2), p. 263.

98. ONAPLAN (1983:3), p. 109. This low proportion of doctors per inhabitants should not be interpreted as a shortage of physicians in the country. On the contrary, unemployment rates are high and migration abroad is common among doctors. In 1970, there were 1,551 doctors in the country, about 1 per 2,600 inhabitants. The supply of doctors in 1970-80 was expected to increase with 4,000, a figure which would exceed the demand. A considerable number of doctors emigrate to foreign countries. 57 and 64 percent of the doctors graduated in the periods of 1960-64 and 1965-70, respectively, emigrated abroad (OIT (1975), p. 239). Even more serious is the inadequacy of the nursing staff. Fewer nurses than doctors graduate annually. Nurses are underpaid and working conditions in the public hospitals are depressing (Bell (1981), p. 193).

99. ONAPLAN (1983:3), p. 110.

100. ONAPLAN (1983:2), p. 291.

101. Ibid., p. 298.

102. SESPAS (1982), p. 58.

103. Ibid., pp. 59-60. The high increase in the number of rural clinics has not been accompanied by equally improved health service in the countryside. Many peasants believe the building of the rural clinics was just a political gesture, since many lack even a bed.

104. ONAPLAN (1983:3), p. 113.

105. Around 33.5 percent of the rural population has "easy access" to drinking water compared with 85 percent of the urban population (ONAPLAN (1983:2), pp. 277-78).

106. ONAPLAN (1983:3), pp. 80-81. Cf. Bell (1981), pp. 193-95.

107. Lundahl (1979), p. 446.

108. ONAPLAN (1983:3), pp. 116 and 131.

109. IEPD (1983:2), pp. 16-17.

110. Ibid.

111. Hobsbawm (1972), p. 30.

112. Marx (1977:2), p. 481.

113. Among the peasant leaders we often find people such as ex-soldiers, herdsmen, small artisans, priests, day-laborers, or even bandits, i.e., persons who have liberated themselves from the rules of the society (Hobsbawm (1972), p. 35).

114. See González (1985).

115. Concho Primo is an imaginary figure who stands as a symbol for all the rural *caudillos* who roamed the country until the appearance of Trujillo in the thirties (Cassá (1983), p. 196). See also Rodríguez Demorizi (1982), pp. 90-92.

116. Cassá (1983), pp. 259-60.

117. Clausner (1970), p. 442.

118. Hobsbawm (1972), p. 38.

119. Calder (1984), Chapters 5 and 6, presents a detailed description of the peasants' resistance against the US invaders. Before the *gavillero* war, passive resistance of peasants against the plantations was also common. For an account of these actions see Baud (1987).

120. Similar gangs of rural bandits, the so-called "cacos," existed in Haiti and were suppressed by the US occupying forces in that country. (See Lundahl (1979), p. 336.)

121. Wallace (1956), pp. 264-281.

122. What really happened is still very unclear. US embassy observers were convinced that the peasants had been unarmed and taken by surprise, they called the incident a cold-blooded massacre, "a wanton killing" (Martin (1975), p. 291). (For a description of these religious movements see Deive (1978), pp. 107-205, De la Mota (1980), pp. 209-215, Martin (1975), pp. 289-292, "Ahora" (1982), pp. 10-12 and Lundahl and Lundius (1987).)

123. Its leaders strove after political positions. In order to secure votes from the peasants, in the elections of 1962 a local representative for the *Unión Cívica National* (UCN) went as far as to promise the leader, Plinio Ventura, the vice-presidency of the country if UCN won (Lundahl and Lundius (1987)).

124. One of the most progressive laws ever issued in the country was law No. 532 of 1969 for the Promotion of Agriculture and Betterment of Rural Life. In 1960, there existed in the country 28 peasant associations. In 1976, this number had risen to 1,413 (of which 111 were cooperatives). The majority of the associations exist in regions where most of the farms are of the *minifundio* type (Eusebio Pol (1980), p. 57 and pp. 35 and 39).

125. Hobsbawm (1967), p. 53.

126. The armed insurrection of April 1965 was backed with great enthusiasm and active participation by the urban poor. This movement was crushed by the US military intervention in the country. In April 1984, urban riots shook the Dominican society. Private and public properties were sacked and destroyed. The intervention of the military forces left at least 100 dead, several hundred wounded and more than 4,000 arrested (Black (1986), p. 140).

5

Produce Marketing and Price Policies

The Dominican peasants are highly integrated in the market economy. Most of the peasants' production is sold in the market and most of the goods consumed by the peasants are also acquired in the market. The strong market orientation implies that the living standard of the Dominican peasants can be influenced by the performance of the market. The presence of market imperfections can negatively affect the level of income of the peasantry. The Dominican peasant participates to a very limited extent in the marketing of his product and marketing activities are generally carried out by different intermediaries. Imperfections in the produce market arise if the intermediaries exercise monopsonistic or monopolistic exploitation of the peasants. Under these conditions, the peasants will receive lower prices for the products they sell and pay higher prices for the products they consume than would be the case under competitive conditions.

A common view among Dominican authorities is that the peasants are being exploited and cheated by the intermediaries, and the precarious economic situation of the peasantry is generally blamed on the activities of the intermediaries. This has been one of the arguments for the increasing participation of the state in the marketing system. In this chapter, we shall analyze whether the Dominican peasants are subject to monopsonistic or monopolistic exploitation by the intermediaries. We shall first consider the degree of participation of the peasants in the market. Thereafter, we shall describe the main characteristics of the produce market and analyze the different marketing channels for agricultural products. Thirdly, we shall discuss whether competitive conditions prevail in the produce market and consider different factors which may give rise to market imperfections. Finally, we shall present a critical exposition of the activities of the state in the marketing system and analyze whether these activities have contributed to improving the marketing system and the level of income of the peasants.

The Peasants and the Market

The Dominican peasants have for a long time been integrated in the market economy. They have never produced everything they need or consumed all that they produce. Even if the Dominican peasants lived practically isolated until the end of the nineteenth century, they could always acquire certain goods, such as simple working tools, clothes and some food items, mainly through traveling salesmen with whom the peasants traded agricultural surpluses.

Due to the relative underpopulation and the low level of urbanization that prevailed in the country, for a long time, the Dominican peasantry did not develop any market tradition to speak of, in the sense that the peasant did not personally transfer his products to the urban markets or other rural areas. In the Cibao area, which is traditionally the most heavily populated and productive area of the country, with the exception of a certain amount of food crops, most agricultural output was intended for the international market. Tobacco was the most important crop, followed by coffee and cocoa. Until the development of the sugar industry, these products along with precious wood and cattle hides made up the bulk of the country's exports.

The main commercial towns were Santiago and Puerto Plata. The commercial activities in these towns were almost exclusively carried out by foreign merchants, mainly Germans, who had a monopoly of the tobacco trade.[1] With the exception of the tobacco market, the peasants participated to only a limited extent in urban market activities. Referring to the market activities of the town of Puerto Plata, an American observer in the 1870s relates:

> We first went to the "Plaza Mercado" or market square, and a more ridiculous sight cannot be imagined, for here, in a square about one-fourth of an acre, was held the daily market. A few rude booths, made of thatch and poles, composed the butcher's stalls, in which were exposed fearful specimens of various meats. Around the square were seated groups of women and children, with cloths spread upon the ground, upon which were displayed various fruits in limited quantities, herbs, salad, eggs six to eight in a lot, peas by the cupful.[2]

Similar impressions are presented regarding the marketplace of Santo Domingo.[3] Santiago was the town of largest commercial activity.

This town had the largest and busiest marketplace in the country and many peasants brought in different products for sale.[4]

By the end of the century, the Dominican peasant was well integrated in the international markets producing the bulk of exports which by this time consisted of tobacco, cocoa and coffee. The bulk of these crops was produced on small farms and was commercialized by a network of intermediaries who traveled by animals in the mountainous zones between Puerto Plata and Santiago, and the plains around La Vega, areas where most of the products were grown.[5] The intermediaries provided advances in cash and goods which the peasant paid by the end of the harvest. Although the peasants produced the bulk of exports, which by this time had become the country's main source of income, they lived an isolated existence, cut off from the urban centers and left at the mercy of the intermediaries in order to obtain credit and the complementary goods for their subsistence.[6]

In 1883, referring to the production of tobacco and praising the benefits of this crop in comparison with cocoa or coffee for which the peasant had to wait a long time in order to be able to enjoy the fruits of the yield, Pedro F. Bonó extensively described the importance of the intermediaries in the marketing of this product. After obtaining cash advances from importers in St. Thomas, England or Germany, large Dominican merchants advanced money and merchandise to producers through a network of intermediaries who were established near the production zones. Bonó describes the different advantages that the producers had from these advances and how they favored the rural population in general. Credit facilities were given to the peasants without any written agreement. This procedure raised certain problems for the peasants, who in many cases could be ruined by the deal.[7] The same procedure was followed in coffee and cocoa production and later in the marketing of food crops to urban areas.

As a result of the growth of the sugar industry, a network of communications was established in the Dominican economy which led to the integration of many peasant communities into a wider market. The newly developed towns as well as the large numbers of workers engaged in this industry increased the demand for food crops. In order to satisfy this demand, production became more diversified. The construction of roads under the American occupation (1916-24), was of importance for the marketing of agricultural products for internal consumption and exports.

However, these improvements did not result in the greater participation of the peasant in the marketing of his products. The intermediaries still exist and at present, they constitute the main marketing source for the peasant production and the major suppliers of services such as credit, transport, information, etc. Direct participation of the peasants in the marketing of their products is practically non-existent. In 1976, only 3 of the country's approximately 103 market places, had direct producer participation.[8] The limited participation of the Dominican peasants in the marketing of their products may be due to the extreme isolation under which the peasants lived for a long time, the high degree of specialization, the small size of the production units and the concentration of trade in the hands of few urban merchants.

General Characteristics of the Dominican Produce Markets

In the Dominican Republic, the majority of foodstuffs and a considerable proportion of export crops are produced on small farms while large farms are mostly devoted to sugar cane production, cattle breeding and, to a lesser extent, other export crops. These two production units present a sharp differentiation in relation to access to resources, technology level, market orientation and organization. Large producers are market oriented and direct their products mainly to the international market. Small producers run a family enterprise. They produce both for own consumption, for the domestic market and for the international market.

The commercialization processes confronted by small- and large-farm products are very different. While the latter may reach the final consumer or the international market in one or two steps, the former have to go through a long commercialization chain. As will be shown, this commercialization system contains a series of deficiencies which may affect the level of income of small producers.

In the Dominican Republic, the bulk of food crops are grown on small and medium-sized farms. Between 80 and 90 percent of the production of onions, pigeon peas, sweet potatoes, corn, yams and manioc, and between 40 and 70 percent of the production of garlic, rice, potatoes, plantains and tomatoes is carried out on farms of a size of less than 3 hectares (50 *tareas*).[9] With the exception of sugar cane, the bulk of agricultural exports is also produced on small and medium-sized farms. In the case of coffee, the second export crop of importance after sugar, 95.6 percent of the coffee farms are of a size less than 6 hectares.[10] Tobacco, the third important export crop, is also cultivated mainly on small farms. Eighty-four percent of the tobacco-growing farms are of a size of less than 6 hectares.[11] Cocoa is the fourth important export crop. Eighty-four percent of the cocoa farms are of a size of less than 5 hectares.[12]

The small size of the production units and the low level of education and organization of the peasants largely limit their opportunity to take advantage of the higher prices paid at the large urban markets.

The small quantity that the peasant can offer for sale does not allow him to incur transport costs. Besides, his dependence on the crop for cash income does not permit him to wait for better market conditions. In many cases, the crop is sold long before it is harvested. Furthermore, the limited access of the peasant to financial means forces him to depend on local intermediaries for the maintenance of his family and to carry on production. Generally, the intermediaries provide the peasants with advances in cash or in consumption goods. In turn, the peasant may sell his crop to these intermediaries and by doing so may lose the opportunity of selling his crop on more advantageous terms.

The Dominican peasant thus relies on the intermediaries for the marketing of his products. This fact has given rise to the hypothesis that the peasants are being exploited by the intermediaries. Operational plans within the Secretariat of Agriculture (SEA) provide evidence that the policy decisions are based upon a perception of widespread exploitation.[13] The notion that the Dominican intermediaries reap monopsony profits may also be deduced from a comparison that, for example, Jerry LaGra makes between the marketing system of the Dominican Republic and other Caribbean islands.[14] According to LaGra, the most important factors that differentiate the Dominican marketing system from that of the French and English speaking countries of the Caribbean can be summarized as follows:

a) In the Dominican Republic, the traditional intermediaries are male truck drivers (*camioneros*), often operating with considerable capital and handling large volumes of products, from a pickup load to a full truck load. In other Caribbean countries, the traditional intermediaries are predominantly women operating with limited capital and handling small amounts of products, around 100 pounds.

b) While in the Dominican Republic, the intermediaries (*camioneros*) are few in number and there is little "entry and exit" in trade, in other Caribbean countries, the number of intermediaries is large and there is "much entry and exit" in trade.

c) In the Dominican Republic, the *camioneros* sell in bulk in wholesale markets and their marketing margins are frequently substantial. In other Caribbean countries, the intermediaries sell at the retail level and obtain only small marketing margins.

The assumption that the presence of the intermediaries in the marketing system implies a high degree of exploitation of the producers has weighed heavily on the decision of the state to intervene and actively participate, through INESPRE (*Instituto de Estabilización de Precios*), in the marketing of agricultural products. However, no general study of the marketing system of the Dominican Republic exists on the basis of which one could support or reject the exploitation hypothesis.

The Produce Marketing System

The commercialization of agricultural products is carried out through a number of interrelated markets. The system includes five different market categories: the local, the regional, the interregional, the agroindustrial and the export market.

The most important market, in terms of the volume of products handled, is the **interregional** market. The most important market of this type is located in Santo Domingo where the bulk of the agricultural production is commercialized through two large wholesale markets. Most agricultural products entering Santo Domingo are received by these two markets. These markets deal in agricultural products both at the wholesale and retail levels. Around both markets, a zone of intensive commercial activities has developed. Most of the largest warehouses of the country are concentrated in these zones, complementing the activities of the markets by supplying grains and manufactured goods. The retailers of Santo Domingo obtain their products in these zones. The variety and quality of the products attract buyers from remote regions of the country and from neighboring Haiti.

However, the performance of these markets suggests that some inefficiency exists in the commercialization channels. Disregarding demand in the region of origin of the product, transport costs and the possible deterioration of the products, most of the agricultural output in the country is transported to Santo Domingo where, after quotation, a new distribution process starts. It is very common that the products return to the same region from where they first came. In 1976, it was found that 49 percent of the total volume of agricultural products entering Santo Domingo was received by the two largest markets. At the same time, between 23 and 31 percent of the volume of the agricultural products received was distributed to other regions of the country.[15] According to the SEA-IICA report *Diagnóstico del Sector de Mercadeo Agrícola en la República Dominicana*, the reason for this practice is the absence of regional wholesale markets, especially for perishable agricultural products for which the country lacks a national standardization, or a wholesaler price-setting system from which producers could obtain market information. Consequently, producers and intermediaries transport their products to the Santo Domingo market since they believe they will obtain a higher quotation for their products in this market, and that the size of the market will minimize the risk of saturation.[16]

The second market in importance is the **regional** market. Existing regional markets are of the "rotative" type. These markets sell agricultural products and other consumer goods on a specific day of the week in different towns of a region. Many participants in these markets are female sellers who travel on specific days of the week to different towns. This type of market is only found in regions near the Haitian border and resembles the Haitian rotative market system.[17]

Local market places exist in more than half of the municipal towns.[18] In 1976, there were 103 public markets in the country, of which 7 were located in Santo Domingo and 4 in Santiago. Only 15 public markets were located in rural areas. Public markets are mainly consumer oriented and offer limited services to producers. The number of markets existing in the Dominican Republic is extremely low if compared with other Caribbean countries. In Haiti, a country half the size of the Dominican Republic, there were 519 markets in 1975 of which 86 percent were of a semi-rural type.[19] The different market structures of these two countries may be due to different historical factors and to the fact that the Dominican Republic has a relatively more developed road and communication system.[20] The lack of nearby marketplaces implies that the peasants have to rely on the intermediaries for the sale of their products since, given the small quantity produced by each individual peasant, it is too costly for them to transport their products to the interregional markets.

Another market of some importance is the **agroindustrial** market. Some agricultural products, such as industrial tomatoes, peanuts and pigeon peas are bought and sold through this market. These industries provide incentives such as credit facilities, fertilizers and soil preparation and therefore attract many small producers for whom these facilities would otherwise be absent. For small producers, the agroindustries represent a secure market with stable prices.[21]

The **export** market is also important for small peasants' products. With the exception of some fruits and vegetables, which are produced by direct contract between producers and export firms, small producers reach this market through a long chain of rural and urban intermediaries. Large producers are in direct contact with the export firms or reach them through larger urban intermediaries.

The Marketing Chain

In the Dominican Republic, there are nearly 350,000 farms of a size of less than ten hectares. The majority of the agricultural products are produced on these farms. The marketing of these products is carried out by a chain of intermediaries who buy the products at the farms and see to it that the products reach the urban consumers and the exporters. The services provided by these intermediaries include gathering, transport, information, credit and at times, selection and packing.

The marketing chain varies with the size and the type of production. In the case of food products, small quantities are generally sold to a local intermediary who is often the owner of a small shop (*pulpería*) where the peasant acquires foodstuffs which he does not produce or has run out of stock after harvest. Larger quantities are sold to rural storekeepers (*acopiadores*) and/or to truck drivers. Truck drivers employ a network of intermediary agents in charge of locating and dealing with the producers and at times gathering and transporting the products from the farm to the roads where they can be picked up by the trucks. The products are then transported to and sold in the urban markets, mainly the Santo Domingo market. Most drivers deliver their cargo to a professional seller with whom they maintain close relations and who receives a commission for this service. These professional sellers sell the product to the wholesalers who in turn sell the products both at wholesale and retail levels. With the exception of rice, all food crops follow the marketing pattern described above. The marketing of rice is totally controlled by INESPRE, although some intermediaries intervene in the marketing process. In the case of the agroindustrial products, some intermediaries may intervene, but in some cases, such as industrial tomatoes, the industry takes care of packing and transport of the product.

The sketch in Figure 5.1 is representative of the marketing channels used for food crops. The central figure in this marketing chain is the truck driver (*camionero*). The *camionero* is the link between rural and urban marketing channels. Most *camioneros* are urban residents who travel to different areas of the country. Some of the *camioneros* hire their drivers. As a rule they also hire their trucks. Others own one or more trucks and only hire their drivers. Generally the *camioneros* travel with one or more assistants, who help them by controlling purchases and sales and assist laborers to load and unload the products.[22]

It should be noted that Figure 5.1 mainly refers to small farm production. As stated above, large farm production has a shorter marketing process since these farms may have direct access to transport and thereby to urban markets. There may be some cases where the number of intermediaries may be larger. This may be the case for those products which are distributed to the different regions of the country through the large urban marketplace channels.

FIGURE 5.1   The Marketing Chain for Food Crops

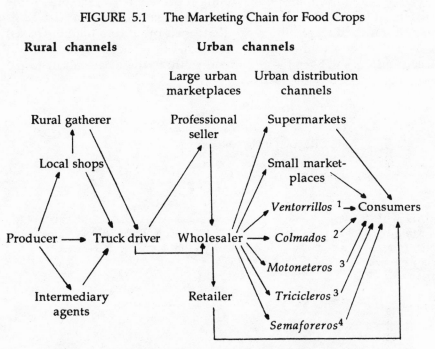

1)   *Ventorrillos* are small stands where fresh vegetables and fruits are sold. They are generally located in low-income urban neighborhoods.

2)   *Colmados* are small shops with an assortment of consumer goods. They are the urban equivalent of the *pulperías*.

3)   *Motoneteros* and *tricicleros* are ambulatory vendors. The former have a three-wheeled moped with a small platform on the back. The latter have a three-mainly vegetables and fruits.

4)   *Semaforeros* are sellers located at street corners, usually by traffic lights.

In the urban areas, agricultural products reach the consumers through a variety of retail sellers who obtain their assortments at the large urban marketplaces. The high- income urban population acquire their products mainly from supermarkets, public markets and traveling vendors who frequent the rich neighborhoods selling fresh vegetables and fruits from a *triciclo*, and at times from a basket carried on the head as is the case of female vendors. Lower income groups obtain their products from the *colmados* and *ventorrillos*, located in the different neighborhoods.

Figure 5.2 shows that the marketing process for rice, in spite of the participation of INESPRE, follows the same pattern as other agricultural products in the sense that small producers (*minifundistas*) channel their crops through the intermediaries while medium-size and large producers deliver the product directly to the local mill or to the larger ones located in the towns.

FIGURE 5.2   The Marketing Chain for Rice

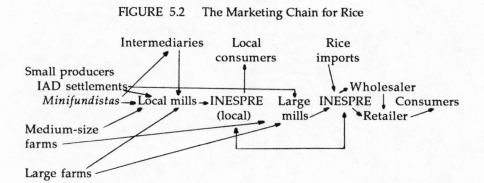

As Figure 5.3 shows, the marketing system for export crops also follows different channels depending on the size of the farms. Small producers market their products through a chain of intermediaries, while large producers reach the export markets directly through the export houses. The sketch in Figure 5.3 applies mainly to coffee and cocoa production. These two crops are mainly produced by small peasants. Coffee and cocoa, when produced in very small quantities, are sold in the form of berries and kernels to the local shops, which in many cases act as small-scale intermediaries as the peasants deliver their products in order to acquire consumption goods or to pay for those goods bought on credit. The peasant can also sell the crop to a small local intermediary agent who, in turn, delivers the product to smaller intermediaries. Some of these buyers may have access to a mechanic or motor-driven coffee-huller and/or a cement floor for drying coffee and cocoa in the sun. The product is then sacked and transported to major urban intermediaries, who in turn sell to the large export firms through which the products reach the international market.

123

FIGURE 5.3   The Marketing Chain for Export Crops

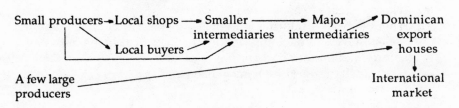

In the case of tobacco, the marketing process also includes a chain of intermediaries. However, in this case the chain is slightly shorter as tobacco production is concentrated in a specific geographical zone. The export firms install storehouses (*almacenes*) close to the tobacco-producing zones. Each of these houses selects 30 to 80 intermediaries (*corredores*) and provides them with cash in order to advance money to producers at sowing time and later on in order to buy their crops. After straining and drying, the tobacco leaves[23] the product is packed in *cerones* and sold to the intermediaries. Small peasants usually sell tobacco on strings in the local shops or exchange them for goods, the shopowner in his turn sells the strings to the intermediaries.

The marketing of export products follows different channels compared with those of the domestically consumed products. Export crops are not sold via the marketplaces but reach the large export firms through different intermediaries.

The Performance of the Marketing System

The existence of imperfections in the marketing system may lead to inefficiencies and to exploitation of the peasants. Inefficiencies may arise if perfect competition does not prevail in the commodity and factor markets involved in the marketing system, e.g., if monopsony power is exercised by the buyer of peasant products and/or if monopoly is exercised by the sellers of the products consumed by the peasants. Then, the income received by the peasant from his products would be lower and the price paid for the products he consumes would be higher than if conditions of perfect competition prevailed.

Perfect competition exists where, among others, the following conditions are fulfilled:[24]

a) There is a large number of buyers and sellers.
b) The quantity of the goods bought by any buyer or sold by any seller is so small in relation to the total quantity traded that changes in these quantities leave market prices unaffected.
c) There is freedom of entry.
d) There is perfect information, in the sense that all buyers and all sellers have complete information of the prices being asked and offered in all other parts of the market.
e) The traded products are homogeneous.

Although most markets do not in reality fulfill the requirements of perfect competition, it could be worthwhile to discuss to what extent the somewhat unrealistic assumptions underlying perfect competition prevail in the Dominican produce market. By means of such a discussion we may gain some insight into the workings of the market.

In this section, we shall discuss whether the above characteristics are absent from the marketing process of the products produced by the peasants and of those goods that are consumed by the peasants. As stated above, there is a general belief in the Dominican Republic that the peasants are being exploited by the intermediaries and different measures have been pursued by the state through direct participation in the marketing process. However, most of these measures have been taken without previously determining the real level of exploitation of the peasants by the intermediaries. It is generally assumed that the profit margins obtained by the intermediaries are extremely high, thus lowering peasant income.

Profit Margins

Data on net profit margins of the different agents participating in the marketing process of agricultural goods do not exist. The only available data concern the share of the final price received by different intermediaries. Table 5.1 below shows the share of final prices received by the main agents engaged in the marketing process of 17 agricultural products for domestic consumption. The figures for 1976 show that for nine of these products, the producers obtain less than 50 percent of the price at which the product is sold to the consumers. The percentage of the price obtained by the producer for the other eight products varies between 50 and 73. The products with the highest shares to the producer are onions and rice, while the lowest producer's share is obtained on grapes. The producer's share varies depending on whether or not the product is perishable. Thus, grains provide the highest shares for the producer. In 1976, they amounted to 72, 66, and 65 to 71 percent for rice, corn and beans respectively. Table 5.1 shows the shares for 1976 and 1984. With the exception of some products, the shares received by the different marketing agents in these years are more or less the same.

TABLE 5.1   Shares of Final Prices in Food Crop Marketing, 1976, 1984
(Percent)

Product	Producer		Truck Driver and/or Rural Storer		Factory		INESPRE		Wholesaler		Retailer	
	1976	1984	1976	1984	1976	1984	1976	1984	1976	1984	1976	1984
Rice	72	73	2	0	9	10	1	6	3	5	13	6
Corn	66	n.a.	6	n.a.	0	0	0	0	8	n.a.	20	n.a.
Red beans	71	67	10	14	0	0	0	0	4	4	15	15
Red beans*	65	n.a.	0	n.a.	0	0	2	0	18	n.a.	15	n.a.
Plantain (Barahona type)	47	n.a.	7	n.a.	0	0	0	0	6	n.a.	40	n.a.
Plantain (Cibao type)	40	50	20	13	0	0	0	0	10	5	30	32
Manioc	60	50	13	19	0	0	0	0	7	6	20	25
Sweet Potatoes	45	43	16	21	0	0	0	0	5	7	34	29
Potatoes	40	50	17	13	0	0	0	0	5	7	38	30
Salad Tomatoes	46	45	0	0	0	0	0	0	4	3	50	52
Onions	73	n.a.	7	n.a.	0	0	0	0	2	n.a.	18	n.a.
Garlic	60	n.a.	16	n.a.	0	0	0	0	1	n.a.	22	n.a.
Pigeon Peas	47	42	0	5	0	0	0	0	28	3	25	50
Papaya	40	n.a.	0	n.a.	0	0	0	0	34	n.a.	26	n.a.
Pineapple	44	n.a.	16	n.a.	0	0	0	0	0	n.a.	40	n.a.
Orange	50	n.a.	7	n.a.	0	0	0	0	10	n.a.	33	n.a.
Grape	33	n.a.	14	n.a.	0	0	0	0	11	n.a.	42	n.a.
Yams	n.a.	50	n.a.	10	0	0	0	0	n.a.	7	n.a.	33

*Commercialized through INESPRE.

n.a.: information not available.

Source: For 1976, SEA-IICA (1977); for 1984, SEA-IICA (1984); various tables and graphs.

Thus, in the case of half of the products, more than 50 percent was added to the price between producers and urban consumers. These are however gross margins. In order to obtain net margins, the costs of the different intermediaries must be deducted. As shown in Table 5.1, the largest margins are obtained by retailers, especially in the case of fruits and vegetables. This may be due to the fact that this group of intermediaries bear the highest risk in the marketing process. These goods are highly perishable and are generally sold in very small quantities to the consumers. The margins obtained by the rest of the intermediaries may not be so high once the cost incurred in gathering, storing and transporting the goods are deducted. Besides, many of these intermediaries provide other services to the producers such as money lending and credit, the cost of which must also be deducted from their gross margins. Labor may also account for a considerable part of the costs incurred by the intermediaries. Agricultural production is widely dispersed and only very small quantities are produced by thousands of *minifundistas*. Different intermediary agents must thus intervene in the gathering process.

Looking at the share of final prices alone, it is not possible to ascertain whether these margins are a result of monopsony power. After deducting the costs incurred in the process of gathering, selecting and transporting the product, plus the implicit wages acquired by the different agents intervening in these processes, profit margins may shrink significantly. Thus, on the basis of these data, it is difficult to determine the existence of exploitative profits, or at what level in the marketing chain, exploitation of the peasants takes place. Nevertheless, this is the most complete information available in the country concerning the marketing of agricultural products and it is possible that it serves as an important source for policy makers.[25]

No detailed information exists on the profit margins obtained in the marketing of export crops produced by the peasants. We have, however, gathered some information on gross margins in the marketing of coffee and cocoa, which are the major export crops produced by small peasants.

The shares in Table 5.2 are a simplification, since the marketing chain can be much longer. It should, however, be kept in mind that the producer's shares presented above refer to small producers and are based on a very small sample.

In order to obtain net profits, we have to take account of the marketing costs of the intermediaries. In the case of small *compradores*, labor and transport costs from the farm to the larger *comprador* must be deducted. The larger *comprador* bears various marketing costs. It is this intermediary who generally hulls, cleans and dries the coffee. He is often the owner of a small factory for hulling coffee which includes a large cement drying-floor, a motor-driven huller, and a warehouse for storing coffee until it is transported by truck to the exporters. The larger *compradores* also bear the risk of money lending, since it is through them that the exporters channel the cash advances needed in order to by the harvest.

TABLE 5.2   Estimated Shares of Export Prices in Coffee Marketing, 1971-1972 *

(in Percentage of Final Prices)

Small Producers	Small Compradores	Larger Compradores	Exporters
63	5	14	18

*Based on prices for the December-March harvest.

Source: Calculated from Sharpe (1977), Table 2.6, p. 38.

The producer's shares in cocoa marketing are higher than those in coffee.[26] Marketing cocoa is less costly, since only limited processing is required. Cocoa only needs to be dried and sacked before it is trucked to the exporter. As in the case of coffee, the small *comprador* bears the labor and transport costs from the farm to a larger *comprador*. The latter generally possesses a cement drying-floor and a warehouse. He is also the major supplier of credit to producers. The urban intermediary may incur storage and transport costs, while the exporter faces costs such as interest, export taxes, export documents, etc.

TABLE 5.3   Shares of Export Prices in Cocoa Marketing, 1984

Producers	Small Compradores	Larger Rural Compradores	Larger Urban Compradores	Exporters
73	2	3	2	20

Source: SEA (1984:1), p. 18.

Table 5.4 indicates the net profit margins obtained by different intermediaries. From each 100 pounds sold, profit margins range from 2.40 pesos for small intermediaries to 4.48 pesos for exporters. However, marketing costs are not specified and it is not clear whether the salaries of the different intermediaries are included in marketing costs or in net profit margins.[27] These profit margins are apparently low, especially if we consider that the number of export firms is low and that the market presents oligopsonistic characteristics (see below). The rate of return on the exporter's capital is less than 3 percent on each transaction.[28] This rate increases depending on how often the exporter's capital turns over, that is, depending on the time lapse from when the cocoa exporter buys the product until he receives payment from abroad.

TABLE 5.4   Selling Price, Marketing Cost and Net Profit Margins of the Different Intermediaries in Cocoa Marketing, 1984 (DR$ per 100 pounds)

	Selling Price*	Marketing Cost	Net Margin
Producer	130.00	-	-
Small *Comprador*	133.50	1.10	2.40
Larger Rural *Comprador*	138.50	2.30	2.70
Larger Urban *Comprador*	142.50	1.30	2.70
Exporter	177.12	30.14	4.48

*These prices refer to the Northeast region. In the Eastern region, due to lack of fermentation and drying before selling, the price paid to the producers can be as low as 80 pesos per 100 pounds.

Source: SEA (1984:1), p. 18.

Degree of Competition among Intermediaries

a) Number of Buyers and Sellers

In the case of food products, the principal agent in the marketing system is the truck driver. In 1977, most of the 4,700 trucks transporting agricultural products were concentrated to certain geographical areas or products.[29] The number of sellers may be around 300,000. In the

Dominican Republic there are about 315,000 *minifundistas* and 63,000 middle holders.[30] The majority of these producers cultivate food crops for sale in the market.

In 1980, the produce flow from producing areas to the capital engaged 400 pickups and trucks each day, carrying an average of 2,000 metric tons of agricultural products.[31] Competition among truck drivers is generally believed not to be substantial since most of these intermediaries are specialized on visiting particular areas of the country and buy specific products. However, this can easily be a result of competition since a *camionero* cannot be in all places and buy all kinds of products. In order to compete, he needs to have a profound knowledge of specific products and areas.[32] We should also keep in mind the important role that the *camionero* plays as a credit source for the producers. In order to minimize risk, a good knowledge of his clientele is also needed.

In the case of exports, oligopsony prevails. Very few firms dominate this market. In 1967, there were 167 coffee exporting firms in the country. However, the market is almost completely dominated by twelve firms, of which four account for more than fifty percent of the market. As shown in Table 5.5, the most important of these four firms is INDUBAN (Industrias Banilejas) which has annually exported between 20 and 30 percent of the coffee. Until 1983, the second, third and fourth ranks were alternatively occupied by the firms Américo Melo, Muné & Cía. and J. Paiewonsky. In 1983, however, a relatively new firm, R. Peña, ranked second among all coffee exporters, displacing Paiewonsky from second position in 1977-78 to third in 1983-84. Muné and Melo ranked third and fourth, respectively, in 1977-78. By 1983-84, these firms were relegated to the sixth and ninth positions.

The coffee export market works under oligopsonistic conditions, i.e., there is always the possibility of competition between existing buyers. Besides, new entrants can always challenge the existing equilibrium. Today, fierce competition is reported to exist among the large export firms. In order to increase their coffee stock some firms offer up to 4 pesos more than other firms per *quintal*.[33] However, in a historical perspective, the prevalence of these exporting firms in leading positions is not determined by competition alone. The quota system in coffee export, in operation until 1985, also influenced their position. Until 1982, quotas were assigned according to the stock of coffee each firm had at the moment of quota distribution. During the period 1982-84, the quotas were assigned according to the export record during the last five years. Since 1984, this system has changed back to being based on the size of the stock. According to the authorities, the system based on export records tended to perpetuate the concentration of exports to the largest firms.[34] In 1985, due to the high prices of coffee on the international market, the quota system was abolished and it remains to be seen whether by means of competition alone the four firms which dominated the market in 1984 will be able to keep their positions as leading exporters.

TABLE 5.5   The Largest Coffee Exporters and Their Market Shares, 1967-68, 1977-78 and 1983-84

	1967 - 1968		1977 - 1978		1983 - 1984	
Rank	Firm	% of tot. exports	Firm	% of tot. exports	Firm	% of tot. exports
1	INDUBAN*	20.9	INDUBAN	31.3	INDUBAN	23.8
2	Américo Melo	10.1	J. Paiewonsky	10.4	R. Peña	12.9
3	Muné & Cía.	8.6	Muné & Cía.	9.4	J. Paiewonsky	8.9
4	J. Paiewonsky	7.2	Américo Melo	7.8	J. F. Pérez	6.7
5	Bordas	4.5	Isa	6.7	Ass. V. Trina	6.0
6	Isa	4.5	Comercial Roig	6.2	Muné & Cía.	5.3
7	Toral Hnos.	3.4	J. F. Pérez	4.5	Nazario Risek	5.3
8	Franjul	2.7	Nazario Risek	4.4	Comercial Roig	3.5
9	Curaçao T. Co.	2.6	Font Gamundi	3.0	Américo Melo	3.4
10	Font Gamundi	2.4	Ass. V. Trina	1.8	Font Gamundi	2.5
11	J. F. Pérez	1.6	S. B. Genao	1.3	Mejía & Mejía	1.8
		68.5		86.8		80.1

*Includes Cafetalera del Sur, Industrias Banilejas C. x A. and Jesús Ma. Paniagua.

Source: SEA, Departamento de Café, División de Estudios Sociales, and Linares, (1984) and (1985).

In the case of cocoa, the concentration of exports is even greater. As Table 5.6 shows, the market has traditionally been dominated by four large firms: Roig, Risek, Muné and Paiewonsky, accounting for around 90 percent of total cocoa exports. All these four firms have also traditionally been powerful coffee exporters. In contrast to coffee exports, the leading cocoa exporters have been able to keep their positions unchanged for the period of 1974-83.

TABLE 5.6   Cocoa Exporters and Their Market Shares, 1974 and 1983

	1974		1983	
Rank	Firm	% of tot. exports	Firm	% of tot. exports
1	Roig	40.8	Roig	37.0
2	Muné	35.7	Muné	25.9
3	Risek	14.9	Risek	19.8
4	Paiewonsky	5.3	Paiewonsky	6.6
5	García & Mejía	1.9	García & Mejía	4.5
6	R. Araujo	1.1	Gamundi	3.7
7			T. González	0.9
8			J. Vásquez	0.2
9			Impex Dom.	0.1
		99.7		98.9

Source: SEA, Departamento de Cacao, División de Comercialización.

Tobacco exports are carried out by 13 to 15 export houses.[35] Unfortunately we have not been able to obtain information about the variation of their market shares over time.

The different export firms obtain their products through a chain of intermediaries whose number may vary from product to product. In the case of coffee and cocoa, the exporters buy the product through independent *compradores* in the countryside. These *compradores* either buy directly from the peasants or more often employ smaller *compradores* on a commission basis to do the buying. These smaller *compradores* may in turn also employ others as their buyers. At the rural level, competition exists between the small *compradores*. However, according to Sharpe, the price the peasants receive for their coffee depends "on the number of other compradores buying in the area, price-fixing agreements among these 'compradores,' the knowledge the peasants have of prices, and the peasants' moral and economic indebtedness to a particular comprador."[36] Similar practices are reported in the marketing of cocoa.[37]

Many of the smaller intermediaries at the rural level are merchants who, apart from buying the peasants products, also sell the commodities that the peasants consume. A rural merchant generally owns a local shop (*pulpería*), where food, liquors, tobacco, household hardware, kerosene, pans and simple household and farm implements are sold, generally on a credit basis. More than one *pulpería* may exist in a small village. Their assortment is more or less the same and is usually very limited. The *pulpería* owner usually maintains a good relationship with his clientele and is often the only credit source available for food and other items consumed by the peasants. The peasants often pay by offering the *pulpería* owner part of their production.[38] Competition seems to be intense among the small intermediaries who buy the products of the peasants as well as among those selling the products the peasants consume. The main reason for this is that trade activity ranks high as a livelihood and many small producers tend to move into trade whenever possible. In this respect, Gerald Murray states:

> Trade is seeing a more lucrative pursuit than small scale production and consequently many small scale producers clearly aspire to (and many actually do) get a foothold in local trade ... many of them turn into buyers at harvest time, purchasing produce from neighbors and transporting it to sell to truckers or other intermediaries; but also some actually set up small *bodegas* and *pulperías* in their communities so that even tiny hamlets may have three or four business establishments.[39]

b) Quantity Traded

A necessary condition for competition to prevail in a market is that the quantity traded by each participant is small enough to ensure that changes in this quantity leave prices unchanged. Most food and export crops are produced in small quantities by a large number of *minifundistas*. Thus, a change in the quantity produced by a single seller will not affect prices. As stated above, in rural areas the quantity of export crops traded by each participant is small and the activity of a single buyer or a single seller cannot affect prices. In relation to export firms, prices of export crops are determined by the world market and Dominican exports are not large enough to influence prices in this market.

In the case of food crops, the producers sell their products to *corredores* or *buscones*, i.e., intermediaries who buy the products directly at the farms and bring them to the *camioneros*. The peasants can also bring their products to the roadside and sell directly to the *camioneros*. The *camioneros* then bring the products to the different urban marketplaces. At these markets, quantities vary from a pickup load to a truckload. However, the number of *camioneros* at the urban marketplace is sufficiently large to ensure that the presence of a single truck or pickup is unlikely to affect prices at this market.[40]

c) Freedom of Entry

The large amount of goods handled by the *camioneros* implies that a relatively large amount of capital is needed in order to enter the produce market. A traveling intermediary must be able to hire or buy a truck, employ assisting personnel and have access to financial means large enough in order to buy products in bulk and make cash advances to producers. Thus, the Dominican produce market is characterized by a high degree of specialization and capitalization which may limit the freedom of entry to the market. Although there are no syndicates that prevent outsiders from moving into this market, the possession of capital is only one of the limiting aspects. Equally important are personal relationships with the producers. The following passage about a plantain intermediary may be illustrative:

> Plantains are both perennial and perishable; this means that the intermediary has a continuous supply and that storage is impossible. Mariano has established permanent relationships with seven or eight producers. These producers take scheduled turns in harvesting their plantains, and Mariano provides the transporting service for each one, completing the circle every two or three weeks ... Because of rapidly fluctuating market conditions, each load has a different price, and bargaining enters into every transaction. If market conditions are good, Mariano generally accedes to the producer's demand; the opposite is true under unfavorable market conditions. In the case of impasse between the two, Mariano would take the bean *sin precio* (without having set the price) and the producer's share would depend on the price Mariano got in the urban market. But the producer will in no case sell to another viajante [traveler]. [41]

The same applies to local rural merchants and storekeepers. Although the *pulperías* present a relatively small choice, some starting capital is needed in order to enter this market. Rural merchants generally obtain credit from large urban merchants and the opportunity to obtain this credit is largely determined by the moral and economic status of the client.[42]

d) Information

An important prerequisite for competition is that both buyers and sellers have sufficient information on prices, quantities and qualities of the products offered in the market. If sufficient information is not available to the different parties, the possibility of monopsony (oligopsony) and monopoly (oligopoly) will arise.

The centralization of the Dominican marketing system facilitates the creation and diffusion of market information. Price information is fairly institutionalized. The Secretariat of Agriculture (SEA) produces and distributes price bulletins weekly - one for producers and one for consumers of agricultural products. Price information is also diffused by radio announcements. Information is collected on a daily basis by the SEA price informants who pay daily visits to the urban wholesaler and retailer markets and obtain information from the intermediaries.[43] Most peasants get information through the traveling intermediaries and the radio. Thus, the level of information among Dominican peasants is relatively good. Whether the peasants could make advantageous use of this information depends on their ability and/or bargaining opportunity vis-à-vis the intermediary. The scope for bargaining may be limited by the ties of the peasant to the intermediary through credit and cash advances, the generally lower educational level of the peasant and the economic limitations he confronts. These limitations often imply that many peasants have to sell out of urgent need and in this case, although having good information on prices, his bargaining power is significantly lowered.

e) Homogeneity

If competition is to prevail, it is essential that the units of the goods sold by different sellers are identical, i.e., the product must be homogeneous. Lack of homogeneity may affect the price-setting process.

In the Dominican Republic, selection of the products does not take place at the farm level but producers sell a mixture of high- and low-grade products. Consequently most products that are sold are of a very uneven quality. The absence of grading standards and selection norms may imply considerable variability in prices. Most intermediaries make a visual judgement of the quality of the products. The quality and moisture content of grains are, for example, estimated visually and by using a bite test. Grains may be shaken softly in one hand and the sound made may have a significant impact on the price offered by the intermediary. The presence of foreign matter such as stones, husk and soil is also estimated visually and if established leads to a volume or weight discount.

Another homogeneity problem is related to the system of measurements and weights. In the Dominican Republic, no standard measurement scheme exists; measures and weights vary from region to region and according to the different products. Intermediaries generally buy the product in one determined measure and sell in the urban markets in another measure. A generalized practice among intermediaries is the purchasing of grains in quintals, each equivalent to 110 pounds, but they pay only for 100 pounds. There is an extensive list of different measures and weights which produces a great deal of confusion especially for the peasantry who is generally not acquainted with the measurement schemes prevailing in urban markets. In these markets, the metric system is widely used whereas in rural areas, a range of different measures prevails. In the case of grains, measures such as *cajón, carga, cerón, argana*, and quintals of 50, 55 and 60 kilos, are widely used.[44]

When qualities and measures are not homogeneous, the opportunities for the intermediaries to cheat the peasants increase. However, this homogeneity problem is overcome by the haggling process. Due to differences in qualities and measurement, no single price prevails in the market. By a process of bidding and asking, the buyer and seller agree on a price that both consider acceptable. Through this process, the quality and quantity of the particular item is examined and discussed. Generally, the price asked by the seller lies far above the price that both he and the buyer believe to be the real price.[45]

Haggling is a widespread practice in the Dominican Republic. Almost no seller, whether a peasant, a street vendor or a large storekeeper in town, asks for the real price. He does not do so since he must keep a margin in order to offer the client the customary *rebaja* or discount.

Sources of Monopsony and Monopoly Power

The level of competition in the produce market may also be affected by the presence of different power factors. Power factors may lower the supply elasticity and thereby generate conditions of monopsony, i.e., sellers may be unable to sell their products other than to one buyer. Clifton Wharton, in his study of monopsony in Malayan rubber, has identified seven types of power factors:[46]

1. *Legal power.* A firm is given the exclusive right to the use of the commodity. The producers are thereby forced to sell to the monopsonist and is unable to sell the product elsewhere.

In the Dominican Republic, licensed intermediaries do not exist; however, the monopolization of INESPRE in the marketing of rice may exemplify this type of power.

2. *Illegal power.* The intermediaries may use force, threats or physical coercion which prevent sellers from seeking alternative buyers.

The presence of this factor is difficult to check. There are, however, some instances where sellers may feel threatened by an intermediary, especially in the case where the latter is also a merchant. The peasant may feel obliged to sell his crop to the merchant since he may feel the threat of not obtaining future credit for food supplies. Such cases have been reported among some coffee producers.[47]

3. *Economic power*. The intermediary may enjoy monopsony through the control of inputs such as credit. Meeting the needs of the producers through cash advances and loans is a source for securing the crops. Another source of economic power and thereby of monopsony, may be the control of transport or processing facilities. Economic power is also present when the possibility of entry is coupled with a relatively large amount of capital. This may impede the entry of other intermediaries and competition is thereby limited.

As will be seen in Chapter 7, the provision of credit is a common practice among Dominican intermediaries, such as *camioneros* and *pulpería* owners. Whether the provision of credit is a source of monopsony power in the Dominican produce market is a debated question. In the case of beans, a study shows that credit provided by the intermediaries, in order to bind the peasant into compulsory sales arrangements, was not in evidence.[48] In the case of coffee, Kenneth Sharpe states that this is a common practice.[49]

Most *camioneros* agree that money lending is an effective strategy for securing supply. Loans are generally interest free. Thus, the provision of credit constitutes a major competition factor among intermediaries. The loans give the lender a preferential position in buying the produce of the borrower. However, if another buyer offers a higher price, the producer will sell to the other buyer, but will have to return the money to the lender with a 3 to 4 percent monthly interest. Although the borrower is not forced to sell to the lender, provided that the price he offers is fair, he generally does so *en agradecimiento* (out of gratitude).[50]

The control of transport or processing facilities seems not to be a source of monopsony power. Generally there is more than one *camionero* buying products in an area and the producer is able to choose the more convenient offer. A study concerning the production of beans reported transport services as relatively unimportant. Producers would be willing to transport their crop to the nearest town if the price there was greater than the price at the farm plus transportation costs.[51] Monopsony power is unlikely to arise from the possession of processing facilities. For example, in the case of coffee washing factories, washing is not a compulsory operation since the product can easily be sold in cherries.

4. *Technical and natural power*. This refers to the access the intermediary has to technical facilities, such as telephones, gas, water, etc., or to problems related to market location and price information.

In the Dominican Republic, technical factors may not be so relevant since the nature of the products in question does not allow this type of power to arise. The centralization of the marketing system and the location of many producers in remote areas of the country may give rise to natural power. This is, however, overcome by the knowledge that the traveling intermediary possesses of his own area of operation. Once the crop of a producer who lives far away from the road is due, he informs a friend living by the road who in turn informs the *camionero*. When the deal is made, the producer transports the products to the road by mule or donkey.[52]

5. *Cultural power*. In many cases, sellers and buyers may be related through family - or sociocultural - ties and this may prevent the sellers from seeking other buyers outside the local sphere. This type of power has a similar effect to that of illegal or legal power in the sense that the seller is committed to one buyer.

Evidence to support the existence of such power in the Dominican produce market is not available. Although in many cases the intermediary may not be directly related to the producer through family ties, similar relations are likely to develop since most intermediaries try to develop a good relationship with the producers. This relationship tends to be strengthened long before the sale of the crop. The intermediary facilitates cash advances and seeks to foster a good relationship with the producer, in order to minimize risk. This means that a peasant may be committed to a particular buyer, but it also implies that the buyer is unwilling to fleece his client since this may damage his reputation in the area.

6. *Psychological power*. This ranges from mentally coercive activities such as propagandizing, brainwashing or advertising. These factors may prevent sellers from behaving in a rational manner and may influence their choice pattern. Psychological power also arises when sellers try to maintain the good will of the buyer in order to secure future loans and cash advances. This type of power is also at work among intermediaries who likewise try to maintain a good relationship with the sellers in fear of social sanctions. The same type of power is also present among the intermediaries themselves who may avoid obtaining new customers due to threats of economic warfare from other buyers.

We have not come across any data which could sustain the existence of mentally coercive activities in the Dominican produce market. However, the great dependency of producers on credit and cash advances from the intermediaries may give rise to some sort of psychological power. But this is likely to be at work among both sellers and buyers. In order to secure these facilities, sellers tend to try to preserve good relations with the intermediaries. In the same fashion, in order to maintain this relationship, the intermediaries will tend to exercise their power in a rather covert fashion, as he endeavors to establish a good reputation among the producers.

7. *Informational and educational power.* This may arise if producers possess poor knowledge of the sale and price alternatives. Lack of this knowledge may be due to low levels of education, economic sophistication, or poor communication.

In the Dominican Republic, the truck drivers and their agents are likely to have more information than the peasants about the market and prices since the former are in daily contact with the urban markets. However, the Dominican peasant seems to be fairly well informed about the market since nearly all peasants have access to information via radio and different intermediaries. Among bean producers, for example, no less than a dozen different sources of price information have been reported.[53]

Summary

In the above section, we tried to analyze whether monopsony and/or monopoly practices exist in the Dominican marketing system or whether, on the contrary, the activities in this market are carried out under competitive conditions. The scarcity of data does not allow definite conclusions, however, although with some limitations, most of the essential prerequisites for competition were found to be in operation. There seems to be a high degree of competition among the small intermediaries who buy the products the peasants produce and among those selling the products the peasants consume. Trade is ranked high as a livelihood in the rural areas and there is some evidence that many peasants engage in trade on a small-scale basis. Thus, at this level, no barriers to entry seem to exist.

The larger intermediaries, the *camionero* in the case of food crops, and the *acopiador rural* in the case of export crops, usually hire other small intermediaries (*buscones*) to locate the prospective seller. These small *compradores* work on a commission basis and this may tend to increase competition. At the rural level, the quantities traded are small and they do therefore not affect prices. At the market level, the number of *camioneros* at the market is sufficiently large to ensure that a single truck driver is unable to affect prices. The level of information is relatively good since the peasants receive price information via radio and the intermediaries on a daily basis. The problem of homogeneity is overcome by the haggling process. Through this mechanism, price differences account for differences in quantity and quality. These characteristics tend to preclude the creation of monopoly or monopsony power.

The Dominican marketing system involves a substantial number of intermediaries, both small and large. The *camioneros* and the export firms belong to the latter category. The former constitute the link between rural and urban areas and are the most important element in the marketing system of food crops. At this level, freedom of entry may be limited since a large amount of money is needed to enter this market. Besides hiring or buying a truck, the *camionero* must have access to financial means in order to acquire large amounts of products and provide credit to the producers.

In the case of the export firms, it was shown that oligopsonistic conditions prevail. For decades, the export market for coffee and cocoa has been dominated by four large export firms. Competition is reported to be high among these firms. Entry into this market is limited by the amount of money needed and, in the case of coffee, by the system of assignation of export quotas.

We also discussed the existence of power factors that may generate conditions of monopsony in the produce market. Of the seven different power factors discussed, some evidence suggests that two of them may be present in the Dominican produce market: legal power, represented by INESPRE's total monopolization of rice marketing; and economic power in the sense that the larger intermediaries may enjoy monopsony by providing credit to the producers. The latter, however, need not necessarily be the case. The evidence suggests that meeting the capital needs of the producers through cash advances and loans is a means of securing the crop. Thus, the provision of credit constitutes an important competition factor among the intermediaries. Whether the peasant is obliged or not to sell his crop to the lender is a debated question. My own experience is that they usually do not do so if the price offered is below the going market price.

The Participation of the State

The state participates actively in the commercialization process through the Integrated Rural Service Centers (*Centros de Servicios*

Rurales Integrados, CENSERI) under the auspices of the Secretariat of Agriculture (SEA), and through the Price Stabilization Institute (INESPRE). The CENSERI are rural centers managed by peasant associations. Each center includes a storehouse and a rural shop. Those centers provide information on prices but their impact at the national level is still very limited. INESPRE is the leading institution in the commercialization of agricultural products. INESPRE regulates the prices of various agricultural products and controls the imports of food staples to the country. At present, this institution regulates marketing and prices of more than a dozen agricultural commodities. At the same time, it actively participates in the marketing of basic foodstuffs at the consumer level.

Although government intervention in the marketing system dates from 1939,[54] it was not until after the creation of INESPRE in 1969 that the Dominican government took a firm grasp of the marketing of important agricultural products. INESPRE's main goals are to implement price regulations at the farm level and promote production, to protect consumers through price stabilization and to reduce marketing margins received by intermediaries. Since 1973, and until 1986, INESPRE had total control over the marketing of rice, which moved from producers, through rice mills, to INESPRE and through this institution it reached the wholesaler, retailer and final consumers. INESPRE also participates in the marketing of beans, corn and to a lesser extent, onions, garlic, potatoes, plantains, eggs, and small amounts of root crops. INESPRE is also the primary carrier of stocks and the monopolist importer of basic food commodities, such as corn, edible oils, nonfat dry milk and some other processed foods.

In order to accomplish its goal of stabilizing prices, INESPRE has been heavily dependent on food imports. Imports of agricultural products have been subject to low tariff rates. The bulk of INESPRE imports have been carried out at zero nominal tariff, with the exception of processed products, such as meat and tomato paste, which pay a minimum tariff of 5 percent.[55] Agricultural imports also received an implicit import subsidy due to the overvaluation of the currency.[56] Although INESPRE has been successful at stabilizing prices, its policies have been highly criticized since they have been mainly geared to suit the urban consumer while small producers have been faced with reduced prices and incomes.[57]

INESPRE's Activities and Price Policies

Since its creation, INESPRE's major involvement has been in the marketing of agricultural products. However, in later years, the institute also participates in direct purchases from producers and in social programs.

Table 5.7 shows the wide range of agricultural products covered by INESPRE's marketing activities. However, most of INESPRE's resources have been concentrated in the marketing of four products: rice, sugar, vegetable oils and corn. In 1983, these products accounted for 83 percent of INESPRE's purchases.

TABLE 5.7   INESPRE's Commodity Transactions, 1983

Commodity	Total Sales (DR$ million)	Total Purchases (DR$ million)	Share of Imports (%)
Polished rice	158.1	142.2	0.0
Black beans	2.8	2.0	0.0
Soybean oil	20.2	19.4	100.0
Cottonseed oil	14.8	13.2	100.0
Sugar (various types)	80.9	75.5	0.0
Onions	1.2	0.7	0.0
Corn	31.4	27.6	88.0
Wheat bran	3.6	3.0	100.0
Sorghum	3.2	3.3	0.0
Potatoes	0.5	0.3	0.0
Eggs	0.6	0.5	0.0
Poultry meat	3.1	2.9	0.0
Nonfat dry milk	5.1	4.7	100.0
Butter oil	4.3	3.3	100.0
Animal fats	0.5	0.5	100.0
Soybean meal	3.1	3.0	100.0
Pigeon peas	1.1	0.0	0.0
Other products	2.1	2.2	0.0
Total	336.6	304.3	

Gross Operating Margin DR$ 32.3 million

Source: World Bank (1985), p. 35.

Rice represented nearly half of INESPRE's sales and purchase operations. It is such an important product, both for consumers and producers, that rice price policies can affect the standard of living of urban consumers and largely influence the level of income and employment in rural areas.[58]

INESPRE has been successful at stabilizing rice prices. Domestic prices have been more stable than international prices. This is partly due to the fact that INESPRE has secured imported rice through PL-480 and the Commodity Credit Corporation (CCC) program at lower and less fluctuating prices than the world price. At the same time, INESPRE's rice imports were carried out using currency at the official exchange rate. In this way, imported rice appeared cheaper than domestically produced rice. Most years, INESPRE's sales price of rice has been below the price of domestic purchase, but above the price of imported rice.[59]

In order to provide cheap rice to the consumers, the institute resumed piling up a rice stock in the harvest season and then releasing it during the off season. However, since INESPRE's rice operations were not profitable, large subsidies were needed in order to pay for the cost of these stocks, as well as to keep prices low for the rice consumers. In order to meet its own expenses and subsidize consumer prices the institute developed a system of cross subsidies in which large margins for some products were used to subsidize low consumption prices for other products. In 1983, its markup over procurement prices ranged from 7 percent on rice to 70 percent on soya oil.[60]

Profits from vegetable oils have been very important in supplying INESPRE with funds for the financing of its other operations. This policy of cross-subsidies has mainly benefited the urban consumer, but has had a detrimental effect on the producers. The monopsonistic powers conferred upon INESPRE and the regional mills likely depressed prices below the level that would have prevailed under competitive conditions. Production was thus discouraged in the long run. According to a World Bank calculation, the Dominican Republic has a comparative advantage in rice production, but with continued low domestic prices, the export potential may be stifled.[61]

Actually, the price INESPRE paid the rice mills rose more slowly than the costs of production at the farm level. Between 1976 and 1981, the price of milled rice, which determines the farm price of rice, rose with 24 percent, while the prices of fertilizers rose with an average of 81 percent. Price setting policies have made rice production unprofitable at the farm level. For the period 1980-84, the farm price of rice was below the costs of production.[62]

In the case of vegetable oils, INESPRE has to a large extent harmed the domestic production of peanuts, an oil producing crop. As a result the area planted with peanuts, which are mainly cultivated by small peasants, fell from 1.3 million *tareas* in 1974 to 0.7 million in 1982.[63]

INESPRE serves as a monopoly importer that sells its vegetable oil imports to processors and distributors. Profits from the sale of imported oil constitute the bulk of INESPRE's gross profits. INESPRE has therefore a strong incentive to maintain a high level of vegetable oil imports and a low level of domestic production of oilseed. It has used its monopoly power to depress prices for domestic producers and hence provide revenues for its own operations. According to World Bank calculations, the Dominican Republic has a strong advantage in peanut production and therefore there seems to be no economic justification for a continuation of the strong disincentive to domestic production of vegetable oils.[64]

Other important items in INESPRE's marketing activities are corn and animal food. INESPRE captures approximately 15 percent of the domestic production of corn, and nearly 90 percent of INESPRE's sales consists of imported corn. INESPRE has consistently maintained the producer price of corn above the import cost, even at the parallel exchange rate. According to World Bank analysis, the Dominican Republic does not appear to have a comparative advantage in producing corn.[65] INESPRE's corn importing operation has meant a drain on its resources. INESPRE sells imported corn for small or negative margins and these low prices have gone to subsidize animal food and have encouraged livestock production.[66]

Other products for which INESPRE attempts to control the market are sugar and nonfat dry milk.

INESPRE buys sugar from the CEA (*Consejo Estatal del Azúcar*) and monopolizes its distribution. Prices have been well below export prices, even at the official exchange rate. This has led, on some occasions, to a shortage in the domestic market since some businessmen consider it to be more profitable to export their INESPRE assigned quota to neighboring Haiti. INESPRE's margins on sugar sales have not been used to finance INESPRE's operations. All but 5 percent has gone to subsidize the operations of the state owned electricity utility CDE (*Corporación Dominicana de Electricidad*).[67]

INESPRE's participation in milk production presents similar tendencies as those prevalent in the cases of rice and vegetable oils. Programs designed to protect consumers from rising milk prices have depressed the domestic dairy industry by substituting imported milk for domestic production. Producers' prices have been set so low that milk production has become unprofitable.[68] In order to address the shortage of milk, INESPRE was given the exclusive right to import powdered milk in 1979. Since 1982, INESPRE has begun a program of processing milk. This program has increased the availability of milk at controlled prices and provided a substitute for domestically produced milk.[69]

INESPRE's marketing activities have mainly benefited the urban consumers. Another activity intended to benefit urban consumers, and on which the institute has put much emphasis, is the social programs. The most important of these programs is that of *Ventas Populares*. INESPRE sponsors stores in urban areas, where about 20 products are sold at subsidized prices. The program of *Ventas Populares* is highly biased in favor of urban areas, especially the large cities. In 1983, there was a total of 259 stores. Of these, 65 percent were located in Santo Domingo and Santiago. INESPRE's social programs are intended to improve consumption among low-income urban consumers. Besides supporting stores in low-income neighborhoods, the institute also sends trucks into poor areas and sells products such as rice, vegetables and milk directly from these trucks.[70]

Among INESPRE's activities, there are two which directly benefit producers. These are the program of direct purchases from producers and the program of producers' markets. At present, the scope of these programs is still very limited. Through the program of direct purchases from producers, INESPRE purchases about 5 percent of the total agricultural production in the country. The aim of this program is to support farm prices and increase farm income. The major products supported by this program are rice, sorghum and corn. The institute has, however, been unable to make its support price a floor price because of the limited amount it purchases. In the case of sorghum, INESPRE has been able to maintain its support price since it purchases a large portion of this crop. This is also the case of minor products, such as garlic, onions and potatoes, of which INESPRE buys almost the entire crop in some years.[71]

The program of producers' markets began in 1984. INESPRE supplies market location, transportation, publicity and lodging for the producers in the city where the market is to take place. It also helps to sell any product not sold in the market. The producers pay 5 percent of their sales in order to cover some of the operation costs. Two markets operate weekly in Santo Domingo and Santiago, and different producers from different associations are brought every week to these markets. Prices are set above the prices being paid to the producers by the intermediaries in the rural areas, but below consumer prices. In this way, both producers and urban consumers benefit.[72] This is, however, a highly subsidized activity and it is uncertain whether INESPRE, given its financial difficulties, will be able to continue such a program.

Effect of INESPRE's Policies

No evaluation of INESPRE's activities has yet been made. The evidence, however, suggests that INESPRE has failed to meet the goals for which it was created. The institute has been confronted with financial difficulties in carrying out its operations. Its accumulated deficit for the period 1970-1987 amounted to DR$ 515 million. INESPRE has been experiencing losses because of higher storage costs, inventory holdings and higher administrative costs. The institute employed 696 persons in 1978, and by 1983 this figure had grown to 2,982.[73]

The failure of INESPRE to meet its goals is also due to the conflicting character of these goals. As a monopsonist, INESPRE has succeeded in implementing price regulations at the farm level, but has failed to promote production. It has succeeded in protecting consumers through its price stabilization program and the program of *Ventas Populares*, but this has been accomplished to the detriment of rural producers. Rural consumers are nearly all excluded from the benefits of *Ventas Populares*, and, with few exceptions, producers have been penalized by the setting of the price of their products below what would be the case under competitive conditions. At the same time, many peasants have seen their products outstripped by INESPRE's imports.

INESPRE's policies have had a short-run character. Providing cheap food for the urban consumers may be a well-intentioned enterprise. In the short run it may increase nutritional levels and improve income distribution in urban areas. However, it is probable that the negative effects of such a policy in the long run may overcome the positive ones. Maintaining low prices for agricultural products discourages production and reduces income and employment in rural areas. People will be discouraged from staying on the land and migration will be encouraged. The flow of peasants into the cities will further increase the demand for cheap food in urban areas. With reduced agricultural production, in order to meet demand, food imports and subsidies will be needed.

One of the important reasons for INESPRE to participate in the marketing system is to prevent "indiscriminate exploitation" of the peasants by the intermediaries. Through its marketing activities, INESPRE has attempted to reduce the marketing margins of the intermediaries. As a monopsonist, it has eliminated some intermediaries. However, the participation of intermediaries in the marketing of agricultural products in the Dominican Republic is a complex phenomenon. For instance, although INESPRE was the sole buyer of rice, some intermediaries still participated in the marketing of this product. Unable to obtain credit from official sources, in order to carry on production, many peasants request cash advances on their crop

146

from the intermediaries. At the same time, due to its financial difficulties, INESPRE limited the ability of the mills to make resources available to producers.[74]

INESPRE's program of direct purchases and producers markets is limited in scope and cannot significantly influence prices. These programs have little prospect of being developed further because of the large subsidies implied. In this respect, INESPRE's actions against the intermediaries have had a negligible effect.

Conclusions

The Dominican peasants produce mainly in order to sell their products. They have been market oriented for a long time, but their direct participation in the marketing of their products has always been very limited. A major reason for this is the small quantity produced by each individual peasant and the concentration of the marketing system. Marketing activities are generally carried out by a network of intermediaries. These intermediaries provide services, such as transport and credit, to the producers. The dependency of the producers on the intermediaries, not only to sell their products, but also to carry on production, has been a major factor underlying the generalized belief that the peasants are being exploited by the intermediaries. This assumption is often used as one of the arguments for the increasing intervention of the state in the marketing system.

After analyzing the marketing system and the different data available, it proved to be difficult to firmly accept or reject the exploitation hypothesis. The scarcity of data does not allow definite conclusions. The general picture that arises, however, is that marketing activities appear to be carried out under fairly competitive conditions, at least in the case of food products. In the case of export products, it was shown that oligopsonistic conditions prevail in the export market. For decades, the exports of coffee and cocoa have been concentrated to four large export firms. However, competition among these firms appears to be high.

The Dominican marketing system engages a large number of intermediaries, both small and large. Since production is widely spread the large intermediaries employ smaller intermediaries. Competition is considerable among the small intermediaries who buy the products that the peasants produce and among those selling the products that the peasants consume. Many peasants engage in trade as this activity is considered to be profitable. Among the larger intermediaries, freedom of entry tends to be limited by the large amount of money needed to enter the market, in order to buy large amounts of produce and to be able to make cash advances to the producers. Whether credit giving is a source of monopsony power is a debated question. Providing cash advances to the producers is a way of securing the crop. This type of credit is generally interest-free and in most cases the peasants will sell to the intermediary who provided credit. However, the possibility of monopsony power tends to be offset by the fact that the intermediary generally has a good relationship with the peasants, in order to minimize risk, but also in order to be able to compete with other intermediaries. At the same time, the level of information is relatively good among the peasants and this may prevent the intermediaries from cheating the peasantry.

The marketing system for food crops seems to work under relatively competitive conditions, albeit with certain deficiencies. It is difficult to find any decisive evidence of peasants being exploited by the intermediaries. Consequently, it is unfair to blame the poverty of the peasants on the "exploitative practices" of the intermediaries. As we will find in Chapters 6 and 7, other factors such as the restricted access of the peasants to land and financial means are probably more important.

The evidence presented in this chapter suggests that exploitation does not seem to be so evident in the marketing chain for food crops, where the state has intervened to a considerable degree. The direct participation of INESPRE in the marketing system has led to the elimination of some intermediaries, but has not succeeded in providing an alternative to the services that these intermediaries generally offered. If state intervention is intended to increase the welfare of the peasantry, a better strategy would be to improve rural infrastructure, encourage competition among intermediaries, increase producer prices and thus stimulate the peasants to increase output.

The intervention of the state in the marketing system seems to have benefited the urban poor. INESPRE has been successful in stabilizing prices but it has failed to promote production. The policy of providing cheap food for the poor has tended to discourage agricultural production and to reduce income and employment in the rural areas.

Notes

1. Hazard (1873), p. 180.
2. Ibid., pp. 182-84.
3. Ibid., p. 222.
4. Ibid., p. 324.
5. Cassá (1983), pp. 21, 23, 123 and 125. By the end of the nineteenth century, some large farms were integrated in the production of export goods, especially coffee and cocoa (ibid., pp. 142-43).

148

6. See Peynado (1909), p. 59 and Peynado (1919), p. 3.

7. Bonó (1980:1), pp. 196-97.

8. SEA-IICA (1977), Table 9, p. 279. At present, INESPRE is making efforts to develop producers' markets in Santo Domingo and Santiago.

9. ONAPLAN (1983:1), Table 29-A, p. 160.

10. Linares (1984), p. 15 and Table 3.

11. These small farms produce 59 percent of the total tobacco production in the country. (See Ferrán (1976), p. 76.)

12. SEA (1983), p. 11.

13. SEA (1981:2), pp. 14 and 125.

14. LaGra (1983), p. 242. Marchetti (1971), pp. 121-44, emphasizes the exploitative practices of the intermediaries.

15. SEA-IICA (1977), p. 36.

16. Ibid., p. 20. This practice results in inefficiency in the distribution process. In times of low yields, most products tend to be concentrated in Santo Domingo, while other regions will face scarcity. (See ibid., p. 265.)

17. Ibid., pp. 18-19. For a description of the Haitian marketing system, see Lundahl (1979), Chapter 4.

18. The Dominican Republic is administratively divided into 29 provinces and a National District. Each province is divided in *municipios* (town councils). The rural communities of each town are divided in *parajes* or sections. In 1983, there were 96 *municipios* and 639 rural sections. (See ONE (1983).)

19. See Lundahl (1979), p. 150 and Lundahl (1983), p. 193.

20. SEA-IICA (1977), p. 33.

21. However, many peasants state that production is not really profitable and that they cultivate these products because there are no other alternatives. (See ibid., p. 21.) The participation of peasants in these markets is likely to increase since an incentive law (Law 409) for production and processing of agricultural products was promulgated in 1982.

22. LaGra (1983), p. 248.

23. After harvesting, the tobacco leaves are put together on strings of a length of 6 to 8 feet. Each *sarta* or string contains about 150 to 165 tobacco leaves. Straining is mainly done by women in a *rancho* or open cabin located on the farm. The *sartas* are then hung inside the *rancho* for drying. This process takes about 3 weeks. The *sartas* are taken down and are prepared in *trojas*, i.e., the *sartas* are placed one on top of the other in the open cabin where they are left for about 40 days for the fermentation process. During this process, a price is set between the intermediary and the producer. The tobacco is then packed in *cerones* and transported by the intermediary to the gathering house which financed the operation. There, the tobacco is selected, cured, cleaned and dried for export. A small amount is delivered to the manufacturing firms in the country. The Dominican Republic produces two types of tobacco, Creole tobacco and Cuban tobacco. The description above refers mainly to the Creole tobacco which is produced mainly by *minifundistas*. The Cuban tobacco has a slightly more complex drying and curing process. This type is mainly grown by medium and large farms and accounts for 10 percent of total production (Ferrán (1976), pp. 58-68).

24. Cf. Miller (1982), p. 223 and Henderson and Quandt (1971), p. 104. One additional condition which is often stated is that consumers are - from the sellers' point of view - identical (ibid.).

25. The validity of the information in Table 5.1 is questionable since some of the information is based on prices prevailing on a specific market day and not on average prices over a longer time period. Prices at the urban wholesale market are very unstable. For example, if a *camionero* buys products taking into consideration the prices that prevailed in the urban market the day before he traveled, he has no guarantee that this price will prevail the next day. A *camionero* stated: "This is like gambling, you don't know if you will win or lose tomorrow, but if you lose you go on and on until you win. I have been 20 years in this business and I have been able to survive, but many have been ruined." (Darío Jiménez, *Camionero*, Mercado Nuevo, 6 February, 1986.) This particular day, Darío made a loss. He brought in a cargo of 101 quintals of sweet potatoes. He paid DR$ 7.45 per quintal and expected to sell at DR$ 14 per quintal but sold only at DR$ 9.

26. The Dominican producer's share in coffee and cocoa export prices is generally considered to be very low and to be a result of the exploitative practices of the intermediaries. However, if we compare with the situation prevailing in Haiti, this seems not to be the case. The Haitian coffee market works on more or less the same terms as the Dominican. Both markets are characterized as oligopsonistic with periods of collusion and periods of keen competition. However, the Haitian producer's share in coffee export prices was between 40 and 50 percent throughout the period 1960-86 (Seguino (1987), p. 17).

27. Marketing costs are only specified for export firms. However, the salary of the exporter is not accounted for. The marketing cost of an exporter includes the following: banking costs DR$ 0.90, storing 0.16, documents 0.03, package 3.60, transport 0.80, depreciation 0.75, preparation of the product 1.00, contribution to the Cocoa Commission 3.62, taxes 19.28. (See SEA (1984:1), p. 21.)

28. This seems to be very low. However, we do not know how accurate the figures in Table 5.4 are or how representative the year 1984 is.

29. SEA-IICA (1977), p. 265.

30. VII Censo Nacional Agropecuario 1981, in ONE (1982:2), p. 11.

31. LaGra (1983), p. 247.

32. "In every district there are both small and large buyers who go from farm to farm. Competition is strong and peasants will sell to the one that gives the highest offer." (Antonio Núñez, *camionero* from San Juan de la Maguana, Mercado Nuevo, 6 February, 1986.) In a study on the marketing of red beans 1981-82 it is reported that 30 percent of the transactions were conducted through local intermediaries while the rest was channeled through nonlocal intermediaries (Anschel and Wiegand (1983), p. 61).

33. Linares (1984), p. 40.

34. One of the reasons for which the quota system based on stocks was abolished in 1982 was the fact that it proved to be too easy for the large firms to cheat the authorities. At the time of checkups by the authorities, some of the firms possessing large warehouses filled them up with anything but coffee.

Only the top and the front were covered with coffee. (Information obtained at the *División de Estudios Sociales, Departamento de Café*, SEA.)

35. Ferrán (1976), p. 131. Competition among these firms is reported to be strong. (See Alemán (1982), p. 61.)

36. Sharpe (1977), pp. 29-30.

37. SEA (1984:2), p. 6.

38. For a description of the rural merchant see Sharpe (1977), pp. 37 and 137-44.

39. Murray (1974), pp. 17-18. In 1980, about 12 percent of the rural active labor force was engaged in commercial activities. (See Secretariado Técnico (1984:2), p. 5.)

40. During my visit to Manolo, a wholesaler selling sweet potatoes at the Mercado Nuevo in April 4, 1986, I counted 23 *camiones*. Most of them were full with sweet potatoes and some were carrying both sweet potatoes and manioc. These trucks were coming from San Juan de la Maguana and from the Cibao area.

41. Murray (1974), p. 62-63. Murray reports that in 1974, he observed 10 *camioneros* buying and transporting beans from the area of Padre Las Casas. Only two of them were not natives from that area. Since production is scattered across small farms it is necessary that the trucker intermediary has personal contacts in the growing areas in order to carry on the assembly function. One truck owner interviewed by Murray had purchased his beans from approximately ten producers (ibid., pp. 47 and 51).

A good relationship with the producer is also important in order to minimize risk. Darío Jiménez, a *camionero* at the Mercado Nuevo, had bought sweet potatoes a month ago at the prevailing price. In the area of San Juan, where the transaction took place, many peasants prefer to sell this crop by *pieza* or *cuadro* (by the lot area) while the sweet potatoes are still in the ground. The peasant asks for a high price and by a haggling process the buyer and seller agree on a price considered to be fair by both, according to the productivity of the crop. This is checked by taking samples of some plants. In the transaction where Darío was involved, no exact day was specified when he could dig up the sweet potatoes. When he came to the market, after being away for two days, he found out that market conditions were bad. The price had fallen to a level below what he had paid in San Juan. A month had passed and he had not been able to pick up the crop. The peasant, in turn, had been pressing him because he needed the land in order to plant peanuts. Darío had to travel many times to San Juan in order to explain that he could not pick up the crop since the prices on the market were too low. When he came, he brought food and rum and had a good time with the peasants. (Interview with Darío Jiménez, *camionero* at Mercado Nuevo, 4 March, 1986.)

42. A peasant that wants to establish a good *pulpería* must have access to a starting capital of between 1,000 and 3,000 pesos, since he must travel to a general store in town to acquire the goods. To minimize transport costs he must buy a fairly large quantity and be able to keep a stock. However, many peasants often start a business with only a few items. (Interviews with Diógenes

Vargas, and Freddy García, *pulpería* owners at El Mamey, Altamira and Río Grande, Altamira, 27 November, 1985.) See also Sharpe (1977), p. 37.

43. SEA-IICA (1977), p. 64. SEA's information to producers is deficient. Prices at the Santo Domingo market change daily and by the time the information is processed and distributed, the price may be outdated. Some private radio stations also visit the market daily and directly inform on the prices of different products at the Santo Domingo market. Some *camioneros* stated that these radio stations make it hard for them when bargaining with the peasants since at times the price provided by the stations are retail prices. (Interview with Darío Jiménez and Antonio Núñez, Mercado Nuevo, 6 February, 1986.)

44. For a description of the different measures and weights used in Dominican agriculture, see *Ahora* (1977), pp. 14-16, and Cruz Brache (1975), pp. 85-95.

45. In a transaction on sweet potatoes, "El Chino," a peasant in El Coco de Juan de Herrera, asked Darío, the *camionero*, for 1,600 pesos for 15 *tareas* of sweet potatoes. Darío offered 500 pesos, after a long discussion and a minute check of the crop, they agreed on a price that lay within the acceptable price range, 750 pesos. (Interview with Darío Jiménez, *camionero*, Mercado Nuevo, 4 March, 1986.)

46. Wharton (1962) pp. 28-30. For a discussion of these factors in the Haitian produce market see Lundahl (1979), pp. 132-33.

47. See Sharpe (1977), p. 75 and pp. 187-88.

48. Anschel and Wiegand (1983), p. 66.

49. Sharpe (1977), p. 75.

50. Discussion with Darío Jiménez, Antonio Núñez and other *camioneros*. Mercado Nuevo, 4 February, 1986.

51. Anschel and Wiegand (1983), p. 61.

52. Interview with Darío Jiménez, *camionero*. Mercado Nuevo, 4 March, 1986.

53. Anschel and Wiegand (1983), Table 36, p. 57a.

54. In 1939, the Office of Control of Rice and the National Rice Institute were created in order to increase government control over rice production and export. In 1945 the Bank of Agriculture and Industry, which in 1963 was replaced by the Agricultural Bank, was in charge of managing the government warehouses for rice and of fixing production prices for that commodity. In 1957, this bank was entitled to carry out the marketing of rice. Prices and margins were established for producers, intermediaries and retailers. By the late 1960s the Agricultural Bank's resources were exhausted by its activity of marketing and control of rice production. This fact, plus the belief that the marketing system was highly inefficient, set the ground for the creation of INESPRE in 1969 (Allen (1985), pp. 32-33). In 1986, the government transferred the marketing of rice to the Agricultural Bank and INESPRE's activities were significantly reduced. In 1988, the marketing of rice was liberalized. (Consejo Nacional de Agricultura (1989), p. 16).

55. See Quezada (1981), p. 55.

56. A dual exchange system existed in the Dominican Republic until 1984. The official rate has been at par with the US dollar while the parallel exchange

rate increased from 1.12 in 1972 to 1.60 in 1983. At the end of 1984, after the unification of these two markets, the exchange rate increased to 3 pesos for 1 US dollar. Until 1984, INESPRE imports were carried out at the official rate.

57. For an evaluation of INESPRE policies, see Quezada (1981).

58. Rice consumption averages 50 kilos per person per year and absorbs 13 percent of total household expenditures. About three-quarters of the output comes from over 25,000 small farms which give employment to a large number of rural workers. The labor share in the farm-gate cost of rice has been estimated at 55 percent (World Bank (1985), pp. 36-37).

59. Ibid., p. 38, and Allen (1985), p. 80. About 24 percent of the total value of Dominican food imports was provided on concessionary terms. The bill of food imports during this period amounted to US$ 1,500 million. PL-480 programs provide credits with a 20-year repayment period and interest rates between 2 and 3 percent (Plant (1987), p. 142).

60. World Bank (1985), Table 3.2, p. 37.

61. Ibid., p. 40. The monopsonistic power of INESPRE and the rice mills was increased in 1982 when a law was passed prohibiting transport of unmilled rice between regions without INESPRE's consent. (Allen (1985), p. 72.)

62. Ibid., pp. 70-71.

63. Ibid., Table XXXVII, p. 98.

64. World Bank (1985), p. 41.

65. Ibid., p. 42.

66. Allen (1985), p. 108.

67. Ibid., p. 58.

68. A shortage of processed milk in urban areas appeared in 1985. Milk producers were reluctant to sell raw milk to the processors because they could get substantially higher prices by selling raw milk directly to the consumers. By means of pressure from the associated producers and processors, in 1985 a quart of pasteurized milk was risen from DR$ 0.45 to DR$ 0.95.

69. Allen (1985), p. 111.

70. Ibid., pp. 5 and 147.

71. Ibid., p. 4.

72. Ibid., p. 156.

73. Ibid., pp. 42-43 and Dauhajre (1989), table IV, p. 83.

74. In later years, INESPRE allowed the millers to keep a portion of the milled rice as payment for milling rice. The millers sold the rice at controlled prices and absorbed the margin that would have gone to INESPRE (Allen (1985), p. 76). The inability of INESPRE to pay the millers on time generated a deep crisis within the rice producing sector. In January 1986, INESPRE's accumulated debts to the sector were DR$ 70 million to millers, DR$ 15 million to producers and DR$ 20 million to the Agricultural Bank. (See Hoy (1986) and Ultima Hora (1986).)

6

Land Tenure Structure and Reform Attempts

We have suggested above that an important factor behind the increasing level of poverty of the Dominican peasants could be their limited access to land. Indeed, the Dominican Republic has one of the most unequal land distributions in the world. Most of the best agricultural land is concentrated in the hands of a minority, while the overwhelming majority of the peasants only have access to small plots of marginal land. The aim of the present chapter is to analyze the Dominican land tenure structure and its development over time.

The land tenure system found today in the Dominican Republic is of relatively recent origin. Until the end of the nineteenth century land was abundant and inexpensive and, although there were some large landholders, the *latifundio-minifundio* system was still undeveloped. Different actions carried out by the Dominican state largely influenced the development of land rights and encouraged the concentration of land in a few hands.

The present chapter also analyzes the extent to which the agrarian reform program which started in 1961 has influenced the agrarian structure of the country. It is shown that very few of the original goals of the agrarian reform have been realized, not least the goal of increasing rural employment, as very few families have benefited from the program.

Land Tenure Structure

The Dominican Republic has a very varied landscape and a climate suited to almost all sorts of crops. However, ownership conditions and cultivation methods impede a rational use of the agricultural resources.

The quality of land, the use that the cultivator makes of it and his choice of agricultural technology are all dependent on whether the cultivator is a small or a large landholder.

The Dominican agricultural land is mainly divided between *latifundios*, *minifundios* and even *microfundios*. This land tenure system is characteristic of most Latin American countries.[1] A *latifundio* is a large estate where work is mainly performed by hired labor. In the categories of *mini-* and *microfundios*, we find small family farms where the agricultural activity is mainly carried out by family labor. In 1981, the *minifundios* (farms with less than 5 hectares) represented 82 percent of the landed properties, but only occupied 12 percent of the cultivable land. On the other hand, the *latifundios* (farms with more than 50 hectares) represented hardly 2 percent of the landed properties and occupied 55 percent of the cultivable land (see Table 6.4 below). The unequal distribution of land becomes more accentuated if we consider that most of the *minifundios* are located on land of inferior quality.

Four soil categories have been identified in the Dominican Republic. They are determined according to agricultural productivity and potential use as well as actual land tenure and land-use structure:[2]

Category A: Cultivable soils, plain or slightly rugged topography, without irrigation, but with high humidity.

The principal use of the land in category A is the cultivation of sugar cane and cattle-breeding. Large estates predominate in this category. The total land area amounts to 600,000 hectares, mainly located in the central, eastern and northwestern parts of the country. Around 100,000 persons are occupied on 20,000 farms and plantations.

Category B: Cultivable soils, plain or slightly rugged topography, with irrigation.

Category B land is concentrated in the fertile river valleys and the valley of Constanza. It is used mainly for cultivation of rice, sugar cane and plantains, as well as horticulture and cattle-breeding. Large estates, private as well as state owned, in sugar cane and pastures, occupy around 600,000 hectares. Within category B there are also 100,000 farms of small or middle size. The major part of the land is irrigated by canals constructed by the state. The rural population associated with this production system is approximately 350,000 persons.

Category C: Soils of limited use, steep or rugged topography, with no irrigation.

The most common crops are perennial crops such as coffee and cocoa, and annual crops like beans, peanuts and different root crops. The areas within category C cover 800,000 hectares. 250,000 persons live on around 40,000 farms of small or middle size. The lands are not suitable for agriculture, the soil is fertile but too thin and nearly impossible to irrigate artificially. The intensive use, or misuse, of the land has resulted in an alarming erosion. Nevertheless, a high percentage of the country's basic foodstuffs comes from these areas.

Category D: Land with steep topography, no irrigation, high environmental humidity as well as semi-arid zones.

Most farms in the category D are very small, so-called *conucos*. The soil is fit only for permanent vegetation and/or forest. This type of land is to be found in the half-dry zones in the Southwest, or high up on the mountain ranges. There is no information about the size of the population living and working in these particular areas and the extent of the land included in this category. The agricultural activities carried out in these areas are narrow and many of the peasants derive incomes from activities such as producing charcoal or breeding goats. Both activities have a devastating effect on the ecological system.[3]

The distribution of land within categories A and B is very unequal. 70 percent of the farms in these categories have less than 5 hectares and only occupy 14 percent of the cultivable land. These small farms are experiencing increasing fragmentation.[4] An extension of peasant lands is limited by the presence of the large landholdings, private and state-owned, that concentrate on the cultivation of sugar cane or cattle-breeding. The latter activities use the land very extensively.

Categories C and D are characterized by overcultivation of marginal lands. These practices have caused great erosion problems. The agricultural activities on these lands, where the cultivation potential is very low, are gaining increased importance. At present, more than 20 percent of the Dominican land under cultivation is used in an inappropriate manner. These are mountainous areas that are suitable only for afforestation and to some extent for the cultivation of coffee and pasture land.[5]

Although, judging from the extensive cultivation methods used by the small group of *latifundistas*, land is not a scarce resource, it remains a scarce resource for the large amount of *minifundistas* and for the country as a whole. The land scarcity is even greater if we consider the fact that a large proportion of the actual land area under cultivation is unsuitable for cultivation due to low soil fertility and topographic limitations.

The Development of Land Concentration

As we saw in Chapter 4, the Dominican Republic was for many centuries characterized by a low population density, an abundance of land and an extensive use of land resources, mainly through cattle-raising and woodcutting. In theory there existed a legal system of land tenure, but in practice anyone could settle down and use the land as he pleased. The land boundaries were very vague and accurate surveys had never been carried out.

Until the beginning of the twentieth century, the land remained undivided, although proprietorship developed quite legally under a traditional and customary land tenure system: the system of *terrenos comuneros*. Since the property was not physically divided, the shareholder, i.e., the owner of *pesos* or *acciones de tierra*, had almost free access to the fruits of the entire property. He also had the right to settle in any region within the limits of the original property that was not actually claimed or occupied by a previous *peso*-holder. As late as 1907, a publication intended to attract settlers and investors to the Dominican Republic, expressed the conditions in the following way:

> In one portion of a *terreno comunero* valued at two thousand gold pesos, the possessor of a share worth for example ten pesos, is legally entitled to cultivate, according to his own desire, any part of it [i.e., the *terreno comunero*] that is unoccupied, and use for his own purpose as shareholder anything that exists within the mentioned lands, of course with the exception of the installments and improvements done by other shareholders.[6]

It seems that until the end of the nineteenth century the Dominican population was not pressed by the necessity to have legal rights to land. Fertile land existed in abundance and the system of *terrenos comuneros* allowed the population to occupy, exploit and enjoy all the land they needed without causing hardship to any of the actual proprietors.[7] Most families, however, cultivated small areas since, with the exemption of tobacco, most crops were intended mainly for subsistence. Nevertheless, the system of *terrenos comuneros* was always a source of confusion and later, with the increasing value of the land, a source of fraud.[8]

Land Concentration and the State

The Dominican state has always been a major landowner. The state owned the so-called *ejidos*, i.e., municipal land open for common use.[9] In addition, after the withdrawal of the Haitians in 1844, the newly formed Dominican state also became the owner of most of the land that had been expropriated by the former regime.[10] In 1871, the Dominican state possessed from two-thirds to three-quarters of the territory.[11]

From independence and far into the twentieth century, one of the major concerns of the Dominican governments has been to increase the land area under cultivation and develop an agrarian export sector. In order to achieve this goal, different governments ceded state-owned land to any individual or industry that was willing to use the land for agriculture. In 1867, the state was authorized by law to lease or cede any uncultivated state-owned land to any immigrant individual or enterprise in an amount that they were willing to cultivate. Full title to the property was granted as soon as the lands were cultivated with coffee, cocoa, cotton or other major fruits (i.e., export crops). Likewise, by a decree from 1879, the state granted concessions of property title to 50 acres of land to any immigrant that came to the country with the intention of "exploiting the country's wealth." In 1902, a decree conceded the right to any individual or company to use, free of charge, any unoccupied state-owned land. An individual could be given a maximum of 1,200 *tareas*, a company 3,000. At the same time, the beneficiaries were entitled to new concessions as soon as the received land had been put under cultivation. Furthermore, agricultural entrepreneurs were exonerated for a period of 25 years from all customs duties on machinery or other inputs to be used in agricultural activities.[12]

From the end of the nineteenth century foreign companies and individuals started to invest on a major scale in Dominican agriculture. In particular, the sugar sector expanded very rapidly. Large tracts of lands were ceded by the state or bought for infinitesimal prices. Seven of the largest *ingenios* expanded their territory from 79,000 *tareas* in 1893 to nearly 2 million in 1925.[13] The peasants' traditional exploitation of the land was checked by different means. In 1900, cattle breeding outside fenced areas was prohibited and steps were taken in order to divide and abolish the *terrenos comuneros*.[14]

The ownership of the land was still very confused at the beginning of the twentieth century. No central office existed where the record of titles, transfers of property or any legal act involving land was maintained. Acts of transactions of land were drawn up by public notaries who were attached to the different *ayuntamientos* (municipalities). It was not necessary to go to the notary in the district where the land was situated. Any notary in the Republic would suffice. The individual notaries were the only ones who kept a copy of the transactions and their records were often either destroyed or in a state of utter confusion.[15] Most Dominicans did not bother to have their transactions registered, they bought and sold land *"de boca,"* i.e., through verbal agreements.[16] Some simply seized good lands wherever they saw them. Traditionally, a period of thirty years of possession and cultivation of land gave a clear title to the land.[17] However, the inefficient system of land registry made many landowners insecure of their rights, especially those who wanted to produce more than subsistence crops, and many were reluctant to invest in irrigation, drainage and other activities that could increase production over time. Furthermore, in some areas, as the population increased, the confusion of ownership involved in the system of *terrenos comuneros* sometimes led to conflicts between shareholders, since some of them tended to expand their activities beyond what they were entitled to. Moreover they also often forged their land titles, something that was very easily done. The authorities also thought that individual ownership to a determined, and legally guaranteed, piece of land would promote agricultural activities and increase production.[18]

Attempts to survey the land were carried out in 1907 and 1911. In 1912, a law was issued that decreed an obligatory inscription of rural titles. All these efforts could not be fully carried out due to the turbulent political situation that prevailed in the country until the US occupation in 1916.

In 1918, the US military government issued a decree concerning forced registration of titles. If a landowner did not register his title within three months he was forced to pay fines of US$ 3. After six months, the fine was raised to US$ 55 and if he still refused he was severely penalized.[19] This meant that anyone who could prove "efficient occupation" of any state land for 10 years was guaranteed a clear title to it. This represented a significant change compared to the traditional period of 30 years a fact that highly favored the large foreign companies that had recently been established in the country.[20] It was also these companies that were most eager that the surveys and registrations should be carried out. The surveys began in the Southeast where the expansion of the sugar sector was most manifest. The costs of the surveys were borne by the landowners, and when the pace of the surveys threatened to slow down due to a lack of surveyors, the US owned Central Romana advanced funds for the surveys so that twenty-five additional surveyors could be employed.[21] The major sugar companies were also helpful in carrying out the final division of the *terrenos comuneros*. In 1920, the US military government issued an "Executive Order for Land Registration and the Demarcation, Survey and Partition of Terrenos Comuneros."[22]

The costs of the surveys were borne by the landowners. In addition they had to survey the land which they could not prove to be theirs. This cost from 50 cents to three dollars per hectare depending on the quality of the land, i.e., a cost of around US$ 20 if one wanted to survey 100 *tareas* of good land. This was a price that only few could afford. In those days, production was mainly for subsistence and the peasants had very little access to cash. Besides, land was abundant and therefore had very low value. Many peasants considered that the price of the survey was too high and did not survey more than they thought was enough for their family's needs. Cash and credit were not easily obtained. Land that was not claimed belonged to the state, but could be bought by others at a price fixed by the Land Court. Thus, land could be bought cheaply by wealthy and astute landowners.[23]

The structure of land tenure was also affected by another law introduced by the US administration, namely the Land Tax Law of 1918. One of the intentions of this law was to increase production. Owners of idle land would be compelled to cultivate the land in order to pay taxes or to transfer it to others who would be willing to do so. This law was said to favor the smallholders since it would mean "an economic pressure to break up large estates and thereby permit more people to put more land into production."[24] It has however been argued that the land tax favored the large sugar companies. These companies could afford to pay the tax for their huge areas covered with sugar. Likewise they could acquire enormous extensions of land at very low prices, namely land sold by those who did not have the means to put the land into production or that could not afford to pay the tax.[25]

The different actions taken by the Dominican state and later by the US military government, largely encouraged the concentration of land into a few hands. Foreign investors were particularly favored. These actions finally turned the Dominican land into a commodity which was regularly bought and sold. Its demand rose, and so did its price.

The Price of Land

Before the abolition of the *terrenos comuneros* in the 1920s, land had obtained its value solely through its use. Possession of large amounts of land was not so much a sign of high status as was, for example, the possession of cattle. By the beginning of the 1870s, land located near the capital could be bought at an average price of US$ 1 per acre (US$ 0.16 per *tarea*).[26] During the 1920s and the 1930s, the price of land was still very low.

The continuing low price of land enabled many landowners to acquire large tracts of land. Later, land transactions also began to take place among peasants. The wealthier peasants were more apt to concentrate land than their poorer neighbors. In the Cibao area, the price of good tobacco land was around 20 to 40 centavos per *tarea* in the 1920s. By the 1940s, the price of this land had increased to around 5 pesos per *tarea*. Prices continued to increase and reached 20 to 50 pesos per *tarea* in the 1950s. In 1983 they were around 400 pesos.[27] In the area of La Vega, where some of the best lands are to be found, in 1907 the price per *tarea* was 2 to 5 pesos. By 1948, this price had increased to between 40 and 50.[28] Today, the price in this area exceeds 500 pesos.

The price of land differed a lot between the various areas. It first rose in the Southeast region due to the sugar boom at the beginning of the century. Later on the rise was due to population growth or the introduction of new infrastructure. For example, the introduction of artificial irrigation in the San Juan Valley in the 1920s probably increased the price of land in this area.[29]

However scanty, the information seems to indicate that land prices started to increase dramatically around the 1930s. By the 1940s, land was an expensive and relatively scarce factor. It is in this decade that the system of tenancy (*arriendo*) and sharecropping (*arriendo a medias*) starts to appear. Since then, it has continued to gain in importance and today this is nearly the only way a great deal of the rural population has access to land. In the tobacco areas between 50 and 70 percent of the producers are sharecroppers.[30] In 1976, land rent under tenancy arrangements in tobacco areas was between 10 and 20 pesos per year and *tarea*, while under sharecropping arrangements it could be as high as 60 pesos.[31]

The rapid increase in the price of land implies that for many peasants, purchasing a piece of land is nearly impossible due to their low incomes and, as we will see in Chapter 7, their limited opportunities for obtaining credit for investment purposes. Those who actually own land, have been able to do so mainly by means of inheritance.[32] However, most of the peasant plots are already so small that partition for inheritance purposes is no longer possible. This situation worsens as the population grows.

The process of land concentration described above was possible partly because the state, as the major landowner in the country, could dispose of large tracts of lands as it pleased. Until today, the Dominican state has retained its position as the largest landholder in the country. The Trujillo regime (1930-61) gave rise to a huge concentration of land in the hands of the dictator, his relatives and friends. Most of the land Trujillo obtained was bought at bargain prices, but nearly all sales were forced. He obtained land wherever he wanted it - from the state, from *latifundistas* or foreign companies. One of his obsessions was sugar production. He concentrated two-thirds of the annual sugar production in his own hands. The vast sugar plantations, together with extensive pastures and other land areas dedicated to rice cultivation and other lucrative agricultural activities, constituted the enormous land area that ended up as state property on the death of the dictator in 1961.

The concentration of land that emerged during the 1920-1960 period is amazing. The census of 1960 shows that more than 85 percent of the farms were of a size of less than 5 hectares and that they only occupied 20 percent of the cultivated area. By contrast, more than 50 percent of the cultivable area was occupied by farms larger than 33 hectares. These represented less than 3 percent of the total number of farms.[33]

The Land Reform Myth

The unequal distribution of land is usually made responsible for many of the problems afflicting the Dominican Republic. The small peasants, cramped together on marginal lands, are forced to make too intensive use of their land, thereby generating erosion problems and threatening the whole ecological equilibrium. The small land base of the peasantry and the high rates of population growth have led to an overutilization of limited natural resources, thereby generating underemployment and rural migration. At the same time, fertile lands lie untouched by plough or hoe, providing grazing for cattle herds that occupy too much land. Huge areas are used for crops that do not nourish a needy population. At the same time vast tracts of land that could be used intensively to generate work and produce foodstuffs lie underutilized. The distress and worsening conditions of the peasantry cause mass migration to towns. Misery and social unrest hit both towns and countryside. Peasants occupying land and demanding their rights create political unrest, at the same time as the growing slum population of the towns constitutes a constant threat of crime and anarchy.

This picture underlies the main arguments pursued by the supporters of a land reform in the Dominican Republic. Particularly by some of its political leaders.[34] A more equitable division of land was expected not only to reduce social pressures but also to increase production and employment in the agricultural sector.

In the last decades, attempts to carry out an agrarian reform program have been made by different Dominican governments. These attempts were consistent with the general pattern of reformism implemented in Latin American countries since the 1960s. Between 1960 and 1964, fourteen major agrarian reforms were enacted in the region. A central factor behind these measures was the concern among the leading economic and political elites about the potential for rural unrest.[35] However, in the 1970s, the flowering reformism in Latin America slowed down, not least in the Dominican Republic. "Many became convinced that social revolution in the countryside was not necessarily imminent, that peasants were not important enough as a political force to court so assiduously, and that increasing levels of production and productivity on peasant holdings or cooperatives was far more complex and expensive than originally imagined."[36] Gradually, the importance of land redistribution as a solution to rural poverty and increased production was disavowed, and most countries embraced the less political sensitive policy of "integrated rural development."[37]

The Dominican Land Reform Process

Ever since the foundation of the Dominican Republic, the state has been an important landowner, since in theory it has controlled all communal lands. During most of the nineteenth century, there existed an abundance of fertile land and a scarcity of hands to work the land. Ever since the days of the Republic's first president, Pedro Santana, various plans were presented in order to increase agricultural production and populate the countryside. However, these plans were never enacted. A common feature of these plans was the thought of attracting foreign, skilled farmers through the foundation of colonies.

The long wars with Haiti, and the constant enmity towards that country, created a certain hidden meaning behind some of the proposed colonies. The border with Haiti should be populated in order to strengthen the defense of that particular area, as well as hinder the "peaceful penetration" of "black" Haitians across the border. The latter motive may partly explain the existence of certain racist formulations in the project proposals of these times. As late as 1923, a program intended to stimulate "Caucasian migration" was approved by President Juan B. Vicini Burgos.[38]

With the exception of two unsuccessful attempts undertaken during the 1920s, it was Trujillo who put the old idea of "colonies" into practice. During his regime 40 colonies were established, covering 140,780 hectares, divided between 11,451 families.[39] The racist and strategic considerations apparent in some of the previous colony plans were present in Trujillo's program as well. No less than 23 colonies were established along the Haitian border. Eight colonies were founded in Dajabón, on a major route used by Haitians for illegal border crossing. This experiment was unsuccessful since the majority of the settlers had been urban dwellers unskilled in agriculture. Many parcels of land were of low quality, and there was no nearby local market.[40] Failures like that were common. Even if other colonies were located on excellent land, most of them had little economic significance mainly due to bad planning, inadequate infrastructure, lack of credit possibilities and technical assistance.[41] The settlers were a motley crew: former townspeople, small peasants, people with good connections, and many immigrants - Spaniards, Japanese, Jews, Hungarians and others.[42]

Trujillo was murdered on May 30, 1961. Just two months after this event, Joaquín Balaguer, who had become president by the time of the dictator's death,[43] announced the formation of an official commission for the distribution of 22,390 hectares to landless field workers and small peasants.[44] In November the same year, the army seized the Trujillo properties, i.e., his own and his relatives' land, and the Dominican state became the owner of 202,100 hectares, of which 99,240 were promptly made available for agrarian reform purposes.[45] The land reform commission was turned into an autonomous and juridical organ of the government, *Instituto Agrario Dominicano* (IAD).[46] The distribution of land started immediately. Already by the end of the year, 140,771 hectares had been distributed to 84,526 individuals. Each family received a parcel of an average size of 12.3 hectares, more than twice as large as the ones distributed during the years that followed. The settlements in 1961 constituted a record compared with the subsequent years of land reform. In a few months, thousands of families were settled. This represents 18.6 percent of all settlements during the period 1961-83 (see Table 6.1).

The reasons for this haste were mainly political. Balaguer, who was highly compromised through his involvement with the old regime, had to save his political integrity. Many citizens of Santo Domingo went into the streets and demanded his resignation. At the same time, many peasants occupied former Trujillo land. Juan Bosch, leader of the opposition, came back after 24 years in exile and immediately started the campaign for the coming elections. In this campaign the land reform issue was strongly emphasized, and political interest was focused on the rural population. It constituted around 70 percent of the country's inhabitants and represented an important electoral force. A new constitution was passed on 29 December 1961 which stressed the rights of the peasantry, and underlined the necessity of a thorough agrarian reform.[47]

The foundations on which the work of the IAD was to be based were made explicit in the land law of April 27, 1962. This law recognized the social and economic conditions in rural areas which urgently demanded reform. It was pointed out that the opportunities for the peasants' possibilities to raise their living standard were limited by their low access to land and inadequacy of production services, such as access to credit, technical assistance and marketing of the products. A specific objective of the law was to generate new employment opportunities in the sector and to raise rural incomes.[48]

During the 1960s the agrarian reform developed slowly. Most of the distributed land was state-owned, and only a minor part was acquired from private landowners.[49] The IAD functioned throughout this period but often with highly reduced efficiency. Until Balaguer once again gained power in 1966, the country went through different stages of political unrest and near chaos. The legal autonomy of the organization was ignored consistently during the various transfers of executive powers. From 1962 to 1966 the director of the IAD was changed five times, and none of these directors held the office for a sufficient period of time to be able to give the IAD a firm organization and continuity in the carrying out of its projects.[50] However, political unrest was not the only reason for the delays in the implementation of the agrarian reform.

By 1962, most state-owned land had been surveyed. However, in order to carry out the reform, new surveys had to be made. Trujillo had violated all land laws when he acquired "his" land and when the state took possession of the vast Trujillo lands, former owners robbed by Trujillo claimed the right to their old properties. Many of these had been sold and resold since the time they belonged to their rightful owners. The land courts could not resolve the claims in time and the IAD could not wait for the results. This led to a situation where the legal processes concerning ownership of particular lands went on while the same lands were being distributed within the IAD program. As a result, the new settlers became very unsure of their legal rights to the land received through the IAD. In 1966, the IAD estimated that it possessed registered titles to only 50 percent of the distributed land. In order to avoid future legal processes, it did not sign any contracts whatsoever with most of the settlers.[51]

Another problem was that numerous squatters had invaded former Trujillo land and state-owned lands. These occupants had in many cases improved the land and attempts to remove them could have been very risky in a climate characterized by severe political tension.[52]

Balaguer's "Reformism" (1966-78)

In the mid-sixties, the agrarian reform program met with growing criticism. The church was particularly critical of the government because it considered that the distribution of land to the peasants was too slow.[53] The reaction from the church came in a crucial period of Dominican history. In June 1966, Balaguer, with his *Partido Reformista*

(Reformist Party), was back in power and severe political measures were expected. Changes were signalled at all levels of society, and - although political repression was harsh and right-wing terror groups operated all over the country - both the church and some left-wing groups were active in the countryside trying to organize the peasants.[54] Many invasions took place of both state-owned and privately owned land. Most of these actions were, however, carried out by isolated groups of peasants, without coordination and support from popular organizations.[55]

In the end, the government had to take action in order to strengthen and accelerate the land reform. In 1972, a set of new laws was launched. Among them we find law No. 214, intended to limit the extensions of the *latifundios*.[56] However, all sugar land was excluded from this law. Three years after the issue of this law a decree was made prohibiting the further extension of existing sugar-fields. As a matter of fact, this law and the subsequent decree were in reality not applied. By the end of 1974, a new process of land concentration began as a result of rising sugar prices and certain political factors that favored some big landowners. This seems to be confirmed by the figures from the last agricultural census (1981) since the average size of the largest farms, i.e., those with more than thousand hectares, increased 28 percent during the period 1971-81 (see Table 6.4 below).

Law No. 145 of 1975 prohibited acquisition through "purchase, donation, lease, mortgage, or usufruct" of the allotments given by the IAD. The law also forbade other uses of the land than those decreed by the IAD.[57] The most widely implemented law was No. 290 of 1972 that stated that all rice lands exceeding 31.4 hectares in size and irrigated by government-built channels should be turned over to the IAD.[58] The settlers on these rice lands received provisional certificates to part of the land although they were expected to work all the land in common.

During the 1974-78 period, the agrarian reform lost some of the dynamism from the two previous years. It had encountered a setback in 1974 when a legal proposal concerning the expropriation of some of the vast pastures was voted down by the senate. Nevertheless, the reform laws of the early 1970s gave some dynamism to the countryside. For the first time, the state tried to confront itself with the problem of unequal land tenure through a set of radical laws. It took control over most of the production of rice, one of the most important foodstuffs in the country.

The 1970s also witnessed a spectacular rise in the political conscience of the peasantry which had started to organize itself to a higher degree than before.[59] The prospects of obtaining land activated the peasants. The number of petitions for allotments by the IAD rose from 6,467 in 1971 to 16,305 in 1973. The IAD could not satisfy these demands and the land occupations continued. Sometimes this led to fierce encounters between peasants and landowners. Some of the latter even formed defense committees. The number of peasant organizations rose from 59 in 1971 to 120 in 1972.[60] In spite of this dynamism in the rural areas and an increased land distribution in 1972 and 1973, the land reform soon returned to its former slow pace. It reached less than one percent of the target group per annum. Consequently it did not make much progress towards solving the problem of unequal land tenure, or even keeping up with population growth.[61]

Most of the laws had proved to be relatively powerless. Their interpretation and application was rather cryptic. The land reform had been a rather isolated phenomenon. Efforts were concentrated to certain units. In most cases, it has been carried out as a simple distribution of land. The major social aspects indicated in the laws of 1962 had not been fully carried out. Technical assistance and the build-up of social services had been extremely inadequate.[62] These facts were largely emphasized by the promotion of the new approach of "integrated rural development" implemented after 1978.

The "New Approach"

In line with the strategy followed in other Latin American countries, the *Partido Revolucionario Dominicano* (PRD), the party that in 1978 succeeded Balaguer's reformists to power, embraced the policy of integrated rural development. In order to reinforce the agrarian reform, the PRD tried to break the tradition of paternalism and authoritarianism that formerly characterized the reform program. 540 organizations were formed among the settlers and an institute, CECARA (*Centro de Capacitación de Reforma Agraria*), was established in order to inform and assist the peasant committees.[63] Another program launched by the new government was the so-called *Programa de Consolidación de Asentamientos* (Program of Consolidation of the Settlements), a joint project between the government and different foreign aid organizations in order to take measures against the vast neglect of infrastructure and technical assistance that had affected the agrarian reform program. The settlements were to be revised, their dwellings renovated, and schools and shops were to be constructed, as well as irrigation channels.[64]

TABLE 6.1   Agrarian Reform Settlements: Number of Families and Land
Area Settled, 1961-1983*

Year	No. of Families	%	Land Area (in '000 ha.)	%	Land Area per Family (Hectares)
1961	11,451	18.6	140.8	36.8	12.3
1962	863	1.4	3.8	1.0	4.4
1963	719	1.2	4.0	1.0	5.6
1964	2,214	3.6	11.5	3.0	5.2
1965	-	-	-	-	-
1966	321	0.5	2.5	0.6	7.8
1967	1,901	3.1	9.8	2.6	5.1
1968	1,447	2.3	6.9	1.8	4.8
1969	2,057	3.3	9.8	2.5	4.8
1970	1,345	2.2	5.1	1.3	3.8
1971	3,621	5.9	23.8	6.2	6.6
1972	6,498	10.5	37.5	9.8	5.8
1973	8,362	13.6	40.6	10.6	4.8
1974	1,800	2.9	9.1	2.4	5.0
1975	1,930	3.1	9.5	2.5	4.9
1976	3,162	5.1	11.1	2.9	3.5
1977	139	0.2	0.4	0.1	2.9
1978	2,634	4.3	10.4	2.7	3.9
1979	1,962	3.2	8.3	2.2	4.2
1980	1,986	3.2	7.9	2.0	4.0
1981	3,244	5.3	14.9	3.9	4.6
1982	1,556	2.5	5.1	1.3	3.3
1983	2,464	4.0	10.2	2.7	4.1
Total	61,676	100.0	382.8	100.0	

*During the period 1973-76, only part of the settlements were collective.
After 1978 all settlements were collective.

Sources: For 1961-1982, IAD (1983:1), pp. 33 and 37. For 1983, IAD (1983:2), p. 4.

Another important project was the creation of Integrated Rural
Service Centers (CENSERI). This project was intended to develop basic
infrastructure for the benefit of organized peasants. Each center dealt
with three basic types of infrastructure: a) a small consumer store
operated by members of the organization, b) a small retail outlet
selling farm inputs such as seeds, chemical fertilizers, tools, etc., c) an
assembly center where produce is assembled for sale and where

community meetings may be held.[65] The issue of land redistribution, so much emphasized in the 1960s and early 1970s, was relegated to a secondary level. However, the euphoria of the new approach to the solution of the peasants' poverty did not last long. The CENSERI was a project conceived during the first years of the PRD regime, under the Guzmán administration and, as many other projects, was not followed up during the Jorge Blanco administration. By 1986, the project was largely in a state of abandonment due among other reasons to a lack of funds.[66]

FIGURE 6.1   Distributed Land Area and Number of Families Benefited by Land Reform, 1961 - 1983

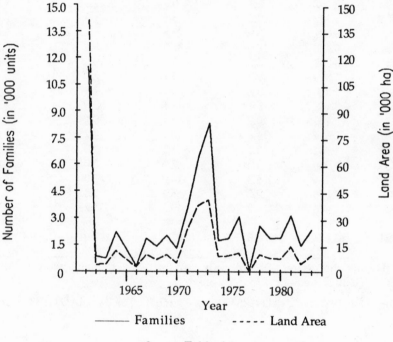

Source: Table 6.1

Table 6.1 and Figure 6.1 above illustrate the process of land redistribution during the period 1961-1983. Until 1983, 383,000 hectares, i.e., 14 percent of the total cultivable land, had been redistributed. In 1975, only 38 percent of the land acquired through the agrarian reform program had been distributed, while 250,000 hectares awaited development.[67] Ten years later, this picture had not changed significantly. It is estimated that only 54 percent of the total land controlled by the IAD is in production.[68]

Production and Employment in Land Reform Settlements

Although the land reform program is crippled by a high degree of inefficiency, its settlements produce an important part of the foodstuffs consumed in the country, even if this production has not increased much since the settlements were established. In 1982, the agrarian reform settlements produced 37.6 percent of the country's total production of shelled rice, 22.3 percent of its vegetables, 30.2 percent of the sorghum, 16.2 percent of the corn and around 16 percent of the manioc, yams, sweet potatoes, potatoes and cocoyam.[69]

The rice plantations have received considerable technical assistance, as well as large amounts of fertilizers and pesticides. Already in 1974, two years after their foundation, the collective settlements showed a production of 3.17 quintals per *tarea* in comparison with the individual settlements which produced 2.20.[70] Collective tenancy was therefore extended to other production activities. It was argued that the system promoted the delivery of public services and production inputs as well as permitted higher yields.[71]

Until 1972 nearly all settlements within the IAD program had been individual, and few of them had obtained any increased output, mainly due to the inability of the SEA and IAD technicians to provide proper services and training to the agrarian reform beneficiaries.[72] On the contrary, the rice cultivators received more attention, partly due to the fact that one of the government's main goals with its agrarian policy had been to make the country self-sufficient in rice. Rice is a crop that needs capital inputs in the form of machinery and fertilizers and the former fragmentation of the land may have led to a decrease in production. However, when the fields were tended collectively and the state provided the necessary inputs, the trend was reversed.[73] In the early 1970s, rice production was also favored by price regulations. In connection with the law of 1972, the regulated price of rice was increased by 13 percent.[74] Production in land reform settlements is highly subsidized. No rent is charged on the land, and no payments are made for technical and management assistance as well as irrigation facilities.

Although the agrarian reform program has succeeded in increasing production of some important crops, its accomplishments regarding employment have been highly disappointing. Underemployment is high among the settlers. In 1981, it was found that 37.5 percent of the agrarian reform beneficiaries had to find complementary work, beside the activities that they carried out on their allotments.[75] The majority of the settlers have continued to use traditional cultivation methods. Accordingly, their yields are low and their earnings barely above the subsistence level.[76]

In 1975, around 400,000 rural families were in desperate need of land.[77] Given the slow pace at which land is being distributed, and the high rates of population growth, the prospects for these families obtaining land are not particularly good. Since 1975, only 17,000 families have been settled. The existence of favoritism in the land distribution process may reduce the employment impact of the program, since this prevents land from being distributed to the most needy. An investigation carried out in a settlement established in 1974 found that many of the settlers had obtained their allotment through friends or on political grounds. (See Table 6.2.)

TABLE 6.2   Means of Getting Allotments in "Las Haras Nacionales en Villa Mella"

Means	% of the settlers
Recommended by the Military or Governmental Functionaries	28.5
Employees of the IAD	1.8
Participated in the Construction of Houses and Facilities	5.4
Bought their Allotments from the Original Beneficiaries	7.1
Transferred from Other Settlements	5.4
Got their Allotment After the Presentation of a Formal Application to the IAD	14.3
Lived or Occupied Land in the Project Area	26.8
Dislodged from Other Areas	3.6
No Answer	7.1

Source: Cuevas (1981), p. 33.

The agrarian reform settlements suffer from a high degree of inefficiency. They have received large subsidies in the form of cheap credit, water supply and technical assistance. However, with the exception of rice, productivity has not increased significantly. Some of the beneficiaries have had to find extra jobs to complement their incomes. At the same time, nearly half of the land area administered by the IAD is still not in production. It is officially admitted that only 25 percent of the settlements have reached the goals laid down in the reform law of 1962.[78]

Summing up

The agrarian reform is highly crippled by administrative deficiencies and by the fact that the available land area for redistribution to the landless is very limited. Sugar cane and livestock production, i.e., the majority of the *latifundios*, are still excluded from expropriation. Considering the poverty that prevails in the Dominican countryside, it is apparent that the agrarian reform, so far, has had a limited effect on alleviating the problem of underemployment that affects Dominican agriculture.

The Dominican land reform has proved to be a myth, since the agrarian structure of the country has been left practically unchanged. The *latifundio-minifundio* system has become even more accentuated after more than two decades of land reform. The program has been very ambitious, on paper, but very little has been achieved in reality. Many of the radical laws that have been issued could not be applied, since some of those who were in charge of their application would be affected by them. Many members of the ruling elite are large landowners. The only tangible effects that these land laws may have had are peasant votes for the particular party that is sponsoring them and fears of expropriation among some *latifundistas.*

In spite of attempts at land reforms, the fact remains that from the Trujillo era up to the present day, not much has changed in the Dominican land tenure system. Trujillo significantly altered the agrarian structure of the country, as a considerable portion of the cultivable land ended up in the hands of the dictator and his family. After his death, some of Trujillo's land was redistributed through the land reform program but most of it remained in the state owned sugar estates. In the chaos that followed after the fall of the 30 year old dictatorship, many landless field workers and small peasants saw their chance and simply occupied the land they needed. Table 6.3 shows the land ownership structure by tenure in 1975. It can be seen that the state remains the largest single landowner of the country.

The concentration of land that developed with the rise of the sugar industry and that increased with the later actions of Trujillo is still predominant in the Dominican Republic. Indeed it seems to have become more accentuated. At present, more than 80 percent of the landed properties are concentrated in 12 percent of the total cultivable land and, as we saw at the beginning of this chapter, most of the land occupied by small farms is of marginal quality. At the same time, less than 2 percent of the landed properties occupy 55 percent of the cultivable area.[79]

TABLE 6.3   Land Ownership by Tenure, 1975

	Land Area (Hectares)	% of Cultivable Land
State owned farms	33,677	1.2
Unoccupied state land	127,393	4.7
Illegally occupied state land	126,562	4.6
State-owned sugar land	113,273	4.1
Privately owned sugar land	68,566	2.5
Settlements within the Agrarian Reform Program	305,462	11.2
Privately owned farms	1,960,254	71.6
Agricultural Bank holdings	1,049	negligible
Total farmland	2,736,436	100.0

Source: VI Censo Nacional Agropecuario, in World Bank (1978:1), p. 397.

The majority of the peasant holdings are constantly decreasing in size, owing to, inter alia, population growth and the so-called "partible inheritance system," i.e., that the land of deceased parents is divided equally among all the children.[80] This situation is worsened by the fact that many peasants receive their income from land that is not suitable for agricultural use. Their growing families force them to use this land to the utmost, and when it is exhausted they have to move to new virgin land. The problem is that such land hardly exists any longer. As early as 1968, it was officially acknowledged that the prospects for enlarging the area exploited within the framework of traditional extensive agriculture were insignificant. The country's agricultural frontiers had been exhausted.[81]

Table 6.4 shows the Dominican land tenure structure in 1971 and 1981. The table clearly indicates that during that decade the average size of the small peasants' holdings decreased, while at the same time their number increased. This could be due to land partition through inheritance but also, and maybe more important, to the effects of erosion. As will be shown in Chapter 9, erosion affects mainly the minifundios. On the other hand, the middle holders (5 to 50 hectares) have slightly expanded their holdings,[82] while the number and average size of farms in the 50 to 1,000 hectares category has decreased. This may partly be due to the effects of recent agrarian reforms.

TABLE 6.4   Land Tenure Structure in the Dominican Republic, 1971 and 1981

		1971			
Size of Holdings in Hectares	No. of Holdings	%	Size in Hectares	%	Average Size in Hectares
<0.5	49,651	16.29	12,208	0.45	0.2
0.5-5	185,292	60.79	339,639	12.41	1.8
5.1-10	33,803	11.09	231,376	8.45	6.8
10.1-50	28,987	9.51	587,839	21.48	20.3
50.1-100	3,974	1.30	268,026	9.79	67.4
100.1-200	1,791	0.59	249,338	9.11	139.2
200.1-500	884	0.29	268,039	9.80	301.2
500.1-1000	222	0.07	147,784	5.40	665.7
1000 and more	216	0.07	632,216	23.10	2,926.9
Total	304,820	100.00	2,736,465	100.00	9.0

		1981			
Size of Holdings in Hectares	No. of Holdings	%	Size in Hectares	%	Average Size in Hectares
<0.5	61,670	16.00	12,543	0.47	0.2
0.5-5	252,995	65.70	313,620	11.72	1.2
5.1-10	32,543	8.45	231,832	8.66	7.1
10.1-50	30,815	8.00	640,487	23.93	20.8
50.1-100	4,081	1.06	271,853	10.16	66.6
100.1-200	1,825	0.47	251,199	9.38	137.6
200.1-500	786	0.20	231,623	8.65	294.7
500.1-1000	184	0.05	121,333	4.53	659.4
1000 and more	161	0.04	602,216	22.50	3,740.5
Total	385,060	100.00	2,676,706	100.00	7.0

Source: VI and VII Censo Nacional Agropecuario, in ONE (1982:2), p. 11.

174

However, the same period witnessed some land concentration among the biggest landowners, i.e., the limited group of owners with more than 1,000 hectares. Although the number of holdings within this category decreased from 216 to 161, the average size of the farms increased from 2,616 hectares to 3,740. The figures in Table 6.4 also indicate that the total land area on farms has decreased by 2 percent during the 1971-81 period. It is not clear whether this decrease is due to erosion or simply to statistical inconsistencies between the two censuses.

FIGURE 6.2   Land Distribution in the Dominican Republic, 1960, 1971 and 1981

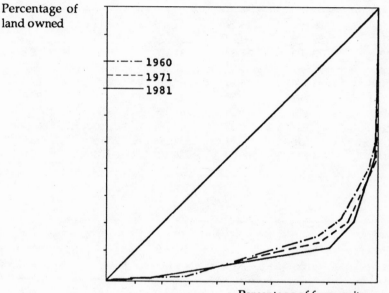

Percentage of land owned

— · — 1960
— — — 1971
———— 1981

Percentage of farm units

Sources: For 1960, Cassá (1982), Table 11-2. For 1971 and 1981, Table 6.4.

In Figure 6.2, the information of Table 6.4 as well as the corresponding figures for 1960 have been translated into Lorenz curves.[83] The curve for 1981 lies slightly outside the one for 1971. The curve for 1971 also lies slightly outside the one for 1960. This indicates that the concentration of land in the Dominican Republic has increased slightly during the last two decades. The Gini coefficients are 0.82 (1960), 0.84 (1971) and 0.85 (1981). However, concentration has not affected all farm sizes. In some segments the Lorenz curves for 1981 and 1971 coincide -

indicating that the share of the smallest farms did not change - and intersect the 1960 curve, indicating that a few *latifundios* decreased in size during that decade. However, it may be concluded that, in spite of the agrarian reform, the Dominican land tenure structure has not undergone any significant change during the period 1960-1981.

Land Tenure and Market Imperfections

As in most Latin American countries, the land tenure structure of the Dominican Republic generates imperfections in the land market since most land resources are concentrated in a few hands. As a result, land prices diverge from the social opportunity cost of land.[84] The few large landowners that control the supply of land also influence the market price of land. At the local level, the large landowner behaves as a monopolist and will therefore offer for sale or rent less land at a higher price than under perfect competition. There exists a series of local monopolies in the land market. On average, there are about 45,000 *minifundistas* for each *latifundista*.[85]

The greater need for land among the *minifundistas* and the landless peasants means that their demand elasticity is lower than for the *latifundistas*. The latter can therefore behave as a price discriminator. The peasants are then forced to pay a higher price than the implicit price paid by the *latifundista*. This price will be above the competitive level while the price faced by the *latifundista* will be below that level,[86] i.e.:

$$r_m > r > r_l \tag{6.1}$$

where r is the hypothetical competitive price of land, and r_m and r_l are the (implicit) prices of land paid by *minifundistas* and *latifundistas*, respectively.

Under the present land tenure structure, land becomes an abundant factor for the *latifundista* and a scarce factor for the *minifundista*, i.e., while land is a cheap production factor for the former, it is extremely expensive for the latter and its price may in some cases be even infinite. Land is generally sold in large parcels and most peasants cannot even afford to bid for it. At the same time, the large landowners do not use their land efficiently. In 1969, 86 percent of the land controlled by the largest *latifundistas* was not in crops but in poorly utilized natural pastures and woods. Furthermore, this group seems not to be very interested in agricultural activities. In 1969, 299 out of 465 farmers with more than 315 hectares (64 percent) did not consider agriculture as their main occupation.[87]

As will be shown later on in this work, this market structure affects the allocation of resources and the methods of production. The underutilization of resources in agriculture is intimately related to the *latifundio-minifundio* system. This land tenure system also influences the performance of the credit and the labor market. The interrelation of these markets and its effects on agricultural production and employment will be discussed in greater detail in Chapter 9. However, before we come to that discussion, we must have a clear understanding of the performance of each market.

Conclusions

The figures we have presented in this chapter show that the Dominican Republic has a very unequal distribution of land, ranking among the countries with the most unequal land ownership structures in the world. Hundreds of thousands of small producers are cramped together on marginal lands. Others are forced to lease land and pay a high price for it. At the same time, some of the best lands are being poorly used by a few large landowners.

However, the land tenure structure found today in the Dominican Republic has not been the result of "the smooth workings of the market," i.e., a process where land is bought and sold at prices determined by demand and supply factors. It is mainly the outcome of a process where the actions of different governments on land rights and agricultural development have encouraged the concentration of land. It is particularly during the twentieth century that the land tenure structure has developed into a major problem. Before that, the population was small, land was abundant and cheap, production was concentrated to free-roaming cattle and subsistence agriculture. The appearance of the sugar enterprises at the end of the nineteenth century and the subsequent introduction of cadastral surveys generated increasing land prices and social unrest in the countryside. In this process, many peasants were evicted from the land they thought to be theirs.

Throughout Dominican history, the state has been the major landowner and today, its importance has not diminished. At the beginning of the twentieth century, the state favored large agricultural entrepreneurs and facilitated their access to fertile lands by means of various land laws and by ceding state-owned lands to them on very generous terms. Accordingly, the Dominican state has had a decisive influence in the creation and perpetuation of the Dominican land tenure structure. During the Trujillo regime, the land ownership structure underwent significant changes. Trujillo became the largest landowner of the country. After his death, the Dominican state took over the vast Trujillo lands and once again recuperated its position as the largest landowner. Since then, the state has tried to change the land tenure structure of the country through the implementation of an agrarian reform program.

The achievements of this program are, however, not especially impressive. Land redistribution has been carried out at a very slow pace and few families have benefited. The agrarian reform settlements have received large subsidies but they show no significant increase in labor productivity. After more than two decades of agrarian reform, the Dominican land tenure structure remains unchanged, and the evidence suggests that, at least in the case of the largest landowners, the degree of land concentration has even increased. At the same time, the number of *minifundios* is increasing and their average size decreasing.

The concentration of land that prevails in the Dominican Republic implies that the Dominican land market is highly imperfect. Those who control the supply of land also influence the price of land. As a result, different producers face different land prices. As we will see in the following, the limited access of the Dominican peasants to productive land is one of the major factors behind their increasing level of poverty and undoubtedly constitutes an important push factor for rural-urban migration.

Notes

1. See Feder (1971), Griffin (1969) and (1976:1), Barraclough and Domike (1966).

2. See ONAPLAN (1983:1), pp. 77-81. This soil classification is somewhat tentative. The figures presented below are rough estimates and should not be compared with the figures in Table 6.4 which are based on actual ownership structure.

3. Ibid., p. 80.

4. Ibid., p. 121.

5. Ibid., p. 114.

6. Dechamps (1907), p. 131.

7. See Moya Pons (1985), p. 197.

8. Baud (1986), p. 26.

9. In English texts, the *ejidos* or *bienes comunales* are often translated as "common land" while the *"terrenos comuneros"* are called "communal land." See for instance, Clausner (1970), pp. 236 and 253.

10. During the occupation, the Haitians seized land from those landholders that had left the country. They also took possession of the majority of the land that belonged to the church. See ISA (1979), p. 9.

11. Some of these lands were held by individuals under questionable titles or with no title at all (Clausner (1970), p. 252). The exact figure on the amount of land owned by the state during this period is not really known. (See Boin and Serulle (1979), pp. 125-26.)

12. See ISA (1979), pp. 10-15. The law of 1902 also facilitated the import of *braceros* (sugar cane cutters) and exonerated the workers from obligatory military service. See Lluberes (1983), p. 22.

13. Baud (1987), pp. 8-9.

14. ISA (1979), p. 16.

15. Clausner (1970), pp. 246, 248 and 251.

16. ISA (1979), p. 12.

17. Clausner (1970), p. 248.

18. See Bonó (1980:2), pp. 263-66.

19. Clausner (1970), p. 363.

20. See Cassá (1983), p. 224.

21. Clausner (1970), pp. 367-68.

22. The system used was the so-called Torrens system. According to this system, a register of deeds was established in the principal city of each district where all notaries had to deposit in triplicate all documents concerning real property. These documents were checked by an "Examiner of Titles" and if the titles were found to be correct, they were entered in the "Registration Book of the Register of Deeds" and copies were sent to a land court established in the capital. If documentation of titles did not exist, the land was surveyed at the cost of the landowners and divided between the shareholders in accordance with how much land they had fenced or kept under cultivation. The Examiner of Titles called hearings at which all parties were given the opportunity to present evidence and argument. The results of the examiner's investigations were sent to the land court that passed a verdict based on these results (Clausner (1970), 366-85).

23. See ibid., pp. 367 and 385 and Baud (1984), pp. 104-05.

24. Clausner (1970), p. 348.

25. Cassá (1983), p. 224.

26. Calculated from *Informe de la Comisión de Investigation de los E.U.A. en Santo Domingo en 1871*, (1960), p. 471. (An acre = 6.4 *tareas*.) For different land measurements units used in the Dominican Republic, see Schoenrich (1977), p. 361.

27. These prices refer to the area of Villa González. See Baud (1984), p. 106. Information on prices is scanty. There is no systematic survey on land prices, rents or sharecropping in the country.

28. These are current prices (Clausner (1970), p. 425). During the Trujillo regime, land prices were highly distorted. In many cases Trujillo bought the land he wanted at prices or payment conditions set by the dictator himself or his army. For example, in the area of La Vega, Trujillo seized a large farm from one of his enemies. This time he just sent one of his brothers and an armed band. Later, Trujillo sold this land to some of his friends at prices between 2 and 6 pesos per *tarea*. The market price of this land was 40 to 60 pesos per *tarea*. (See ibid., pp. 424-29.) Most of the land Trujillo owned was bought at

ridiculous prices. For a detailed presentation of Trujillo's properties see Rivera (1986). Cf. also Bosch (1985).

29. Cf. Garrido Puello (1981), p. 103.

30. This refers to the area of Villa González (Baud (1984), p. 107). The most common sharecropping arrangements in the Dominican Republic is that of *arriendo a medias*. This means that the sharecropper cultivates a determined portion of land with seeds allotted by the landowner. The latter also advances money to the sharecropper for the acquisition of fertilizers, labor expenses, etc. When the yield is sold, the advanced money is discounted and the rest of the money is divided 50-50 between the landowner and the sharecropper. In 1972, tenancy and sharecropping arrangements were prohibited by Law No. 289. But the effects of this law have been negligible (ibid.).

31. Ferrán (1976), p. 100 and 102. Baud (1984), p. 108, also presents some figures on rent under tenancy arrangements: DR$ 1 per *tarea* in the 1940s and DR$ 10 to DR$ 15 in 1983. It is however not clear if these figures refer to the rent per year and *tarea*.

32. See Baud (1984), p. 106 and Crouch (1981), pp. 31-32.

33. Calculated from Cassá (1982), Table 11.2. Unfortunately, I have been unable to find the census of 1935 in order to make a comparison.

34. See for instance Balaguer's speeches in Cassá (1986), pp. 467-86.

35. A critical factor which provided an impulse towards agrarian reformism was the influence of the US government through the Alliance for Progress. The fear of the spread of the Cuban revolution to other countries of the region was an important element in the initiation of the Alliance for Progress in 1961. The Alliance made economic aid conditional on the demonstration of commitment to changes in land tenure structure and improved rural living conditions. (See Grindle (1986), p. 142.) For the importance of the Alliance on the implementation of the agrarian reform in the Dominican Republic see Martin (1975), especially the US ambassador's speech of June 19, 1963, in ibid., pp. 719-28.

36. Grindle (1986), p. 142.

37. In the Dominican Republic, this new approach is exemplified by the implementation of the project Centro de Servicios Rurales Integrados (CENSERI). The new approach is mainly oriented towards increasing the peasants' living standard by providing them with direct inputs and infrastructure to improve production, without altering the structure of land holding. For a description of this type of program in major Latin American countries, see Grindle (1986), pp. 161-74.

38. SEA (1924), pp. 132-33. The project proposer recommended the government to conduct a "vigorous campaign in Copenhagen, Stockholm and Christiania." (Ibid.)

39. IAD (1983:2), p. 5.

40. Clausner (1970), pp. 436-37.

41. IAD (1983:2), p. 5.

42. Trujillo welcomed every chance of receiving immigrants. Spaniards arrived after the civil war, Jewish refugees came just before the outbreak of

180

World War II, and Hungarians arrived after the revolt in 1956. Gardiner (1979), pp. 36, 90, 200, 204, 164 and 190.

43. Moya Pons (1980), p. 622. Even if Trujillo concentrated all power, he sometimes left the presidency to others in order to give an impression of constitutionalism. Balaguer was president, for the first time, from August 3, 1960 until January 16, 1962.

44. Clausner (1970), p. 437.

45. Ibid., pp. 445-46.

46. Ibid., p. 439.

47. Ibid., p. 446.

48. IAD (1981:2), pp. 7-10.

49. ONAPLAN (1983:1), p. 108.

50. Clausner (1970), pp. 470-71. The carrying out of the agrarian reform program was also hindered by different organizational rigidities. (See Barraclough (1970), pp. 36 and 52-54.)

51. Ibid., p. 488.

52. Ibid., p. 444.

53. Not all catholic priests were involved in the criticism. For the majority of the clergy, active pursuit of social change was contrary to their cultural convictions and class origins. The most active groups were the Jesuits, among them, the influential "radio priest" Cipriano Cabero who over his transmitter announced that "invasion of unoccupied land, state or private, by hungry campesinos is socially just" (Clausner (1970), p. 496) and parish-priests like Varona in El Seybo who stated that "God gave them [the peasants] the right and the responsibility to resist and defend themselves." (Wipfler (1978), p. 417.) These groups had a vast influence on public opinion and pressed the government to take a stand. Wipfler gives an exhaustive description of the Dominican church's position during these years. (See ibid., pp. 367-450.)

54. It is estimated that 650 persons were assassinated for political reasons between 1966 and 1970 (Alcántara Z. (1981), pp. 60 and 64).

55. Ibid., p. 66. In 1975, 153,955 hectares had been illegally occupied by peasants. The occupations have not stopped since that time. For example, only during the period January-October 1981, no less than 39 occupations were carried out. (See Dore Cabral (1982), p. 166.) Many observers see the determination of the land occupying peasants as the real force behind the agrarian reform, since they provoke the state to act in order to avoid conflicts in the countryside. (See ibid.)

56. Dore Cabral (1979), p. 22 and ONAPLAN (1983:1), pp. 108 and 111. For a review of the different land reform laws in the Dominican Republic see Illy (1983), pp. 265-91.

57. IAD (1981:2), p. 22.

58. Ibid., p. 103. It seems that this law was not applied to its full extent. See Dore Cabral (1982), p. 164.

59. Alcántara Z. (1981), p. 98.

60. Ibid., p. 99. By 1980, there existed in the country 2,324 peasants' organizations with a total of 95,861 members. See ONAPLAN (1983:1), p. 97.

61. World Bank (1978:1), p. 16.

62. Alcántara Z. (1981), p. 119.
63. IAD (1983:2), p. 9. See also ONAPLAN (1983:1), p. 109.
64. Ibid., p. 35.
65. LaGra (1983), p. 263.
66. Information obtained at *Departamento de Economía Agropecuaria*, SEA.
67. World Bank (1978:1), p. 17.
68. The alleged reason is that "the Institute does not have enough financial means or operative capacity to do better." (Silvestre Alba de Moya, head of *Asociación de Hacendados y Agricultures*, a large farmer association. Interview in *Hoy*, 30 November, 1985, p. 6-A, Santo Domingo.) Cf. IAD (1983:2), p. 8.
69. IAD (1983:2), p. 10.
70. Dore Cabral (1979), p. 22.
71. Quezada (1981), pp. 90 and 93.
72. Graber (1978), p. 113.
73. In 1979 the IAD settlements produced 25 percent of the country's total production; in 1982, 38 percent. In 1979, 1.4 million quintals of white rice were produced. In 1983, this figure had increased to 2.1 million (IAD (1983:2), p. 36).
74. Quezada (1981), p. 93.
75. Alcántara Z. (1981), p. 91.
76. World Bank (1978:1), p. 16.
77. Ibid.
78. IAD (1983:2), p. 10.
79. This is one of the most unequal land ownership structures in the world. According to its Gini coefficient, the Dominican Republic ranks 12th in a sample of 54 countries. The Gini index calculated for these countries was based on data from around 1960. See Taylor and Hudson (1972), pp. 267-68.
80. Sharpe (1977), p. 45.
81. ONAPLAN (1968), p. 119.
82. A "middle" holder is mainly an agriculturalist who is able to work exclusively on his own land, and does not have to get employment in other farms. His income is enough, or exceeds his level of subsistence. This , however depends on the quality of the soil, on the access to the market and to different inputs (IEPD (1983:2), p. 8).
83. Figures for 1960 in Cassá (1982), Table 11-2.
84. See Griffin (1969), pp. 70-77. In Chapters 6 to 9 we draw on Griffin's (1969) study.
85. In 1981, the number of *latifundistas* (producers with more than 50 hectares) was 7,037 while the *minifundistas* (producers with less than 5 hectares) amounted to 314,665 (see Table 6.4).
86. For a discussion on the principles of price formation on this type of land market see Lundahl (1984), pp. 528-30.
87. Alemán (1982), pp. 20-21 and 30.

7

Agricultural Credit

In this chapter, we will discuss the problem of credit in the Dominican agricultural sector. We will analyze the opportunities for savings and the demand and supply of credit in the sector, i.e., we will attempt to determine the extent to which peasants may be able to save, their need for credit, the purposes for which they may be expected to borrow and the sources from which they may obtain their loans. We will analyze how financial funds are distributed among producers, as well as the sources from, and the conditions under which different producers obtain their loans.

It is argued that the Dominican credit market is highly imperfect and that the distribution of financial resources is very unequal. The policy of cheap institutional credit mostly benefits large producers while the peasants are largely excluded. This policy has tended to worsen the distribution of income in the rural areas.

Savings Opportunities

In the Dominican agricultural sector, the availability of funds for capital formation is largely inadequate. The level of investment is exceedingly low and in consequence, most agricultural activities are still carried out with very rudimentary production techniques and low productivity. Poverty is widespread among the rural population. There is substantial inequality in income distribution in the agricultural sector, an inadequate structure of land ownership and a highly unequal distribution of most agricultural resources. As a result, most income generated in the sector is concentrated in few hands. In 1970, 2 percent of the families in the agricultural sector received 34.9 percent of the total agricultural income, while 49.2 percent of the families in the sector only received 15.7 percent of the total agricultural income.[1] The same year, total agricultural income amounted to DR$ 350.1 million but, according to the Secretariat of Agriculture (SEA), only 73 percent of this income remains in the rural areas. The remaining 27 percent is classified as urban income since it is generated on farms belonging to absentee landowners.[2] As Table 7.1 below shows, the unequal distribution of income in the agricultural sector limits the opportunities for savings in the sector.

TABLE 7.1   Rural Family Income and Expenditure in 1973

Monthly Income Level	Average No. of Families (%)	Average Monthly Income (in DR$)	Monthly Expenditure (in DR$)	Savings Ratio (%)
Less than 50	49.9	35.07	62.42	-78
50 - 100	25.8	85.62	95.89	-12
100.01-300	18.5	207.79	216.10	-4
300.01 and above	5.8	1,025.42	994.66	3

Source: SEA (1976), Table 4, p. 17 and Table 9-A, p. 205.

The figures in Table 7.1 should, however, be taken with great reservations since it is not possible for a family to go on facing negative savings over a long time period. They seem to be the result of a single observation and may not therefore reflect the fluctuating character of family income in the agricultural sector. However, they do provide some insight into the savings opportunities open to the different income groups. The greatest savings opportunity is found among those families receiving above 300 pesos a month. However, only 6 percent of rural families earn that much and, as mentioned above, the income received by some of these families is considered as urban and so are their savings.[3]

According to Table 7.1, in 1973, 94 percent of rural families had monthly expenditures that exceeded their monthly income. In order to cover this budget deficit, the peasant has to obtain credit. However, this deficit cannot go on year after year since the peasant will then confront accumulated debts. Extra income, in the form of remittances from relatives working in town or abroad, may offer the possibility of breaking out of this circle of debt. As will be shown in Chapter 10, most peasant families have relatives in towns, mainly women working as maids, and some have relatives working in the US or Venezuela. Most of these workers pay regular visits to their relatives bringing presents in cash or goods. The peasants can also raise extra income by selling a pig or a cow. These assets generally represent peasants' "savings."

No detailed data exist on savings in the rural sector. The low level of income of the majority of the rural population, plus the fact that many peasants depend on credit to finance consumption, may suggest that the possibilities for rural savings, especially among the poorest families, are very limited. However, most peasant families manage some savings. Although Dominican peasants are almost always heavily indebted, they usually manage to hold assets as a means of protection against periods of distress. This may include sickness, death of a family member or any other extraordinary expenditure. Assets often consist of pigs or cattle. The coexistence of indebtedness and asset holdings seems to be a common characteristic of most peasant societies.[4]

Another type of savings common among poor families is putting the money into a *san*, a kind of rotating credit association which is similar to those found under different names in many other countries.[5] The *san* is an informal savings device where a group of participants (generally 10 to 12 persons) make regular contributions to a fund that is given to each member in turn. The fund is administered by the organizer or "owner" of the *san*. Contributions are generally made monthly and the *san* lasts until each member has had his turn. Douglas Norvell and R. V. Billingsley have illustrated the way in which the *san* is played as follows:

> Assume that a *san* group is composed of ten players and a leader who sets the amount to be received by the winner at $100. In turn, players agree to contribute $11 at each of ten weekly meetings. On the Monday of the first week a number from 1 to 10 is assigned to each player. Each player gives $11 to the leader, who then selects one of the numbers. The player with the winning number receives $100. The remaining $10 is retained by the leader. The winning player's number is cast out, but he continues to contribute until the ten drawings have been held. Each Monday, the process will be repeated until the game has run its course. Eventually everybody wins so the advantage of being the winner is in acquiring funds early in the game.[6]

The cost of *san* as a saving device or as a credit mobilization scheme may appear to be high, especially for the recipient of the final rounds. However, given the limited savings opportunities available to poor families, the *san* is an effective way of forcing oneself to save. Besides, given the high rates of interest prevailing in the informal credit market (see below) the *san* may prove to be a cheap way of obtaining credit for the winners of the first rounds. The *san* is sometimes played without interest charges, but in this case, the first turn goes to the organizer. There also exist commodity or article *sanes*. In this type of *san*, members make regular cash contributions to the organizer and each participant in turn will receive the agreed article.

The fact that most rural families are poor and that most of them rely on credit have led policymakers and development planners to believe that these families do not save. However, although no quantitative data exist, many rural families do save. A study from 1983 reported that in a rural community, no less than 30 percent of the families reported to play or had played *sanes*.[7] Savings is a major tool of risk management. Keeping assets or playing *san* are ways of securing protection in times of crisis or unexpected expenditures. The seasonal character of agricultural income forces the rural family to continuously balance the flow of income and expenditures. A way of managing this balance is through savings and borrowings.

Some evidence suggests that rural households in low-income countries have a high average propensity to save. A key element in saving mobilization is, however, the attractiveness of the reward paid on savings.[8] Concerning saving propensities in rural areas, Michael Lipton argues that they are generally higher than shown by the available figures. Non-monetized activities, which can be considered as farm saving embodied directly in investment, are generally not accounted for.[9]

The Demand for Credit

There is a great need for credit in agricultural production, both for large farmers and peasants. This necessity is characteristic of agricultural production itself, with long gestation periods between planting and harvesting. Credit is essential to improve productivity and push agricultural development in general. In the Dominican case, the need for credit is greater among small peasants since, as shown, their earnings are so meager that the possibilities of generating an investable surplus are very limited.

The rate of time preference (or degree of impatience) for present over future income tends to be high among the poor and, as we will see later, this fact tends to make for high interest rates in the informal rural credit market where most peasants procure their credit. The size of income is a major characteristic underlying an individual's impatience. As Irving Fisher explains it:

In general, it may be said that, other things being equal, the smaller the income, the higher the preference for present over future income; that is, the greater the impatience to acquire income as early as possible. It is true, of course, that a permanently small income implies a keen appreciation of future wants as well as of immediate wants. Poverty bears down heavily on all portions of a man's expected life. But it increases the want for immediate income *even more* than it increases the want for future income.[10]

Considering the fact that he can only obtain cash income at harvest time, the peasant's demand for credit, especially to finance consumption, is very high. The long gestation period inherent in agricultural production implies that a peasant can harvest one, two, or at most, three times a year, depending on the character of the crop. Income will be available only at the time when the harvest is sold, but consumption for the subsistence of the peasant and his family cannot, for biological reasons, coincide with the peasants' seasonal income pattern. This fact, combined with the scantiness of income generated by the harvest, are the principal reasons why small peasants have to depend so much on credit. Credit is also needed to buy production inputs such as fertilizers and seeds, but this concerns mostly large and medium-size producers, since the majority of the Dominican peasants rarely can afford commercialized inputs. Apart from his small plot, only seeds and plants (generally laid up from last harvest) and some hand tools constitute the peasants' means of production.

Credit requirements depend on the type and extension of production, the family size and its basic needs. In slash and burn cultivation the amount of credit required for production purposes varies with the size of the land cleared. If the size of the family is not large enough to carry out all of the work, cash is needed both to cover the family's daily consumption and to pay for the extra labor needed for clearing, fencing, planting, weeding and harvesting. Table 7.2 illustrates production costs of a middle holder in 1971. (Note that the information in this table refers to a new plot cleared by this particular peasant.)

Referring to the credit need of this particular producer, Sharpe states:

> ... his children are still too young to work, so he had to hire others to help for two days in early August and four days at harvest time. These six days cost him (including food plus wages) $8.75. His total preharvest costs (labor and nonlabor) were thus $37.85. But most of these costs had to be met at least three months before he had his first cash crop, the beans. More seriously, Chaguito had to feed and care for his family during these months.[11]

TABLE 7.2   Typical Costs for Clearing, Planting, and Harvesting a One-Acre
             Cultivated Plot

Task	Days of Labor	Nonlabor Costs (in DR$)	Month
Cutting underbrush and felling trees	4		late June
Burning the brush and trees	2		early August
Clearing and cleaning off after burning	4		early August
Placing a fence with 2-foot high base of horizontally laid rails and 3 strands of barbed wire (about 3 rolls of wire at $6/roll)	12	18.00	mid-August
Planting (bean seeds cost $9.60 and corn $1.50 at this time; plantain bulbs, sweet potatoes, yucca, and small coffee plants are all readily available from his own conuco or that of a neighbor without cost; days of labor include labor of digging up and transporting these plantain bulbs, etc.)	8	11.10	early September
Weeding	4		mid-October
Harvesting (calculation for bean harvest; other crops are not harvested as such, except coffee after 4 years, in a conuco this size but rather picked daily to meet family's food needs)	6		early December
Total days of labor	40		
Total nonlabor costs		29.10	

Source: Sharpe (1977), p. 43.

This producer also had some land in coffee production. Financing
coffee production is somewhat more complicated than financing
subsistence crops. Cash is needed to finance production long before
harvest. Usually there is a delay of three or four weeks between the
time the coffee is picked and the time it is removed from the berry,
dried and finally sold. Cash is needed in order to pay the pickers and
provide them with at least one meal a day. Furthermore, during the
period of waiting for the harvest, the producer must also provide the
daily cash expenses of the family.

As Table 7.3 shows, in 1971, this producer had cash income of DR$
791.00 while his expenses amounted to DR$ 730.39, including production

costs (18 percent) and consumption. Although with an annual cash surplus of DR$ 60.61, this producer had to borrow. Because of the seasonal nature of the crops, he faced seven months of shortage of cash.[12] All producers in the village studied by Sharpe faced a cash shortage for up to eight months of the year. In order to sustain their families and meet production expenses they had to depend on credit.[13]

TABLE 7.3   Cash and Expenditure Flow of a Middle Holder,* 1971
(in DR$)

Income:	
Selling coffee	665.00
Selling tobacco	16.00
Money sent from family in New York City	110.00
Total year's cash income	791.00
Expenses:	
Food	528.56
Paying labor	129.75
Clothing, medicine, transport and others	72.75
Total year's cash income	730.39
Total year's surplus	**60.61**

*Size of household: 12.

Source: Sharpe (1977), Table 3.5, pp. 56-57.

Among small peasants, loans are generally taken for consumption purposes but the use of the loan varies with the type of crop and the degree of extension work in the area. Thus, a small coffee or cocoa grower - given the long gestation period of the crop, its relatively low requirement of commercialized inputs and the scarcity of extension work in small producers' areas - is likely to allocate most of his credit to current consumption. The case of a small rice or tomato grower is different. These are short-cycle products with relatively high requirements regarding commercialized inputs. Due to the active role played by the agroindustries and government actions through the agrarian reform program, these producers have access to some extension work. Thus, peasants growing short-cycle products allocate part of their loans to the purchase of modern inputs. However, a significant part may still be used for consumption purposes. In a study of rice growers, it was found that these producers devote an important proportion of the credit received from rice factories to pay for their families' needs.[14]

Table 7.4 shows the distribution of rice-factory credit by use category and farm size. It is somewhat surprising that producers in the category of 51 to 500 *tareas* spend a higher percentage of their loans on family needs than producers with farms of less than 50 *tareas*. A possible explanation could be that small producers include some "family needs" in the category of "other." It could also be that the larger producers finance part of their production activities with credit from formal institutions.

TABLE 7.4   Credit Supplied by Rice Factories by Farm Size and Uses, 1975 (Percent)

Size of Farms (in Tareas)	Family Needs	Hiring or Purchase of Machinery	Purchase of Fertilizers	Purchase of Seeds	Labor	Other
Less than 50	3.1	39.2	18.2	4.8	21.3	13.4
51 to 100	8.3	11.7	13.0	4.7	60.8	1.5
101 to 500	9.7	9.7	31.3	7.3	42.0	-
501 to 2,000	4.2	20.8	10.4	2.1	41.7	20.8

Source: SEA-IICA (1977), p. 69.

In sum, the demand for credit among rural families is high for a variety of reasons. A major reason for taking a loan is to feed the family during the period elapsing between planting and harvesting. Loans are also needed to pay production expenses and to cover unforeseen events such as sickness, funerals and harvest failure.

The Supply of Credit

As pointed out above, there is a great demand for credit in the agricultural sector. Dominican producers may obtain their credit from two main sources: the formal and the informal credit market. These two credit sources are also identified as official or organized, and unofficial or unorganized credit markets, respectively, and their characteristics are common to most underdeveloped countries.[15] The formal market consists of agricultural banks, commercial banks and cooperatives. The informal credit market often includes a variety of sources: local merchants, shopkeepers, traders, specialist moneylenders, landowners, relatives and friends.

The functioning of the two markets differs substantially. The most salient characteristics differentiating these two markets are: the rate of interest, the credit-borrower relationship and the size of the loan. Interest rates in the formal market are relatively low and are determined by the government, whereas in the informal market, interest rates may be very high and are generally determined by the interaction of demand and supply in the local market. In the formal market, the creditor-borrower relationship is of an impersonal, official or bureaucratic character, while in the informal market, it is of a more personal and non-bureaucratic character. Generally, the average size of loans in the formal market is larger than in the informal market.

TABLE 7.5   Agricultural Credit in 1975

Sources	Value (in thousand DR $)	Percent
Formal	90,515	66.3
BA	78,034	57.2
Private Banks*	1,509	1.1
Cooperatives	5,623	4.1
SEA	2,606	1.9
ODC**	137	0.1
FDD	2,606	1.9
Informal	45,829	33.7
Private persons***	37,989	28.0
Peanut industry	4,000	2.9
Factories	1,097	0.8
Sugar mills	549	0.4
"Lavador" (soap) industry	411	0.3
Producers association	1,783	1.3
TOTAL	136, 344	100.0

*Excludes credit for marketing activities.
**Office of Community Development.
***Includes relatives and other persons.

Source: SEA-IICA (1977), p. 65.

In the Dominican Republic, agricultural credit is provided by a variety of sources. Table 7.5 shows the distribution of agricultural credit by source in 1975. Formal or official agricultural credit sources are represented by the *Banco Agrícola* (Agricultural Bank), and special institutions as cooperatives and the Dominican Development Foundation (FDD). The *Banco Agrícola* is funded by government capital transfer and by foreign sources. Commercial banks' agricultural lendings originate in their own deposits and, to a lesser extent from the *Fondo de Inversiones para el Desarrollo Económico* (FIDE),[16] a Central Bank fund. The other institutions listed above are financed by this fund. Informal credit sources are represented by agroindustries, factories, truck drivers, shopkeepers (*pulperías*), moneylenders and relatives. Lendings from these sources originate from their own working capital. However, some of these sources, such as the agroindustries and professional traders, may have access to formal credit sources and thereby act as intermediary agents through which formal credit is channeled into rural areas.[17]

As can be seen, the most important credit sources in the sector are the *Banco Agrícola* (BA), providing 57 percent of the total credit[18] and private persons accounting for 28 percent of the total credit. Table 7.5 also shows that the participation of private banks in financing agricultural activities is very limited. In the late 1970s, only between 6 and 8 percent of the commercial banks' loan portfolio were allocated to the sector. These loans were mainly for livestock production and marketing activities.[19]

An important source in the informal credit market, not included in Table 7.5, is that of local shopkeepers. Local shops (*pulperías*) provide credit (traditionally known as *fiao*) to small peasants mainly for consumption purposes. There do not exist any empirical data concerning this activity, but no one acquainted with rural reality would doubt the importance of this source providing facilities to peasants' families for the daily supply of food.[20]

The Distribution of Institutional Credit

In general, the Dominican agricultural sector suffers from a low availability of funds for financing its different production activities. This is one of the main problems obstructing development in the sector. However, the unequal distribution of available funds, between different producers deeply aggravates the problem. Most institutional (formal) credit in the sector primarily benefits large producers and only a very small proportion of the available funds is allocated to small producers. Due to the governmental effort to increase production in the agrarian reform settlements, a considerable amount of the available official credit has been allocated to these settlements (see Table 7.8 below). With the exception of the small group of peasants who have benefited from the agrarian reform, the majority of the Dominican peasants have to rely on informal credit sources: traders, rice mills, local shopkeepers, etc. Low availability and unequal distribution of financial means are problems affecting rural development in most Third World countries:

In most countries the amount of credit available in rural areas is inadequate, and what little credit is available through organized institutions tends to be rationed among those with secure titles to land and supplied at a relatively low rate of interest. The majority of rural population must seek credit in the unorganized capital market and pay a high price for it ...[21]

In the Dominican Republic, the leading institution providing credit to the agricultural sector is the *Banco Agrícola*. In the following we will take a closer look at this credit source in order to see how this bank distributes its available funds among the sectors' producers.

TABLE 7.6   Formalized Banco Agrícola Credit to the Agricultural Sector, 1973-1987

(in 1973 prices)

Year	Total Sector Credit (in DR $ Million)	Crop-production Credit (in DR$ Million)	Crop-production Credit as Percentage of Total Sector Credit	Total Area Receiving Credit ('000 Tareas)	Credit/ Tarea (DR$)
1973-74	51.7	36.9	71.5	2,433	21.2
1975-76	59.1	43.4	73.5	2,968	19.9
1977-78	63.0	50.1	79.5	3,381	18.6
1979-80	92.5	69.8	75.5	4,724	19.6
1981-82	61.3	47.8	78.0	2,717	22.5
1983-84	61.8	47.3	76.5	2,305	26.8
1985-86	48.4	38.2	79.0	1,756	27.5
1987	65.4	49.0	75.0	2,905	22.5

Source: Calculated from SEA (1988), Tables 117 and 118, Consejo Nacional de Agricultura (1989), Tomo II, Ch. 3.2, Table 10 and Ceara (1989), Table 11.

Although far from satisfying the sector's total credit demand, the amount of loans provided by the *Banco Agrícola* increased at the average rate of 6 percent per annum during the period 1973-87. As shown in Table 7.6, the real value of *Banco Agrícola* loans increased steadily during the 1970s. However, due to the high rate of inflation in the 1980s, there was a slowdown in the rate of increase during the 1981-87 period. The land area in crops amounted to about 630,000 hectares (approximately 10 million *tareas*) in 1971.[22] Assuming from Table 7.6, that total sector credit is allocated to crop production, then *Banco Agrícola* credit has only covered an average of 29 percent of the total land area in crops.

Banco Agrícola credit covers both crop and livestock production. In absolute terms, loans to crop production are the most important ones. As Table 7.6 shows, this subsector captures around three-quarters of the total value of *Banco Agrícola* credit to the sector. The remaining quarter is devoted mainly to livestock production.

If we look at the total *approved Banco Agrícola* credit during the period January-September 1980, crop production only received 79.5 percent of the value of the total loans although it captured 93 percent of the total number of loans. For livestock, the situation was the opposite. This subsector only captured 7 percent of the total number of loans but received 20.5 percent of the value of total agricultural loans. During the same period, the average amount per loan to crop production was DR$ 2.1 million, whereas the corresponding figure for livestock was as high as DR$ 8.9 million.[23] The most important crops receiving credit in 1980 were rice, coffee and plantains. 32 percent of the total crop production credit was allocated to rice production while coffee and plantains received 21 and 4 percent respectively.[24]

Although the total *Banco Agrícola* credit to the sector has increased during the last decade, the land area receiving credit has not increased in the same proportion. In 1987, the total land area receiving credit was smaller than in 1975-76. The amount of credit per *tarea* averaged 22 pesos per annum during the 1973-1987 period (see Table 7.6).

The figures above refer to the distribution of agricultural credit among different production activities in the sector. They are mainly related to the question of: "Credit for what?" Now, we shall try to look at another distribution problem affecting agricultural credit, specifically, that referring to the question of credit for whom?

Table 7.7 indicates that loans from the *Banco Agrícola* mostly benefit large farms and, to some extent, medium-sized ones. Large farms, representing only 2 percent of the total number of farms, received 8 percent of the total value of *Banco Agrícola* loans in 1973, whereas small farms, which represent 77 percent of the total number of farms, only received 33 percent. In 1975, the situation for small farms improved a bit while the proportion of credit allocated to large farms doubled. The neglect of the peasants by formal credit sources is nothing new. During the 1960-73 period, the real amount of agricultural credit available more than tripled. However, some evidence suggests that very little of this massive increase in formal credit filtered down to the non-wealthy.[25]

TABLE 7.7   Number and Value of Banco Agrícola Loans by Farm Size, 1973 and 1975

No. of Farms * (in %) 1971	Farm Size** (in Tareas)	1973			1975		
		No. of Loans	Value ('000 DR$)	%	No. of Loans	Value ('000 DR$)	%
Small farms (77 %)	1 to 10	1,661	1,119		2,022	900	
	11 - 50	19,756	7,521	33	29,526	16,611	41
	51 - 100	7,433	5,799		10,895	14,461	
Medium-size farms (21 %)	101 - 250	2,261	3,386		2,426	5,226	
	251 - 500	696	2,984	15	732	4,224	12
Large farms (2 %)	501 - 1000	294	1,292		274	3,840	
	1,001 - 5,000	115	1,653		143	7,700	
	5,001 - 10,000	146	229	8	6	58	17
	10,001 and above	60	283		2	1,278	
	No area estimated	7,324	19,088	44	7,944	23,738	30
TOTAL		39,746	43,356	100	53,970	78,036	100

*These are approximate figures. Farm-size categories included in the *Banco Agrícola* credit data differ from farm-size categories in the 1971 agricultural census.
**(1 tarea = 0.063 hectares).

Source: World Bank (1978:1), pp. 390, 393.

The distribution of credit between agricultural activities influences the distribution of credit among producers. A salient feature in the Dominican land use pattern is that the proportion of the total land in crops decreases as the size of the farm increases. Thus, while small peasants devote about 78 percent of their land to crop production, the corresponding figure for large farmers is 23 percent.[26]

The skewed credit distribution will be better understood if we consider that in 1971 there were in the Dominican Republic 49,700 farms of a size less than 8 *tareas* (16% of total farms) while a further 185,300 farms (61% of total farms) were of a size between 8 and 80 *tareas*.[27] We can see that the *Banco Agrícola* credit supply to the small peasants is very limited. Assuming that the total *Banco Agrícola* loans to producers with less than 10 *tareas* were distributed as one loan per farm then, in 1973, a maximum 3 percent of the nearly 50,000 *minifundistas* received *Banco Agrícola* loans.

The effort of the government to increase production in the reform settlements has significantly changed the allocation of *Banco Agrícola* credits in later years. As Table 7.8 shows, in 1981 37 percent of the total value of these bank credits was allocated to the agrarian reform settlements. The corresponding figure for 1985 was 47 percent. Credit in the agrarian settlements is mainly allocated to rice production. This crop received 61 and 78 percent of total agrarian reform credit in 1981 and 1982, respectively.[28]

If we consider that from 1975 to 1983 only 16,000 families were settled on agrarian reform land, the allocation of *Banco Agrícola* credit to the *minifundistas* has not undergone any significant increase. On the contrary, as can be seen from Tables 7.7 and 7.8, there has been a tendency towards a concentration of *Banco Agrícola* credits in fewer hands. The value of total *Banco Agrícola* credits to the sector increased by 91 percent between 1975 and 1981. However, during this period the total number of loans decreased by 32 percent.

The distribution between the different farm-size categories in 1981 presents some changes in relation to 1975. In 1981, 54 percent of total *Banco Agrícola* credit was allocated to small farms compared with 41 percent in 1975. This improvement is mainly due to the large share of credit received by agrarian reform farms. Agrarian reform farms within this farm category obtained 17 percent of total *Banco Agrícola* credit to the sector. Credit allocation to medium-size farms decreased significantly between 1975 and 1981. The allocation to large farms was increased from 17 to 36 percent of total in 1975 and 1981, respectively. This large increase is probably due to the fact that in 1981, 18 percent of total *Banco Agrícola* loans was allocated to agrarian reform farms included in the category of large farms.[29]

The above exposition of the formal credit market indicates that the available financial means in this market are largely inadequate given the importance of credit in the agricultural sector. The low availability of funds is worsened by the way credit is distributed

TABLE 7.8 Number and Value of Total Banco Agrícola Loans and Loans to Agrarian Reform Settlements, by Farm Size, 1981

No. of Farms* (in %) 1981	Farm Size (in Tareas)	Total BA Loans			BA Loans to Reform Settlements		Reform Settlements Loans as Percentage of Total BA Loans
		No. of Loans	Value ('000 DR$)	%	No. of Loans	Value ('000 DR$)	
Small farms (82 %)	1 to 10	7,696	33,791		850	8,304	
	11 - 50	10,020	35,741	54	1,788	12,237	17
	51 - 100	3,158	11,383		1,081	4,968	
Medium-size farms (16 %)	101 - 250	1,852	5,341	6	920	2,513	2
	251 - 500	812	3,608		12	22	
Large farms (2 %)	501 - 1,000	3,425	15,369		934	5,625	
	1,001 - 5,000	7,866	38,730	36	3,733	21,220	18
	5,001 - 10,000	21	57		13	19	
	10,000 and above	140	246		6	13	
	No area estimated	1,622	5,081	3	525	884	-
Total		36,612	149,347	100	9,862	55,805	37

* These are approximate figures. Farm-size categories included in *Banco Agrícola* credit data differ from farm-size categories included in the 1981 agricultural census.
Source: Banco Agrícola (1983), pp. 16, 40

between different production activities and farm sizes. Institutional credit has mainly benefited large farms and, in more recent years, the agrarian reform settlements. This implies that the majority of producers cannot benefit from this credit source.

According to Claudio González-Vega,[30] this unequal distribution of agricultural credit is characteristic of most formal financial institutions in poor countries. These institutions generally provide credit at very low interest rates. As a result, an excess demand for cheap credit arises and this situation forces the lender to ration the credit through non-market means. The allocation of loans is generally concentrated to the large and less risky borrowers, i.e., those that can offer some type of security. Under these conditions, small producers with few assets to offer will be penalized. As will be shown below, interest rates charged by the *Banco Agrícola* are very low, and given the rate of inflation prevailing in the country, *Banco Agrícola* loans have been negatively priced.

Informal Credit Sources

The low level of income and the seasonality of the income flow force most peasants to resort to credit. As shown above, very few peasants have access to formal financial institutions. In order to finance production and consumption, the peasants have to resort to their most feasible credit source: intermediaries, local merchants, *pulperías*, moneylenders and *compadres*.[31] Quantitative data about the activities of these alternative credit sources (informal credit market) are scarce but, without doubt, a great amount of agricultural credit is supplied by these sources.[32]

Apart from professional moneylenders, truck drivers, etc., there are a number of firms in the country devoted to processing and commercializing agricultural products. Among these are rice factories and agroindustries processing tomatoes, peanuts and pigeon peas. Through their field representatives (*peritos*) these firms supply credit, technical assistance, agricultural inputs and other services to producers. In exchange for these facilities, the peasant agrees with the firm to sell his yield. In practically all regions of the country there is a great dependency of producers on intermediaries for supply of credit in the form of inputs or for consumption purposes. Some of these intermediaries charge interest rates of between 2 and 10 percent per month.[33]

Among the informal credit sources, rice factories are very important. In 1976, 131 rice factories were operating in the country.[34] These factories provide credit to rice growers in order to secure their rice supply. About 29 percent of the total credit received by the rice growers originated from this source.[35] Factory loans are mainly in cash (94 percent of the value) and a small part (6 percent) in inputs, mainly fertilizers and seeds. Inputs are provided according to farm size. No explicit interest is charged but prices are established by factory owners. At times, input prices can be up to 50 percent higher than the corresponding market price.[36] Credit is given to a certain "client circle" which every factory has acquired. The size of loans depends on the paying capacity of the clients which is determined by the estimated rice production. There is no legal agreement underlying credit transactions, but factories have developed a system to control their clients. Field agents (*peritos*) periodically visit rice growers in order to check yield development.

A similar situation is found among tobacco producers. Credit is mainly obtained through intermediaries who on behalf of the tobacco exporting firms advance cash to the producers in order to secure the purchase of the crop. Generally, no interest is charged on these loans.[37] Probably the borrower may later on obtain lower prices for his products. The difference between these prices and the corresponding market prices would be equivalent to the interest that the peasant is willing to pay for the loan. As we saw in Chapter 5, for the intermediaries, extending credit is a way of securing the crop. At the rural level, the number of buyers is generally large and price information is rather good. In Chapter 5, we also argued that the peasant is not compelled to sell his crop to the lender intermediary, although he generally does so out of gratitude. However, if the deal is not convenient, the peasant can as well sell to another intermediary and repay the loan with interest.

A common practice in rural credit transactions is that some peasants sell the future yield to a local merchant or intermediary at prices that may be below the going market prices.[38] This transaction involves a risk premium. Thus, the difference between the market price and the price actually received by the producer accounts for the risk involved in the outcome of the yield and in possible price fluctuations. These risks are transferred to the buyer. This practice is called *venta a la flor* and is very common among small peasants cultivating long cycle products such as coffee and cacao.

Table 7.9 illustrates the different sources from which a sample of 230 small tobacco growers obtained credit. The largest credit suppliers were local shops and intermediaries.

In spite of the high interest charged by some informal credit sources, most producers procure their loans in this market. The financial services of informal intermediaries in underdeveloped countries are often costly, but when rural borrowers are presented with a choice between cheap formal and expensive informal credit, they often choose the informal.[39] Some researchers argue that the average borrowing cost from informal sources is much less than is widely thought. For the new borrower of small amounts, these informal borrowing costs may be very similar to the total borrowing cost of acquiring formal loans.[40] Informal lenders generally deal with a reduced number of borrowers. This facilitates lending decisions and reduces both lenders' and borrowers' transaction costs. In the Dominican Republic, informal lenders are generally entrepreneurs who usually combine several roles: traders, rice millers and storekeepers. These entrepreneurs generally regard the provision of credit as a necessary cost element in the enterprise.

TABLE 7.9   Credit Sources of 230 Small Tobacco Producers* during the 1971-72 Harvest

Source	Annual Interest Rate (Percent)	Number of Producers Receiving Credit	%
Relatives and friends	0	179	78
Local shops	0	209	91
Peasant organizations	0	76	33
Intermediaries	No explicit interest (but commitment to sell the crop)	200	87
Bank	8 to 10	48	21
Moneylenders	180 to 240	32	14

*Half of these producers had farms of less than 2 hectares. The remaining half had farms of between 2 and 5 hectares.

Source: Ferrán (1976), pp. 86-95.

Most peasants resort to these credit sources attracted by the facility with which they can obtain a loan and by the different services these sources provide. For example, an investigation carried out in 1984 in three rural communities concluded that the services provided by the different informal credit sources are highly appreciated by the peasants and that the image of usurer, as the rural moneylender is generally perceived in urban circles, is not truthful. Accordingly, "the informal sector is perceived by the community as serious, responsible, consulted and listened to ..."[41]

The Cost of Credit

As stated above, interest rates in the formal credit market are officially fixed, whereas in the informal credit market interest rates are determined locally by demand and supply forces. Interest rates on loans through the banking system have been fixed since 1919. A ceiling interest rate of 12 percent annually was then settled and has remained the same ever since. Given the rate of inflation prevailing in the country (the annual average rate of inflation in the 1970s was 11 percent and in the early 1980s 15 percent)[42] it follows that *Banco Agrícola* loans are obtained at practically zero interest. Actually, nominal interest rates on *Banco Agrícola* loans range from 6 to 12 percent per annum. The corresponding figures for the informal credit market are 2 to 20 percent per month,[43] i.e., the interest rate in the informal credit market can be as high as 20 times the maximum interest rate permitted in the country. We do not know, however, which proportion of informal market loans that falls within the higher range of interest rates. As we have seen, there is a variety of credit sources, some charging interest rates explicitly, others implicitly. The scanty information seems, however, to suggest that interest rates in this market are high.

It is hard to see the logic underlying the government decision to keep interest rates at the rigid 12 percent ceiling. In practice, what this policy does, is to provide gratuitous credit to the rich while the poor have to bear the higher interest rates charged by informal credit sources. This policy may also be affecting the reluctance of the commercial banks to increase lending to the sector, thus limiting further the supply of funds. According to the World Bank report, if commercial bank lending to agriculture is to be increased, the legal ceiling has to be removed in order to make lending to the sector more attractive.[44]

Part of the rationale behind the low interest rates charged by formal agricultural lending institutions in underdeveloped countries is to redistribute income in favor of the poor and to increase production. In most cases, however, the opposite result has been obtained. Cheap credit generally benefits a small number of large borrowers while a large number of small potential borrowers are excluded. "By distorting the allocative functions of interest rates, these policies have prevented savings from being channeled to their most socially profitable uses."[45]

Another important argument behind cheap formal credit policies is the widespread stereotype belief that peasants are exploited by intermediaries or rural moneylenders as these charge unscrupulously high interest rates. In the following sections we shall try to take a closer look at different factors that may aid us to explain why interest rates are high in the informal credit market of the Dominican Republic.

Supply Factors

In the Dominican agricultural sector, there is practically no institution that deals simultaneously with both savings and lendings. The main lender to the sector is the *Banco Agrícola*. However this source obtains its funds from governmental and international sources. Thus, there do not exist any institutional arrangements between savers and investors in agriculture.[46] In the informal sector, the intermediaries or the agroindustry in question offer loans out of their own pockets, thus bearing the lender's risk. Traders and industries may, however, have access to formal urban credit markets and may in this sense play an intermediary role between the formal urban credit market and the informal rural credit market.

The lender's risk could be an important factor behind the high interest rates charged by informal credit sources. This risk is based mainly on two components: the moral reputation of the borrower and the margin of security he can provide. The first component may not be difficult to determine since the rural lender usually has a very good knowledge of the individuals he deals with. The latter may vary from borrower to borrower. In many cases the assets that could be taken over in cases of default are too small or the borrower possesses no title to the land he occupies. A low margin of security may therefore mean a high mark-up in the interest rate.[47] However, as pointed out above, the Dominican rural moneylenders usually develop a good contact with their clients and no security is needed as the size and length of the loans are related to the crops. In this sense, the risk of the lender may be mainly based on the outcome of the harvest. Climatological changes may affect the volume of the peasant crops and variations in prices may affect the value of the crops. If these changes are negative, the peasant in question may incur involuntary default. Thus, with the exception of involuntary default, the risks of lending tend to be minimized since the Dominican rural lenders tend to have good knowledge of the paying capacity of each client. The following quotation illustrates this fact:

> ... buying a peasant's coffee demands financing his preharvest production costs and household needs, and such capital advances easily can be lost. As one exporter explained: "The peasant might even have the best intentions, but his situation is such that if a child gets sick, he's just not going to have the money to pay back what I advanced him." The exporters prefer to advance capital to independent middlemen - usually local commerciantes [sic] with the economic position to guarantee such advances - and let these compradores absorb the risk. These local middlemen have direct knowledge of their clientele (who can be trusted, who has the production to guarantee and [sic] advance) and can control

much of the regional coffee market through advances of credit and cash.[48]

The high average rate of interest charged cannot be fully explained in terms of risk premia as compensation for possible defaults, since the lenders usually have a good knowledge of their clientele and are able to use this knowledge either to charge high interest rates to the less reliable clients or to deny them the loan altogether.

Another important factor to consider on the supply side of the informal credit market is the opportunity cost of lending, i.e., the alternative use that the moneylenders could make of their loanable funds. This may influence the interest rates, since lenders are expected to charge rates which are at least as high as the rate of return they could obtain by investing in other activities. Since the lenders consist mainly of traders and their intermediaries, these could have the alternative of holding commodity stocks rather than lending. This could be feasible in the case of grains. The rate of return realizable on commodity stocks mainly depends on the seasonal variation in the prices of these commodities and the cost of holding stocks. The variation in prices would depend on the elasticities of demand and supply of the commodities in question and the cost of holding stocks will depend on the storage facilities of the trader. If the price variation is high and the cost of holding stocks is low, the rate of return would be high.[49] However, in the Dominican Republic, the possibilities of stockholding are relatively limited. In the case of rice, until 1986, the Price Stabilization Institute (INESPRE) had a total monopoly on the commercialization of this commodity and rice factories had to deliver all rice production to INESPRE. In the case of coffee and cocoa, holding stocks may be risky, especially for small local traders, since these are export crops and it is difficult to foresee the development of the international markets.

Thus, stockholding seems not to be a feasible alternative to moneylending in Dominican agriculture and thereby it cannot significantly influence the rate of interest charged by the intermediaries. Apart from stockholding, there are very few alternatives where a rural moneylender could place his financial resources. He could, however, engage in agricultural production or invest in urban activities. If the rate of return in these activities is high, the opportunity cost of the loans that may be extended by these lenders will also be high. Lenders could, for example, invest in land, cattle and urban real estate, or simply make savings deposits. The three first alternatives may be connected with high transaction costs. Savings deposits do not seem to be an attractive alternative. In 1970-74 the legal ceiling on interest rates paid on saving deposits was on a level of 4 percent per year for commercial banks and 6 percent for savings and loan associations.[50]

Interest rates can be influenced by the degree of competition among lenders. Lack of competition among lenders may generate monopoly profits in the credit market. In this case, interest rates are likely to be higher than would be the case under competitive conditions. However, moneylending in rural Dominican Republic is generally a complementary activity. Credit is mainly supplied by traders and local shopkeepers. Thus, the functions of moneylending, marketing and merchandizing are generally carried out by the same agent. This symbiosis of the rural credit and produce markets is very important for an understanding of the working of the Dominican informal credit market. The intermediary-trader is first and foremost a buyer of agricultural products, and he lends or "advances money" to producers in order to secure the crops. As argued in Chapter 5, competition seems to prevail among the intermediaries. In the case of professional moneylenders, competition is likely to prevail. Loans are generally small and anyone with money can enter this market.

Another important factor that can influence the interest rate is the administrative cost to lenders. However, the personal and short-term character of the loans tends to minimize this cost.

Contrary to what is generally believed, the high interest rates prevailing in the Dominican informal rural credit market are not likely to be the result of usury or monopolistic practices of the moneylenders. Some of the lender's risk tend to be minimized and the opportunity cost and the administrative costs of lending tend to be low. No monopoly profits arise since the number of potential lenders is likely to be high.

Demand Factors

On the demand side, the distribution of income and wealth largely influences the necessity of borrowing. In an agrarian economy like that of the Dominican Republic, where land ownership is very unequally distributed, the demand for credit is likely to be high. The existence of a large number of producers in need of cash, in relation to a relatively lower amount of loanable funds, may be a major factor behind the high interest rates charged in the informal credit market. In an economy where the majority of the producers barely meet their subsistence requirements, borrowers may be willing to pay high interest rates since they are likely to attach a higher value to present than to future consumption. Thus, "the rate of interest expresses a price in the exchange between present and future goods."[51]

After payment of past debts, what is left over from one harvest is often not sufficient to meet the needs of the family and finance production. In order to subsist and keep on producing, the peasant is expected to be willing to pay a high rate of interest. His rate of time preference is likely to be high. He is more interested in satisfying present needs than future ones.[52]

The rate of time preference is influenced by the size of income, the distribution of income over time and the uncertainty with respect to income. As shown, rural incomes are close to the subsistence level and most peasants face shortages of cash during most of the year. The urgency to meet present needs implies a high rate of time preference, at least during the months of income shortage, i.e., in the short-run perspective. The small size of income and the uncertainty of future income tend to make for a high rate of time preference since peasants are likely to appreciate an addition to an immediate income than to a more remote uncertain income.[53]

It may seem strange that peasants possessing assets prefer to borrow at high interest rates instead of selling their assets. A cheaper way to meet temporary cash shortage could be selling assets at need periods and repurchasing them after harvest. However, there are both economic and psychological reasons which prevent most peasants from doing so. Firstly, the peasant may be faced with the problem of indivisibility of assets. The cash he needs may not correspond to the value of the assets. Secondly, assets (generally cattle and pigs) are often kept as a kind of security. Peasants are reluctant to sell them except during acute crises when no alternative means of raising cash is available.[54] In the case of land, many peasants attach an emotional and social worth to their land. Land ownership is a source of social prestige and personal security. Selling land is generally associated with high transaction costs and risk. Surveying land costs money and the transaction may imply legal complications since ownership of land is not always clear. Furthermore, many peasants may fear they would not be able to repurchase land in the same area where they live.

It should be kept in mind that the loans the peasants need are relatively small and of a short-term character. There is a wide range of sources from which he may obtain these loans. Some of these charge no interest, such as relatives and friends. Others do, according to the size and length of the loans. Before selling his assets, the peasant is likely to exhaust the possibility of borrowing from these sources. Another important factor to be considered is the social and personal ties present in rural areas. Rural lenders are in daily contact with their clients, and in many cases they may also be related through family ties or lifelong friendship.

Thus, demand factors largely influence the interest rates charged in the informal credit market. These rates would not be so high were there not a large number of borrowers in desperate need of credit and willing to pay for it.

Imperfections in the Credit Market

The Dominican credit market is highly fragmented. Small and large producers have access to credit on very different terms. The former obtain their loans mainly from informal credit sources where interest rates are generally high, while the latter receive cheap credit from formal credit sources. Fragmented capital markets tend to worsen the distribution of income over time. The privileged group of producers with access to cheap credit can increase their incomes in different ways: through the profits received by the loans, through the free transfer of income implicit in underpriced credit, and through the resource transfer implicit in partial or total default.[55] The larger the size of the loan, the larger will the implicit subsidy be.

The performance of the rural credit market is intimately related to the land market. The concentration of large amounts of land in the hands of the *latifundista* allows him to have access to the organized credit market where interest rates are generally low and, due to the high rate of inflation, even negative in real terms. He can use land as a collateral, thus minimizing the risk for the lender.[56] The *minifundista*, on the other hand, possesses too little land to be used as collateral and is to a large extent excluded from the organized credit market. He has to rely on informal credit sources where interest rates may be 20 times as high. Thus, the *latifundista* tends to pay interest rates which are lower than the rate that will prevail were the capital market unified and competitive, whereas the *minifundista* often pays interest rates which are higher than the competitive rate:

$$i_m > i > i_l , \tag{7.1}$$

where i is the social cost of capital or the interest rate that will prevail under competitive conditions, and i_m and i_l are the interest rates paid by *minifundistas* and *latifundistas*, respectively.

Conclusions

The analysis in the present chapter has shown that there is a low availability of institutional funds for financing agricultural production and that the possibilities of financing capital formation by rural savings alone are very small. There is a great demand for credit to finance both consumption and production. Producers may obtain their loans from two different sources: the formal and the informal credit markets. Small producers obtain their loans mainly from informal credit sources where interest rates tend to be high, while large farmers obtain them from formal credit sources at very low interest rates.

The low availability of funds for financing production in the agricultural sector is deeply aggravated by the unequal distribution of available institutional funds between different producers. The policy of cheap institutional credit has mostly benefited large-scale farmers and, more recently, agrarian reform settlements. The agrarian reform is a politically important program and this may be the main reason behind the large amount of credit that has been allocated to the settlements. Besides, the settlements are administered by the *Instituto Agrario Dominicano* (IAD) and any application for credit has the support of this institution. The policy of cheap credit implemented by the *Banco Agrícola* has been an important determinant of the limited access that small producers have to this credit source and the high degree of concentration of the *Banco Agrícola* loan portfolio. Through the rationing mechanism loans have been allocated to the wealthier and less risky borrowers. This policy has tended to worsen the distribution of income in the rural areas. Large producers have benefited from subsidized credit while the overwhelming majority of the peasants have to procure their loans in the informal credit market and pay high interest rates.

Different factors may influence interest rates charged in the informal market. On the supply side, the simultaneous practice of moneylending and marketing activities of the intermediaries is generally argued to be a source of exploitation. However, credit is used among intermediaries as a means of attracting sellers. At the rural level, the number of intermediaries is generally large, the loans are small and of a very short-term character. Thus, the possibility of reaping monopoly profits on moneylending activities is not high. Other factors, such as risk, may be more important for explaining the high interest rates charged by some intermediaries. On the demand side, the rate of time preference among borrowers is likely to be high, since poor peasants generally attach a higher value to present than to future income. Hence, the demand for credit, in a short-run perspective, tends to be high and this in turn tends to make for high interest rates.

The issues discussed in this chapter show that the Dominican credit market is highly imperfect, since different producers face different interest rates. The imperfections in the credit market are largely the result of the government credit policies. The situation prevailing in the credit market is related to that of the land market. While *latifundistas* pay interest rates which lie below the equilibrium rate that would prevail in an unified and competitive credit market, the *minifundistas* pay interest rates above the equilibrium rate. As will be shown in Chapter 9, these market imperfections tend to lower the level of investment, employment and income in the sector and thus indirectly constitute an important push factor behind the rural-urban migration.

Notes

1. SEA (1976), Table 12-A, p. 211.

2. Ibid., pp. 27-28 and Table 12-A, p. 211.

3. The figures in Table 7.1 should be considered as approximations. Different figures on the same issue can be found in Del Rosario (1982), Table 10-B, p. 27. These figures are based on the same source as the SEA figures, namely the Central Bank survey on income and expenditure structure.

4. See Lewis (1955), p. 277. Until 1978, the most common assets among Dominican peasants were pigs. That year, a disease affected the pig population and the authorities decided to exterminate it. In order to implement this measure, the military forces had to intervene since many peasants were reluctant to sacrifice their pigs and see their "savings" vanish. That many peasant families manage some savings appears also to be confirmed by the accomplishments of the Rural Savings Mobilization Project implemented by the *Banco Agrícola* in 1984. In one and a half years, the number of savings accounts amounted to 23,735 with a total balance of more than 7 million pesos. 78% of the accounts had balances of DR$100.00 or less (Poyo (1986), pp. 13 and 35).

5. See Bouman (1977), pp. 181-218 and Bouman (1984), pp. 232-47. For a description of a similar rotating savings association, *sangue*, in Haiti see Laguerre (1976). The *san*, as a saving device, is very popular in the Dominican Republic (cf. Norvell and Wehrly (1969)). The practice of *san* probably originates from West Africa where the Yoruba term *esusu* denotes a similar phenomenon (Deive (1977), p. 34).

6. Norvell and Billingsley (1971), p. 396.

7. Cabrera (1984), p. 84.

8. See Adams (1978).

9. Lipton (1977), pp. 246-7.

10. Fisher (1930), p. 72.

11. Sharpe (1977), p. 42.

12. Ibid., pp. 54-57. The figures in Table 7.3 are only approximations, see ibid., note 11, p. 229.

13. This village is located in the central Cibao area. Coffee is the major crop. 55 percent of the households were small holders, 21 percent middle holders and 14 percent were relatively large holders. Around 10 percent of the heads of households were agricultural day laborers. This latter group may have some land but it produces neither enough food to meet family needs nor cash crops

for sale. Day laborers are faced with the problem of seasonality, and in order to feed their families they also depend on credit until the harvest comes. (See ibid., pp. 46-59.) For an exposition of the credit needs of tobacco growers in the Cibao area, see Ferrán (1976), pp. 85-90.

14. SEA-IICA (1977), p. 69.

15. For a discussion of these two credit sources, see Griffin (1974), pp. 229-34 and Tun Wai (1956), (1957).

16. FIDE was created in 1966 with the purpose of providing a channel in the Central Bank through which foreign and domestic funds could be transferred to different finance sources. (Cf. World Bank (1978:1), p. 23.)

17. These are the so-called bridge loans which have been widely used by rice mills, coffee exporters and more recently by melon exporting firms. (See Ladman and Liz (1988)). Tobacco exporters also use bridge loans (cf. Ferrán (1976), p. 145).

18. The importance of the *Banco Agrícola* as the leading credit source for agricultural activities has decreased relatively in the last decades. During the period 1955-59, the *Banco Agrícola* proportion of the total agricultural credit reached an average of 85.2 percent. In the period 1970-75, this proportion had fallen to an average of 60 percent. (See World Bank (1978:1), Table 7.9, p. 389.) In 1984, *Banco Agrícola* loans to the sector accounted for 69 percent of total agricultural credit. (See SEA (1986), Table 32, p. 66.)

19. Consejo Nacional de Agricultura (1984), pp. 5-6.

20. See Sharpe (1977), Chapters 4 and 5, and Ferrán (1976), pp. 88-89. In 1977, a local shopkeeper in the village of Rio Verde - La Vega was found to have more than 30 percent of his fixed and working capital on "fiao" (Ferrán (1976), p. 89).

21. Griffin (1974), p. 230. For a discussion on agricultural credit rationing, see González-Vega (1984), pp. 78-95.

22. This excludes land under sugar cane production. (See Chapter 9, Table 9.2.) This crop does not receive credit from *Banco Agrícola*. The State Sugar Council as well as the private mills procure their loans from other sources.

23. SEA (1981:1), p. 30. There is a clear bias towards livestock. Credit is not the only agricultural resource concentrated in this branch. In 1971, 63.4 percent of the total area under cultivation was occupied by pastures while the corresponding area in crops (excluding sugar) only amounted to 28 percent. However, in this same year, crops (excluding sugar) contributed with 31 percent of the total value of agricultural production and generated 52 percent of total employment in the sector, while livestock only contributed with 29 percent and 15 percent of total sector production and employment respectively. (See Chapter 9, Table 9.2 and World Bank (1978:1), Table 8, p. 14.)

24. SEA (1981:1), p. 30.

25. Ladman and Adams (1978).

26. See Chapter 9, Table 9.1.

27. See Chapter 6, Table 6.4.

28. See Banco Agrícola (1983), pp. 33-34 and Consejo Nacional de Agricultura (1989), Tomo II, Ch. 3.1, Table 12.

29. The average size of farms within the agrarian reform program is about 5 hectares. (See Chapter 6, Table 6.1.) Since 1978, all settlements were administered as collectives by IAD. Some settlements may obtain *Banco Agrícola* loans as collectives and this may be the reason why we find agrarian reform farms within the category of large farms.

30. See González-Vega (1984), p. 84.

31.*Compadrazgo* (literally, co-parenthood), is a relationship whereby a person becomes the godparent of a friend's or relative's child, thus binding the adults through special socio-economic and religious obligations. *Compadre* is the reciprocal term by which a male parent and a godparent address one another. (See Anschel and Wiegand (1983), p. 22.) For an analysis of the *compadrazgo* as institution see Gudeman (1972), pp. 45-71.

32. In 1975, it was estimated that 46 percent of the total agricultural credit was provided by informal sources. (See ONAPLAN (1983:1), p. 170.)

33. SEA-IICA (1977), p. 22.

34. Ibid., pp. 68-70.

35. This amount may be underestimated. Considering that small farmers produce 74.4 percent of the total rice production in the country and that the institutional credit supply to small producers has been very limited, it is possible that the proportion of credit supplied by these factories was higher than what the producers reported. Since the *Banco Agrícola* clients are generally not allowed to make use of this type of credit many producers are reluctant to give information on this subject. (See SEA-IICA (1977), p. 68.) However, the increased supply of *Banco Agrícola* credit to rice production on agrarian reform settlements may have reduced the dependence of rice growers on factory loans.

36. Ibid., p. 69.

37. See Ferrán (1976), p. 119. A similar situation is found among coffee growers. These producers largely depend on intermediaries for cash advances. Usually no interests are charged on these loans, but the borrower is expected to sell his crops to the lender. (See Sharpe (1977), Chapter 4 and Cabrera (1984), p. 55.) The same situation is found among cocoa growers. (See SEA (1984:1), p. 6.)

38. Pre-harvest sales are a very common practice among Dominican peasants. (See Sharpe (1977), p. 62.)

39. See Bouman (1984), pp. 242-43.

40. See Adams (1984), p. 66.

41. Ramírez E. (1984), p. 71. However, one has to keep in mind that this study is limited to three communities and cannot serve as a basis for generalizations. For a different view see Marchetti (1971), p. 127.

42. Calculated from Dauhajre (1984), Table 23, p. 68.

43. See World Bank (1978:1), p. 24.

44. Ibid.

45. González-Vega (1984), p. 78.

46. This is a common feature of most agrarian economies (Rao and Joshi (1979), p. 111). See also Adams et al. (1984) and González-Vega (1982). It was not until 1984 that the *Banco Agrícola* initiated a program to mobilize rural savings.

47. For a discussion of the lender's risk as a determinant of the rate of interest in agrarian economies see Rao and Joshi (1979), pp. 111-14.

48. Sharpe (1977), p. 37.

49. For a discussion on commodity stocks as an alternative to lending, see Rao and Joshi (1979), pp. 89.

50. World Bank (1978:1), p. 9. The real return on saving deposits is even lower, if one considers that the average rate of inflation during this period was around 13 percent. Ibid., p. 452.

51. Fisher (1930), p. 61.

52. For a discussion of the rate of time preference as a determinant of the rate of interest in a rural informal market, see Lundahl (1979), pp. 513-20.

53. Fisher (1930), p. 77. See also Lundahl (1979), p. 519.

54. Sharpe relates the situation of a small holder who, in order to pay accumulated debts and meet expenses when his wife gave birth, "was forced to sell a young pig and a calf which he had been painstakingly raising to build his stock." (Sharpe (1977), pp. 51-54.)

55. *Banco Agrícola* loans present a high rate of default. In 1983, DR$ 53 million of *Banco Agrícola* due portfolio (*cartera vencida*) were in default (*morosos*). (Consejo Nacional de Agricultura (1984), p. 7.) During the 1979-1983 period, the rate of default averaged 30% per annum (Cuevas and Poyo (1986), Table 6, p. 14). For a discussion on cheap agricultural credit and income distribution see González-Vega (1984), pp. 120-32.

56. In 1981, the *Banco Agrícola* extended 34,491 loans. These loans were extended under five different security categories. Only one was extended without guarantee. (See Banco Agrícola (1983), p. 13.)

8

The Use of Haitian Labor *

The employment problem in the Dominican Republic cannot be fully understood without taking into consideration the participation of Haitian workers in the labor market. As we saw in Chapter 2, underutilization of labor in the Dominican Republic is very high, especially in the agricultural sector. Rural workers are subject to high levels of underemployment at the same time as the most important agricultural activities face a tremendous labor scarcity. This labor shortage is continuously filled through imports of Haitian labor. In Chapter 2 we also argued that if Dominican workers prefer to face underemployment in the rural areas or to migrate to the cities risking unemployment, it must be because the working conditions and the wages paid for these agricultural activities are not sufficiently attractive. In this chapter, we will try to shed some light on the major paradox of the Dominican labor market, namely the coexistence of unemployment and underemployment with massive imports of labor. We start with an historical account of the participation of Haitian workers in and their importance for the Dominican economy. Thereafter, we analyze the Haitian immigration in economic terms and examine its impact on the Dominican labor market.

Labor imports are not new in the Dominican Republic. Ever since the rise of the Dominican sugar industry, the participation of foreign workers has been significant, and it has been increasing in importance throughout the years. Both historical and economic factors have played an important role in this situation.

Haiti and the Dominican Republic share the physical territory of the island of Hispaniola. They do not share it equally, however, as the

*This chapter draws upon material from Luhdahl and Vargas, "Haitian Migration to the Dominican Republic," in Lundahl, The Haitian Economy: Man, Land and Markets (London: Routledge, 1983).

Dominicans possess some two-thirds, with only half as much left to a Haitian population which is only slightly lower than the Dominican one. Both countries are poor, although poverty is not shared alike. Haiti is the poorest country in Latin America with a gross national product per capita which was estimated by the World Bank to equal some US$ 320 in 1984 whereas the corresponding figure for the Dominican Republic was 3 times as high, or US$ 970, according to the same source.[1] This income gap has led to a steady stream of temporary and permanent migrants from Haiti to the Dominican Republic for a full century.

In 1980, the number of Haitians living in the Dominican Republic was estimated to be 200,000, with some 70,000 in the labor force.[2] The Haitian immigrants have mainly been working in the sugar sector. However, in the last decade, the participation of Haitian workers in other agricultural and urban activities has been increasing.

In the Dominican Republic, sugar is the most important economic activity. Until recently, it has traditionally accounted for 40 to 60 percent of exports.[3] (The increased exploitation of minerals - ferronickel, gold and silver - and the boom experienced by tourism and the duty-free industrial zones has implied that the share of sugar exports has decreased during the last decade.) In terms of employment as well, the sugar industry is the largest single employer in the country, representing more than 70 percent of total industrial employment[4] and about 20 percent of agricultural employment.[5]

This chapter analyzes the different factors determining the high participation of Haitian workers in Dominican agricultural activities. It is shown that the presence of these workers constitutes an important factor in the performance of the Dominican labor market. It tends to press agricultural wages downwards, thereby discouraging Dominican workers from participating in certain agricultural activities.

The Rise of Sugar and the Use of Haitian Labor

As we recall from Chapter 4, the Dominican Republic was sparsely populated for a long time. A virtual mass emigration arose from the first Haitian invasions in 1801 and 1805. The population of Santo Domingo declined from some 125,000 in 1789 to 63,000 in 1819.[6] Venezuela, Colombia, Puerto Rico and, particularly, Cuba, all received large numbers of immigrants. A contemporary observer noted that: "All of the Spanish population decided to emigrate to other lands, and the only ones who did not leave were those who absolutely could not do so."[7]

The result was that in the 30 years up to 1819, the Dominican population was reduced by almost 50 percent. The Haitian occupation (1822-44) added another reason for emigration.[8] The population vacuum was filled by Haitians. By 1841, the population had increased to 130,000 as a result of Haitian immigration,[9] which was coupled during this period with the confiscation of landed property from Dominican emigrants and the outright annexation of a part of the Dominican territory as well.[10]

In spite of the Haitian immigration, the Dominican Republic continued to be sparsely populated at the beginning of the 1870s. In 1871, the total population of the country was estimated to be some 150,000.[11] Thus, mainly land-intensive goods, such as timber and cattle, were produced.

In the coastal region southwest of Santo Domingo, there were, however, some sugar plantations which continued to cultivate sugar cane and produce sugar by means of the traditional wooden sugar mills.[12] These plantations, however, faced a problem when it came to obtaining labor,[13] since cultivation and the manufacture of sugar were activities that required concentrated efforts.

Sugar soon became the most important product of the Dominican Republic - a fact that was to have an enormous importance for migration from Haiti, up to the present time. The expansion of Dominican sugar production began when large numbers of Cubans came into the country as a result of the aborted Cuban attempt to rid that island of Spanish sovereignty between 1868 and 1878.[14] During the course of a few years, some 5,000 Cuban exiles arrived in the Dominican Republic.[15] Some of these were planters who had brought some money that was invested in cane land and in modern machinery for sugar manufacturing using steam engines and railroads to transport the cane. The traditional animal-powered *trapiches* were replaced by modern *ingenios*. The first of these was founded in 1875 and during the next seven years another 30 sugar plantations were founded, representing an investment of 21 million Dominican pesos or US$ 6 million.[16]

The Cubans were soon followed by other foreigners, notably Americans. The *ingenios* quickly proved their superiority to the *trapiches*. The lower cost entailed in sugar production in the former quickly put the latter out of business. Overall sugar output, destined mainly for the United States market, increased rapidly, from some 8 million pounds in 1880 to 35 million pounds in 1886 and 100 million pounds in 1905.[17]

The new large-scale sugar technology required large amounts of labor. During the harvest season, the demand for labor was so great that it was possible to "gain in a few days the wage that before was gained only in weeks ... and even in months."[18] In three years, nominal wages increased 80 percent, and wages increased from 50 cents a day in 1880 to 90 cents in 1883.[19] In this way, many Dominican peasants were encouraged to leave their homesteads and move to the new sugar area, east of Santo Domingo, temporarily or permanently.[20]

The domestic supply of labor was, however, not large enough to satisfy the demand from sugar plantations and *ingenios;* immigrants were attracted as well. In the first place, the Dominican Republic was sparsely populated when sugar production began to expand. The subsequent rise in population figures was, to a large extent, due to immigration.[21] Secondly, work in the cane fields and in the sugar mills was highly temporary. Outside the harvest season there was nothing to do.

To some extent, this presented a conflict for those Dominicans who in addition to the work offered by the sugar companies also had some land to work.[22] The participation of Dominican workers in the sugar plantations soon came to an end, however. In 1884, due to lower prices and strong competition from European sugar producers, the Dominican sugar industry confronted its first crisis. Many producers were ruined and some *ingenios* were temporarily closed down. Those that managed to stay in production could no longer afford the high wages paid. At the same time, due to the monetary fluctuations that prevailed in the country in the late 1880s, and the high rate of inflation in the 1890s, real wages were significantly lowered and became therefore unattractive to the Dominican peasants.[23]

Finally, owing to the higher population pressure elsewhere - especially on the Haitian side of the border[24] - immigrant workers were prepared to work for lower wages than Dominicans. The first immigrants, known as *cocolos,*[25] came from the British West Indian islands. In 1884, Eugenio María de Hostos calculated that 35 *ingenios* used 5,500 domestic and 500 foreign day laborers.[26] By 1902, the number of *cocolos* working in the ingenios was around 4,500. The increasing number of immigrant workers attracted the attention of Dominican newspapers which argued about the depressing effect of immigration on wages. Accordingly, the sugar industry paid wages which were 50 percent lower than the wages the companies paid during the period when Dominicans were employed. The tendency to employ foreign workers continued. In 1919, 9,600 foreign *braceros,* cane-cutters, were hired by the sugar companies.[27] The *cocolos* were soon outcompeted by Haitian immigrants. The latter were less costly for the sugar producers. They only had to cross the border while the *cocolos* had to be brought by boat.[28] As early as 1885 the number of Haitians in the sugar industry was large enough to call forth vehement protests from Dominicans who suggested that immigration of Haitians ought to be stopped on racial grounds.[29]

Although hard data are scarce, since the immigration of Haitians was more or less uncontrolled, there is no doubt that immigration figures rose substantially as the sugar industry expanded during the next few decades. Between 1916 and 1925 the Ministry of Agriculture and Immigration published information regarding Haitian immigration in its *Memorias*.[30] The 1919-20 *Memoria* indicated that 10,124 Haitians were legally in the country, and the 1920 Dominican census recorded a total of 28,258 Haitian residents.[31] These figures are far from reality, since they do not take any account of the uncontrolled, clandestine migration.

During the American occupation of the Dominican Republic, from 1916 to 1924, active encouragement was given to the expansion of the sugar industry and hence to the demand for labor. During the First World War, the European beet sugar producers in for example Germany, France, Russia and Rumania were put out of competition. An excess demand for sugar ensued in the international market with prices in the Dominican Republic rising from US$ 5.50 per *quintal* (100 kilos) in 1914 to 12.50 in 1918 and 22.50 in 1920.[32] During this "Dance of the Millions," economic and social life in the Dominican Republic received a tremendous impetus from sugar production:

During this short period, some towns like Santiago, La Vega, San Pedro de Macorís and Puerto Plata became urban in a true sense. Sugar made of Macorís a city with large houses of reinforced concrete and streetcars in the streets to transport passengers. Puerto Plata and Santiago with tobacco and La Vega and Sánchez with cocoa, favored by the railroads, were also converted into noisy commercial centers where day after day new buildings and stores were erected and the families who had commercial interests became rich over night.[33]

Some cities installed electric lights and, for the first time, paved their streets and constructed sewerage systems, while the social clubs also proliferated, literary societies were founded and theaters and parks were constructed.[34]

The expansion of sugar production was also facilitated by a number of political measures. Some of these dated from the period before the occupation. As shown in Chapter 4, the Dominican government conferred important advantages on American investors by granting tax exemption on their products, and by lowering machinery and port duties for foreign investors to half of what local investors paid.[35] Most important of all, whenever roads, railroads or ports were deemed to be important for foreign enterprise, the Dominican government undertook to expropriate the necessary land. The *terrenos comuneros* were also subdivided so that the expanding sugar corporations could acquire the necessary land tracts for their operations. In 1919, a list was devised of 245 goods that could be imported free of duty and of 700 goods where only low duties had to be paid.[36] This favored sugar production in two ways. In the first place, machinery for the sugar *centrales* could now be imported without the payment of duty and secondly, since tobacco, cocoa and coffee could also be imported freely, relative prices were shifted in favor of sugar.

The sugar plantations did not fail to expand. When coffee and cocoa growers were ruined as a result of exposure to low-cost foreign competition and an export tax on these two products,[37] their land had to be sold, usually to sugar interests. The land legislation also facilitated this expansion. The American-owned Central Romana company, for example, was able to obtain title to what had hitherto been two whole villages. Some 150 Dominican families were evicted and the villages were burned to leave room for sugar production.[38] This type of transaction, together with different unpopular actions carried out by the American occupation forces, triggered off a peasant rebellion in 1920. It subsequently was put down by the Americans.

The occupation forces proceeded to regulate the labor supply directly. During the United States occupation of Haiti, the American administration actively encouraged emigration from that country. Haiti was considered to be overpopulated. In itself this was sufficient reason for the Americans to try to stimulate emigration. However, there was also a purely financial reason. Those who left the country legally had to pay an emigration tax, the proceeds of which were mainly used to liquidate the Haitian foreign debt which had been consolidated during the occupation into American hands.[39]

On the Dominican side, complementary measures were taken. In 1919, the American Military Governor issued a series of executive orders which all aimed at ensuring the supply of workers for the sugar industry (and for public works). Thus, it became prohibited to induce Dominican workers to leave the country or to transport them if the purpose was to employ them abroad. Haitian immigrants were not allowed to leave the Dominican Republic before the *zafra* for which they had come had finished. After that, however, the employers were to ensure that the Haitians departed no later than within a month.[40]

In spite of these regulations, the individual sugar *centrales* could not always be certain that enough labor would be forthcoming for the harvest. Thus, a letter from the Santa Fé sugar *ingenio* voiced the following complaints to the Department of Agriculture and Immigration:

> We have met the insuperable difficulty ... that the majority of the workers imported during this period that have not been repatriated have not remained with this sugar mill. Some have spread to the neighboring mills, others have returned by themselves to their respective countries without giving notice, others are dedicated in other places to tasks which differ from the agricultural ones, working in docks, factories, work-shops and warehouses situated in different localities.[41]

Other observers, however, held a different opinion:

> A Haitian day-laborer at home is paid 30 American cents by the Public Works Department, and 20 to 30 outside. The writer is positive, after surveys in both countries, that the Haitian profits by his move but that his presence has a bad effect on wage levels in Santo Domingo ... At any rate the Dominicans would be glad to dispense with their 100,000 or so of annual Haitian visitors. This alien and undesired element is about a tenth of the population of the country ...

> Cheap imported seasonal labor digs a pit of subsistence wages at the feet of the Dominican worker in the interest of the sugar business.[42]

The most interesting information conveyed by the quotation is the one regarding the wage level. If the figures given are reasonably correct, the movement of Haitians across the border would have tended to lead to a wage rate equalization between the Dominican Republic and Haiti. In the latter country, the average wage for unskilled labor was about 20 US cents in 1923.[43]

The Post-Occupation Period

When the American occupation of the Dominican Republic ended, in 1924, the Dominican economy was highly dependent on sugar production.[44] Sugar has continued to be the most important economic activity up to the present day. By the same token, Haitian immigration has maintained its importance. Both sugar production and migration have been subject to fluctuations, due on the one hand to the price level prevailing in the international sugar market and on the other to the state of relative political ease or tension between Haiti and the Dominican Republic. However, clandestine migration has hardly ever ceased even though at times the legal migratory flow has been interrupted.

The cane-cutters were not the only Haitians to migrate to the Dominican Republic during the 1920s and 1930s. Many other Haitians crossed over the vaguely defined borderline between the two countries. It was not until 1935 that the Haitian-Dominican border was finally demarcated.[45]

Parts of the western Dominican Republic became "Haitianized." Haitian money circulated freely and was accepted as legal tender even in Santiago. In the south Haitian money penetrated all the way to Azua.[46] The 1935 census reveals a figure of 52,657 Haitian immigrants, of whom 41,000 were qualified as *jornaleros*. Almost 50,000 lived in rural areas.[47] Hence virtually all those who did not count as family dependents were either sugar workers or squatter farmers. Some were also active in retail commerce.

The "Haitianization" of the border area did not fail to provoke anti-Haitian feelings in the Dominican Republic and measures were gradually taken to bring this process to a halt. As early as 1900, Hostos had suggested that the Dominican government should be instrumental in bringing colonists to the frontier to strengthen the Dominican influence and seven years later a law was passed which allocated government funds to such colonization. In 1925, a government commission was appointed to select suitable areas for agricultural colonies in order to stop the Haitian penetration.[48]

These measures failed to have any effect. In the mid-1930s, the price of sugar in the world market was rising slowly after having reached its lowest level so far during the twentieth century in 1933.[49] Haitians kept slipping into the Dominican Republic, legally or illegally, to work in the sugar industry.[50] In 1937, however, Haitian immigration came to an immediate stop. During that year, for reasons that are not quite clear, Trujillo unleashed a massacre of Haitian immigrants.[51]

The act consisted in indiscriminate butchering of from 15,000 to 25,000 Haitians - men, women and children - with machetes, clubs, knives, bayonets and (more seldom) firearms[52] at the beginning of October 1937, mainly along the border river Massacre, but also further eastward into Dominican territory, as far away as San Pedro de Macorís, Samaná Bay and Barahona.[53] This terrible deed which was carried out at the direct orders of *el Benefactor* sent many thousands of Haitians fleeing back to their country.

During the same month, the border between Haiti and the Dominican Republic was closed. The movement of Haitians across the border was stopped - but only temporarily. Although great care was taken by Trujillo to hide the facts of the massacre,[54] the news soon leaked to the world. The matter had to be settled via a symbolic payment of US$ 750,000.[55]

For some years Trujillo continued his efforts to repatriate Haitians. Between 1937 and 1944 a deportation program was in operation. This program officially required that an indemnity be paid to the Haitians who had improved the lands they were working before repatriation could take place, but in practice many Haitians were deported without payment up to the 1944-5 *zafra*.[56] To complement the deportation program, a 1938 law put a $500 head tax on all non-white immigrants to the Dominican Republic.[57] Four years later, a Haitian law also attempted to regulate the flow of migration.[58]

During the same year, Trujillo began a Dominicanization program. By constructing a number of villages along the border, backed by a series of military posts, Dominican families were given land in agricultural colonies and the town of Elías Piña was completely modernized and furnished with a host of public facilities and infrastructural arrangements. Roads were constructed and irrigation canals were dug. As a result, the border area was settled by Dominicans and the zone was incorporated with the rest of the country.[59]

Neither of these measures was efficient in preventing migration. The year after the massacre, 1938, Haitians again crossed the border in secrecy to work in the Dominican sugar industry,[60] and during the 1944-5 harvest season, the Haitian and Dominican governments again agreed that Haitian workers could hold jobs on the Dominican side of the frontier.[61] It is impossible to say how quickly the pre-1937 level of migration was reattained. The estimates of the number of Haitians working in Dominican agriculture in 1938 vary between 20,000 and 60,000. The latter figure includes the families of the workers.[62] In 1943 the number of Haitian cane-cutters was estimated to be some 30,000.[63] However, the reliability of these figures and their possible significance cannot be easily appreciated since the methods of estimation are likely to differ considerably.

The attitude of Trujillo towards Haitian immigration may have changed during the 1950s. As the Second World War was coming to an end, he perceived that the profit level of the sugar industry was sufficiently high to warrant an inroad. In 1949 he had the Ingenio Catarey, near Villa Altagracia, constructed as his private property. This was followed a year later by the Central Río Haina which was to be the largest sugar mill in the country. In addition to these construction activities, foreign-owned sugar estates and *ingenios* were also purchased until he controlled a majority of the sugar-producing companies in the country. Only the Casa Vicini and the South Puerto Rico Sugar Company (which owned the Central Romana) remained outside Trujillo's sugar empire,[64] which controlled 63 percent of the industry.[65] It seems that a major strategy followed by Trujillo in order

222

to force foreigners to sell their sugar enterprises was to enact in 1951 the Dominican Republic's first labor code. Trujillo campaigned for the application of the new labor laws on the privately owned sugar properties while overlooking the conditions endured by the workers in his own properties. Many private mill owners were accused of violating numerous articles of the Labor Code and were intimidated by the dictator to sell their properties.[66]

In 1952, Haiti and the Dominican Republic signed a recruitment treaty which was renewed in 1959.[67] Table 8.1 shows the number of workers who officially migrated during this period to work in Catarey, Río Haina and Central Romana in the 1950s.[68] Needless to say, all these figures (which are flows) are underestimates since they do not take illegal migration into account.

TABLE 8.1   Legal Migration of Haitian Sugar Workers to the Dominican Republic, 1952-58

Fiscal Year *	Number of Workers
1952-53	16,500
1953-54	9,800
1954-55	3,850
1955-56	2,800
1956-57	3,800
1957-58	3,500

*The Haitian fiscal year starts on 1 October.

Source: Edouard (1969), pp. 195-96.

Between 1957 and 1963 an estimated 30,000 workers crossed the border each year.[69] Allegedly the flow was maintained by means of various payments to Haiti's president, François Duvalier. "Dominican sugar mills ... paid Duvalier's contractors first of all $15 per head for each cane cutter delivered. Half of each cane worker's wages was then paid to him in Dominican pesos and half was sent to Haiti in dollars."[70] There, it was kept by the Duvalier officials.[71]

The Post-Trujillo Period

The Duvalier labor racket was brought to an end in 1963, when relations between the two countries deteriorated drastically, almost to the point of warfare, apparently because of Duvalier's attempts to drag Haitian political refugees out of the Dominican embassy.[72] Crossing the border became difficult since Duvalier created a war zone of three miles from which peasants, cattle and huts were removed and where anybody subsequently found there was simply shot.[73] It seems, however, that not even these drastic measures sufficed to bring migration to a standstill. Even during 1964, it was reported that some 3,000 Haitian sugar cane-workers were brought into the Dominican Republic.[74]

Three years later, the traffic was again in full swing. In 1966, a contract had been signed by the Haitian and Dominican governments according to which the Duvalier government was paid 60 dollars per cane-worker provided.[75] The following year, the Central Romana, which at that time accounted for some 30 percent of total employment in the sugar sector, employed 12,578 Haitians. Altogether, some 30,000 Haitian cane-cutters were estimated to be employed by Dominican firms.[76] In 1970, 42,142 Haitians lived legally in Dominican territory, but in addition some 45,000 were believed to have been in the country illegally, bringing the total to almost 90,000 people.[77] This figure may, however, be an underestimate. The *Oficina Nacional de Planificación* estimated that the true number was 100,000 in 1968 and the Dominican Border Commission gave a figure that was even higher: 200,000.[78] However, this figure presumably includes people of Haitian descent born in the Dominican Republic.[79] A third figure, of 300,000, estimated by Robert Rotberg, appears to be on the high side.[80]

Table 8.2 shows the number of Haitian cane-cutters who immigrated legally under contracts supervised by the Consejo Estatal del Azúcar (CEA) between 1966-67 and 1983-84.[81]

Table 8.2 is based on information from the CEA itself, both the number of workers and the amount of money received by the Haitian government may be underestimated. Only during the 1977-78 *zafra* was the work carried out exclusively by means of clandestine workers.[82] At that time, the Haitian government raised the price of Haitian cane-workers to 70 dollars, and as a result President Balaguer refused to allow any recruitment of Haitians and called upon the Dominicans to work in the harvest.[83] This temporary disagreement was, however, soon forgotten. The Haitian government received US$ 82 per worker supplied for the 1978-79 *zafra* and US$ 173 per head the following year. For 1980-81, some US$ 182 was paid for each of the 16,000 workers imported by agreement with the Haitian government.[84]

TABLE 8.2   Legal Immigration of Haitian Sugar Workers and Payments
to the Haitian Government, 1966-67 - 1983-84

Year of Zafra	Number of Legal Immigrants	Payments to the Haitian Government (in US$)
1966-67	14,000	n.a.
1967-68	10,000	n.a.
1968-69	n.a.	n.a.
1969-70	12,000	n.a.
1970-71	n.a	n.a.
1971-72	12,000	n.a.
1972-73	12,000	n.a.
1973-74	12,000	n.a.
1974-75	n.a.	n.a.
1975-76	12,000	n.a.
1976-77	12,000	n.a.
1977-78	0	0
1978-79	15,000	1,250,000
1979-80	16,000	n.a.
1980-81	16,000	1,600,000
1981-82	19,000	1,900,000
1982-83	19,000	2,250,000
1983-84	19,000	2,250,000

n.a.: information not available.

Sources: 1967-80: Veras (1983), p. 41. 1980-84: Veras (1985), p. 143.

The demand for Haitian labor in the sugar industry has recently
been estimated to exceed 100,000 during the harvest season. The CEA
alone requires about 70,000 and the central Romana a further 20,000
during the six months of the zafra. To this, we have to add the demand
from the Vicini mills and from the colonos or outgrowers who also
depend almost exclusively on Haitian workers.[85] As Table 8.2 shows,
only up to 19,000 are officially imported from Haiti and the number of
Haitians permanently living in the bateyes[86] were 26,100 in 1980 (see
Table 8.3 below). Then, if the above estimates are correct, the legal
supply falls short of demand by over 50,000 workers every year.
According to Roger Plant, who on behalf of the Anti-Slavery Society
investigated the situation of the Haitian workers in the Dominican
Republic in 1982, it is the way in which this latter group of workers are
recruited which has caused great international scandal.[87] In 1979 the
case of the Haitian migrant workers in the Dominican Republic was
taken up by the Anti-Slavery Society before the United Nations and in

1983 the ILO sent a commission of enquiry to the Dominican Republic in order to investigate allegations of violations of the Forced Labor Convention on the part of the Dominican Government. These charges were based on reports of how the Haitian workers had been recruited. In order to supply the sugar plantations, Haitians residing illegally in the Dominican Republic were systematically persecuted by the military and forced to work on the sugar plantations under threat of deportation. In 1983, the ILO Commission reported:

> Particularly in the Northern region, the Commission received testimony of arrests and harassment of the kind alleged, involving both forcible transport to the State-owned plantations in the area and confiscation of workers' money and belongings by members of the armed forces. In that region, there appeared to exist an organized atmosphere of repression on the part of the military, in concert with the local employers of labour, to keep the Haitians on the plantations and to force them to work there under threat of deportation ... this situation is contrary to the obligations of the Dominican Republic under the two (ILO) Conventions relating to forced labour.[88]

In spite of international denunciation, the practice of forced labor has continued and the evidences suggest that it has even escalated in recent years.[89] The import of Haitian *braceros* was highly affected by the political crisis that shook Haiti in 1985-86 and culminated with the fall of the Duvalier regime in January 1986. Under these circumstances, it proved impossible for the Haitian authorities to recruit the workers and thus fulfill the agreement made between the former Haitian government and the Dominican government. This incident brought about a political crisis between the two governments. The Dominican authorities had already advanced US$ 2 million to Duvalier and the new Haitian authorities did not want to recognize this debt since the sum was appropriated by Duvalier himself and, presumably, brought out of the country when he left it. At last, the issue was settled and the Haitian authorities agreed to pay back the 2 million.

An internal crisis then broke out in the Dominican Republic.[90] The 1985-86 *zafra* had already been delayed for some months and if *braceros* could not be recruited, the harvest could be easily lost. The government started a campaign to recruit Dominican workers but with very little success.[91] At the same time, Dominican military forces brought Haitian nationals living in the country to compulsory work in the sugar fields. This situation provoked the protest of the Catholic Church and other organizations in the country and in Haiti as well.[92]

In the end, the *zafra* was carried out mainly by Haitian residents, military brigades and public sector employees.[93]

The difficulties confronted by the Dominican government to carry out the 1985-86 zafra once again revived the question of the Haitian presence in Dominican territory. Traditionally, Dominicans have accepted the Haitian presence in the sugar sector as "natural," but when Haitians lately have begun to offer their services in other sectors as well, old fears of being overrun by the neighboring country have been revived in the internal Dominican debate. Some argue that since most of the Haitians residing in the country are illegal, they should either be repatriated or forced to work in the sugar fields since it was for that duty they were brought into the country. Newspaper articles pointed out that there were more than 500,000 Haitians residing in the Dominican Republic and, "although coming with the obligation to work in the *zafra,* most of them are dedicated to coffee picking, domestic work and witchcraft or the sale of lottery tickets, sweets and clothes."[94]

TABLE 8.3   Haitians Residing in Rural Areas of the Dominican Republic in 1980

	Total	In the Labor Force
In *bateyes* of the CEA	54,020	14,600
In *bateyes* of private *ingenios*	31,050	11,500
Coffee workers not taking part in the sugar harvest	9,380	4,690
Workers in other *fincas*	18,700	9,350
Total in rural areas:	113,150	40,140

Source: ONAPLAN (1981:2), p. 23.

The real number of Haitians residing today in the Dominican Republic is not quite clear. The above figure could be an exaggeration. In 1975, some 100,000 Haitians who had emigrated since 1950 were estimated to live permanently in the Dominican Republic.[95] This figure, however, appears to be an underestimate when seen in the light of what is by far the most reliable investigation of the quantitative aspects of Haitian immigration, undertaken by the *Oficina Nacional de Planificación* (ONAPLAN) in 1980.[96] This survey included those sugar workers who lived in the *bateyes* of the CEA and private *ingenios*, as well as those working on coffee *fincas* who did not also take part in the sugar harvest and, finally, those working elsewhere in Dominican agriculture. The distribution is shown in Table 8.3. ONAPLAN arrived at a total number of Haitians in the Dominican countryside of 113,150; 40,140 of whom were workers, the rest being family members. The survey did not include the urban districts but since it is well known that a substantial number of Haitians lived in Santo Domingo, La Romana, Higüey, San Pedro de Macorís, Santiago, Barahona and other cities, it was concluded that the number of Haitians in the country as a whole was not lower than 200,000, with some 70,000 in the labor force.

Now that we have some idea regarding the historical pattern and the magnitude of Haitian migration to the Dominican Republic, we may go on to analyze the causes in economic terms. As a starting point, we will give an account of the conditions meeting the migrants once they have crossed the border and the Dominican attitudes towards Haitian migrants.

Living Conditions of Haitian *Braceros* in the Dominican Republic

The majority of the Haitian immigrants in the Dominican Republic are *braceros* who work in the sugar sector. The living conditions meeting these people on the Dominican side of the border are extremely onerous. In 1979, the United Nations Anti-Slavery Society for the Protection of Human Rights[97] denounced that "the conditions of Haitian migrant workers could be compared only with slavery."[98] Such evidence is, however, not new in the history of Haitian migration to the Dominican Republic. The living conditions facing the Haitians once they have crossed the border have never been good. Writing in the early 1950s, Jean Price-Mars gave the following description of the situation:

The mills employing them provided a sui generis statute which meant that they belonged to the enterprise. Thereafter they no longer had the right or the freedom to leave the place to which they were attached and even less could they steal away from the task that had been assigned to them. The police took them as soon as they were found outside their sugar mill territory because they could not present the national *cédula* (their identity card), being equipped only with a residence permit delivered by the director of the enterprise to which they were attached.

They were paid according to the whims of the employer and, when the cutting season had ended, the employer could stop all wage payments. Then the poor immigrant was obliged to accept any task at any wage in order not to perish by hunger, and if, by chance, he did not find anything to do, he was forced to become a beggar, led astray into plundering. If the heavy arm of the law did not send him to jail, then the all too fast revolver sent him to join his equals in the cemetery of unknown tombs.[99]

Later observers give similar accounts. Roland Wingfield describes the scene in the early 1960s:

The life of the Haitian migrant worker in the Dominican Republic is reminiscent of slavery days. Their work consists of cutting or carting cane from dawn to dusk. The companies provide them shacks and hammocks but they have to shift for themselves for food. It is incredible how they subsist on a meager diet of a little rice and beans which they cook themselves on open-fires with occasionally some bread and very rarely some meat. They get their energy from the cane that they chew all day long while working. They are intent on saving money on a salary of a few dollars a week. They generally keep to themselves, gamble or play cards with each other. Some manage to cohabit with Dominican women but in this case they generally return to Haiti empty-handed or don't return at all ... The return trip is at the expense of the worker and sometimes uses up half of his savings. Some actually walk all the way back. Since the majority are illiterate, they are occasionally short-changed when converting their Dominican pesos into Haitian gourdes ...[100]

In 1973, a survey of the conditions of the sugar workers employed by the leading mills in the Dominican Republic found that only 58 percent of the houses inhabited by the workers (67 percent of whom were Haitian) had wooden floors, only 56 percent of all the houses used gas lighting and only 57 percent possessed any latrines. Altogether 36 percent of the people living under these conditions had to use the cane fields or other open fields instead. In addition, no clean drinking water was provided but the workers had to use a public trough which was also employed for washing animals.[101]

As for the contemporary situation, this is described in the report of the Anti-Slavery Society:

At the border, they are put on trucks and taken to a fenced staging post where they wait to be purchased either by colonos (Dominican private landowners) or by the representatives of the three main sugar producers ... En route the only nourishment provided is cane juice or brown sugar. At the staging post the Haitian workers are sold for 10 pesos ... each and taken by truck to the purchaser's farm.

On the farms the workers live in camps under conditions of extreme squalor, deprivation and danger to health. A family of five will share a 12' x 12' room furnished with a large bed, a table and a coal burner on the floor for cooking. There is neither electricity nor running water. Water for drinking is often from a polluted stream and a single latrine must suffice for forty people.

Wages are paid not by the hour but by the weight of cane cut and loaded. The rate is $1.30 per ton. A very strong, skilled cutter can cut three tons in a day but this does not guarantee the wage he will earn. The cutter is illiterate and cannot verify that the weigher's receipt is correct and the weigher is out to make a profit. A weigher who does not regularly send more cane to the mill than cutters are paid for will lose his job. As the cane dries it looses weight. This is not only an inducement to the weigher to cheat but also handicaps the cutter when he has to wait for transport to load his cane. The receipts can only be cashed fortnightly and the family needs money more often and so must borrow. They can sell their receipts but at a loss of 10% of their value. Every worker interviewed in a particular sample said this was a common occurrence ...

Conditions in the work-camps throughout the country are uniformly characterized by gross overcrowding and, though a few of the State Sugar Council (CEA) estates do have lavatories, the absence of hygiene and sanitation is otherwise pervasive. These conditions, coupled with poor clothing and malnutrition induced by an insufficient and unbalanced diet, result in the permanent existence and spread of acute and chronic diseases, most of which could be avoided and brought under control ...[102]

The terrible conditions endured by the Haitian migrant workers in the Dominican Republic are described in detail by Roger Plant.[103] The living and working conditions of these workers violate most of the postulates of the Dominican Labor Code and the guarantees stipulated in the recruitment contract are totally ignored. After describing the situation of these workers Plant concludes:

But it was not so much the poverty of the living quarters that caught my attention, as the fact that no attempt had been made to provide the Haitians with any amenities which might make their life more bearable ... In the CEA bateyes nothing had been done to give the Haitian encampments anything but a prison-like atmosphere. The Haitians were housed in small cell-like rooms in long prefabricated concrete blocks, with doors that could be padlocked if need be.[104]

Dominican Attitudes towards Haitians

The conclusion to be drawn from the descriptions in the previous section is that the Haitian cane-workers have had to work and live under conditions that have made it completely impossible to meet any basic needs in terms of food, clothes, shelter or otherwise. In addition, we must take into account the treatment accorded the Haitians from the point of view of human relations.

The Haitian immigrants, apart from confronting the difficult living and working conditions to which they are submitted, have to endure the scorn and humiliation of a society which considers itself different and superior. For many Dominicans, Haitians are inferior beings: ugly, dirty, barbaric, corrupt and superstitious. Through generations, this view of the Haitian has been nourished through hearsay and by literature based on a racist conception of history. These beliefs are widely held by the Dominican population, encouraged by mass media and by the consent of the authorities.

The Dominican prejudices concerning the Haitians are based upon, among other things, misinterpretations of Haitian religious beliefs (voodoo) which in themselves contain many traces of the African heritage. The old racist clichés of Africa mix with the Dominican beliefs. Thus, the Haitian is seen as a cannibal, whose life is immersed in witchcraft. He is endowed with supernatural powers and has relations with the devil. Rich, upper-class Haitians who do not practice voodoo are seen as decent and well educated.

In accordance with the view of the Haitian as a savage from the jungle his culture is also considered as inferior. The destiny of the Haitian is to disappear. His way of life, his conformity, his acceptance of his destiny, all this shows that he does not have any aspiration in life and the root of this evil is sought in his racial inferiority.[105] According to Marcio Veloz Maggiolo, there is an oral tradition behind all these beliefs, cultivated with a certain sadism.[106]

The attitudes of Dominicans towards Haitians must be seen in a historical perspective. They have their origin in the continuous Haitian invasions during the nineteenth century, especially the occupation of 1822-44. The mistrust and hatred that Dominicans felt at that time was nourished and increased by rational ideologists who preached nationalism with racist overtones. Dominican nationality was synonymous with white race, Spanish culture and Christianity, while the Haitians represented the black race, Africa, voodooism and superstition.[107]

This racist ideology has contributed to perpetuate alienation among the non-white population in the country. Although the majority of the Dominican population are blacks and mulattoes, the African inheritance is usually rejected. They are Dominicans, and only the Haitian can be identified as a real Negro. There is a deliberate confusion of racial definitions in the Dominican Republic. No one is considered as black. People are either white, light Indian, dark Indian, *mestizo* or *moreno*, but never black.

The African ancestry, and the centuries of slavery to which the blacks were submitted, is a forgotten chapter in Dominican history. The Dominican population knows very little about its African origins. Only the European and Indian influences are recognized. Slavery is generally ignored and so are the circumstances under which it was abolished in the country. Dominican historians, in general, do not acknowledge that it was the Haitians who put an end to slavery in the Dominican Republic. Instead they stress the brutality of the Haitian army and indulge in descriptions of Haitian "cruelties" towards the Dominican population. Thus the Dominicans are ignorant of the role of the Haitians in the liberation of the slaves.[108]

The contemptuous attitude towards Haitians is deeply rooted in the "Haitiphobia" which developed during the different Haitian raids in the nineteenth century, but its modern version was created during the Trujillo era. During this period, most Dominican writers and intellectuals saw a potential enemy in the Haitians. The continuous Haitian migration was seen as a permanent threat for the "preservation of the race," morality, language and customs of the Dominican people: "This immigrant is of the worst kind. Totally black, almost naked, nearly always hungry and sick, nomadic tribes deprived of everything, dark caravans bringing misery, superstition, immorality, voodoo, Africanization ..."[109] The quotation is from a well known Dominican historian. Another prominent colleague of his presents an identical view:

> This type is frankly undesirable. Being of a purely African race, he cannot represent any ethnic incentive at all to us ... [he is] a badly nourished and worse clad man; he is feeble, although very prolific, given his low level of living. For this very reason, the Haitian who encroaches upon us lives contaminated by numerous and capital vices and is necessarily affected by sickness and physiological deficiencies which are endemic at the bottom of that society.[110]

Anti-Haitianism was preached loudly during the Trujillo era and the massacre of 1937 can be interpreted as an attempt to put an end to the Haitian presence in the country. This incident was hailed by Trujillist ideologists. Joaquín Balaguer, later president of the Dominican Republic, approved of Trujillo's action with the following words:

> The problem of the race is the principal problem of the Dominican Republic ... If the nationalization of the border is implemented as planned by President Trujillo, then the future of the Dominican

Republic has been ensured. The glory that Trujillo shall receive by
initiating, conducting and bringing the process of nationalization to a
fortunate end will not be inferior to the glory corresponding to that of the
creators of the Republic.[111]

The obscure tradition of prejudices against the Haitian immigrants
is carried on today as well, as Haitians continue to work in sugar cane-
cutting and other agricultural activities. It is kept alive by politicians
who try to blame the high levels of unemployment persisting in the
country on the presence of Haitian nationals in the country. A good case
in point is Elías Wessin y Wessin, leader of a right-wing party, who,
using an exaggerated estimate of the number of Haitians living in the
Dominican Republic - 500,000 - stated that action ought to be taken to
stop this "pacific invasion."[112] The country's present president, Joaquín
Balaguer, as late as in 1983 exposed a wide range of racist prejudices
and fears of Dominicans being overrun by the "racially inferior"
Haitians. In his book *"La isla al revés"* he delivers notions such as: " ...
the black race when it finds itself in a primitive, social condition,
reproduces itself in a geometric progression very similar to that of the
most prolific plants."[113] It is not at all uncommon to find anti-Haitian
"news" in the newspapers which keeps the prejudices alive.[114]
Naturally, the situation under which the Haitian cane-workers are
forced to live and work in the Dominican Republic helps to preserve
and encourage prejudices Dominicans have about the culture and way of
life of the Haitian people in general. At the same time, these
prejudices reinforce the Dominicans attitude towards cane-cutting
which is generally considered as a slave activity.

Effects of Haitian Migration on the Dominican Labor Market

After this description of the living conditions confronting the
Haitians in the Dominican Republic and the Dominican attitudes
towards Haitians, two questions arise:

1. Why are Haitians, in spite of the bad living conditions and the
   often hostile attitudes they meet, attracted to the Dominican
   Republic?
2. Why are Haitians, and not Dominicans, hired if the Dominican
   attitudes towards Haitians are so negative?

To answer these questions, we must look at what determines the
supply of Haitian and Dominican sugar workers.

The Supply of Haitian Migrants

In traditional labor market analysis, migration takes place when wage differences are sufficiently large to outweigh the costs connected with migration between two areas. In the well-known Harris-Todaro model of rural-urban migration, for example, movement takes place when the expected urban wage (the wage rate in formal employment weighted by the probability of getting a job) exceeds what the migrant earns at his place of origin.[115] The same should apply in the situation of the Haitian migrant. As long as a Haitian perceives that he can earn more during the relevant time period in the Dominican Republic than at home, and this difference is not outweighed by the costs he incurs by migrating, we should expect him to move. As we have seen in the foregoing, these costs are not only pecuniary (e.g., transport costs) but also of a social kind. The migrant has to break from his customary environment and go to live for longer or shorter periods under difficult conditions where discrimination against his nationality is widespread.

How large are the wage or income differentials that induce Haitians to move across the border? Unfortunately, little is known in quantitative terms, but it is possible to arrive at some approximations of the relevant figures. Around 1973, the average daily wage for a sugar cane-cutter in the Dominican Republic was 2 pesos. During a good sugar year the *zafra* lasts for some 200 days.[116] Thus, the annual income in 1973 for a cutter who did not undertake any other work amounted to 400 pesos, or as many US dollars at the official exchange rate. If the parallel market exchange rate (assumed to represent the equilibrium rate) of 1.20 pesos per dollar is used, the figure becomes US$ 333.

For Haiti, the data are not as good. Clarence Zuvekas has provided what appears to be the best estimate (based on World Bank data).[117] According to this, per capita personal income in rural districts lay around US$ 96 in 1975. Assuming, as the World Bank does, in its calculations of income distribution figures for 1970, that the ratio between personal income per capita and income per person employed in agriculture is approximately 1 to 3,[118] this gives us a figure of US$ 288 per worker for the entire year. Adjusting for inflation between 1973 and 1975, assuming that no other changes took place,[119] we arrive at a 1973 figure for Haiti of US$ 203 for the average member of rural labor force in Haiti.[120]

No doubts it is these differences in earnings between the two countries that attracts the Haitians to work in the Dominican Republic. Plant reports that

> ... all Haitians interviewed had come with the expectation of realizing significant savings. I received markedly different claims of the amounts

that had been saved in the past, and which they expected to save during the current harvest. A few claimed to have put aside $200 or more. Others denied saving anything, or gave a figure in the region of 20 to 30 Dominican pesos. From my own estimates, the average saving at that time was a paltry sum of between 30 and 80 pesos for six months of back-breaking work.[121]

In 1985, the wages for cane workers were increased to 2.83 pesos per ton. Assuming a worker could cut an average of two tons per day, his earnings will still be below the minimum wages for agricultural workers which at this time was 8 pesos per day. Furthermore, in the last few years, following the agreement of the Dominican government with the IMF, food staples have experienced significant price increases at the same time as the Dominican peso has been heavily devalued. Thus, the possibilities for the Haitian migrants to realize significant savings have been diminished. Still, in January 1986, in spite of the fact that fierce violence struck both urban and rural areas of Haiti at the same time as the Haitian church and the students strongly protested against the recruitment process and the treatment given to Haitian workers in the Dominican Republic, thousands of Haitian peasants made their way to the Leogâne market place to register for the next harvest. It was not until the degree of violence had reached its climax which culminated with the death of three peasants, that the Haitian government gave up the recruitment process.[122]

The Supply of Dominicans

The second question posed at the beginning of the present section was why Haitian and not Dominican workers are hired by the sugar producers.[123] The employment situation in the Dominican Republic is characterized by substantial underemployment in rural areas.[124] Of course, the level of underemployment varies throughout the year depending on the season, but even so it does not disappear completely even during the busiest months of the year.[125] Consequently, one would expect that the sugar industry would be able to procure workers within the Dominican Republic itself without having to resort to Haitian immigrants. However, this is not the case. The Haitians have played a very important role in Dominican sugar production for a full century and continue to do so today. The inquiry undertaken by the *Oficina National de Planificación*, referred to above, found that more than 77 percent of the labor force in the 12 state-owned sugar mills consisted of Haitians in 1980.[126] The Dominicans are found mainly in supervisory positions and positions requiring special skills.

To explain this extensive use of Haitians, we must look not only at the supply of Haitian workers, but also at that of Dominicans. It is well known that it is difficult to recruit Dominicans to the sugar industry. The survey of the Dominican labor market undertaken by the International Labor Office in the early 1970s offers some reflections on this subject. In the first place, it was found that more than 80 percent of the rural labor force consisted of people who owned some land. Only 20 percent were landless. Of those owning land some 60 percent were cultivating 2 hectares or less. This group supplemented their incomes with work outside their farmsteads. Such work could be found for example in the sugar industry, although these *minifundistas* are not as a rule particularly interested in that type of work. They work instead on the farms of those who have more land. In this way, they manage to keep busy for only six months per year. The remainder of the time they are idle.[127]

This period of idleness coincides to some extent with the period during which the sugar harvest takes place. Nevertheless, the *minifundistas* are not particularly eager to work on the sugar estates. According to the ILO mission, the reason for this decision is that the *minifundistas* cannot leave their farms for any great length of time to work on the sugar estates. Moreover, the *minifundistas* live in regions other than those where the sugar estates are located. The highest rural population densities are found in the Cibao Valley and in the Valle del Yaque del Sur but the sugar estates are in the eastern parts of the country where the population density is low.[128] At the same time, the Haitians provide efficient competition in the rural labor market. They are ready to work long hours for low wages and to live under the conditions described above.

The ILO mission sums up the situation by referring to the existence of a vicious circle in the sugar labor market:

The imports of Haitian braceros and the resistance of the small farmers of other regions to abandon their own cultivations during five or six months reinforce and influence each other reciprocally. The sugar enterprises bring braceros because of their - justified - fear that the Dominicans will not come from the zones where they live and the Dominicans manifest strong resistance and strong prejudices against cutting cane because they know that the enterprises have imported braceros and that, consequently, no vacant jobs exist. The Dominicans do not come to the cane-cutting because of the low wages that are paid and the bad living conditions that are offered, and wages remain low and living conditions bad because the imports of cutters continue. The original circumstances and factors reinforce each other in this manner, reciprocally, in a vicious circle.[129]

236

The situation may also be illustrated with the aid of Figure 8.1. On the horizontal axis we measure the demand and supply in the sugar labor market. On the vertical axis we have the wage rate and the marginal revenue product of labor to the sugar industry (the demand curve for labor).

FIGURE 8.1   Wage Rate Determination in the Sugar Labor Market

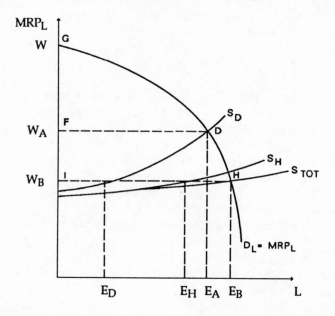

If only Dominicans had been employed in the sector, with given inputs of land and capital E_A workers would have been employed at a wage rate of w_A. However, in addition to the supply of Dominican workers (given by the S_D curve), we also have a supply curve for Haitian workers (S_H). This curve starts at a point on the vertical axis which lies below the corresponding point of the S_D curve. In addition, the S_H curve is less steep than the S_D curve which indicates that it takes a smaller wage increase to obtain a given number of Haitians at the margin than it takes to obtain the same number of Dominicans. Adding the two supply curves horizontally gives the total supply of labor (S_{TOT}). The intersection of the latter curve with the demand (marginal revenue product) curve gives the total employment E_B which is higher than when no Haitians are allowed, and the wage rate w_B, which is lower. By recruiting Haitians, the sugar companies can increase their surplus over wages from DFG in the figure to HIG, and with given inputs of land and capital also their profits. By moving leftwards from the intersection point H until we reach the S_H and S_D curves respectively, we also find that a comparatively large number of Haitians (E_H) and few Dominicans (E_D) are employed. (The situation illustrated in Figure 8.1 also applies to other producers employing Haitian workers). At least in the short run, when the possibilities of substituting capital for labor are limited, we should expect the demand curve to be very steep, demand being highly inelastic. In this perspective, low wages appear to be mainly a supply-side phenomenon.

In some Latin American countries, the unequal distribution of land, in combination with the few alternative employment opportunities available in the rural areas, could imply that in certain areas *latifundistas* enjoy monopsony power in the labor market.[130] However, in the Dominican case, the wages paid by the *latifundistas* would, at the margin, tend to be equal to the returns the *minifundista* obtain by working his own land. In this sense, the imperfections illustrated in equations (6.1) and (7.1) in relation to the land and credit markets, respectively, are not likely to arise in the labor market, and we have:

$$w_m = w = w_l, \tag{8.1}$$

where w represents the "competitive" wage level in agriculture and w_m and w_l are the wages paid by *minifundistas* and *latifundistas* respectively. Moreover, as illustrated in Figure 8.1, the massive imports of Haitian workers tend to lower the general level of wages in the sector. The low bargaining power of the rural worker (Dominican and Haitian alike), who is generally illiterate, unorganized and competing with a large number of other workers, weakens the possibility to enforce minimum wage legislation in the rural areas.[131] As we have shown, agricultural wages are, in general, considerably below the legal established minimum, especially in the case of the Haitian workers.

The increasing criticism, both on the domestic and the international level, of the working and living conditions endured by the Haitian cane-cutters has caused a great deal of embarrassment for the Dominican authorities. At the same time, the fear that the recent political changes in Haiti may have a negative effect on the supply of Haitian *braceros* has increased the pressure on the Dominican government to "Dominicanize" the *zafra*. However, a precondition for a "Dominicanization" of the *zafra* is that wages are increased to a level attractive to Dominicans and that the living conditions in the *bateyes* are significantly improved. These conditions can hardly be attained in a situation where the sugar industry is confronting one of its deepest crises. Due to protectionist policies in Europe and the United States and the increasing competition from US corn-syrup producers, sugar prices have been falling since the mid-seventies. The world market price fell from a level of US$ 0.30/lb. in 1974 to US$ 0.05/lb. in 1984.[132] Dominican producers' average production cost of raw sugar was estimated at US$ 0.09/lb. in 1976.[133] In 1974, when large profits were made by the sugar producers, the government authorized the sugar companies to retain part of the taxes to improve productivity and the living conditions of their workers.[134] However, as shown above, the results of this measure have been negligible.

Conclusions

The migration of Haitians to the Dominican Republic dates from the colonial era. However, the modern phase of this migration began with the rise of the sugar *ingenios* during the last third of the nineteenth century. The substitution of *ingenios* for small *trapiches* that had traditionally been used for the production of sugar led to an increased demand for labor. The Dominican supply of labor was inadequate. However, large numbers of Haitians were recruited, legally or illegally. This pattern has persisted ever since. Deterioration of political relations between Haiti and the Dominican Republic as well as fluctuations in world market sugar prices have influenced the magnitude of the migration, but the flow has never been completely stopped. It is estimated that a minimum of 200,000 Haitians were residing, permanently or temporarily, in the Dominican Republic in 1980.

The living conditions confronting the sugar workers in the Dominican Republic are extremely onerous most of the time. Various observers have classified them as reminiscent of slavery. The living quarters are utterly primitive. Sanitary facilities are lacking and drinking water is difficult to obtain. The cane-cutters work long days for low wages. All kinds of diseases are common. The Haitian immigrants also have to endure the attitude of the Dominicans who consider Haitians to be inferior beings, different in color and culture, utterly alien and a negative influence on Dominican society.

In spite of these facts, the majority of the sugar workers are Haitians. Attracted by the difference in earnings between the two countries, thousands of Haitians every year cross the border, legally or illegally. These people manage to outcompete the Dominicans for jobs, especially in the sugar industry, but also in other branches of agriculture. Most of the Dominican rural labor force consists of people who have some land to cultivate and who therefore, given the low wages in the sugar industry and the living conditions prevailing there, prefer to stay on their farms or to migrate to the cities. For these reasons, the majority of the sugar workers in the Dominican Republic are Haitians.

The presence of a huge number of workers, whose difficult economic situation forces them to accept low wages and endure living conditions that Dominicans do not accept, tends to lower the general level of wages in the agricultural sector. This discourages the Dominican rural workers from participating in certain agricultural activities. Thus, indirectly, the increasing use of Haitian labor in Dominican agriculture constitutes another push factor of migration.

Notes

1. World Bank (1986), Table 1, p. 180.

2. ONAPLAN (1981:2), p. 38.

3. Banco Central, *Boletín Mensual*, various issues. The importance of sugar in total exports decreased from 44% in 1971-75 to 10% in 1984-87. (Ceara (1989), Table 19, p. 40.)

4. Refers to the period 1971-79. (ONAPLAN (1983:2), p. 55.)

5. Refers to 1971. (See Chapter 9, Table 9.2.)

6. Hoetink (1971), p. 43.

7. Heredia y Mieses (1955), p. 162.

8. For details see Moya Pons (1972), especially Chapter 2.

9. Candler (1842), p. 132.

10. Palmer (1976), pp. 67, 69.

11. Hoetink (1971), p. 44.

12. Around Baní at the beginning of the 1870s some 100 of these *trapiches* were to be seen and around Azua some 100-200 (ibid., p. 19). Samuel Hazard, who visited the Dominican Republic in 1871, mentions on the subject of the *trapiches* that "these were actually the only kind of sugar-mills I saw in operation in any part of my journey in St Domingo" (Hazard (1873), p. 370).

13. Hoetink (1971), p. 44.

14. For details regarding this war, see e.g. Thomas (1971), Chapters 20-22.

15. Moya Pons (1980), pp. 407-8.

16. Ibid., p. 409.

17. Knight (1928), p. 25.

18. Eugenio María de Hostos, quoted by Hoetink (1971), p. 33.

19. Del Castillo (1982), p. 7.

20. As a result, a lack of fruits, vegetables and other food crops was observed, for example, in the capital (Hoetink (1971), pp. 33-35).

21. Ibid., p. 44.

22. This is however, not to say that the sugar industry did not attract domestic workers.

23. Del Castillo (1982), pp. 9-13 and Báez E. (1978), p. 45. See also Baud (1986), pp. 30-31.

24. During the last quarter of the nineteenth century, land had clearly become a scarce factor in Haiti, as a result of population growth. (Cf. Lundahl (1982), where the determinants of Haitian migration to Cuba during the 1890-1934 period are discussed. On the supply or push side, the same factors were active in promoting migration to the Dominican Republic.)

25. Hoetink (1971), p. 64.

26. Quoted by ibid., p. 31.

27. Del Castillo (1982), p. 15.

28. Another reason for preferring Haitians was that the *cocolos*, unlike the Haitians, could more loudly demand their legal rights since they counted on the protection of the British authorities. (Cf. Del Castillo (1979), pp. 3-43.)

29. Hoetink (1971), p. 64.

30. The publication of these *Memorias de la Secretaría de Estado de Agricultura e Inmigración* was discontinued in 1926.

31. Acosta (1981), p. 136 and *Primer censo nacional 1920* (1923), p. 147, respectively.

32. Moya Pons (1980), p. 480.

33. Ibid.

34. Spitzer (1972), p. 331.

35. Knight (1928), pp. 47-48. Ibid., Chapter 12, gives details regarding the expansion.

36. Spitzer (1972), pp. 253-54.

37. Jiménes Grullón (1965), p. 168.

38. Knight (1928), p. 350.

39. Lundahl (1982). For details regarding the American debt policy, see Lundahl (1979), pp. 370-72.

40. Hernández (1973), pp. 56-61.

41. Quoted by ibid., p. 61.

42. Knight (1928), p. 158.

43. Millspaugh (1931), p. 143.

44. Moya Pons (1980), p. 494.

45. Palmer (1976), pp. 84-86.

46. Moya Pons (1980), p. 519. However, one has to keep in mind that the "penetration" was not one-sided. The Dominican presence was also strong in Haiti. Dominican cattle and goods were sold on Haitian markets (Baud (1986), pp. 34-35) and some Dominicans owned land in Haiti. (Cf. Lundahl and Lundius (1987).)

47. Hernández (1973), pp. 53-54. The absolute figures are probably not too reliable.

48. Machado Báez (1955), pp. 230-31.

49. Lundahl (1979), pp. 281-82.

50. Hicks (1946), p. 104, estimates that more than 200,000 Haitians were at this time living in the Dominican Republic. This figure appears to be exaggerated, however.

51. Heinl and Heinl (1978), p. 528.

52. Explicit orders had been given not to use firearms so that the killings, which were carried out by Dominican soldiers, could later be blamed on "angry Dominican farmers" (Hicks (1946), p. 113).

53. For details regarding the massacre see e.g. Hicks (1946), Chapter 12; Galíndez (1962), pp. 196-201; Crassweller (1966), pp. 149-64; Heinl and Heinl (1978), pp. 525-30. See also García (1983), Castor (1983) and Cuello (1985).

54. Thus, the British minister in Ciudad Trujillo reported that "care was taken not to molest Haitians working or living on foreign-owned property or in towns where foreign witnesses might be." Quoted by Heinl and Heinl (1978), p. 528. This meant that, the Haitian *braceros* at the American-owned ingenios were spared (García (1983), p. 33).

55. Vincent (1938), pp. 219-25; Pierre-Charles (1965), pp. 111-12. In reality the indemnity was reduced to US$ 550,000 (Crassweller (1966), pp. 158-59).

56. Palmer (1976), p. 88.

57. Ibid., p. 90.

58. Ibid., p. 91.

59. Ibid., Moya Pons (1980), p. 520.

60. Wingfield (1966), p. 97.

61. Hernández (1973), p. 56.

62. The former figure derives from Bosch (1979), p. 259. The latter, which is probably an overstatement (Corten (1970), p. 714) comes from Romain (1959), p. 33.

63. Jiménez Grullón (1943), p. 22.

64. Moya Pons (1980), p. 517. The Central Romana was sold to the multinational Gulf and Western in 1967. Later, in 1984, it was sold to a Cuban American Corporation (Plant (1987), p. 35).

65. Franco (1967), p. 76.

66. Plant (1987), pp. 22-23.

67. Veras (1983), p. 53.

68. Edouard (1969), p. 195.

69. Gingras (1967), p. 115.

70. Ibid., p. 115.

71. Ibid., pp. 115-16.

72. For details, see e.g. Diederich and Burt (1972), Chapters 13-14; and Heinl and Heinl (1978), Chapter 14. An account of the events on the Dominican side

is given by John Bartlow Martin (1975), Chapter 18. Martin was at the time United States Ambassador to the Dominican Republic.

73. Heinl and Heinl (1978), p. 638.

74. Gingras (1967), p. 115.

75. Veras (1981), Anti-Slavery Society (1979), p. 4. Cf. also Pierre-Charles (1969), pp. 120-21.

76. Corten (1970), p. 716.

77. Díaz Santana (1976), p. 129.

78. Ibid.

79. Segal (1975:1), p. 212.

80. Rotberg and Clague (1971), p. 249. Cf. Segal (1975:1), p. 212.

81. The 1966 agreement between the Haitian and Dominican governments expired in 1971 and was never renewed, but both governments have continued to act according to it (Veras (1981) and (1983), p. 53).

82. It was stated officially that the *zafra* had been "Dominicanized" but this was not true. Finally it was recognized that more than 16,000 Haitians were working in the seven *centrales* of La Romana, Caei, Colón, Angelina, Barahona, Monte Llano and Amistad. (The daily newspaper *El Caribe* on 30 July 1971 provided a figure of 16,288 Haitians. Hernández (1973), p. 65.)

83. Anti-Slavery Society (1979), p. 4.

84. Veras (1982), pp. 40-41.

85. Plant (1987), p. 66. This seems to be, however, an overestimation, especially when compared with the findings of the ONAPLAN survey from 1980. (See ONAPLAN, 1981:2.)

86. A *batey* is a small community located in the neighborhood of a sugar mill.

87. Plant (1987), p. 66.

88. ILO Official Bulletin, Vol. LXVI, Report of Commission of Enquiry, 1983, p. 135. Quoted by Plant (1987), pp. 70-71.

89. See ibid., especially Chapter 6 and Moya Pons et al. (1986), pp. 194-96. Since 1986, the clandestine recruitment of Haitians has been intensified. This became evident when in January 1989, a truck carrying Haitians from the border to CEA cane fields was involved in an accident where 48 were killed and 33 were severely injured. Apparently no one took responsibility for the recruitment of these workers. (*Listín Diario* , 28-01-1989.)

90. See Dominican newspapers during the period January-April 1986, especially *Hoy* (2-2-1986; 21-2-1986; 4-3-1986; 5-3-1986; 6-3-1986; 12-3-1986; 14-3-1986; 15-3-1986).

91. In March 1986, President Jorge Blanco recognized that only five of the CEA *ingenios* were operating. These employed a total of 8,866 *braceros* of whom only 2,137 were Dominican and the rest were Haitian nationals. (See newspaper *Hoy* 6-3-86.)

92. See Amigo del Hogar (1986), pp. 17-19 and 37-39 and Plant (1987), pp. 85-90.

93. Military groups and civilian government workers were integrated to the *zafra* attending a call from President Jorge Blanco. (See newspaper *El Nacional* 11-2-1986, p. 38 and *Ultima Hora* 10-2-1986. See also *Ahora* (1986), p. 17-19.) The difficulties to recruit cane cutters have continued. In 1989, it was estimated that only 11,000 out of the 40,000 needed *braceros* were at work. The *braceros* were leaving the cane fields for the better paid urban construction activities. (See newspaper *El Siglo* 15-5-1989.)

94. See Newspaper *Hoy*, 2-2-1986, p. 3. Recently, the minister of labor declared that there are one million Haitian nationals residing in the Dominican Republic and that less than 10 percent had legal status. (See newspaper *El Caribe*, 26-4-89.)

95. Segal (1975:1), p. 198.

96. ONAPLAN (1981:2).

97. Anti-Slavery Society (1979). Some argue that the actual living conditions of cane workers are much worse than those that existed under slavery. (Moya Pons et al. (1986), pp. 196-99.)

98. Anti-Slavery Society (1974), p. 1.

99. Price-Mars (1953), pp. 329-30.

100. Wingfield (1966), pp. 98-99, 100.

101. Sánchez de Bonilla (1973). According to the 1983 survey, living conditions in the *bateyes* have become worse. (See Moya Pons et al. (1986), pp. 465-528.)

102. Anti-Slavery Society (1979), pp. 4-7. The same picture in much more detail emerges from the description in Lemoine (1983). Cf. also the documents contained in World Council of Churches (1980); Veras (1985), pp. 73-104; Madruga (1986), Chapters 7-8; Moya Pons et al. (1986) and Plant (1987).

103. Plant (1987).

104. Ibid., p. 104.

105. Veloz Maggiolo (1977), pp. 105-6.

106. Ibid., p. 106.

107. See Cassá (1976), pp. 61-85.

108. Deive (1979), pp. 67-73.

109. Rodríguez Demorizi (1955), p. 46.

110. Peña Batlle (1954), pp. 67-68.

111. Balaguer (1947), pp. 124-25.

112. Quoted by *Haití Información*, No. 18, February 1980, p. 2.

113. Balaguer (1983), p. 147. See also ibid., p. 156. A great deal of the arguments Balaguer presents in this book are based on obscure sources from the first quarter of this century. In this particular case a book from 1911 by a certain Juan Rogers Commons. An inquiry carried out in 1986, by the *Consejo Nacional de Población y Familia* among different Dominican leaders, shows

244

244

244

244

244

244

244

244

244

244

244

244

244

244

244

244

244

244

244

244

244

244

244

244

244

244

244

244

244

244

244

that 72 percent of these leaders considered that "a pacific invasion of Haitians is taking place in the Dominican Republic." (*Hoy* 17-3-1986.)

114. For example, the front page of *El Nacional* (2 February 1981) relates under the heading of ¡*Haitianos!* an incident in which one hundred Haitian nationals were rounded up by Dominican troops in the northern part of the country. One of the Haitians was said to have a "human head" and "other articles for the practice of witchcraft" among his belongings. After the incident, the prisoners were brought to the sugar cane fields in the eastern part of the country.

115. Harris and Todaro (1970). We will discuss this model further in Chapter 10.

116. OIT (1975), p. 136.

117. Zuvekas (1978), p. 123.

118. International Bank for Reconstruction and Development (1976), Table 1.4.

119. Institut Haïtien de Statistique (1976), p. 32, gives the cost of living index for Port-au-Prince as 187.6 in 1973 and 265.8 in 1975.

120. Corten (1970), pp. 720-22, attempts a similar conclusion based on data for the 1950s and early 1960s and arrives at the conclusion that the difference in what a Haitian could earn at home and by cutting cane in the Dominican Republic may be grossly exaggerated. His conclusion must be taken with a grain of salt, however, since at least the Haitian figures used for the comparison are extremely shaky. It should be noted that these figures (insofar as they are reasonably correct) are equilibrium figures which take the existence of migration into account. Had no migration taken place, the difference would of course have been even greater.

121. Plant (1987), p. 103. According to World Bank figures presented by Plant, by the end of the 1970s, the yearly average per capita income in the rural areas of Haiti was US$ 55. (Ibid., p. 55.)

122. Ibid., p. 88.

123. It is important to note that the Dominican employers do not seem to let whatever prejudices they may hold against Haitians influence their decision to hire them.

124. OIT (1975), pp. 130-34.

125. Ibid., p. 133.

126. ONAPLAN (1981:2), p. 12 and Table 1, p. 13. The corresponding figure in the coffee farms was 29 percent. (Ibid., p. 16).

127. OIT (1975), pp. 131-43.

128. Ibid., p. 136. The alternative for those who leave their farms is not primarily work in the sugar industry, but migration to urban areas. Cf. Vargas (1981).

129. OIT (1975), p. 137.

130. This is, for example, argued by Griffin (1969), pp. 70-80.

131. Minimum wages have been established in the Dominican Republic since 1940. At first, minimum wages in agriculture were limited to export crops, mainly sugar, coffee and cocoa. However, since 1966, minimum wages were established for all agricultural workers at DR$ 2.00 for eight hours of work. It were later increased to DR$ 2.50 in 1974, DR$ 3.50 in 1979 (Quezada (1981), p. 39), DR$ 5.00 in 1984 and DR$ 8.00 in 1985. As a rule, Haitian workers earn wages significantly below the established minimum (cf. Plant (1987), pp. 85, 101, 116). Average wages for agricultural workers in general are estimated to be 40 percent of the legally stipulated minimum wage (Murphy (1988), p. 20).

132. The figure for 1974, in World Bank (1978:1), Table 7:31, p. 411. For 1984, Banco Central (1985), p. 178.

133. World Bank (1978:1), p. 38.

134. Ibid., p. 40. Law 13 of 1974 authorized the companies to retain part of the tax if sugar prices were to exceed 20 cents/lb. (ibid.).

9

The Effects of Market Distortions

As we saw in the previous chapters, most of the agricultural land in the Dominican Republic is concentrated in the hands of a minority. A few large landowners, including the state, control the supply of land and thereby exercise monopoly power in the land market. This land tenure system also influences the performance of the credit market. Credit tends to be concentrated in the hands of the *latifundistas* since these can use the land as collateral while small peasants cannot. This market structure affects the allocation of resources and the methods of production. The utilization of resources in agriculture is thus intimately related to the *latifundio-minifundio* system.

The aim of the present chapter is to discuss how these market imperfections influence the allocation of resources, output and employment in the agricultural sector. First, we will analyze the land tenure and land use patterns in relation to labor demand in the agricultural sector. The extent to which imperfections in the credit market have influenced the introduction of modern technology and the demand for labor in the sector will also be dealt with. We shall furthermore discuss how the interaction between the growth of population, the land tenure structure, the land use pattern and the cultivation methods have aggravated the erosion and deforestation problems in the country. It will be argued that the prevailing land tenure structure and land use pattern in the Dominican Republic is not compatible with efficient use of labor resources.

Factor Market Imperfections

In Chapter 6, we argued that the Dominican land market is highly imperfect. The Dominican Republic has a very unequal land distribution. 82 percent of the landed properties only occupy 12 percent of the cultivable land while, on the other extreme, less than 2 percent of the landed properties occupy 55 percent of the cultivable land. Moreover, the large farms are generally located on the flat and irrigated lands while the small farms are confined to the steeper slopes of the hills and mountains. In Chapter 6, we also showed that the land tenure structure found today in the Dominican Republic is mainly the outcome of a process where different government decrees on land rights and agricultural development encouraged the concentration of land. Through this process, the large landowners could acquire land at very low prices. Furthermore, the existence of local monopolies in the land market and the different demand elasticities exhibited by small and large landowners imply that *minifundistas* pay higher prices and rents than *latifundistas*. In addition, since prices of most agricultural products have been controlled and land taxes are non-existent, there has been very little incentive for *latifundistas* to use the land efficiently. In other words, the opportunity cost of land for the *latifundistas* is low.

The distortions in the land market have also influenced the allocation of agricultural credit. As we showed in Chapter 7, the Dominican credit market is highly fragmented. Small and large producers have access to credit on very different terms. The former obtain their loans mainly from informal credit sources where interest rates are generally high, while the latter receive credit from formal credit sources where interest rates are low and, due to the high rate of inflation, even negative in real terms. One of the reasons for the existence of this fragmented credit market is that the policy of cheap credit implemented by the *Banco Agrícola* has led to a rationing mechanism whereby loans tend to be allocated to the wealthier and less risky borrowers. The concentration of large amounts of land in the hands of the *latifundista* allows him to use land as collateral, thus minimizing the risk of lending. The *minifundista* on the other hand, possesses too little land to be used as collateral and is to a large extent excluded from the organized credit market. Thus, the *latifundista* tends to pay interest rates which are lower than the rate that would prevail were the capital market unified and competitive, whereas the *minifundista* is likely to pay interest rates which are higher than the competitive rate.

In Chapter 8, and also in Chapter 2, we discussed the Dominican rural labor market. We argued that since few alternative rural occupations are available, the large numbers of Dominican rural workers in combination with massive imports of Haitian workers tend to make for a low level of wages in the sector. As a result of this situation, agricultural wages are generally below the legally established minimum and seem more or less to reflect the competitive character of the labor market. Thus, contrary to the situation found in the land and credit markets, we find no divergence between the wages paid by small and large producers.

The characteristics of the factor markets summarized above can be expressed as follows[1]:

$$r_m > r > r_l, \tag{6.1}$$
$$i_m > i > i_l, \tag{7.1}$$
$$w_m = w = w_l, \tag{8.1}$$

where r, i and w are the hypothetical competitive prices of land, capital and labor, respectively; and r_m, i_m, w_m and r_l, i_l, w_l represent the actual or implicit prices paid for the different factors by *minifundistas* and *latifundistas*, respectively.

The presence of imperfections in the land and credit markets implies that the *minifundistas* and *latifundistas* will face different sets of relative factor prices:

$$(r/w)_l < (r/w)_m \tag{9.1}$$

and

$$(i/w)_l < (i/w)_m. \tag{9.2}$$

As we argued in the preceding chapters, there has been a high concentration of landownership and, as discussed above, for the *latifundistas* land is relatively abundant and its opportunity cost is low while for the *minifundistas*, land is extremely scarce and prices are prohibitive. But at the same time, the large producers have been able to procure credit even at negative interest rates. We do not have any data to determine whether $(i/r)_l$ exceeds or falls short of $(i/r)_m$.

Given the relative factor prices described in (9.1) and (9.2), the two sets of producers will combine production factors in entirely different ways. The *latifundista* will tend to employ less labor (N) per unit of land (T) than will the *minifundista*. The former will combine more capital (K) with labor than the latter and the capital-land ratio is indeterminate, that is,

$$(T/N)_l > (T/N)_m, \tag{9.3}$$

and

$$(K/N)_l > (K/N)_m, \tag{9.4}$$

$$(K/T)_l \gtrless (K/T)_m, \tag{9.5}$$

depending on whether

$$(i/r)_l \underset{<}{\overset{>}{=}} (i/r)_m \qquad\qquad (9.6)$$

These factor combinations influence the composition of output on the two types of farms. The *latifundistas* will tend to produce relatively more capital-intensive crops (e.g. irrigated sugar cane) and to use land extensively (e.g. by grazing cattle on natural pastures). The *minifundistas*, on the other hand, will tend to produce more labor-intensive crops such as foodgrains and other food crops. As the evidence presented below shows, the unequal access of producers to production factors not only influences the output mix, but also the land use pattern and the general level of employment, production techniques and production level in the agricultural sector.

Imperfections, Land Use and Agricultural Employment

The Land Use Pattern

The divergent factor prices faced by *latifundistas* and *minifundistas* influence the land use pattern in the agricultural sector. On the *latifundios*, land has been used mainly for pasture and the cultivation of sugar cane. In 1976, more than half of the total land area under cultivation was in pasture, and around 11 percent was occupied by sugar cane.[2] Due to factor price distortions, land is used very inefficiently in these activities,[3] in spite of the scarcity of land confronted by the country as a whole and by the *minifundistas* in particular. The same year, only 12 percent of the total cultivable land was dedicated to food production.[4] Food crops are mainly grown on the *minifundios*. As will be shown later in this chapter, this land use pattern largely influences the demand for labor in the sector. Livestock production is the least labor-intensive activity, and the sugar cane, which requires large amounts of labor, mainly uses imported Haitian workers.

The divergent factor prices faced by *latifundistas* and *minifundistas* have influenced the techniques of production adopted by these producers: on the *minifundia* labor-intensive techniques are being used while on the *latifundia* production techniques are land-intensive. The highest percentage of farmland given over to the cultivation of both annual and perennial crops[5] is found among middle and small cultivators, i.e., peasants with less than 30 hectares. As shown in Table 9.1, farms of a size of less than 5 hectares devote 47 percent of their total land area to annual crops and more than 30 percent to perennial crops, including traditional export crops. The intensive use of land resources within this group of farms can also be seen by the absence of fallow land. As will be shown later, the shrinking land base of the *minifundista* has led to an ever more intensive land use pattern, shortening the fallow period and creating serious erosion problems. Table 9.1 also shows that the middle size farms (5 to 30 hectares) dedicate approximately the same proportion of land to the different crops and can afford some land in fallow. On the other hand, the large farms (above 30 hectares) dedicate 76 percent of the land to pastures and only 8 percent to food production.

TABLE 9.1   Land Use Related to Farm Size (Percentage of Available Land According to Category of Use, 1976)

	Farm size (in hectares)			
	1.5-4.9	5-31.2	≥31.3	Average
Annual crops	46.9	25.6	8.0	18.1
Perennial crops	31.2	23.7	14.9	19.3
Improved pastures	6.3	25.0	45.8	34.3
Natural pastures	15.5	23.7	30.0	26.5
Fallow land	0.0	1.9	1.4	1.2

Source: ONAPLAN (1983:1), p. 119.

Almost all food crops are produced by small and middle size cultivators. In 1976, it was estimated that more than 70 percent of the farms producing sweet potatoes, pigeon peas, beans, corn and cassava, and between 40 and 70 percent of the farms producing garlic, rice, onions, potatoes, plantains, bananas and tomatoes were of a size of less than 3 hectares. There are no specific figures on yams and peanuts, but it seems as if a large part of these crops is cultivated on small farms.[6]

Land Use and Employment

The land use pattern is intimately related to the generation of employment in the sector. Seasonal and perennial crops have the highest demand for labor. These crops, with the exception of sugar cane, are mainly produced on small and middle size farms. The bulk of agricultural employment is generated on these farms. As Table 9.2 shows, 82 percent of the total labor demand in the sector is concentrated

TABLE 9.2   Land Use and Labor Requirement in Agriculture, 1970-1971

| Crops | Cultivated Area | | Labor Necessity | | |
	Thousand Hectares	%	Million Man-days	%	Man-days per Hectare
Perennial:					
Sugar cane	195.0	8.6	13.7	19.8	70
Coffee	135.0	6.0	10.8	15.6	80
Cocoa	68.3	3.0	3.8	5.5	55
Plantains	95.3	4.2	10.5	15.2	110
Others	39.5	1.7	3.1	4.5	78
Total perennial crops	533.0	23.6	41.9	60.5	78
Seasonal: (production mainly for the market)					
Rice	81.6	3.6	3.7	5.3	45
Tobacco	18.3	0.8	2.4	3.5	131
Peanuts	51.0	2.2	1.8	2.6	35
Seasonal: (production for the market and subsistence)					
Corn	24.9	1.1	1.2	1.7	48
Beans	23.0	1.0	1.2	1.7	52
Potatoes	8.4	0.4	0.7	1.0	83
Cassava	14.7	0.6	1.2	1.7	81
Others	70.1	3.1	2.9	4.2	41
Total seasonal crops	292.0	12.9	15.1	21.8	51
Pastures [1]	1,432.0	63.4	12.2	17.6	8
Total	2,257.0[2]	100.0	69.2[3]	100.0	30

1: Includes livestock production and pasture conservation.

2: In 1971, the total cultivable area amounted to 2.7 million hectares. Of this, 2.3 million were under cultivation, 0.1 were in fallow and 0.3 in forest.

3: In 1971, the total labor demand in the agricultural sector amounted to 83.1 million man-days. Of this, 69.2 million represented direct labor requirement and 13.9 million represented indirect additional labor requirement. According to the ILO mission, this later category corresponded to employment in complementary agricultural activities related to small farms.

Source: OIT (1975), Tables 54-57, pp. 146-48.

on seasonal and perennial crops. At the other extreme, we have livestock production. This activity occupies 63 percent of the total cultivated land area but its labor requirements only represent 18 percent of the total labor demand in the sector.

The highest labor requirement is found in such crops as tobacco, plantain, potatoes, cassava, coffee and sugar cane. There, the number of man-days per hectare ranges from 131 - in the case of tobacco - to 70 - in the case of sugar cane. Perennial crops present the highest labor requirement, using an average of 78 man-days per hectare, while the corresponding figure for seasonal crops is 51 man-days per hectare. The lowest labor requirement is found in livestock production. This activity uses 8 man-days per hectare.[7] Considering that seasonal crops produce more than one harvest per year, the figures on man-days requirements in this crop category seem to be too low. It is therefore uncertain whether these figures have been calculated on a yearly basis.

The above figures indicate, however, that labor demand in the agricultural sector is mainly generated in small and middle size farms where the more labor-intensive crops are cultivated. A disproportionately low amount of the total cultivated land, about 28 percent, is devoted to seasonal and perennial (not sugar cane) crops,[8] whereas 63 and 9 percent respectively of the total cultivated land area is devoted to pastures and sugar cane. These two crops are mainly cultivated on large farms. As shown above, livestock production has a very low labor requirement and sugar cane, although presenting high labor requirements, uses very little Dominican labor (see Chapter 8).

Thus, monopoly power in the land market influences the land use pattern in the sector and this in turn affects the demand for rural labor.

Market Imperfections and Technology in Dominican Agriculture

Credit and Technology

The concentration of land in the hands of a few landowners also influences the credit market. As we saw in Chapter 7, the *latifundistas* can use land as collateral and obtain subsidized credit from official sources. The *minifundistas*, on the other hand, have to pay high interest rates to informal credit sources. This situation tends to affect the introduction of technology in agriculture.

The introduction of a new technology is largely determined by the relative factor prices of the production factors, especially that of capital and labor. In a situation where all producers of a certain crop face the same factor prices, *ceteris paribus*, these producers will use the same technique. This is, however, not the case in a situation such as the one prevailing in Dominican agriculture, where producers face different factor prices. Such a situation may influence the choice of technology in agricultural activities. The case can be illustrated with the aid of Figure 9.1.

On the vertical axis we have the employment of capital (K), and on the horizontal axis, the employment of labor (N).

FIGURE 9.1   The Choice of Technique

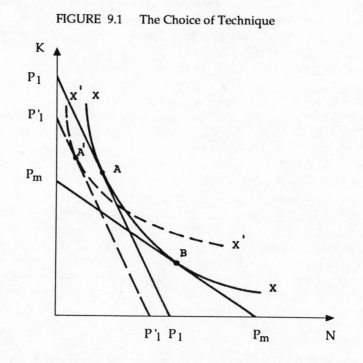

Let us assume that the isoquant XX represents the different possible combinations of labor (N) and capital (K) for the production of a given amount of a certain crop. Assume further that the relative price of labor and capital faced by the *latifundistas* is given by the price line P_lP_l while the relative factor price faced by the *minifundistas* is given by the price line P_mP_m. Given these factor price lines, the *latifundistas* will choose the factor combination given by point A while the *minifundistas* will choose technique B. As can be seen, technique A is relatively more capital-intensive than technique B.

The new technologies available tend to be intensive in the use of material inputs and are therefore mainly adopted by large producers.[9] This is the case, for example, for food grains, notably rice. The biological characteristics of the new seed varieties require an abundant supply of water, fertilizers and pesticides. Thus, this technique will be adopted only by those producers who enjoy relatively cheap credit and material inputs.

This type of "landlord-biased" technology is represented by the isoquant X'X' and will be adopted by *latifundistas* only. These producers will face lower costs by choosing a technique such as that represented by point A', where the price line $P'_1P'_1$ (parallel to P_1P_1) is tangential to the new isoquant. This technique is economically irrelevant for the *minifundistas*. Were these producers to adopt techniques as those given by isoquant X'X', then they would face higher costs since this isoquant will have a point of tangency with a price line which lies northeast of P_mP_m. Thus, while the *latifundistas* can afford the new technology X'X', the *minifundistas* will continue with technology XX.

The Use of Modern Technology in Dominican Agriculture

As illustrated in the above figure, we would expect a higher use of modern technology (machinery, fertilizers, improved seeds, etc.) among large Dominican producers. It seems to be so, at least in the case of machinery. As Table 9.3 shows, 20 percent of the total credit received by the largest farms (above 2,000 *tareas*) was devoted to purchase and/or hire machinery. The corresponding figure for small farms (less than 100 *tareas*) was 6 percent. An opposite situation is found in the case of fertilizers and seeds. Small farms allocate substantially more of the obtained credit to buy these inputs than large farms do although this is mainly due to the fact that most of the small producers who receive credit are agrarian reform program beneficiaries. Most of this credit is used to finance the production of rice which requires a large amount of such inputs. However, most of the land area using fertilizers in the country is concentrated in large farms. For example, in 1971, sugar cane production occupied 69 percent of the total land area using fertilizers.[10]

Irrigation facilities are less unequally distributed. In 1975, as much as 47 percent of the state irrigated land was given over to rice, a crop mainly cultivated on agrarian reform settlements. The corresponding figures for pastures and sugar cane were 15 and 9 percent, respectively.[11] A factor that may have influenced the distribution of irrigation facilities is the application of Law 134 of 1971 or *Ley de quota aparte*. This law implied that the beneficiaries of state irrigation facilities were *compelled* to pay the state with a share of the irrigated land. This share varied between 25, 50 and 80 percent of the irrigable land depending, respectively, on whether the land in question was used for food crops, for pastures or was uncultivated.[12] The land received by the state was intended for redistribution through the agrarian reform program. Before the implementation, in 1972, of the agrarian reform on the large rice farms, irrigation facilities were largely concentrated to these producers.

The use of modern inputs is generally very limited among the peasantry. As pointed out above, the main producers of food crops and, to some extent, of export crops, are small peasants. Many of them live on the mountain slopes, far away from the services offered by the state and other organizations. Their production methods are often inadequate and their access to modern machinery is highly restricted. They are, for topographical reasons, often hindered in the use of machines. Many peasants hire oxen, as well as tractors. In 1983, the Ministry of Agriculture provided 323 tractors for hire at 9 centers spread across the country.[13] This service is very insufficient and only reaches farmers living in central areas.

TABLE 9.3   Use of Agricultural Credit by Farm Size, 1978
(Percent)

Uses	Farm Size (in tareas)					
	≤50	51-100	101-500	501-2,000	>2,000	Average
Construction	2.4	4.5	7.1	8.2	4.3	4.7
Fertilizers and pesticides	23.6	20.7	16.6	17.4	7.1	20.2
Seeds	19.6	18.2	15.7	7.9	4.2	17.3
Labor	27.5	30.2	28.6	28.4	23.1	28.4
Family needs	17.9	16.1	16.4	11.4	2.8	16.6
Hiring or purchase of machinery	5.6	5.5	5.0	4.0	20.0	5.6
Purchase of livestock	0.2	0.9	5.7	16.6	38.5	3.2
Others	3.2	3.9	4.6	6.1	-	4.0

Source: SEA (1981:3), Table 19, p. 67.

Some small producers have access to modern inputs, e.g. in the case of rice and tobacco production. Here growers use fertilizer and pesticides on approximately 95 and 80 percent respectively of the land under cultivation.[14] Furthermore, most rice producers have access to state constructed irrigation systems. However, with the exception of rice, tobacco, garlic, onions, tomatoes and potatoes, all other peasant crops lack - completely, or to a large extent - fertilization and protection through pesticides. In most cases they also lack artificial irrigation.[15]

In general, the agricultural sector as a whole presents a very limited use of modern technology. In spite of the advantage the large producers have had in obtaining cheap credit, and considering that the Dominican currency had been overvalued for a long time, no significant increase in, for instance, agricultural mechanization is found. As Table 9.3 shows, in 1978 less than 6 percent of total agricultural credit was allocated to machinery.[16] Large producers seem to devote most of their credit (38.5 percent) to purchase livestock. The number of tractors operating in the agricultural sector was, in 1983, estimated to be 3,500,[17] in comparison with 34,700 oxen- or horse-maneuvered plows.[18] In 1971, less than 5 percent of the farms used mechanical traction only, 57 percent human traction only, 35 percent animal traction only and 5 percent utilized a combination of animal and mechanical traction. At present, the situation seems to be more or less the same.[19]

Different factors have contributed to maintaining the low level of technology found in Dominican agriculture. As indicated by Figure 9.1, the introduction of techniques is closely related to relative factor prices. On the one hand, the import of Haitian labor has enabled the large sugar producers to secure a labor supply without raising wages. This has prevented the large producers from adapting policies economizing on labor and raising its productivity. On the other hand, the easy access to cheap land resources has induced the large producers to increase production mainly by increasing the land area, disregarding the introduction of technology which may increase labor and land productivity. The case of the sugar producers is illustrative. The land area under sugar cane production increased with 1.6 million *tareas* during the 1973-76 period.[20] The sugar yield per hectare decreased from a level of 77.4 metric tons per hectare in 1963-65 to 47.7 in 1973-75.[21] The productivity among sugar cane cutters is one of the lowest in the world.[22]

Another cause of the general low level of technology could also be the increase in the price of inputs. The price index of agricultural inputs (fertilizers, pesticides, machine oil and seeds) increased from 100 in 1973 to 189.5 in 1979. During this period, the price the peasants received for their products only increased from an index of 100 to 131.9.[23]

In the peasant sector, the limited access of small producers to credit has undoubtedly contributed to limit the introduction of new technology. Another important factor that may have prevented technological change in peasant agriculture is the low level of education of the peasantry. As shown in Chapter 4, rural education has largely been neglected by Dominican governments. There seems to be a strong connection between education and innovation among peasants. More educated peasants are generally more ready to innovate as they could more easily perceive the benefits of improved techniques at the same time as they could more efficiently implement new techniques and thus minimize risk.[24]

Credit, Employment and Output

Although it is difficult to determine the impact of credit on employment,[25] some evidence suggests that in the Dominican Republic there is a tendency for employment to increase when credit per hectare increases. Credit, when allocated to small farms, seems to have a very positive impact on the use of technology and the generation of employment. Credit availability helps the peasants to buy supplementary inputs which in turn enables them to increase labor productivity, production and income.

A survey carried out by the *Secretaría de Estado de Agricultura* (SEA)[26] shows that, for all farms, in the absence of credit, the labor requirement for crops is four times higher than for livestock. When credit is used, employment increases considerably more in crops than in livestock.

The SEA study arrives at two interesting conclusions. Firstly, it suggests that if a rigorous employment policy is to be followed, livestock production has to be relegated to a secondary plane. Secondly, a credit policy oriented towards optimizing employment must be geared towards channeling financial resources to the small farms which are not receiving credit since, *in absolute terms*, these farms present the highest absorption of labor. Hence, at the margin the employment effect, for a given volume of credit per hectare, is most favorable on the small farms.[27] These conclusions indicate that Dominican authorities are aware of the fact that institutional credit has been neglected for those who may make the best use of it in terms of employment generation.

Another study, performed at a more disaggregated level, points out that credit, when allocated to small farms, has a very positive influence on rural employment. In his doctoral dissertation, George A. Munguía[28] evaluated the results of the Tobacco Institute Supervised Credit Program (SCP) and the FAO Extension Education Project. The research was carried out with the help of a multiple regression equation model. For evaluation of the SCP, data were collected from 237 tobacco growers in four different areas of the country. The evaluation of the FAO project included data on all farmers receiving FAO technical assistance and a corresponding number of non-FAO farms as control sample. The findings of the research on SCP farms can be summarized as follows:

a) The credit program made it possible for SCP farmers in the four studied areas to buy more fertilizers and insecticides than the control sample farmers. b) In the four areas studied, output, labor employment and labor productivity increased with the amount of fertilizers employed. c) A more intensive use of labor, when not accompanied by an increase in the amount of fertilizers, did very little to increase production.

For the FAO project, the following results were obtained:

a) Farmers who received technical assistance from FAO agronomists obtained higher yields than farmers in the same area who did not. b) After two years, farmers on the FAO program experienced a substantial increase in the income generated by their small farms. c) Irrigation facilities played a very important role by allowing farmers to apply inexpensive capital inputs and thereby raise land and labor productivities. d) Credit availability helped farmers to buy the very productive capital inputs. e) Employment generally increased with the amount of inexpensive capital inputs used.

The above results suggest that if the government is interested in increasing employment and income in rural areas, it should implement measures towards increasing the allocation of credit to small farmers. Credit makes it feasible for the peasants to acquire supplementary inputs to increase both labor productivity and production and thereby also incomes.

The Static Resource Allocation Effects of Factor Market Distortions

The arguments pursued in the last sections can be summarized in the following way:

Imperfections in the land market affect the allocation of resources and production. The fact that small and large producers face two different sets of relative land-labor prices has made production on large farms more land-intensive, while production on small farms has become more labor-intensive.

Since the use of capital in Dominican agricultural activities is very limited, production in the sector basically is a function of the use of land and labor only. Using production data for 1,802 farms surveyed by SEA in 1976, Norberto Quezada calculated the factor shares in agriculture by estimating the parameters of a Cobb-Douglas production function. Table 9.4 presents the labor, land and capital shares by crops. Ten important peasant crops were included. Estimates of the labor input include expenditures on both hired labor and imputed cost of unpaid family labor. Rent includes payment for rented land and/or imputed costs for owned land. Capital includes expenditures on machinery, irrigation, animal power, seed, fertilizer, and product preparation for marketing.[29]

TABLE 9.4   Estimates of Factor Shares, Selected Crops and All Crops, Dominican Republic, 1976

Crop	Labor	Rent	Capital
Rice	.546	.405	.049
Corn	.637	.328	.035
Peanuts	.724	.272	.004
Red beans	.711	.201	.068
Cocoa	.443	.519	.038
Cassava	.430	.549	.021
Plantains	.065	.935	*
Sweet potato	.798	.108	.092
Sauce tomato	.736	.264	*
All crops	.423	.553	.024

*Parameters not reliable for estimation of factor shares.

Source: Quezada (1981), p. 110.

The low level of capitalization in Dominican peasant agriculture is illustrated by the fact that in most crops labor has the largest factor share, followed by land. For the agricultural sector in general, labor is the most important factor in the production process. Hired labor accounts for 32 percent of all non-cash costs.[30] Family labor is the largest component of total labor used in the sector. It amounts to 44 percent of total labor requirements in sixteen important crops, varying from 18 percent in rice to 77 percent in beans/corn, the labor requirement being higher when the crops are interplanted.[31]

Here it should be pointed out that the presence of factor market distortions can give rise to a series of "pathologies" in the economy. Of greatest importance in the present context is that factor intensities can be reversed. A product may be labor-intensive in the physical sense but land-intensive in the value sense, i.e., the production activity using the largest proportion of labor per unit of land may be paying the largest share of output to land. Factor intensity reversals can give rise to "perverse" price-output and distortion-output responses, i.e., an increase in the relative price of one good may lead to a fall in its output, with the degree of factor market distortions unchanged. Similarly, an increase in the rate of subsidy to one sector may lead to a fall in the output of that sector, with relative output prices unchanged. (These and related issues are discussed in the Appendix to the present chapter.)

If we compare the figures shown in Table 9.4 with those in Table 9.2, it seems that for some crops there is no correspondence between their value and physical intensities. Such is the case of cocoa, cassava and plantains, which although being relatively physically labor-intensive (Table 9.2), pay the largest share of output to land (Table 9.4). The figures in Tables 9.4 and 9.2 may not, however, be comparable since they are based on two different surveys. A better way of checking physical and value intensity correspondence is by comparing Quezada's results in Table 9.4 with SEA figures on physical intensities since these are calculated from the same survey. These figures are presented in Table 9.5 below.

As can be seen, the figures on physical intensities obtained by the ILO survey differ from those obtained by the SEA survey. It is unlikely that these differences could be due to changes in technology between 1971 and 1976. Firstly, no significant technological changes have taken place in Dominican agriculture, and secondly, the period between the two surveys is too short to be used for demonstrating technological change even if such change has taken place. Thus, these differences may be due to a different measurement approach or simply to low quality of the data. Most of the food crops produce more than one harvest per year and it is possible that this is not accurately accounted for in the surveys. Such may be the case for rice and plantains which show the largest differences in labor-land ratios between the surveys.

In column (2) in Table 9.5, the different crops have been ranked according to their physical intensities. In the absence of factor intensity reversals, we would expect value intensities (column (3)) to present the same ranking pattern, i.e., the product with the relatively highest use of labor per unit of land, in this case tomato, should have the highest share of output being paid to labor or, inversely, the product with the lowest share of output being paid to labor, in this case plantains, should present the lowest use of labor per unit of land. This is, however, not the case.

TABLE 9.5   Physical and Value Factor Intensities in Dominican Agriculture

| Crop | Physical Intensity (Man-days per Hectare, N/T) | | Value Intensity (Labor Share in % of Total Value) |
	ILO Figures (1971)	SEA Figures (1976)	(1976)
	(1)	(2)	(3)
Tomato	n.a.	117	73.6
Rice	45	75	54.6
Cassava	81	68	43.0
Sweet potatoes	n.a.	63	79.8
Plantains	110	47	6.5
Beans	52	47	71.1
Peanuts	35	36	72.4
Corn	48	35	63.7
Cocoa	55	20	44.3

Sources: Column (1): Table 9.2. Column (2): SEA (1977), Table 2.6, p. 9. Column (3): Table 9.4.

It is difficult to ascertain whether the lack of correspondence between physical and value intensities, as presented in Table 9.5, is a result of factor intensity reversals. First of all, the quality of the data may present some difficulties. We just pointed out some of the deficiencies concerning physical intensities. It is difficult to know the accuracy of the data on value intensities. As pointed out above, labor and land shares include the imputed cost for unpaid labor and for owned land, respectively. Moreover it is not clear how these imputed values were calculated.

In any case, with the data at hand it is nearly impossible to discuss value intensity reversals. The figures in column (3) have been obtained by using a Cobb-Douglas production function and, as stated in the Appendix, in this type of functions value factor intensity reversals are not possible. The reason is that in Cobb-Douglas functions the elasticity of substitution is constant and equal to 1, so that the relative shares going to land and labor are invariant to both changes in relative commodity prices and changes in the factor price differential.

Thus, on the basis of the figures presented in Table 9.5, we cannot ascertain whether or not we have factor intensity reversals in Dominican agriculture. However, even in the case where factor intensity reversals take place, the likelihood of perverse responses is a debated subject in the theoretical field. Peter Neary has strongly argued against the possibility that the perverse results take place in reality, classifying the issue as a theoretical curiosum (see Appendix). Neary argues that these perverse results follow from comparative-static analysis and, for a variety of plausible adjustment mechanisms, can be ruled out as dynamically unstable and hence are unlikely ever to be observed. In what follows, we simply assume that no such reversals take place and that the different perverse results discussed in the Appendix can be ruled out.

Factor Market Distortions and Agricultural Production

The situation where different producers face different sets of relative factor prices can be illustrated with the aid of the Edgeworth-Bowley box diagram in Figure 9.2.

FIGURE 9.2   Distortions in the Agricultural Sector

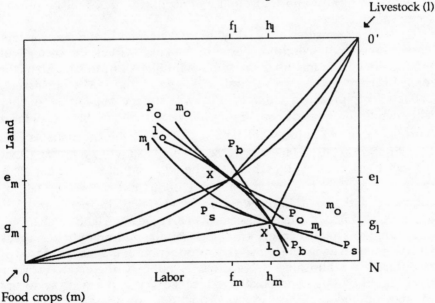

Assume that agricultural production is a function of land and labor only. The area ONO'T represents factor endowments in the agricultural sector. It is assumed that production factors in agriculture are not transferable to other sectors and that these factors are full employed in

264

the sector's two lines of production. Land is measured on the vertical axis and labor on the horizontal axis. Production in the food subsector is measured by a map of isoquants extending from 0, and production in livestock by a map of isoquants extending from 0'. The contract curve 0X0' lies to the right of the diagonal 00' (not drawn), which means that for all relative factor prices (i.e., assuming that factor reversals do not occur), food crop production uses more labor in relation to land than livestock production.

Let us first consider the case where there are no distortions in the factor markets. In the absence of market imperfections, the sector will produce an output mix given by point X in the diagram. Factor intensities are given by the straight lines 0X and 0'X respectively. At this point, the food crop subsector will combine $0e_m$ land with $0f_m$ labor and the livestock subsector will combine $0'e_l$ land with $0'f_l$ labor. At point X, both producers will face the same factor prices as shown by the price line P_0P_0 which is tangential to both isoquants at point X. As long as there are no distortions in the factor markets, the allocation of agricultural resources will be efficient and production in the sector will be both technically and allocatively efficient. Point X will be on the sector's contract curve.

Let us now consider the case where a distortion in the land market exists. If monopoly conditions exist in the land market, the sector will produce an output mix given by some point like X'. At this point, factor intensities are given by the straight lines 0X' and 0'X' respectively. The food crop producing *minifundistas* will combine $0g_m$ land with $0h_m$ labor while the livestock raising *latifundistas* will combine $0'g_l$ land with $0'h_l$ labor. At point X' the *minifundistas* and the *latifundistas* face two different relative factor price sets. This is shown by the fact that the factor price line P_bP_b tangent to the l_0l_0 isoquant is steeper than the price line P_sP_s tangent to the m_1m_1 isoquant. For the *latifundista*, compared with the *minifundista*, land is relatively cheaper than labor and thus production in this subsector will become more land-intensive.

As long as factor markets are imperfect, the allocation of resources will be inefficient in the sense that production could be increased if resources are reallocated. Given that at point X' the relative factor prices faced by large and small producers diverge, the two producers combine production factors in proportion to the relative price they face. These factor prices diverge, however, from the social opportunity cost. Production at X' is inefficient, i.e., X' is outside the contract curve and on a curve *inside* the sector's production possibility curve (see Figure A.2 in the Appendix). This point is not allocatively efficient since the sector could produce an output mix as the one represented by point X where for example the production of food could be increased without decreasing the production of livestock. This is shown by the fact that the isoquant m_1m_1 is closer to 0. At the equilibrium point X', the following relations prevail:

$$r_m > r > r_l \tag{6.1}$$
$$w_m = w = w_l . \tag{8.1}$$

$(w/r)_m < (w/r) < (w/r)_l$, i.e., the ratio of wages to rent in the *minifundio* subsector is less than in the *latifundio* subsector, or equivalently, the factor price line P_sP_s has a less steep slope than the P_bP_b line. The factor price ratio that will prevail with competitive, undistorted, factor markets is less than the one prevailing in the *latifundio* subsector and greater than in the *minifundio* one, i.e., the slope of P_oP_o is less than the slope of P_bP_b and greater than the slope of P_sP_s.

$$(N/T)_m > (N/T)_{Fu} > (N/T)_{Lu} > (N/T)_l \tag{9.7}$$

i.e., line 0X' has a less steep slope than 0'X'.

$(N/T)_{Fu}$ and $(N/T)_{Lu}$ represent the undistorted labor-land ratio of food and livestock production, respectively.

At point X', labor productivity in the *minifundio* subsector is lower than at point X since more labor is combined with less land. The outcome will be that in the absence of migration, too many people will be concentrated to the *minifundio* subsector as compared with the optimal situation depicted in point X. Thus, with the presence of monopoly power in the land market, the agricultural workers have to face lower rewards than would be the case with competitive factor markets.

The Dynamic Effects of Factor Market Distortions

In the previous section we showed that the presence of factor market imperfections results in (static) economic inefficiency in the sense that it is possible to increase the production of any single good without having to reduce the production of some other good. An implication of this argument in the case of the Dominican Republic is that rural workers will face lower incomes. The presence of factor market imperfections also has dynamic effects which affect the level of income in the rural areas. Firstly, factor market imperfections prevent dynamic technological efficiency, i.e., the adoption of new and superior methods of production will be slowed down or not take place at all (see

Figure 9.1). Secondly, as we shall see below, the presence of factor market distortions has dynamic implications which negatively influence the rate of growth of agricultural production. These implications will be more serious if, for example, the degree of distortion in the land market increases over time. However, as we have seen in Chapter 6, the degree of distortion in this market seems not to have changed significantly during the post-Trujillo period. (The Gini coefficient increased from 0.82 in 1960 to 0.85 in 1981). Consequently, we shall henceforth assume that the degree of distortion is constant.

In the following sections, we shall analyze the major dynamic consequences of factor market distortions in the agricultural sector. We start by discussing how the land tenure structure, the land use pattern and the cultivations methods, in combination with the growth of the population and the labor force have resulted in a decumulation of land resources in the peasant sector through an accelerated deforestation and erosion process.

The Cultivation Methods

As discussed above, the introduction of modern techniques in Dominican agriculture has been very limited. So far, the new inputs have only reached cultivators on the flat lands and in the fertile river valleys. The most ancient and harmful agricultural techniques are still used on the already worn down and overpopulated mountain slopes. This situation represents a severe threat to the ecological balance of the island.[32]

As in many tropical and sub-tropical countries, the most common technique used among Dominican peasants is the so-called "slash and burn" technique. This means that an area is cleared by burning the vegetation cover, and then crops are planted in the clearing, often without any other manuring than the ashes. When the yields start to decrease, the plot is abandoned until it regains its fertility. Meanwhile the peasant has to open another plot for cultivation.[33] The capacity for the soil to yield more than one harvest differs from area to area, but the Dominican peasants generally stay on the plot two to three years.[34] The critical factor involved in this technique is that the peasant often has a very limited supply of new land to clear. The technique is not suitable for all types of crops and the peasant tends to use the land to its maximum, shortening the fallow period and thereby increasing the risk for erosion.[35]

The soil of the mountain slopes is often very fertile, but also very sensitive to crude cultivation methods. The simple instruments at the disposal of the peasants often tend to harm the soil or limit its yield, for example, the constant weeding with broad-bladed *machetes* scrapes away the thin top layer, and the hoe many peasants use only penetrates 10-15 centimeters into the ground, which is insufficient to ensure adequate development of the root system.[36] Most of the crops cultivated on these lands are inappropriate to the ecotype, with the possible exception of the cultivation of coffee and cocoa that provide some protection for the soil.

The absence of soil-conservation methods and the shrinking land base of the peasantry, due to population growth and the prevailing *latifundio-minifundio* system, have led to two major problems in the Dominican agriculture: erosion and deforestation. These problems present serious consequences for the country as a whole, but in particular for the peasantry who must face reduced yields and incomes.

The initial step in an erosion process is probably the clearing of land covered with forest. As the population grows, the clearing of forest may take place either because of the need to expand food production and/or because of the need for more wood for fuel purposes. We will first shortly analyze the process whereby the intensification of cropping leads to erosion.

Erosion

Soil fertility is closely related to changes in population density and agricultural techniques. According to Ester Boserup,[37] when a given land area becomes cultivated more frequently, the purpose for which it was hitherto used must be changed and this may create additional activities for which new investments are required. In primitive agriculture, technical changes can take place only when the system of land use is modified. At the same time, some changes in land use can come about only if they are accompanied by introduction of new tools. Accordingly, when forest fallow (fallow period between 20 and 25 years) is replaced by bush fallow (fallow period between 6 and 10 years), the use of the plow becomes indispensable at the same time as the gradual disappearance of roots of trees and bushes in the fallow facilitates its use. It may happen that peasants are well aware of the profitability of shifting to more intensive systems of land use and even have access to tools of a less primitive kind. Still, these changes may not take place until a certain density of population is reached. It may also happen that a peasant population faces a critical increase in density and is without knowledge or without the possibility of utilizing fertilization techniques. The fallow period will then be shortened and, in the absence of improved techniques, this would lead to a decline in crop yields and sometimes to exhaustion of land resources. The peasantry would then have to face the choice between starvation and migration.[38]

In the last decades, the Dominican peasant has been facing a situation very similar to the latter described above. His limited access to improved techniques forces him to rely on traditional production methods and to intensify the pattern of land use. The outcome has been increased erosional problems and low yields. For a considerable number of peasants the choice has been migration.

In the Dominican Republic, erosion has been present throughout the whole of the twentieth century, but the process has accelerated with the growing population, the increasing number of small cultivators, the reduced fallow periods and the deforestation. In 1979, a commission of the *Subsecretaría de Recursos Naturales* investigated the erosion of some areas spread all over the country. It found that the erosion could range from 230 tons per hectare and year to 1,895 tons. The average erosion in the investigated areas was around 1,100 tons.[39] Erosion has been growing steadily during the last three decades and has made a spectacular advance through the vast deforestation in the 1960s. (See below.)

As a rule, the flat lands do not suffer so much from the effects of erosion. Peasants making their living on the slopes, having to survive by constantly seeking new land in replacement of the old, destroyed plots, often look with envy on those who live on the arable plains. But the plains also suffer from inadequate management, unequal land distribution and the fragmentation of already limited landholdings. The increase of salt in the soil ruins many hectares of plain land every year. The reason for this development is that inadequate use of artificial irrigation releases salts that are bound in the earth and transports them to the surface. With time, these salts can hinder the growth of the plants. The magnitude of the problem is made evident by the problems afflicting the state owned sugar cane fields around Barahona where, due to salification, 2,000 hectares of a total of 11,500 have been taken out of production. On the rest of this land, the annual production of sugar cane has decreased from an average of 140 tons per hectare to 95 tons per hectare in only a few years.[40]

Still, the situation is most alarming on the hill and mountain sides. In their search for new land, the peasants have to move higher up, closer and closer to the tops. Soon there is no land left for clearing. When a peasant has used the soil, it must be covered with grass, bushes or trees and then rest for at least 5 years in order to regain its former strength. But since the reserve of cultivable land is running out, the peasant has to press the land even harder than before and try to yield harvests on the soil until only the bare rock is left. He does not have the time or financial means to let soil-protecting crops like coffee and cocoa grow on his land. He must give himself and his growing family food every day, and he must create a reserve of food or money in order to meet the fearful periods between harvests.

The enormous losses of soil caused by erosion are apparent for anyone who happens to walk along the shoreline of Santo Domingo after heavy rain. Hundreds of meters out into the open sea the water is colored light brown, by soil carried from the inland by the rivers, thousands of tons of good earth perish in the seawater just after a few rainy days. The sediments harm the irrigation system and dams. To give but one example, the dam of Tavera receives 275 tons of eroded material per hectare in its basin of 7,370 hectares every year. The accumulation of sediments behind the dam wall is around 18 meters deep. All dams in the country suffer from the same sort of problem.[41]

Deforestation

The indiscriminate cutting down of trees advanced notably in the early 1960s. The pressing need for peasants to get more land to cultivate was one important factor. Another was their need of fuel for cooking.[42] But a major reason for the devastation of the Dominican forests was probably due to the emergence of a political vacuum after the fall of Trujillo. The peasants started to cut down the valuable hardwood and sell it to the local sawmills. Large devastations of the Dominican forests took place before, during the US occupation and during the Trujillo regime as well. But still, the repressive Trujillo administration had some sort of control over the situation, granting rights to felling trees to chosen individuals.[43]

During the turbulent years of the sixties, it was free for anyone to make a profit out of the precious timber. Both peasants and wealthy lumber-mill owners saw their chance. Apparently most of the trees cut down during these years came from communal land and former Trujillo properties. A forced closing down of the country's sawmills and a total prohibition of forest exploitation in 1967 did not improve the situation.[44] The damage was already done. Furthermore, the production of charcoal, concentrated to the poor southwest part of the country, takes a heavy toll on the remaining part of the country's forests and bush vegetation. The felling of trees in order to make charcoal is of huge dimensions. Every year the southwest produces 2.4 million sacks of charcoal. These are bought by truck drivers and brought into the towns. The demand is high and increases steadily due to the high prices of stoves and liquified gas. Most Dominicans have three meals a day and at least one meal includes beans or pigeon peas that have to be boiled for a long time.[45] The consumption of charcoal is concentrated to the towns since the peasants still use firewood.[46] Even if most of the Dominican forests have been destroyed, the reforestation of the damaged areas has nearly not begun. The attempts that have been carried out so far have been limited.[47]

The soil of the mountain slopes is fertile but lies in thin layers. At the moment, the peasants are forced to use this soil to its utmost, and the damages originated from their activities are already striking back at themselves. The soil on the mountainsides needs some sort of protection against wind and rain. Trees and bushes alleviate the effects of evaporation, their roots bind the earth and help it to store humidity.[48] Coffee is a tree crop and offers some of these advantages, but in order to plant food crops, like cassava, beans, plantains and corn, the peasant has to clear most of the permanent vegetation. Besides, these crops do not provide sufficient cover for the ground and do not have the dense and intertwined root system of natural grass.[49] The trees that the peasants leave standing are too wide apart to act as effective barriers against erosion. The result is that the heavy tropical rains hit the unprotected soil, pressing the soil together and decreasing its permeability. The top soil dissolves into a mud that prevents the water from penetrating into the ground. Torrents, caused by the rains, carry the soil into ravines and riverbeds. The sediments that grow on the riverbeds can force the rivers to rise, change their course and inundate fertile land, sterilizing vast areas by depositing sand and gravel.

The Dominican peasants are not ignorant of the negative effects some of their cultivation practices have on the soil. Most of them are, however, unable to change their fate. The problem of erosion and deforestation is intimately related to the absence of improved technology and to the composition of output.

As discussed above, the absence of improved technology among the peasants is largely a consequence of the limited access the peasants have to education and credit. Without credit and knowledge most peasants would, for example, be unable to make terraces. Moreover, the cost implied in soil conservation measures are generally high. For the individual peasant, it may prove impossible to afford these costs, especially since the rewards of such measures are not obtained at once, but in the future. Furthermore, for a peasant struggling for daily survival, working on marginal land, or working as sharecropper or tenant, the prospects of investing on soil conservation methods may not be so appealing. Consequently, if the process of soil destruction is to be reverted, efficient government action is needed. However, as we have seen, the efforts of the Dominican government to control deforestation and erosion have so far been very limited.

The composition of output, on the other hand, is influenced by factors such as population growth, relative commodity prices, access to credit, etc. Thus, whether a peasant cultivates food crops, which tend to erode the soil, or tree crops such as coffee, cocoa or forest, which tend to protect the soil, is determined by these factors.

Erosion and the Composition of Peasant Output

In this section we shall limit our analysis to the *minifundio* subsector. In the presence of market imperfections, the interaction between population growth and erosion mainly affects this subsector. This implies that the new entrants in the rural labor force will have trouble in acquiring land. As argued in Chapter 6, the monopolist landowner may sell or rent land only at a high price. Sometimes the land is not even held mainly for cultivation or grazing purposes, but as a source of status and a way of securing credit and political power. Thus, little land will be added to production in the *minifundio* subsector, but at least some of the new workers will be employed there. This will change factor proportions in this subsector. Production will become more labor-intensive since little new land can be acquired for the new workers.

However, an increase of the labor supply will intensify erosion in the *minifundio* subsector as the land will be worked more intensively. The labor force growth changes the composition of output at given commodity prices. The peasants will tend to produce more of the labor-intensive crops (food crops) and less of the land-intensive crops (export crops). (The relative labor-intensity of different peasant crops can be seen in Table 9.6.) This shift will increase the rate of erosion and the supply of arable land will fall. The increased amount of labor will thus be combined with less productive land and this will result in lowering the productivity of both land and labor.

As a result of population and labor force growth, the land base of the peasants has been shrinking. The concentration of land in the hands of a few large landowners has implied that too much of the increasing agricultural labor force has been forced onto the limited land area in the *minifundio* sector. This has accelerated the erosion process. Since less productive land is available for the peasantry, labor productivity has fallen and so have rural incomes. For a large number of peasants, the escape from this situation has been migration.

The interaction between the use of traditional techniques, population growth and erosion, and the influence these factors have on rural employment is summarized in Figure 9.3.[50] It should be kept in mind that while in Figure 9.2 we denominated *minifundista* production "food" we now specify it further and subdivide it into food crops and export crops (see Table 9.6).

272

TABLE 9.6   Labor Requirements per Crop on Small Farms (0.5 to 5
             Hectares) April 1975 - March 1976

	Man-days per hectare
Food crops	
Cassava - corn*	146
Tomatoes	129
Beans - others	119
Cassava - sweet potatoes	105
Cassava	92
Pigeon peas	91
Rice - others	84
Rice	84
Rice - corn	81
Corn - pigeon peas	81
Cassava - corn	79
Sweet potatoes	76
Banana - coffee	75
Cassava - others	73
Corn - sweet potatoes	70
Peanuts	68
Sweet potatoes - others	66
Corn - others	62
Beans	60
Beans - corn	59
Pigeon peas - others	59
Corn - plantains	56
Plantains	56
Plantains - others	52
Cassava - pigeon peas	52
Peanuts - others	51
Corn - peanuts	49
Corn	48
Corn - beans	43
Corn - cassava	41
Export crops	
Tobacco	113
Tobacco - others	70
Coffee - cocoa	60
Coffee	54
Coffee - others	46
Cocoa	32
Cocoa - coffee	21
Cocoa - others	13

*Interplanted.
Source: SEA (1977), Table 2.7, pp. 10-11.

FIGURE 9.3   Changes in Factor Endowments and the Composition of
Production in the Peasant Sector

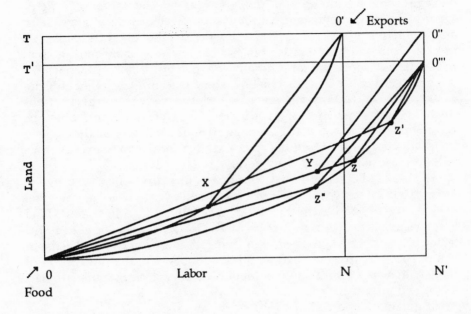

The growth of population increases the supply of labor in the agricultural sector and in the absence of migration most of this increase will be absorbed by the *minifundio* subsector. Initially this subsector has a factor endowment which is given by the box ONO'T. Land is measured on the vertical axis and labor on the horizontal axis. The production of food goods (rice, beans, corn, etc.) is measured by means of a series of isoquants (not shown) extending from O, and export (coffee and cocoa) production by isoquants extending from O'. At the outset, the peasants produce the output mix given by point X in the diagram, with factor intensities given by the straight lines OX and O'X respectively. Export production is land-intensive and food production is labor-intensive, i.e., export products use relatively less labor in relation to land as compared with food products. We assume that this is so for all relative factor prices, i.e., no factor reversals take place.

With the increase of the labor force in the sector, the factor endowment box becomes ON'O"T. Assuming linearly homogeneous production functions and holding commodity and factor prices constant, factor intensities remain unchanged (OY is an extension of OX and O"Y is parallel to O'X), as the production moves to point Y.

According to the Rybczynski theorem,[51] if the supply of one of the factors of production increases while the supply of the other is kept constant, the production of the good using the increased factor intensively will, at constant commodity and factor prices, increase in absolute terms, whereas the production of the other good decreases. At constant commodity and factor prices, the increase of labor must go into production of food, the labor-intensive crop. But if factor proportions are not to change in food production, some land must be released from export crop production. However, in order to keep factor proportions unchanged in this line of production, the released land must be accompanied by some labor. Then, at given relative commodity prices, the production of food will increase and the production of export crops will decrease as exemplified by point Y in the diagram.

As discussed above, the risk for erosion increases when we move to more labor-intensive utilization of the soil. With erosion, the total availability of land will shrink. In this situation, unless new land becomes available, the new box becomes ON'O'''T'. In order to keep the factor proportions in production unchanged, more land as well as labor has to be taken from the export production. Again, the production of food will increase and the production of export crops will fall. The sector will produce at point Z.

At given relative commodity prices, the process described above is *cumulative*. Initially, the growth of population and labor force increases the percentage of the labor-intensive crop and this in turn increases the rate of soil erosion. However, the falling supply of agricultural land gives a further impulse towards a more labor-intensive crop pattern which in turn increases the rate of erosion, etc. At the same time, the population and the labor force continue to grow, etc. The outcome of this process is falling per capita income in the peasant sector.

Until now, we have assumed constant commodity and factor prices. However, an increase in the labor supply is unlikely to leave relative commodity and factor prices unchanged.

Thus, neither Y or Z can be possible equilibrium points. The outcome depends on the development of relative commodity prices. An increase in the relative price of food goods would move us further northeast in the diagram, with Z' as a possible equilibrium point. In this case, the production of subsistence goods increases and the process of erosion is accelerated. If, on the other hand, the relative price of subsistence goods fall, the production of these goods will fall and we move southwest in the diagram, with Z" as a possible equilibrium point. Since the production of export goods, in this case, increases, the process of erosion will be counteracted.

Different factors, such as world market prices, government tax and price policies and population growth, influence relative commodity prices. If as a result of these factors, the relative price of export goods falls, the production of food goods will increase. The price effect will reinforce the Rybczynski effect and consequently also the erosion process. Labor productivity will fall as more labor will be added to the shrinking land base. Labor will be subject to increasingly diminishing returns and the per capita income in the agricultural sector will fall. If the relative price of export goods increases, on the other hand, the production of this good will increase and the erosion process will come to a halt or at least be slowed down.

Thus, the acceleration or counteraction of the erosion process depends on two major factors: a) the Rybczynski effect, and b) the price effect. At constant commodity prices, the Rybczynski effect leads to increased food production which in turn tends to accelerate erosion. The price effect could influence the erosion process negatively or positively depending on the direction of the development of relative prices. If these prices develop in favor of subsistence crops, the price effect will work in the same direction as the Rybczynski effect and the erosion process will be further accelerated. If the relative prices move in favor of exports, it will work in the opposite direction of the Rybczynski effect. In this case, whether the erosion process will be accelerated or counteracted depends on whether the Rybczynski effect is relatively stronger or weaker than the price effect. In the following section, we will take a look at the development of relative prices and discuss to what extent they have influenced the composition of output and thereby the erosion process.

Relative Commodity Prices and the Composition of Output

The relative prices of export and food goods are largely influenced by developments in the world market and by government policies with respect to taxation and domestic prices. The development of world market prices and government taxes on traditional Dominican exports is presented in Figure 9.4 and Table 9.7, respectively. Export prices have been fluctuating to a large extent but show an upward trend, especially from 1973.

Explicit export taxes have changed throughout the 1955-79 period. Taxes on cocoa, tobacco and coffee were discontinued in 1962. Until 1961, coffee and cocoa exports were made through a monopoly controlled by the Trujillo family. During the Trujillo regime, those two export crops were not only subject to high taxes but they also had to be sold to a monopoly with the attending price consequences. Taxes were also discontinued on non-traditional agricultural exports in 1966 as an export promotion tool. Between 1963 and 1974 the majority of export taxes were collected from sugar exports. In 1975 taxes were again levied on coffee and cocoa (Law 199).[52]

FIGURE 9.4   Prices of Dominican Export Crops, 1960-1984

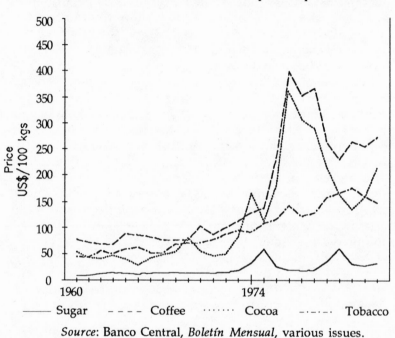

Source: Banco Central, Boletín Mensual, various issues.

Export taxes in the Dominican Republic have been progressive in the sense that the rates go up when world market prices increase. We do not have any data on taxes after 1979, but since export prices have been increasing it is possible that taxes have followed the same trend. High export taxes result in lower prices for the producer of these products.

Another factor affecting producer prices is the overvaluation of the currency. With overvaluation, exporters will receive less domestic currency for a given quantity of exports. In the Dominican Republic, a dual exchange system was in operation until 1985. The official rate was at par with the US dollar. This is the rate at which exporters, until recently, have had to convert all their export earnings to domestic currency. The peso had been at par with the US dollar since 1947, while the parallel rate offered a constantly increasing premium on the dollar (see Table 9.8). Until a few years ago,[53] exporters had to convert all their foreign exchange earnings at the official rate, which meant a clear loss for the exporter compared to what he would have achieved had the official rate been allowed to reflect the true scarcity of foreign exchange. Thus, besides explicit export taxes, export crops have been subject to increasing implicit taxes arising from the overvaluation of the currency.

TABLE 9.7   Export Tax Rates,* 1956-1979. (Annual Averages in Percent ad Valorem)

Years	Sugar	Coffee	Cocoa	Tobacco
1956-60	2.44	24.03	20.64	6.14
1961-65	3.76	1.01	2.26	1.39
1966-70	7.64	-	-	-
1971-75	16.76	0.29	0.20	-
1975-79	10.23	17.53	18.16	-

*Does not include "other taxes" (documents, export permits, loading charges, and so forth).

From 1967 to 1973 a DR$ 0.015 per kilogram tax was levied on exports as part of the International Coffee Agreement.

Source: Quezada (1981), Tables 2.8 and 2.9, pp. 67-68.

The performance of the marketing system for export crops also influences the price received by producers. As argued in Chapter 5, the commerce for coffee, cocoa and tobacco can be described as being oligopsonistic in the local market. This may result in lower prices at least for the small producers who have to go through a long marketing chain.

In the case of food crops, the marketing system was considered to be rather competitive. Most of these crops, however, have been subject to price controls. The Price Stabilization Institute (INESPRE) regulates marketing and prices of more than a dozen agricultural commodities. In order to accomplish its goal of stabilizing prices, INESPRE has been heavily dependent on food imports. Most of these imports have been carried out at zero nominal tariff. At the same time, they have received an implicit import subsidy due to the overvaluation of the currency. INESPRE's policies have tended to lower the prices received by food crops producers. (See Chapter 5.)

TABLE 9.8   Price of the US Dollar in the Parallel Market, 1960-1988
(Annual Averages)

Year	DR$
1960-64	1.09
1965-69	1.09
1970-74	1.14
1975-79	1.21
1980-84	1.68
1985-88	3.95

Sources: 1960 to 1979: Quezada (1981), Table 2.10, p. 73; 1980 to 1988: Banco Central, *Boletín Mensual*.

Relative Prices and the Composition of Output in the Peasant Sector

The above factors influence not only the prices received by producers of export and food crops, respectively, but also, (assuming that producers are responsive to price changes) the composition of output. Table 9.9 presents producer prices for peasants export crops and food crops, respectively, for the period 1960-79.

TABLE 9.9   Producer Price Index for Selected Crops, 1960-1979
(Annual Averages, 1960 = 100)

Year	Food Crops					Export Crops		
	Rice	Corn	Beans	Peanuts	Plantains	Coffee	Cocoa	Tobacco
1960	100	100	100	100	100	100	100	100
1961-1965	95	101	122	101	203	176	123	120
1966-1970	93	122	128	103	336	174	186	150
1971-1975	116	175	207	125	483	266	304	230
1976-1979	160	219	332	172	1,029	n.a.	n.a.	n.a.

Sources: Calculated from World Bank (1978:1), Table 7.19, p. 399 and Quezada (1981), Table 1A, p. 238.

The table has to be interpreted with extreme caution but, if anything, the figures seem to indicate that (excluding plantains, for which producer prices have increased significantly and considering that rice, corn, beans and peanuts amount to approximately 45 percent of total food crops production) for the two product groups as a whole, the price of food crops has fallen in terms of export crops (see Figure 9.5 below). We do not have any figures on producer prices for export crops for the period 1976-79, but assuming that these prices follow the trend in world market prices presented in Figure 9.4, producer prices should have continued to show an upward trend.

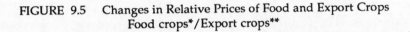

FIGURE 9.5   Changes in Relative Prices of Food and Export Crops
Food crops*/Export crops**

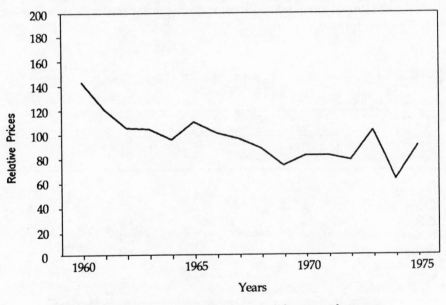

*Weighted producer prices for rice, corn, beans and peanuts.
**Weighted producer prices for coffee, cocoa and tobacco.

Source: Table 9.11.

Provided that the supplies of export and food crops are not unresponsive to changes in relative prices, the increase in the relative price of export crops should have induced the peasants to shift out of production of food goods and to go into the production of coffee and cocoa instead. Thus, according to the model outlined above, this should tend to slow the rate of erosion down as a result of less intensive use of the soil. But has this really happened in the Dominican Republic? In order to answer this question we should look at the allocation of land between the different crops. We do not have any data in relation to shifts in the allocation of peasant land between different crops. However, some data are available for the total cultivable land of the country and these are presented in Table 9.10.

As the table indicates, the percentage of land in food production has decreased while it has increased slightly in export crops. However, the shift seems not to have been from food crops into export crops but into pasture land. In contrast to the diminishing land area in food crops, there has been a spectacular increase in pasture for livestock production. The figures also show that the percentage of land area occupied by forest and fallow has shrunk significantly, indicating the country's limited possibility to continue with its traditional extensive land use pattern.

TABLE 9.10   Dominican Land Use, 1960 and 1976
(thousands of hectares)

	1960		1976	
	Hectares	%	Hectares	%
Food crops	350	16.9	328	12.0
Export crops	396	19.1	577	21.1
Pastures	757	36.5	1,445	52.8
Forest	280	13.5	222	8.1
Fallow land	290	14.0	164	6.0
Total	2,073	100.0	2,736	100.0

Source: IAD (1983:2), p. 18.

The increase in the percentage of land used for export crops may be explained by the increase in the land area in sugar cane. As we recall, the land area used for this crop (produced mainly on large farms) increased by more than 100 thousand hectares during the period 1973-1976. Thus, the decrease in the percentage of land area in food production is probably not a result of a shift in the composition of small peasant production. It could be due, on the one hand, to the diminished land area in the hands of the *minifundistas* who are the major producers of this type of crops (as we recall from Chapter 6, Table 6.4, the land area in farms of less than 5 hectares decreased from 351,800 hectares in 1971 to 326,100 in 1981) and, on the other hand, to a shift of larger producers away from food crops and into pasture.

Now, if the relative price of peasant export crops has increased in terms of food crops, is it likely that small producers have not shifted production away from food crops and into export crops? This may very well be the case. The model used above easily allows for the situation where the changes in relative prices have not been large enough to lead to a shift in production. It is also possible that this type of shift will only take place if relative prices increase steadily during a very long period and in this case a shift in production would take place in the very long run. The data available are not adequate to check any of these possibilities. However, the cultivation of cocoa and coffee implies a long gestation period and in the absence of financial resources, a shift to this type of crop may not be feasible. The conditions prevailing in the credit market only allow the peasants to procure credit for very short periods and at high interest rates (see Chapter 7). Another reason for maintaining the level of production of food crops in spite of the possible fall in relative prices is that more than one harvest per year can be produced. At the same time, many of these crops can be interplanted. This means that both food and cash can be obtained more regularly throughout the year.

A third factor which may prevent an increase in the land area devoted to export crops in the *minifundio* subsector is the decreasing size of this type of farm. The average size of farms in this category fell from 2.0 hectares in 1971 to 1.5 in 1981 (see Table 6.4 in Chapter 6). It would be difficult for new producers in this category of farms to afford the cultivation of both export and food crops as has traditionally been the case.

To sum up the argument, changes in the composition of output in the peasant sector depend on two factors: changes in factor endowments (the Rybczynski effect) and changes in the relative price between food and export crops (the price effect). The available data, if anything, indicate that the relative price of food has decreased and, according to the model, this should have led to a shift in the composition of peasants' output in favor of export crops, i.e., the price effect has been in the opposite direction to the Rybczynski effect. Hence, whether the erosion process has increased or not depends on the relative strength of these effects. The empirical evidence, in so far as it can be interpreted, seems to indicate that the Rybczynski effect has outweighed the price effect. There is virtually no indication of peasants having shifted away from food crop production.

Thus, if the figures discussed above are not too erroneous and if the peasants have continued to grow food crops in spite of the fall in relative prices, the process of erosion should also have accelerated during the period 1960-80, and this in turn may have accentuated the low level of productivity and incomes in the peasant sector.

Relative Prices and the Composition of Production in the Large Farms

In 1976, producers with more than 31 hectares devoted 76 percent of their land to pastures and only 8 percent to food crops (Table 9.1). We do not know what the situation in 1960 was like, but this large proportion of land area in pasture may be partly due to a shift away from food crops, forest and fallow land, and to the incorporation of new land into pasture as Table 9.10 seems to indicate.

Now, can this shift in the composition of production in large farms be explained in terms of relative prices? In Table 9.11, the development of producer prices for sugar cane and beef (mainly produced on large farms) is compared with a weighted index for export crops (coffee, cocoa and tobacco) and food crops (rice, beans, corn and peanuts), mainly produced on small farms. The producer prices for sugar cane have been increasing steadily since 1960. This could explain the increase of the land area for this crop. However, sugar cane and grazing are, in a sense, complementary activities since a large number of oxen are used in the transportation of sugar cane. Thus, an increase in the production of sugar cane is likely to increase the demand for oxen and this in turn may tend to increase the land area in pasture. In the case of beef, producer prices increased from an index of 100 in 1966 to 167 in 1975. But this increase is much lower than the increase in the weighted index for food crops and export crops, respectively, during the same period. Thus, the enormous increase in the percentage of land area used for pasture can hardly be explained in terms of the development of relative prices.

The explanation has to be sought elsewhere. An important factor could be the large incentives given to livestock producers since the early 1960s. The *Banco Agrícola*, in cooperation with the Alliance for Progress program, provided incentives for the production of meat for export by providing credit. The number of loans to these producers increased from 7 in 1961 to 2,926 in 1963. During the same period, the average size of these loans increased from DR$ 231 to DR$ 1,356. This policy continued during the 1970s. The average size of loans to livestock increased from DR$ 1,629 in 1970 to DR$ 4,175 in 1977. At the same time, the government provided different incentives to these producers. In 1968, export taxes on meat were reduced from DR$ 16.00 to DR$ 5.00

per animal.[54] Milk producers were, however, not equally privileged. Milk production was subject to price control at the same time as the milk processing firms were allowed to import milk. This may have discouraged some producers from raising livestock.[55]

However, many of these producers are absentee landowners for whom it may be more handy to keep land in pasture than to venture into production of food crops. The higher risk involved in the production of food crops plus the restrictive price policies implemented by the government may further discourage these producers. There are also some indications that peasants who choose to migrate often tend to let their land lie in pasture, and since migration has increased during the last decades, this could also have contributed to the increased amount of land used for pasture.[56]

TABLE 9.11   Weighted Producer Price Index* for Selected Food Crops and Export Crops, and Producer Price Index for Sugar and Beef, 1960-1975

(1966=100)

	1960-65	66	67	68	69	70	71	72	73	74	75
Food crops**	100	100	103	102	103	104	104	105	125	150	183
Export crops***	90	100	108	117	141	129	129	137	124	245	207
Sugar	84	100	99	107	107	114	114	130	143	243	370
Beef	-	100	96	96	95	111	119	125	149	166	167

*Weighted according to the relative and average importance of the production of the different items over the period.
**Include rice, corn, beans and peanuts.
***Include coffee, cocoa and tobacco.

Sources: Calculated from World Bank (1978:1), Table 7.1, p. 378 and Table 7.19, p. 399, and Quezada (1981), Table 1A, p. 238 and Table 5A, p. 242.

Agricultural Production

One of the implications of the preceding argument is that the rate of growth of agricultural output will be reduced. During the last decades, the performance of the agricultural sector has been highly disappointing. Production, if it has not declined, has been stagnant, especially in the case of most food crops. Total agricultural production decreased with 3.6 percent during the period 1962-68.[57] This trend seems to have continued during the 1970s. As Table 9.12 shows, for the majority of the products, the growth of output has lagged behind the growth of population during the period 1973-82. As we recall, the rate of growth of population was 2.9 percent during the 1971-81 period.

TABLE 9.12   Volume Index of the Principal Agricultural Products, 1973-1982 (1973 = 100)

	1973	1974-76	1977-79	1980-82	Average Annual Rate of Growth 1973-82
Rice	100	116	127	145	4.5
Beans (red)	100	95	116	115	3.9
Corn	100	105	103	93	-0.1
Peanut oil*	100	71	76	67	0.6
Plantains	100	91	101	123	3.9
Potatoes	100	95	51	65	- 0.7
Sweet potatoes	100	87	67	50	- 9.0
Cassava	100	75	95	50	- 2.1
Calabash	100	101	91	82	- 5.6
Pigeon peas	100	107	107	124	3.7
Onions	100	134	144	191	16.1
Salad tomatoes	100	99	67	73	0.9
Pork	100	106	127	0	2.7
Milk	100	98	106	124	4.0
Beef	100	92	103	116	2.7
Sugar*	100	105	102	90	0.4
Coffee*	100	85	115	124	10.4
Cocoa*	100	115	111	97	1.6

*Does not include production data for 1982.

Source: Subsecretaría Técnica de Planificación Sectorial (SEA), in IEPD (1983:2), Table 2, p. 11.

According to FAO figures, in 1984, total agricultural production - and food production per capita - was at a lower level than in 1971. Food production per capita fell from an index of 106 in 1971 to 96 in 1984. The corresponding figures for total agricultural production per capita was 103 in 1971 and 93 in 1984.[58]

Likely explanations for the stagnation or decline of agricultural production are the imperfect transferability of production factors (in this case, land and credit) in combination with population growth, and the price policy pursued by the Dominican government. Firstly, the limited access to land confronted by the peasantry in combination with population and labor force growth, has led small producers to shift into more labor-intensive production methods. This has tended to accelerate the erosion process and hence to decrease the supply of arable land. At the same time, the limited access these producers have to credit limits the possibilities of investment. Hence, the peasants have ended up with a lower output per unit of land and thus lower income. Lower income implies lower possibilities of savings and investments which in turn tend to reduce further the rate of agricultural growth

Secondly, the concentration of land and credit resources in the hands of a few large landowners has led this group of producers to use these resources inefficiently. The level of agricultural investments among them has also been low and this in turn has contributed to maintain a low level of productivity and growth. Finally, the government policy of keeping food prices artificially low is likely to have discouraged both small and large producers from increasing production.

The production of rice has, however, increased significantly. This is mainly due to the concentrated efforts of the government on the agrarian reform settlements which produce a large proportion of this crop. Other products presenting positive growth rates are milk and beef. However, considering the large increase in the amount of land given over to pasture, these increases are not so impressive.[59]

In any case, the supply of food has been unable to catch up with the population growth. This food deficit has led to increased imports of food staples. The country is presently exporting a variety of agricultural products, traditional ones like sugar, coffee, cocoa and tobacco and non-traditional ones like sweet-potatoes, yams, cassava, cocoyam, pigeon peas, calabash and beef, but at the same time, it imports huge quantities of foodstuffs. (See Table 9.13.) In 1980, agricultural exports represented 48 percent of the agricultural GNP and amounted to DR$ 230 million. The same year, the import of agricultural products amounted to DR$ 113 million.[60] But if the trade balance proved to be favorable for agricultural production taken as a whole, it showed a deficit for foodstuffs in general, since the traditional agricultural export products accounted for the largest part of export incomes. The exports of food staples in relation to the total exports decreased in current prices from 9.5 percent in 1970 to 8.8 percent in 1981, while food imports represented 14 percent of the total imports during the same period. The deficit in the balance of trade for food staples reached DR$ 49 million in 1979, DR$ 117 in 1981, and was calculated to be DR$ 219 million in 1983.[61]

TABLE 9.13   Volume Index of Dominican Imports of Some Food Staples, 1972-1983*

(1972=100)

	Rice	Beans	Corn	Peanut, Soy, and Cotton Oil	Value Index of Total INESPRE Imports** (at Current Prices)
1972	100	100	100	100	100
1973	345	266	208	58	190
1974	843	46	250	116	384
1975	575	159	129	89	195
1976	371	130	234	124	177
1977	726	90	294	118	264
1978	122	64	82	147	157
1979	-	155	291	238	283
1980	472	348	604	219	414
1981	732	-	574	234	475
1982	-	-	617	229	249
1983	-	-	831	237	288

*Refers to imports carried out by the Price Stabilization Institute (INESPRE).
**Includes powdered milk, wheat and minor food items.

Source: INESPRE (1984), pp. 85-96.

Conclusions

The major argument pursued in this chapter is that the unequal distribution of land generates imperfections in the land market, and indirectly influences the performance of the credit market. These market imperfections have prevented an efficient allocation of agricultural resources. The outcome has been stagnant agricultural production and falling rural incomes.

The unequal distribution of resources has influenced the land use pattern and the output mix. While the *latifundistas* use land-intensive production methods, the *minifundistas* use labor-intensive methods. Hence, the former tend to cultivate land-intensive crops, mainly pastures, while the latter have tend to grow labor-intensive crops, mainly food crops. Thus, monopoly power in the land market has influenced the land use pattern in agriculture and this in turn has affected the demand for labor. As more land is put into pasture, the total demand for labor increases at a slower rate than would be the case if more land were put into the cultivation of food crops. In the absence of alternative employment, the man/land ratio in the *minifundio* subsector increases and this in turn tends to press down the level of rural wages. A large farm crop which demands high labor inputs is sugar cane, but the sugar plantations rely mainly on Haitian workers. The presence of these workers, whose status as immigrants implies an even lower bargaining power than that of the Dominicans, tends to lower further the level of wages in the sector.

Imperfections in the credit market have negatively influenced the introduction of modern technology in the agricultural sector in general, and in the peasant sector in particular. Dominican agriculture presents a very low level of investment and this has contributed to maintain low productivity and growth in the sector.

Traditional land use and cultivation patterns in combination with population and labor force growth have increased the problems of erosion and deforestation, thereby reducing further the land base of the country in general and of the peasantry in particular. The concentration of land in the hands of the *latifundistas* has implied that the increasing agricultural labor force has been added to a more or less constant supply of land. As a result, labor productivity in the peasant sector has been falling and so have rural incomes. The cultivation of marginal land has been intensified at the same time as the peasants are forced to move higher up onto the mountain slopes. This, in combination with an increased demand for charcoal and firewood, has led to the felling of trees on the mountainsides. The result has been an accelerated erosion process.

The tendency for erosion to increase was shown to be dependent on two factors: the effects of changes in factor endowments (the Rybczynski effect), and the effects of changes in relative commodity prices (the price effect). In the Dominican case, the increase in the rural labor force in combination with a rigid land tenure system has led to a shift towards more labor-intensive crops in the peasant sector. This shift has tended to increase erosion. The changes in relative prices may, on the other hand, have been in favor of land-intensive crops, notably coffee and cocoa, which if cultivated, tend to counteract erosion. However, there seems to be no evidence of peasants having shifted to these types of crops. Different factors, such as low short-run elasticities of supply of export crops and the difficulty of obtaining credit, may have prevented the peasants from making this shift. Thus, the Rybczynski effect seems to have outweighed the price effect and hence the peasants have been confronted with a diminished supply of arable land.

The falling supply of arable land gives a further impulse towards a more labor-intensive utilization of the land which in turn increases the

rate of erosion. At the same time, the population and labor force
continue to grow, the man/land ratio increases further. More trees will
be felled on the mountains, either because of the need to open up new
land or because of the need for charcoal and firewood, and the rate of
erosion increases. In the absence of significant measures to check erosion,
the peasants will inevitably be facing decreasing incomes. The costs
involved in erosion control are generally high, especially since the
benefits are not enjoined at once but in the future. For the individual
peasant family, whose income barely meets subsistence requirements,
these costs are probably high. The situation could possibly be changed
by government action. However, the measures taken by the Dominican
government in order to check erosion have been negligible.

The shrinking land base of the peasantry due, on one hand, to the
land tenure system of the country and, on the other hand, to population
growth in combination with unchanged technology, undoubtedly
constitutes an important push factor behind the rural-urban migration.

Notes

1. This section draws on Griffin (1969), pp. 78-80 and Griffin (1976:1), pp. 161-63.

2. In 1976, 4.5 million *tareas* (300,000 hectares) out of a total of 2.7 million hectares were dedicated to sugar cane. (See Rodríguez (1984), p. 34.)

3. ONAPLAN (1983:1), p. 121. In the case of pastures, the average stocking rate is one animal per hectare and could thus easily be doubled or tripled with better management (World Bank (1978:1), p. 16).

4. IAD (1983:2), p. 18.

5. The most important perennial crops are coffee, cocoa, plantains, bananas, coconuts and citrus fruits, i.e., tree-crops (World Bank (1978:1), p. 394). The ILO mission makes the following division: perennial crops: sugar cane, coffee, cocoa, plantains, others; annual (seasonal) crops: rice, tobacco, peanuts, corn, beans, potatoes, cassava, others (OIT (1975), p. 147).

6. ONAPLAN (1983:1), p. 159 and Table 29-A, p. 160.

7. Similar findings are reported by the SEA survey of 1976. However, the crops with the highest labor requirements were found to be tomatoes, tobacco and rice (SEA (1977), p. XII). Sugar cane production is not considered in this survey.

8. This amount includes some large farms as well, mainly producing export crops such as coffee and cocoa.

9. Griffin (1974), pp. 51-52.

10. Dore Cabral (1979), p. 21. In this year, fertilizers were used in only 22 percent of the land area devoted to the most important crops (ibid.).

11. World Bank (1978:1), Table 17, p. 32. State irrigated land is serviced by state owned and state maintained canals. Such land may be privately owned (ibid.). The present irrigated area is 178,300 hectares, equivalent to around 60

percent of the land suitable for irrigation. Most of the irrigation canals were built after 1966. The existing irrigation system confronts serious technical and economic problems (Isa (1985)). See also World Bank, (1978:1), pp. 32-36.

12. See Dore Cabral (1979), pp. 58-59.

13. ONAPLAN (1983:4), Table 20, p. 48. A big problem concerning all machinery used in Dominican agriculture is the wide range of different trademarks in use. This makes it hard to get adequate service and necessary spare parts. In 1975, there existed 23 importers of agricultural machinery, and not less than 70 different trade marks. Most of the workshops were concentrated to the capital and most of the manuals were not written in Spanish. Between 1960 and 1969, 3,300 tractors were imported, mainly from the US and Europe, and 2,217 motocultivators or small tractors mainly from Asian countries (OIT (1975), pp. 137-38).

14. ONAPLAN (1983:1), p. 161 and Table 29-B, p. 162. Some food crops are said to receive fertilization in 0-10 percent of the cultivated area. About half of the most important food crops apply pesticides in 40 to 90 percent of the cultivated area. However, in all cases, fertilizers and pesticides are reported to be applied with deficiencies (ibid.).

15. Ibid. Besides rice, other peasant crops with high access to irrigation facilities are plantains and beans, occupying 9 and 6 percent, respectively, of state irrigated land (World Bank, (1978:1), Table 17, p. 32).

16. The figures in Table 9.3 are based on a single observation. In later years, the situation seems to be unchanged. In 1981, less than 2 percent of the agricultural bank credit to the sector was dedicated to purchase agricultural equipment (ONAPLAN (1983:4), p. 6).

17. Ibid., p. 153. Some sources give higher figures, probably due to the fact that tractors not in use are counted as well. It is estimated that the lifespan of a tractor in the Dominican Republic is around 8 years. For a comparison see Duarte (1980), Table 2.22, p. 171, who presents the figure of 8,853 tractors in 1971.

18. Alcántara Z. (1981), p. 45.

19. ONAPLAN (1983:4), p. 32.

20. Rodríguez (1984), p. 34.

21. World Bank (1978:1), Table 18, p. 37.

22. Cane cutters in the Dominican Republic manage, on average, 1.5 tons a day. The corresponding figure in Australia is 12-15 tons per worker a day; in South Africa and Jamaica, 7 tons a day; in Mexico, Peru and Puerto Rico, 5-6 tons a day (Veras (1983), Table 18, p. 155).

23. ONAPLAN (1983:1), Table 30, p. 166.

24. Cf. Lundahl, (1979), pp. 607-10. See also Schultz, (1964), pp. 18-23.

25. The impact of a loan is very difficult to determine with certainty. Measurement of the impact of a loan requires the collection of information on all changes in the sources and uses of liquidity that are contemporary with loan receipt and then a comparison of the "with" and "without" loan situation (Adams et al. (1984), p. 3).

26. SEA (1977), Tables 4.19 and 4.24, pp. 55 and 58.

27. Ibid., Table 4.21, p. 56.

28. Munguía (1975), pp. 68-124 and 134-167.

29. Quezada (1981), pp. 106 and 108.

30. Ibid., p. 111.

31. Ibid., p. 113 and Table 3.6, p. 112.

32. In his study on the area of Elías Piña, Palmer reports that even the most rudimentary methods of preventing soil erosion are lacking. Crop rotation and limited interplanting are the only techniques practiced (Palmer (1976), p. 172).

33. Cf. e.g. Wolf (1966), pp. 20-22 for a description of this technique.

34. ONAPLAN (1983:1), p. 123.

35. Wolf (1966), p. 22. See also Boserup (1965).

36. Sharpe (1977), p. 41. See also Lundahl (1979), p. 63.

37. Boserup (1965).

38. Ibid., pp. 13-15, 23-24 and 41.

39. IAD (1981:1), p. 26. These may be approximate figures. According to other sources, erosion ranges from 200 to 1,400 tons per hectare and year. (See US AID (1981), figure V-4, p. 40.)

40. US AID (1981), p. 65.

41. Ibid., pp. 49-60 and 63-64.

42. It is estimated that 80 percent of the Dominican households depend on energy extracted from wood (Casanovas (1983), p. 3). Palmer (1976), pp. 115-18, gives an account of the different factors that contributed to deforestation in the border area during the period 1900-61.

43. Law No. 6787 of 1945 prohibited the cutting of trees on mountaintops and around rivers, springs, lakes and ponds (Palmer (1976), p. 122).

44. ONAPLAN (1983:1), p. 139.

45. US AID (1981), p. 101. The total annual production of charcoal is estimated to be 4.8 million sacks, equivalent to 622,900 metric tons of wood. There does not exist any reforestation of these areas, and the abundance of goats (the cow of the very poor) in the area constitutes a further threat to soil regeneration (ibid., pp. 101 and 105).

46. Practical restrictions to the charcoal commerce do not exist. The government tried to block the transportation of charcoal but did not succeed (ibid., p. 100).

47. It is estimated that the country loses 2,000 hectares of forest per year. However, during the period 1969-78, the government had only afforestated 1,919 hectares (ONAPLAN (1983:1), p. 140-41). A reforestation program is intended by the project *Plan Sierra*. This project covers an area of around 2,000 square kilometers with highly eroded and overpopulated mountain slopes. For a description of this project, see Santos (1980).

48. For a description of tropical mountain soil see Webster and Wilson (1966). See also Lundahl (1979), p. 209.

49. Lundahl (1979), p. 210.

50. This analysis draws on ibid., pp. 221-23.

51. Cf. Rybczynski (1955). A formalization of the theorem in algebraical terms is found in Södersten (1964), Chapter 3.

52. Quezada (1981), p. 66. For an account of the different tax laws on traditional exports during the period 1960-86, see Consejo Nacional de Agricultura (1989), tomo II, pp.781-82.

53. In 1984, the Dominican peso was *de facto* devalued and the two markets were unified. Traditional exports were however penalized since, by government disposition, exporters of these crops were receiving 1.48 pesos for each dollar exported while the market rate was nearly 3 pesos for one dollar. (See Pérez Minaya (1985).)

54. ISA (1979), pp. 192-96.

55. Some of the milk producers dedicated their land to sugar cane production, others dedicated themselves to financial business (ibid., pp. 236-40).

56. Grasmuck (1982), p. 395.

57. Economía Dominicana (1976), p. 93. Other factors, such as the political unrest during 1963 and 1965 and the droughts of 1967 and 1968, may partly be responsible for this decrease in production.

58. Calculated from FAO (1975), pp. 85-87 for 1971-74 and FAO (1985), pp. 87 and 89 for 1973-84. (1974-76=100). It should be noted, that the FAO (Production Year Book) figures imply a very high level of aggregation and may therefore be somewhat shaky.

59. Meat exports represented 6 percent of the total value of food exports and a negligible percentage of total exports. (ONAPLAN (1983:1), pp. 86 and 81). Milk production is also deficient. Since 1980, INESPRE has been importing increasing quantities of milk (INESPRE (1984), pp. 93-96).

60. ONAPLAN (1983:1), p. 81.

61. Ibid., p. 83.

Appendix to Chapter 9

In this Appendix, we shall discuss some important issues related to factor market distortions.

The presence of factor market distortions can give rise to different "pathologies" in the economy.[1] Among the structural effects[2] of factor market distortions we shall consider the following: a) the shrinkage of the production possibility curve, b) the possibility that the production possibility curve becomes concave, c) non-tangency, i.e., non-equivalence of the marginal rates of transformation and substitution, d) the possible reversal of the product factor intensities and, e) the possibility of a "perverse" price-output response and a "perverse" distortion-output response.

As stated in the main text, the existence of factor intensity reversals is difficult to determine empirically, especially in underdeveloped countries where access to reliable data is very limited. However, for the interested reader, and in order to make the analysis self-contained, we will give a brief review of the theoretical discussion concerning this issue.

We shall first consider the problem of shrinkage of the production possibilities curve and its non-tangency with the product price line.

The Shrinkage Effect

For every point on the contract curve representing an input combination there is a corresponding point on the production possibility curve. This is illustrated in Figure A.1 using the box diagram we have worked with in the main text.[3]

The curve OXYO' is the contract curve that will prevail in the economy when no distortions in factor market exist. Given a point on the contract curve, such as X, a point on the production possibility frontier can be determined. At point X, isoquants m_0 and l_0 are tangential to each other. The isoquant m_0 intersects the diagonal at point R, and therefore, measuring the output of food along NO', the quantity of food produced is given by the distance NB. On the other hand, the l_0

isoquant intersects the diagonal at point Z, and therefore, if we choose to measure livestock along ON, the quantity of livestock produced is given by the distance NC. Extending the lines BR and CZ until they meet, we obtain point D. In the same fashion, if we consider another point on the contract curve such as Y, and follow the same procedure, we will obtain point E. We can go on in an analogous fashion and read several points that correspond to input combinations on the contract curve. If we join all these points we get a curve such as ODEO'. This is the production-possibility curve.

FIGURE A.1   The Derivation of the Shrinkage Effect

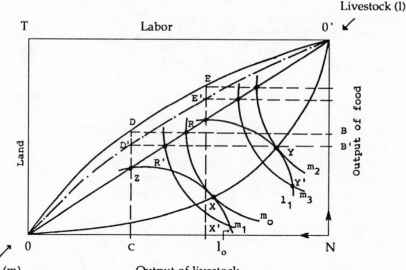

Food (m)   Output of livestock

The same procedure can be followed in the situation where factor market distortions prevail. In this case, the economy does not produce on the contract curve, but the isoquants will cut each other, for example at point X'. As before, the isoquant l_0 intersects the diagonal at Z and the quantity of livestock produced is still given by NC. However, due to the differential paid by the *minifundistas* on land, the input combinations for this producers are now given by isoquant m_1. Then the intersection point is R' instead of R and the quantity of food produced is given by NB'. Extending the line B'R' until we meet the line CD we obtain point D'. Following the same procedure, if we consider point Y' where the same distortion exists, we obtain point E'. Both D' and E' lie inside the production possibility curve ODEO'. If the same procedure is followed for every pair of isoquants showing the same distortion, and all these points are joined, we get the distorted production possibility curve OD'E'O'.

The shrinkage effect is also illustrated in Figure A.2 where both the undistorted and the distorted production possibility curves are shown. Curve BX'C lies inside the optimum curve BXC, except at the two specialization points B and C. Point X indicates no distortion while X' indicates that the *minifundio* (food) subsector is paying a differential for land.

FIGURE A.2   The Shrinkage Effect

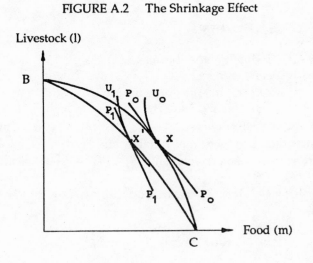

The production possibility curve that arises in the presence of factor market distortions need not be convex, as in Figure A.2. The curve can be concave, or convex in one section and concave in another.[4]

The Non-Tangency Effect

The 2x2 model illustrated in Figure 9.2 can be formulated as follows:
Production functions:

$$m = m(T_m, N_m) ,$$
(A.1)

$$l = l(T_l, N_l) .$$
(A.2)

Endowment constraints:

$$T_m + T_l = \overline{T} \ , \tag{A.3}$$

$$N_m + N_l = \overline{N} \ . \tag{A.4}$$

First order conditions for profit maximization:

$$w_m = m_N P_m \ , \tag{A.5}$$

$$w_l = l_N P_l \ , \tag{A.6}$$

$$r_m = m_T P_m \ , \tag{A.7}$$

$$r_l = l_T P_l \ , \tag{A.8}$$

where m and l indicate food (*minifundio* subsector) and livestock (*latifundio* subsector), respectively; T_m, T_l and N_m and N_l represent land and labor used in the production of food and livestock, respectively; w_m, r_m and w_l, r_l are the rewards to labor and land in the *minifundio* and the *latifundio* subsectors, respectively; m_N, m_T and l_N, l_T are the marginal productivities of labor and land in the production of food and livestock, respectively and, P_m, P_l are the prices of the two goods.

Taking the total derivatives of equations (A.1), (A.2), (A.3) and (A.4), we get:

$$dm = m_T dT_m + m_N dN_m \ , \tag{A.9}$$

$$dl = l_T dT_l + l_N dN_l \ , \tag{A.10}$$

$$dT_m = - dT_l \ , \tag{A.11}$$

$$dN_m = - dN_l \ . \tag{A.12}$$

Substituting equations (A.5) to (A.8), (A.11) and (A.12) into equations (A.9) and (A.10) yields:

$$dm = - (r_m/P_m)dT_l - (w_m/P_m)dN_l \ , \tag{A.13}$$

$$dl = (r_l/P_l)dT_l + (w_l/P_l)dN_l \ . \tag{A.14}$$

Dividing equation (A.14) with (A.13), we obtain the slope of the production possibility curve:

$$\frac{dl}{dm} = -\frac{P_m}{P_l}\left[\frac{r_l dT_l + w_l dN_l}{r_m dT_l + w_m dN_l}\right] .$$

(A.15)

The marginal rate of transformation (MRT), i.e., the slope of the production possibility curve (dl/dm), will coincide with the marginal rate of substitution (MRS), i.e., the slope of the price line (P_m/P_l) when the bracketed term in (A.15) equals 1, i.e., when $w_m = w_l$ and $r_m = r_l$.

However, in the presence of distortions, such as in our case, where $(r_l/r_m) < 1$, the bracketed term will be less than 1 and $|MRT| < |MRS|$. This is illustrated in Figure A.2 where the slope of the price line P_1P_1 = MRS is steeper than MRT, the slope of the inner transformation curve BX'C at X'. In other words, the relative market price of l is less than its opportunity cost because of the lower factor market costs to l.

The Factor Market and Supply Response

Assume that the production functions governing the production of goods l and m are linearly homogeneous and that the labor-land ratios (N/T) in each subsector are denoted by t_l and t_m. Assume further that in the absence of distortions food is labor-intensive. In the presence of a distortion, the *latifundistas* benefit from a differential $\lambda = r_l/r_m < 1$ for land, i.e.:

$$r_l = \lambda r_m ,$$

(A.16)

$$w_l = w_m .$$

(A.17)

In the presence of factor market distortions, two types of factor intensities must be distinguished: those in the physical sense and those in the value sense.[5]

PH represents the physical definition of relative factor intensity, i.e., the difference in labor-land ratios in the two subsectors:

$$PH = t_l - t_m .$$

(A.18)

VA represents the value definition of relative factor intensity, i.e., the difference in shares of labor relative to land in the two subsectors:

$$VA = \frac{w_l N_l}{r_l T_l} - \frac{w_m N_m}{r_m T_m} = (w/r)_l t_l - (w/r)_m t_m .$$

(A.19)

The production line with the largest share of the value of output going to land is said to be land-intensive in the value sense.

In the absence of distortions (when $\lambda = 1$), PH and VA always have the same sign. In that case, the production activity with the greatest relative use of labor per unit of land also has the largest share of output being paid to labor. If $\lambda \neq 1$, PH and VA may have different signs. If so, a product is relatively land-intensive according to one definition and labor-intensive according to the other, i.e., the production activity with the greatest relative use of labor will pay the largest share of output to land, and vice versa.

In the presence of distortions, when $\lambda \neq 1$, PH and VA intensities of the products may be reversed. Stephen Magee[6] has identified four sets of non-specialized factor market equilibria in the Edgeworth-Bowley box. These are illustrated in Figure A.3.

FIGURE A.3   Sets of Non-specialized Factor Market Equilibria

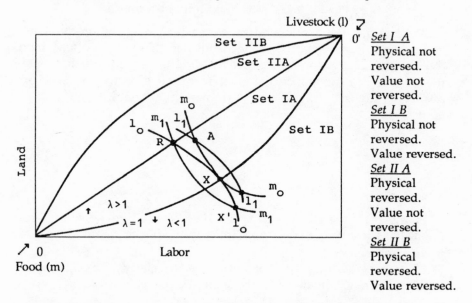

Set I A
Physical not reversed.
Value not reversed.
Set I B
Physical not reversed.
Value reversed.
Set II A
Physical reversed.
Value not reversed.
Set II B
Physical reversed.
Value reversed.

The four sets in Figure A.3 denote non-specialized factor market equilibria for which the original value and physical intensities (such as those given by point X) may be reversed or may not be reversed. It can be seen that the only region where the physical and value intensities correspond is that between the non-distorted contract curve 0X0' and the diagonal 00'. At point A, for example, $|\lambda| = |(w/r)_m| / |(w/r)_l| > 1$, i.e., the factor-price line (not drawn) tangential to the isoquant l_1l_1, is less steep than the factor-price line (not drawn), tangential to m_0m_0.

Substituting equations (A.16) and (A.17) into equation (A.19), VA can be rewritten as

$$VA = (w/r)_l t_l - (w/r)_l \lambda t_m = (w/r)_l (t_l - \lambda t_m). \qquad (A.20)$$

By multiplying and dividing by t_l, we can rearrange equation (A. 20) so that

$$VA = (w/r)_l t_m \left[\frac{t_l}{t_m} - \lambda \right]. \qquad (A. 21)$$

At all points below the diagonal in Figure A.3, t_l/t_m is less than 1, i.e. by assumption, food is PH labor-intensive and livestock is PH land-intensive. But at all points above the non-distorted contract curve 0X0', λ is greater than 1. Thus, the bracketed term in (A.21) then is negative. Consequently, the physical and value intensities always correspond in the region between the non-distorted contract curve and the diagonal. This is, however, not the case at point X'. At this point, $\lambda = (w/r)_m/(w/r)_l < 1$, i.e., the slope of the l_0l_0 isoquant is steeper than the slope of the m_1m_1 isoquant.

Since at all points below the diagonal, t_l/t_m is less than 1, the sign of the bracketed term in (A.21) is indeterminate and the possibility for value intensity reversal will appear. VA may be positive or negative depending on whether

$$\frac{t_l}{t_m} \begin{array}{c} > \\ < \end{array} \lambda. \qquad (A. 21)$$

If $\lambda < (t_l/t_m)$, VA will be positive and the correspondence between PH and VA will be broken.[7] In this case, for example, the product with the greatest relative use of labor per unit of land will have the lowest share of output being paid to labor. In our case, this means that, in the presence of value intensity reversals, the *minifundio* subsector which is labor-intensive in physical terms, will be land-intensive in the value sense. That is, in the presence of value intensity reversals, the *minifundistas* will pay the largest share of output to land.

Different authors have shown that the presence of factor intensity reversals has important consequences for the behavior of the system to price and differential changes.[8] Accordingly, given the present formulation, where the differential is multiplicative, in the presence of factor intensity reversals, outputs will respond perversely to changes in relative prices, i.e., an increase in the relative price of a product will lead to a decrease rather than to an increase in the production of that good. An increase in $P = (P_m/P_l)$ (with the differential λ held constant) increases the supply of m if the physical and value intensities correspond and reduces m if they do not. Consequently, the supply response of outputs to changes in P is normal if, and only if, neither the physical nor the value intensities reverse (Set IA in Figure A.3) or both reverse (Set IIB), and the response is abnormal or perverse if, and only if, relative factor intensities reverse in the physical sense only (Set IIA) or relative factor intensities reverse in the value sense only (Set IB).

In the same fashion, the response of outputs to changes in the differential λ (with product prices P constant) is normal or perverse depending on whether PH and VA intensities correspond or not, that is, an increase in a differential paid by a production activity on either factor reduces output if factor intensities do not reverse (the normal case) and increases output if they do (the perverse case).[9]

The likelihood of factor intensity reversals depends on the characteristics of the production function. For homothetic production functions (i.e., where factor proportions are independent of the level of production), the ratio of the isoquant slopes along the diagonal (the ratio of the $m_1 m_1$ and $l_o l_o$ isoquants at point R) yields the differential λ required to reverse the PH factor intensities. The value of λ required to cross the diagonal and give a PH reversal becomes smaller the higher the product elasticities of factor substitution S_m and S_l (i.e., the percentage change in N/T for a given percentage change in w/r) and the more similar the initial factor intensities of the products.[10]

It seems that no generalization about the possibility of VA intensity reversals is possible.[11] This is determined by the relative elasticities of substitution in the two subsectors. If the production function is of the Cobb-Douglas type, VA factor intensity reversals are impossible since the relative shares going to land and labor, and hence the VA factor intensities, are invariant to changes in either prices P or the differential λ.[12] Thus, the possibility of VA reversal considered in Set IB in Figure A.3 is nil if the elasticities of factor substitution equal 1, i.e., $S_m = S_l = -1$.

In general, if λ is held constant and P varies, the value factor intensities never reverse if S_m and S_l are constant and equal (as in the Cobb-Douglas case), reverse once if S_m and S_l are constant and different, and may reverse more than once in all other cases.[13]

The Likelihood of Perverse Responses

Before ending this appendix, a word should be said about Peter Neary's argument concerning the possibilities that the perverse results discussed above take place in reality. According to Neary, "all these paradoxes are theoretical curiosa which will 'almost never' be observed in real world economies."[14] Using a 2x2 model, Neary shows that if, for example, capital adjusts sluggishly in the short run, an equilibrium where the PH and VA factor intensities do not correspond in a small open economy must be locally unstable. Accordingly, the perverse output response to prices follows from comparative-static analysis and, for a variety of plausible adjustment mechanisms, can be ruled out as dynamically unstable and hence unlikely to be observed.

However, Horst Herberg and Murray Kemp[15] argue that what is interesting is not whether the small open economy is stable or not, but whether the larger system, within which that economy is included and where commodity prices are endogenously determined, is; that is, instability of a partial system does not preclude stability of the larger system. Neary argues,[16] however, that Herberg's and Kemp's reasoning is not valid because it violates Samuelson's Correspondence Principle, whereby the comparative static behavior of a system is seen to be closely related to its dynamic stability properties.[17]

The existence of factor intensity reversals is, in our case, an empirical issue. As we noted in the main text, however, it is difficult - particularly in underdeveloped countries - to establish the existence of reversals. The empirical study of such phenomena is obstructed by several factors. First, it depends on the type of production function chosen. Using - as is common - a Cobb-Douglas function, the possibility of value reversal is ruled out *ex hypothesi*. Second, the existence of heterogeneous factors of production, which in the estimation are treated as homogeneous, may indicate that reversals have occurred when in reality they have not. Finally, and perhaps more serious, the study of reversals requires access to reliable data. If there is any subject for which such data are unlikely to exist, it is the agricultural sector in underdeveloped countries. In short, since it is possible and likely that perverse results never occur, we will therefore not take them into consideration in our analysis.

Notes

1. Bhagwati and Srinivasan (1983), Chapters 20 and 21.
2. Following Bhagwati, Magee (1976), p. 4 classifies the effects of factor market distortions into structural and welfare effects.

3. The derivation of the production possibility curve in the presence of factor market distortions is found in Johnson (1966), pp. 687-88, and Magee (1976), pp. 47-49.

4. Bhagwati and Srinivasan (1971), Jones (1971), Herberg and Kemp (1971), Herberg, Kemp and Magee (1971) and Magee (1976).

5. Definitions in Magee (1976), p. 22 following Jones (1971).

6. Magee (1976), pp. 23-24.

7. In the case of Set IB, value reversal will occur if $\lambda < t_l/t_m$ and will do not if $\lambda > t_l/t_m < 1$. Similarly, since at all points above the diagonal t_l/t_m is greater than 1, in the case of Set IIB (where $\lambda > 1$), value reversals will occur if $\lambda > t_l/t_m$.

8. For references see Magee (1973), pp. 20-21, and Magee (1976), Chs. 2 and 3.

9. Normal and perverse output responses to price changes are not necessarily related to the concavity or convexity of the transformation curve. For different propositions linking the shape of the transformation curve to the factor market and production functions see Magee (1973), pp. 27-28, and Magee (1976), pp. 57-58).

10. Magee (1976), p. 39.

11. Ibid.

12. Herberg and Kemp (1971). Since the elasticity of substitution in a Cobb-Douglas production function is constant and equals unity, the labor-land ratio and the factor share change proportionally.

13. Herberg, Kemp and Magee (1971).

14. Neary (1978), p. 672.

15. Herberg and Kemp (1980).

16. Neary (1980).

17. Samuelson (1979), Chapter 10.

10

Rural Out-Migration and the Allurement of the Modern Sector

The major parts of this work have been dedicated to an analysis of the rural economy. The focus of our study has, so far, been on the performance of the agricultural sector and its inability to generate productive employment for the rural population. In Chapter 2, we showed that the agricultural sector has been unable to efficiently employ its increasing labor force. In the subsequent chapters, we analyzed the major factors obstructing an efficient use of labor resources in that sector.

The deteriorating economic situation in the rural areas has forced many peasants to migrate from the countryside into the cities, or abroad. Rural-urban migration has been a response to the pressure on land and the increasing unprofitability and risk, involved in agricultural activities. At the same time, it is also a reaction to the higher wages and the relatively better living and working conditions offered in the urban areas. In Chapter 2, we also showed that, throughout the last decades, the migration of peasants to the cities has been increasing steadily, in spite of the high level of unemployment persisting in the urban areas.

The aim of the present chapter is to identify some of the major urban factors (pull factors) that have attracted the peasants into the cities. We begin by presenting the magnitude and the distribution of migration in different cities of the Dominican Republic. Thereafter, some of the consequences of rural-urban migration, namely the concentration of the population in marginalized urban neighborhoods (slums), are presented.

In a third section, we discuss the Dominican industrialization process, and the different policies which may have encouraged workers to migrate to the cities. The extent to which the urban (industrial) sector has been able to absorb the increasing urban labor force is also considered. It will be shown that, in terms of employment generation, the industrialization policies pursued in the country have been inadequate. Most workers have not been able to obtain jobs in the organized, or formal, labor market, but have instead found employment in the informal labor market. The importance and characteristics of these two markets will also be analyzed.

In a fourth section, the major factors influencing the migration decision are discussed. It will be argued that this decision is based on a perceived value of migration where economic factors play a major role. However other factors of a more individual, or psychological, character are also important. In a final section, the migration of Dominicans abroad is considered, as well as the influence of this migration on the remaining population. Finally, we present a short discussion of the economic effects of migration.

The Migration Flow

Since the 1950s, the migration of the Dominican peasants into the cities has been steady. In 1920, 83 percent of the Dominican population lived in rural areas and in 1950, 76 percent of the population still lived in the countryside. By 1981, however, this figure had dropped to 48 percent.[1] The Dominican Republic conforms to the pattern found in most Latin American countries where, since 1950, a tremendous exodus of peasants into the cities has been taking place. In 1950, 61 percent of the Latin American population lived in rural areas. By 1970 the rural population of Latin America had dropped to 44 percent of the total.[2] Similar patterns are found in population growth. Latin America's total population increased approximately 2.8 percent annually between 1960 and 1970, whereas rural regions grew by only 1.3 percent per annum.[3] The corresponding figures for the Dominican Republic are 2.9 and 1.2, respectively.[4] It is difficult to ascertain to what extent these differences in urban-rural population growth are due to rural-urban migration. However, it is estimated that between one-third and one-half of the urban growth in most underdeveloped countries is due to rural-urban migration.[5]

The Dominican Republic has experienced an unprecedented increase in population during the last three decades. In 1950, the Dominican population was around two million. By 1981, this figure had increased to nearly 6 million. Actually, the Dominican Republic has one of the highest population densities in Latin America, 117 persons per km^2. Due to the high rate of growth of the population and to rural-urban migration, the urban population has increased very rapidly since the 1950s, doubling its size every ten years.[6] The cities with the highest population increase are Santo Domingo (the capital) and Santiago, the second city in importance. Table 10.1 presents the urban population growth by size of cities.

TABLE 10.1   Urban Population by Size of Cities

Size of Cities (number of inhabitants)	No. of Cities in 1970	Population (in thousands)				Percentage Increase in Relation to the Previous Census		
		1950	1960	1970	1981	1960	1970	1981
More than 50,000:								
Santo Domingo		181.5	370.0	673.5	1,313.2	104	82	95
Santiago		56.6	85.6	155.0	278.6	51	81	80
30,000 - 49,999	7	103.6	151.4	257.7	n.a.	46	70	n.a.
20,000 - 29,999	5	40.9	75.5	122.3	n.a.	85	62	n.a.
10,000 - 19,999	7	26.7	50.7	89.4	n.a.	90	56	n.a.
Less than 10,000	77	99.1	188.8	295.3	n.a.	90	56	n.a.
Municipal Capitals	98	508.4	922.1	1,593.2	2,936.0	81	73	95

Sources: For 1950-1970, OIT (1975), Table 33, p. 92. For 1981, ONE (1982:1).

It can be observed that in the period 1950-60, all cities, regardless of their size, experienced a rapid increase in population. In Santo Domingo, which tops the list, the population increased by 104 percent during that period. During the period 1960-70, the trend changed with demographic growth being mainly concentrated to the largest cities, i.e., cities above 30,000 inhabitants, while cities of less than 30,000 inhabitants experienced a relative decline. In relation to its extraordinary demographic growth in the 1950-60 period, Santo Domingo also experienced a relative decline. During the period 1960-70, this city increased its population by 82 percent. However, the demographic growth of Santo Domingo speeded up again during the 1970-81 period. During this decade, the population of this city increased by 95 percent.

The urban demographic pattern portrayed in Table 10.1 seems to indicate that migration in the Dominican Republic has been a step migration. In the first decade of large migration movements (1950-60), rural migrants settled to a large extent in smaller towns, while in the latter decades, many of these migrants moved towards larger cities.

The rapid expansion of urban areas during the 1950s took place in spite of Trujillo's restrictive measures against rural migration. In 1953, a law was passed stating that no peasant, or other rural resident, may move to urban centers without permission from the central government. Nevertheless, an inquiry carried out in 1976 in five slum districts of Santo Domingo found that 91 percent of the family heads residing in that city were migrants, and that 46 percent of them had arrived in the 1950s.[7] Thus, there was substantial rural-urban migration throughout that decade. A temporary decrease took place in the mid-1960s during the chaotic years that followed after the fall of Juan Bosch in 1963 and culminated with the April revolution in 1965. These incidents may have slowed down the migration flow into the major cities, and especially to Santo Domingo. With the return of Joaquín Balaguer in 1966, the migratory movement regained importance and has continued uninterrupted up to the present.

Traditionally Santiago, located in an agricultural district, has received most of its migrants from rural areas whereas Santo Domingo has drawn a majority of its migrants from other urban centers. In 1978, 62 percent of the migrants in Santo Domingo came from urban areas. For most migrants, Santo Domingo is the main attraction at a national level. Lately, there are some indications that an increasing number of peasants choose to move directly to this city.[8]

Apart from internal migration, the Dominican Republic has also experienced a large international migration. For the period 1960-70, the migration of Dominicans, mainly to the US, is estimated to be approximately 15 percent of the natural population increase.[9] The migration of Dominicans abroad will be dealt with in a later section.

Selectivity of Migration

Among the migrants arriving in urban centers, the major selective factors at work would appear to be those of age and education.[10] It is generally the younger and better educated sections of the population that leave for the cities. This may be due to the fact that these groups tend to discern, more easily than others, the limited opportunities provided by their original environment. In 1978, 78 percent of the migrants to Santo Domingo were under 25 years of age and the majority had more than five years of schooling.[11]

Most of the migrants to Santo Domingo were women (56 percent). Many women migrate to the cities in search of jobs as domestic servants. In 1979, 32 percent of the total employed female population of Santo Domingo worked as maids.[12]

The City Slums

As stated above, during recent decades, most Dominican cities have been growing at an accelerating pace. However, the urbanization process has not been able to keep up with urban population growth and a large portion of the population lives on the outskirts of the cities in crowded and improvised settlements. As a result, most cities have been going through a ruralization process in the sense that these new districts, or *barrios marginados*, more resemble improvised rural settlements than urban communities.

These demographic phenomena affect nearly all large cities in underdeveloped countries. *Favelas* in Rio de Janeiro, *callampas* in Santiago de Chile, *barriadas* in Lima, *colonias proletarias* in Mexico City, *ranchos* in Caracas, *villas miserias* in Buenos Aires, *bidonvilles* in Port-au-Prince...or *barrios marginados* in Santo Domingo, all refer to the same phenomenon: the spontaneous settlement of rural migrants in the city. Nowadays, these settlements constitute a new form of urbanity in nearly all underdeveloped countries. In most Latin American countries, squatters constitute between one-fifth and one-half of the total urban population.[13]

The most salient characteristics of these urban settlements are: the wretched appearance of the lodgings, the distant location from urban commercial centers, the lack of water mains and sewer systems, the lack of sanitation, the overcrowded conditions and the illegal character of the settlements.

In Santo Domingo, around 56 percent of the population lives in *barrios marginados*. This population is cramped together in an area which represents 16 percent of the total area of the city.[14] These *barrios* generally lack water mains and sewer systems and their population lives under very unhealthy conditions. In 1979, only 25 percent of the total urban population had access to sewer system[15] and in the capital only 40 percent had running water in their houses.[16] In 1981, in a *barrio* in Santo Domingo with around 35,000 inhabitants, only 30 percent had access to communal latrines, 4 percent had access to communal toilets, and 5 percent had no access at all to either communal latrines or toilets. 83 percent of the families were illegally occupying the land where they had built their houses. The illegal character of the settlements is a major factor contributing to the deteriorating appearance of the lodgings, since the settlers fear they can be dislodged by the authorities at any time.[17]

The level of income of some of the families living in the *barrios* is very low. In 1983, these families had an average of 128 pesos per month to live on. Of this income, 80 percent was spent on food. The rest was spent on rent, health care, clothing and transport.[18] Most of the workers are unable to get a steady job in the formal labor market. In order to subsist, all family members have to find a way to earn a living, including the children. Many slum children spend the day "working in the city." They work as shoe-shiners, sell newspapers, peanuts and sweets, generally prepared by their mothers. Some of them spend the days digging in the garbage cans of the rich neighborhoods, looking for food waste and collecting the plastic bags in which the better-off people usually wrap their garbage.[19] Another common activity among slum children is to stand by the traffic-lights and clean the windscreens of cars when the light is red, while others just beg.

The urban industrialization and modernization process that gained force during the 1950s has probably constituted a major attraction influencing the peasants' decision to move into the cities. However, it is evident from the dire poverty encountered by many migrants in the city slums that this expanding sector of the Dominican economy has been unable to absorb all the applicants for urban employment that have sought their fortune in the cities. In the next section we shall try to describe the performance of the industrial sector in the Dominican Republic and indicate why it has been unable to generate sufficient employment to the increasing labor force.

The Urban (Industrial) Sector

The Dominican industrialization process could be said to have started with the establishment of the sugar industry in the 1870s. However, this industry mainly represented a rather isolated enclave which had very little connection with the rest of an economy that was largely based on agricultural activities. This industry was essentially foreign owned. Capital as well as labor came from abroad. Most profits were repatriated and investments were mainly concentrated in the growth of infrastructure around the fast developing sugar industry.[20] The activity of the urban sector was mainly of an administrative and commercial character. Some foreign-owned banks operated in the capital but were chiefly related to the financial activities of the sugar industry and some local traders.

After the World War I, the price of sugar fell on the world market and a deep economic crisis struck the Dominican Republic during the 1920s. The economy was far from recuperation when the stock market crash came in 1929, followed by a devastating hurricane the year after. At this time, apart from the sugar industry, the only industries of importance that existed in the country were a state-owned shoe factory, founded in order to meet the army's needs, and a partly foreign-owned beer brewery.[21] There were also some cigar and liquor factories, a match factory and various small enterprises, mainly artisans' workshops, with few employees.[22]

It was not until the last decade of the Trujillo era that an industrialization policy was pursued in the country. Soon after Trujillo came to power in 1930, the destiny of the Dominican society was to be directed according to the dictator's wishes. He soon monopolized the most profitable branches of the economy. The first step towards his personal enrichment was the monopolization of salt production.[23] Soon after that his interest was directed towards the sugar industry. His engagement in sugar production started in 1948, and by his death in 1961, he controlled two-thirds of the country's total sugar production.

In the 1950s, a small group constituted by Trujillo, his relatives and an inner circle of personal friends controlled nearly all industrial activities in the country. In 1950, an industrial incentive law was promulgated providing tariff protection and tax exemption to the infant industries. The generous tariffs and highly selective government support protected these industries from domestic and foreign competition and generated ample profits for the small group of industry owners.[24] The flourishing industrial sector attracted many workers from the rural areas and many tried their luck in the prosperous and growing towns.

The industrialization policies implemented in the Dominican Republic are very similar to those implemented in most Third World countries. During the World War II, most of these countries were unable to satisfy their import needs at the same time as they experienced a drastic fall in the prices of their exports. A feeling of self-reliance started to grow among these countries and many embarked on an industrialization process. The import-substitution strategies followed were based on high government protection and this has led to a highly inefficient industrial sector. Most of the industries in these countries present high production costs and underutilization of both labor and capital. At the same time, the agricultural sector was largely neglected, as most resources were allocated towards the industrial sector.[25] The Dominican industrialization process which started in the 1950s and was reinforced in the 1960s has similar features.

Industrialization in the Post-Trujillo Period

After Trujillo's death in 1961, his entire industrial empire became state property. His sugar industry came to be administered by the *Consejo Estatal del Azúcar* (CEA) while the rest of his industries is actually controlled by the *Corporación Dominicana de Empresas Estatales* (CORDE). CORDE manages 19 large manufacturing industries, 7 commercial firms, 2 mine enterprises, a real estate company, an agricultural consortium, and a transport (air) company. In 1975, the CORDE consortium had net fixed assets amounting to DR$ 50 million and employed 8,527 persons. The manufacturing industry administered by CORDE accounted for 70 percent of CORDE's total employment.[26]

When Balaguer came to power in 1966, the Dominican industrialization and urbanization process was reactivated. A new strategy was designed in an official document published in 1968. The new strategy recalled the policies of 1950, in its emphasis on self-reliance. However it explicitly considered the problems of employment and income distribution, and the necessity for industrialization in order to confront the population growth and its pressure on land resources.[27] In 1968, an industrial incentive law (Law 299) was promulgated. The new law granted tariff exemption on imports of capital and intermediate goods, and ample fiscal incentives to the selected firms. These industries also enjoyed access to cheap credit and foreign exchange.[28] The new industrialization strategy soon produced results. The growth rates of GDP after 1968 have, on average, been significantly higher than those experienced during the pre-1968 period. For the period 1960-68, the average annual growth rate was 3.9 percent, while for the period 1968-78 it reached 8.6 percent.[29]

It is difficult to ascertain to what extent this high growth rate was a result of the industrial incentive law. Other factors may have been of equal importance. Firstly, with the Balaguer regime, a sense of security grew among the business community after a long period of social and political unrest. Secondly, in the mid-1970s, the prices of the country's main exports increased substantially.[30] Thirdly, the Balaguer administration embarked on a huge construction program and the activities in this sector may have reactivated other sectors of the economy as well. During the period 1968-73, about 60 percent of total gross domestic investment was allocated in the construction sector. During this period, construction activities grew at an annual average of 17 percent.[31]

In the late 1970s, there was a marked decline in the growth rate of the construction sector, as well as other economic activities. The rate of economic growth fell to an average of 4.0 percent during the 1975-82 period.[32] The fall in sugar prices and the increase in oil prices may have contributed to the poor performance of the economy.

The industrialization policies proved to be unsuccessful when it came to the maintenance of stable economic growth. Neither were these policies successful in achieving diversification or decentralization of economic activities. The share of manufacturing in GDP only increased from 13.7 to 15.7 percent during the period 1970 to 1980.[33] The high level of concentration of industrial activities that prevailed during the Trujillo era was still apparent. At present, 3.2 percent of the firms account for 50 percent of the total capital stock, 47 percent of total industrial production and 23 percent of total employment within the sector. On the contrary, small and medium sized firms, account for 85 percent of all industrial enterprises, but only 19 percent of the capital stock, less than 30 percent of the production and nearly 50 percent of the sector's employment.[34]

Nor was the industrialization policy successful in increasing industrial activities in other regions of the country. Most firms were located in the major cities, in spite of the fact that the industrial incentive law of 1968 provided large incentives to firms that established themselves in other regions than Santo Domingo. Firms located in Santo Domingo were to enjoy tariff and tax exemptions for a period of eight years, while firms established in other parts of the country would receive these benefits for a period up to twenty years. These incentives proved to be insufficient to achieve decentralization and by 1973, more than three-quarters of the import substitution industries were located in Santo Domingo.[35] In 1979, this situation had not changed significantly. As Table 10.2 shows, an overwhelming majority of the industrial establishments in the country are found in Santo Domingo.

TABLE 10.2   Localization of Manufacturing Industries

	No. of Establishments	
Localization	(1)	(2)
Santo Domingo	1,308	-
Santiago	259	58
San Cristóbal - Haina	52	11
La Romana	20	31
San Pedro de Macorís	32	82
La Vega	33	14
Puerto Plata	30	11
Rest of country	115	33
Total	1,849	230

(1): No. of establishments according to an inventory made by OSP, Secretary of Industry and Commerce in 1979 (excludes industrial duty-free zones).

(2): No. of establishments in industrial duty-free zones in 1988.

Sources: For column (1), ONAPLAN (1982); for column (2), FED (1989).

The industrialization policies implemented in the late 1960s proved to be highly successful in attracting workers from the rural areas as well as from other urban centers to Santo Domingo. As shown above, the population of this city doubled in a decade's time. The establishment in the late 1970s and the 1980s of duty free industrial zones (Export Processing Zones) in towns like Santiago, San Pedro de Macorís, La Vega, La Romana and Puerto Plata, have also attracted rural migrants to these towns. In the two latter towns, a rapid expanding tourist industry may attract migrants as well.

The Modern Sector and Employment

The industrialization policies were less successful at providing employment for the huge amount of workers who had moved to the urban centers in anticipation of finding improved living conditions. In Santo Domingo, where the industrialization and urbanization efforts were concentrated, the labor force grew at the rate of 6.3 percent during the period 1968-73. This rate is considerably higher than the rate for the country as a whole. During this period, the total labor force grew at an annual rate of 2.7 percent.[36]

In the 1970s, the growth rate of the total urban labor force was three and a half times higher than the growth rate of urban (industrial) employment. While the urban labor force grew at an annual rate of 5.9 percent during the period 1970-81 (see Table 2.2), total industrial employment grew at an average of 1.6 percent annually during the period 1970-79 (see Table 10.3).

Table 10.3 below, shows the index of industrial employment for the period 1960-79. Industrial employment (excluding the sugar industry) increased from an index of 100 in 1970 to 200 in 1979. This is a significant increase, especially compared with the situation before 1970. The average index of industrial employment during this period was 95. The growth of industrial employment in the post-1968 period was, however, unable to keep pace with the growth of the urban labor force. All throughout the 1970s, urban unemployment was around 20 percent. In the 1980s, it had even increased. In 1983, the unemployment rate in Santo Domingo reached 21.4 percent (see Table 2.4).

One of the possible reasons for the persistence of unemployment could be that the economic expansion actually created employment, but that these job opportunities were absorbed by the underemployed rather than by the unemployed. Another important factor that may have contributed to the maintenance of unemployment is the structure and type of growth which characterized the Dominican economy in the 1970s. Growth was concentrated in the capital-intensive industries of the modern sector. This led to greater differences in productivity levels and to a sluggishness in the creation of employment opportunities.

TABLE 10.3   Index of Industrial Employment in the Dominican Republic,*
1960 - 1979

(1970 = 100)

	1960-69	70	71	72	73	74	75	76	77	78	79	Average Annual Growth Rate 70-79
*)	n.a.	100	103	112	119	126	111	102	103	107	118	1.6
**)	95	100	106	122	118	151	166	178	193	185	200	8.1

*Total Industrial employment.
**Industrial employment excluding the sugar sector.

Sources: 1960-69: World Bank (1985), Table 8.1, p. 419; 1970-79: ONAPLAN (1983:2), Table 31, p. 55.

Statute No. 299 conceded exemptions of as much as 100 percent of taxes on profits for those industries that invested their profits in new equipment. In 1973, the capital-labor ratio in the majority of the favored industries was 25 percent higher than the average ratio of the rest of the registered industry, excluding the sugar industry. That year, the import substituting industries had average capital-labor ratio of US$ 10,000 per employed person.[37] For the period 1973-77, these industries presented an average of DR$ 15,748 per employed person.[38]

As a result of government protectionist policies, capital is priced below its opportunity cost. For this reason, some of the privileged industries tend to have an installed capacity which is out of proportion compared to the size of the market which in turn leads to an underutilization of the factors of production. On the other hand, since income is concentrated in a few hands, the internal market grows very slowly - thus reducing the possibilities of fully utilizing the installed production capacity. In 1979, it was estimated that 54 percent of the firms utilized less than 25 percent of their production capacity.[39]

During the period 1968-79, the manufacturing sector, excluding the sugar industry, generated 30,133 jobs. About 29 percent of these jobs were generated in the capital, where most industrial establishments are located. The sugar industry generated very few jobs in the seventies. Employment in this industry increased from an index of 100 in 1970 to 119 in 1973, but then it decreased to an index of 89 in 1979. In the 1980s, urban employment was mainly generated in the duty free industrial zones.[40]

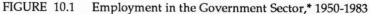

FIGURE 10.1   Employment in the Government Sector,* 1950-1983

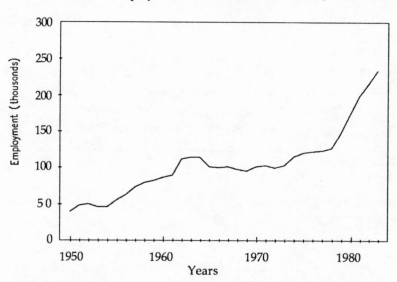

*Excludes employees of the *Consejo Estatal del Azúcar* (CEA) and of *Empresas* CORDE. Settlers at IAD projects and day laborers at CEA and other public enterprises are also excluded.

Source: Dauhajre (1984), Table 5, p. 43.

A major employer in the urban sector is the government. The government sector is generally considered as part of the modern sector since the government employer generally pays wages above the established minimum.[41] As Figure 10.1 shows, employment in the government sector increased steadily in the 1970s, and early 1980s. The index of government employment increased from 100 in 1970 to 232 in 1983.[42] However, these figures do not include the CEA and *Empresas* CORDE, both important government owned industrial conglomerates. As can be seen in Figure 10.1, employment in the government sector increased considerably after 1978. This can be interpreted in relation to the shift of government that took place in August that same year. As pointed out in Chapter 4, the *Partido Revolucionario Dominicano*, PRD, favored increased government employment for both political and economic reasons.

In the government owned industries, political interests seem to have prevailed over internal economic goals. Employment in these industries is reported to be excessive. From being a net contributor to public savings in the early 1970s, these industries became a net drain during the period 1979-82. In 1982, only 5 of 25 enterprises reported positive operating profits.[43]

The Informal Sector

In terms of income and employment generation, the urban sector could be divided into three major subsectors: the modern (industrial) sector, the government sector and the informal sector.[44] In 1983, the informal sector accounted for 45 percent of total urban employment, while the industrial and the government sector contributed with 33 and 22 percent, respectively.[45]

The informal sector includes all urban small-scale activities characterized by low productivity. The participants in the informal sector are persons who have not been integrated in the modern sector and who have to make a living on their own account. The informal sector is often considered to be composed of shoeshiners and ambulatory salesmen. However, the ILO mission estimated that in 1970, the overwhelming majority (90 percent) of the work carried out within the informal sector was "functionally linked to the economic system."[46] Table 10.4, presents the different employment activities included in the informal sector.

TABLE 10.4   Distribution of Employment within the Urban Informal Sector, 1970

Activities	Percentage
Marginal services	10.5
Reparation and preservation	44.3
Services related to the construction sector	6.3
Transport services	4.9
Production	34.0
	100.0

Source: OIT (1975), p. 120.

In 1970, there were around 88,000 workers employed within the informal sector. The majority of these workers (44 percent) dealt with repair and maintenance mechanics. This means that they work with anything from cars and bicycles to watches (*relojeros*). They also work as electricians, cobblers, painters and brick-layers. 34 percent of these workers were occupied with direct production, here we find tailors and dressmakers, carpenters, people who make household utensils out of zinc, basket-makers, artisans, etc.[47] The processing of scrap and used wood is very common. Many people are also engaged in different sorts of services such as barbers, owners of small restaurants and mobile kitchens. About 10 percent of the workers within the informal sector are engaged in marginal services. Many of these workers are ambulatory salesmen, such as the *tricicleros* who sell vegetables and fruits. Others have stationary stands, *ventorrillos*, or work as *paleteros*, selling cigarettes, sweets and chewing gums. Others have a stand selling *fantasías*, i.e., an assortment of combs and trinkets. Some of these salesmen have a more stationary character. A special group is the so called *buhoneros* who have stalls along the pavements in the city centers, many of these sell goods on commission from shop owners and importers. Their assortment is mostly constituted by imported products, clothes, toys and *fantasías*.

Most of the activities within the informal sector are carried out in the streets or in the workers' homes. About 40 percent of the self employed workers worked in the streets, 24 percent in their home, and 36 percent in some form of business premise.[48] The level of income of the self employed or independent workers is low. In 1979, 48 percent of the workers within this category earned less than 125 pesos a month.[49] Seasonal unemployment is very common and incomes are very unstable. As a result, underemployment among these workers is very high. In 1980, it was estimated to be 56.1 percent.[50]

Even if working conditions are unstable, it does not seem as if the group of workers engaged in activities within the informal sector changes over the years. In 1978, 50 percent of the people who were engaged in the informal sector stated that they had been in the same sort of occupation for 7 years, or more.[51] The majority of the workers engaged in the activities mentioned above would probably consider themselves as *chiriperos* (people who do not have a stable job, but do whatever turns up) in the sense that they would prefer a more secure and better paid job.

Another group of workers who may also be included in the informal sector is the so-called occasionals. These workers present the highest level of underemployment (79 percent in 1980, see Table 2.7), and receive the lowest income in urban areas. In 1979, 71.3 percent of them earned less than 50 pesos a month.[52] This group is constituted primarily by *chiriperos*. These workers cannot afford to invest in a *paletera* (a kind of portable counter) or a *ventorrillo* (booth or stall), they walk the streets in order to find something to do, maybe weed a garden, wash a car or run errands for someone. The difference between the occasional and the unemployed is very small, and they can as a matter of fact be considered as unemployed.

The importance of the informal sector is steadily increasing as most workers who are unable to find jobs in the modern sector try to make a living on their own account. According to an official publication, employment in the modern sector (government and industry) in the city of Santo Domingo decreased from 61 percent of total employment in 1980 to 55 percent in 1983. As a consequence, an increasing number of workers seek employment in the informal sector and this has led to a process of informalization of employment. In 1983, 45 percent of the employed workers of Santo Domingo were active within the informal sector, 33 percent were in the private modern sector and 22 percent were employed by the government sector. The increasing activities in the informal sector have led to a fall in average income and productivity of the urban workers. Wages in the informal sector are significantly lower than in the modern sector. In 1983, the average income of a worker in the modern sector was 60 percent higher than in the informal sector.[53]

The Migration Decision

The issues discussed in the previous sections suggest that in spite of the incapacity of the urban sector to provide sufficient employment opportunities, an increasing number of peasants have made the decision to migrate to the cities. At first sight, the decision of the peasants to migrate to cities afflicted by high levels of unemployment, may seem irrational. However, a growing body of evidence suggests that this is far from being the case.

The paradox of continued rural-urban migration in spite of rising urban unemployment in underdeveloped countries has attracted the attention of many social scientists. At present, the most comprehensive model related to the migration decision is the Harris-Todaro model.[54] This model states that the decision of each potential migrant to move to the city or not is based on an implicit "expected" income maximization objective. The principal economic factors involved in the decision to migrate are the urban-rural real wage differential that prevails for different skilled and educational categories of workers and the degree of probability that a migrant will be successful in securing wage employment in any period of time. The combination of these two variables is what basically determines the rate and magnitude of rural-urban migration.

The Harris-Todaro model presents some limitations in the sense that the decision to migrate is based on pure economic factors, while non-economic factors which also exert a major influence on individual decision making are not explicitly taken into account. Michael Todaro, however, on his own, has presented a schematic framework where the interaction of the different factors influencing the migration decision is illustrated. Among these factors we find psychic returns (e.g. urban amenities) and psychic cost (e.g. risks, social adjustment).[55] Todaro states that "migration is stimulated primarily by rational economic considerations of relative benefits and costs, mostly financial but also psychological."[56]

The expected income hypothesis does not explicitly include the various risks involved in the migration decision. According to Oded Stark and David Levhari, the model does not specify how the higher short-run variability in earnings, as a source of direct disutility, and the variability in alternative rural earnings, and in future urban earnings, must figure in the migrant's calculations. According to these authors, the motive for migration may not be expected income maximization per se, but aversion to risks may be a major cause of rural-urban migration. Accordingly, for an optimizing, risk averting small peasant family confronted with a subjective risk-increasing situation, migration of one of its members is a way of controlling risk by diversifying its income portfolio. The risks associated with urban employment diminish with time and may be lower than the risks associated with agricultural activities. Thus, rural-urban migration is largely a manifestation of the risk avoidance attitude of the individual migrant.[57]

Another analytical tool widely used when discussing rural-urban migration is the push-pull hypothesis.[58] This hypothesis suggests that migration occurs because of the socio-economic imbalances existing between city and countryside. The push-pull hypothesis has been underlying most of our discussion in the present work. However, this procedure also presents some limitations. The hypothesis suggests that certain pull factors attract migrants to the cities, while certain push factors expel them from the countryside. Thus, we should expect a higher migration from those areas where push factors are strongest. However, the evidence suggests that it is not necessarily so. A case in point is the southwest region of the Dominican Republic. This region has the country's highest degree of poverty and underemployment, but still it presents the lowest out-migration in the country.[59] Similar cases are reported from different Latin American countries.[60] Although the poorest sector of the rural population is represented, to a high degree, in urban areas, it should be kept in mind that it is members of the relatively better off stratum in the rural society that generally leave. Those who are inclined to leave due to desperate poverty may not even be able to afford the journey.[61]

Certainly, we cannot view the rural-urban migration process only in terms of rural-urban wage differentials or socio-economic imbalances. Other factors of a more individual or psychological nature may be of equal importance.

Factors Influencing the Migration Decision

The most important factors influencing the migration decision of the Dominican peasants are summarized in Table 10.5 below. These factors have been divided into structural and psychological forces of migration and these two categories are subdivided into push and pull factors.

The structural forces constituting the push factors enumerated in Table 10.5 were dealt at length with in the preceding chapters. Here we shall deal with the pull factors. The rural psychological push forces will be discussed in relation to their urban counterparts.

The Pull

Structural Forces. Among the pull factors ranked foremost by the migrants are employment opportunities and higher incomes. In 1978, 57 percent of the migrants to Santo Domingo said they came to this city in search of employment.[62] Despite the harsh situation that prevails in the urban labor market, most migrants manage one way or other to find employment. It should be kept in mind that, although the migrant may be unable to find employment in the modern formal market, where relatively high and institutionally fixed wages prevail, he still has the alternative to find employment in the informal market where entry is easier and incomes are fairly flexible. The evidence suggests that most migrants do manage to get employment and obtain higher incomes than would be the case if they had remained in rural areas. In Santo Domingo, 45 percent of the male migrants who arrived before 1969, and 33 percent of those who arrived during the period 1969-78, had an average monthly income above 200 pesos a month in 1979.[63] (This is above the urban minimum wage which at this time was DR$ 125 per month, and substantially above the average income in the rural areas (see Chapter 2).

Another factor that ranks high in importance is education. Many migrants come to the cities in search of better education opportunities for themselves or their dependants. In Santo Domingo, 14 percent of the migrants interviewed in 1979 gave studies as the main reason for coming to this city.[64]

TABLE 10.5   Structural and Psychological Forces of Migration

	Structural Forces	Psychological Forces
	Rural	
Push	1) Land tenure structures (*latifundio-minifundio*) 2) Insufficient or poor land 3) Lack of complementary production factors (credit, market facilities) 4) Lack of alternative employment 5) Low wages 6) Absence of sanitation and medical facilities 7) Deficient education services 8) Deficient transport and communication 9) Lack of electricity	1) Boredom 2) Small chances of social and economic advancement 3) Decreasing expectations 4) Risk aversion
	Urban	
Pull	1) Higher employment opportunities 2) Higher diversity of jobs 3) Higher wages 4) Better health and medical services 5) Better educational services 6) Better transport and communication 7) More organized labor market (workers' unions, medical insurance, vacation, retirement benefits, etc.) 8) Relatively easier access to electricity and water	1) Higher possibilities for amusements and adventures 2) Higher chances of economic and social advancement 3) Rising expectations 4) Presence of relatives and friends 5) Lower risk

Source: This table draws on Butterworth and Chance (1981), Table 1, p. 44. The contents are, however, extended and adapted to the Dominican situation.

Other important factors of attraction are the availability of public hospitals, better transport and communication, and a relatively easier access to electricity and water. Many migrants emphasize the advantages of being near a hospital which they are able to reach by walking paved streets, or by taking a bus or a *carro público*. These conditions may be compared with the difficulties faced in rural areas, where reaching a doctor is both a time and money consuming enterprise. In order to do so, many peasants have to ride a donkey in order to come to a road where they are able to find transport into a nearby town. By the time they get there the patient may be already dead.

Although most of the slum areas lack, at least in a formal sense, electricity and water pipes, most of the slum dwellers manage to install electricity in their houses. In many cases, the dwellers do not pay for these services since the installations generally are made by themselves, by running cables from a nearby electric stand. The access to potable water is relatively limited. Only 60 percent of the households in Santo Domingo have running water.[65] Slum dwellers generally fetch water at nearby public water pipes.

Another factor of attraction is the different advantages found in the modern formal labor market. Although most migrants may have difficulties in entering this market, the fact is that most of them leave with the hope of finding a stable and secure job either within the private or the government sector. These sectors not only offer more secure and better paid jobs, but also provide workers with the protection of minimum wage laws, social insurance, Christmas bonus, vacations, and, with the exception of government employees, the right to unionize. All these advantages are totally absent in rural areas.[66]

Psychological Factors. The attraction of the city lights as an explanation to migration has been severely criticized. Nevertheless the evidence suggests that this is an important, although not decisive, factor for many migrants to leave the countryside. This is generally true for many young men and women without families of their own, and indeed, it is this group which constitutes the bulk of migrants. These migrants generally complain about the boredom of country life, the lack of *ambiente*, atmosphere, and the low chances for *progreso*, social and economic advancement. This is generally contrasted with the city life, full of *ambiente, movimiento*, i.e., life and movement - the place where the possibility of *progreso* really exists.[67]

Although many migrants may never be able to realize their dreams, their hopes are kept alive by those that meet success in the cities. The slum dwellers are in daily contact with the wealthy section of the urban population. These contacts have a demonstration effect which tends to raise expectations and hopes among the migrants. The demonstration effect is also at work among the migrants themselves. In

1983, around 33 percent of the households in the urban slums had television, 30 percent had refrigerators, and 11 percent had gramophones.[68] The acquisition of sophisticated electric equipment by the urban poor is a sign of progress, a way to demonstrate that one is enjoying the goods of the city. These goods are as a rule absent in the rural areas, not only because of lack of money, but also for lack of electricity.

Nowadays, the presence of relatives in the cities is a prime attraction for migrants. Many of the peasants who come to the cities stay with relatives, and as many as 44 percent of the migrants to Santo Domingo also gave this as the main reason for coming to that city.[69] With the aid of relatives, the newcomers are quickly adapted to the urban environment. In 1979, 52.5 percent of the migrants in Santo Domingo stated that they were introduced by relatives and friends to their way of making a living.[70] Like in the countryside, a system of mutual aid prevails in the city slums and the extended family unit, where every member participates in the maintenance of the group, is of utmost importance for individual survival. In 1979, the aid of relatives was the principal means of subsistence for more than 75 percent of the unemployed workers of Santo Domingo.[71] The presence of relatives and friends in the cities tends to minimize the psychological costs of migration, i.e., the risk involved in moving to an unknown environment and the process of adjustment to city life.

The Perceived Value of Migration

The decision to migrate is based on the prospective migrant's perception of the value of migration, i.e., the *ex ante* gains the migrant will receive by leaving his place of origin.

The perceived value of migration is based on the expected value of migration which is determined by subtracting the cost of migration from the return of migration. This can be formulated as follows:

$$E_M = [(W_U - W_A) + R_P] - [C_U + T + C_P] \qquad (10.1)$$

$$W_U = \frac{N_M}{N_U}\overline{W}_M \ , \ \frac{N_M}{N_U} \leq 1 \text{ (Todaro's urban expected wage)} \qquad (10.2)$$

where:

E_M = Expected value of migration
W_U = Urban expected real wage
W_A = The agricultural real wage

R_P = Psychic returns to migration (*ambiente*, adventure, social advancement, etc.)

C_U = Cost of living in the urban areas

T = Cost of the journey from the migrant's place of origin to the city

C_P = Psychic costs of migration (adaptation difficulties, risk, etc.)

$\overline{W}_M$ = Fixed minimum urban wage

N_M = Total labor (urban and rural migrant) required in the modern (manufacturing) sector.

N_U = Total urban labor force

The first part of equation (10.1) expresses the return of migration which is given by the urban-rural wage differential plus the psychic returns to migration. The second part expresses the cost of migration which includes the urban cost of living, the cost of the journey and the psychic cost of migration.

In the Harris-Todaro model,[72] the urban-rural wage differential $(W_U - W_A)$ is determined by the urban expected wage, W_U, which is equal to the fixed minimum wage $\overline{W}_M$ adjusted for the proportion of the total urban labor force actually employed, N_M / N_U, and the agricultural real wage, W_A, which is equal to the marginal product of labor in agriculture, expressed in terms of the manufactured good. It is assumed that the real wage in manufacturing W_M equals the marginal product of labor (f') in this sector. But W_M is constrained to be greater than, or equal to, the fixed minimum wage:

$$WM = f' \geq \overline{W}_M \qquad (10.3)$$

the possibility of excess demand for labor at the minimum wage is ruled out, i.e., $f' = W_M$. Only in the case of full employment $(N_M = N_U)$ will the expected wage be equal to the minimum wage (i.e., $W_U = \overline{W}_M$).

In the Harris-Todaro model, the migration to urban areas is a positive function of the urban-rural expected wage differential and the equilibrium condition is:

$$W_A = W_U \qquad (10.4)$$

i.e., migration will cease when the expected income differential is zero.[73]

However, even in the case of $W_U - W_A = 0$, we still have non-economic returns, R_P, in equation (10.1), and as long as the prospective migrant perceives these returns to be higher than the cost of migration, rural-urban migration will continue.

The expected present value of migration varies with the level of information that the prospective migrant has about the prospective returns and costs of migration. The migration decision is not adventurous or capricious. It is based on facts related to the information the ' potential migrant has of the possible gains or losses migration entails.

In the Dominican Republic most of the migrants had a satisfactory level of information before they moved. In 1979, 62 percent of the migrants in Santo Domingo stated they had previous information on their prospective life in town before they moved.[74] The flow of information about city life is maintained through the contacts between the migrants and their relatives and friends within their place of origin. Despite the high levels of urban unemployment and the harsh situation endured by most migrants in the city slums, many seem to achieve their expected value of migration. In 1979, 82 percent of the migrants in Santo Domingo and 87 percent in Santiago stated that they were pleased with their decision to move into town and were not willing to move back to their places of origin.[75]

It could be argued that with rural-urban migration as high as it is, the equilibrium condition ($W_U = W_A$) will soon be reached. But this is unlikely to happen since W_U is mainly based on wages in the formal labor market, W_M, and these are generally above the minimum ones that are institutionally fixed and cannot be influenced by what happens in the informal sector. Most of the workers in this sector tend to see their occupation as a second-best alternative, hoping eventually to get a job in the governmental sector or in the private modern sector. The pressure of migrants on the urban labor market is likely to lead to a reduction of wages in the informal sector and, as a consequence, to an increase in income inequalities in urban areas.

The Harris-Todaro model has important policy implications, especially with regards to solutions to the employment problem. Among other things, the model implies that a purely urban solution to urban unemployment tends to increase rather than decrease the pool of urban unemployed:

> The traditional (Keynesian) economic solution to urban unemployment, (i.e., the creation of more urban modern-sector jobs without simultaneous attempts to improve rural incomes and employment opportunities) can lead to the paradoxical situation where more urban employment leads to higher levels of urban and rural unemployment ... Since migration rates are assumed to respond positively to both higher urban wages and higher urban employment opportunities (or probabilities), it follows that for any given positive urban-rural wage differential ... higher urban employment rates will widen the expected differential and induce even higher rates of rural-urban migration ...

Thus, if 100 new jobs are created, there may be as many as 300 new migrants and, therefore, 200 more urban unemployed.[76]

If no measures are taken in order to increase income in the agricultural sector and the quality of life in the villages, migration from the rural areas will continue in spite of the rising unemployment rates in the urban areas.

Migration Abroad

After the Mexicans and Cubans, the Dominicans constitute the third largest immigrant group from Latin America in the United States.[77] The exact number of Dominicans living in this country is difficult to estimate, since the majority is constituted by illegal immigrants. In 1978, the number of Dominicans living in the city of New York alone, was estimated to be between 300,000 and 500,000.[78]

Until the 1950s, the migration of Dominicans to the US was of limited proportions. Those who migrated were mainly political refugees and students. During that decade, the migration started to change character, most people migrated for the purpose of work. During that decade, about 1,000 Dominicans migrated annually to the US.[79] During the following decades migration has been increasing steadily. Table 10.6 presents the migration of Dominicans to the US in the period 1960-80.

The total annual migration of Dominicans to the US largely exceeds the figures in Table 10.6, since a considerable number of those with non-immigrant visa remain in the US. In 1981, it was estimated that around 20,000 Dominicans leave every year in order to work in the US.[80]

The number of non-immigrant visas granted by the US consulate in Santo Domingo increased from an average of 60,000 annually in the 1960s to 150,000 in the 1970s.[81] This gives a hint of the magnitude of illegal migration. However, it is not only persons with non-immigrant visas who illegally migrate to the US. About 60 percent of those applying for non-immigrant visa are refused by the US consulate[82] and a large portion of these applicants manage to get into US territory by other means. These means range from buying falsified visas, to the venture of crossing the open sea in small boats to Puerto Rico or the Bahamas.

In the 1970s, Venezuela was also an important area of migration for Dominican workers. In 1983, it was estimated that around 60,000 Dominicans lived there.[83]

TABLE 10.6   Officially Admitted Dominican Immigrants to the US, 1960-
1980

Years	Average Annual Migration
1960-69	7,575
1969-73	13,726
1973-80	15,332

Source: Bray (1983), p. 4.

As in the case of internal migration, selective factors also operate in international migration. It is the young and the better educated part of the population that migrate abroad. In 1978, 84 percent of the Dominican migrants in the US stated that they had come to the US before the age of 40.[84] According to the Commission on Western Hemisphere Immigration, the Dominican Republic is one of the Latin American countries with the highest migration rate of highly trained personnel to the US.[85]

The majority of Dominicans who migrate abroad are of urban origin. In 1979, it was estimated that 52 percent of the US-bound immigrants were from the urban middle class stratum, 24 percent were from rural areas while the rest came from the lower social strata of the urban population.[86]

The pull and push factors which influence internal migration are also at work in relation to international migration. The majority of the migrants left their places of origin in search of employment and higher income. Another important reason is education and the presence of relatives abroad.

TABLE 10.7   Reasons for Dominican Migration to the US

Reason	Percent
Unemployment	27
Search for higher incomes	24
Education	22
To join relatives	17

Source: Ugalde et al. (1978), p. 9.

Unemployment in the place of origin is a major factor influencing the decision to migrate abroad. About 58 percent of those who migrated from the city of Santiago were unemployed before they left for New York. Of these, 29 percent had been unemployed for more than two years. These high rates of unemployment may partly be due to the fact that many of the migrants are fairly highly educated. Some probably waited to get a job suited to their education. As in many underdeveloped countries, unemployment among professionals is not uncommon in the Dominican Republic.

The "Absent Dominicans" and Those They Left Behind

Most of the Dominicans that have migrated to the United States keep close contacts with their relatives in the Dominican Republic and pay regular visits to their place of origin. Most of the migrants see their stay in the United States as transitory. They work hard and save in order to return to their home country. Return migration is relatively high. About 44 percent of the migrants return after some years.[87]

Nearly all migrants manage to get jobs and adapt quickly to the new environment. Most migrants to the United States live in neighborhoods where they are surrounded by relatives and friends. In New York, for example, you find districts in Queens or on the Lower East Side of Manhattan, where Dominicans live close together in communities that reflect their homeland. They shop in *colmados* that bear the name of their villages, they attend meetings of Dominican parties, read Dominican newspapers and play the Dominican lottery. Few learn English and the majority feel more attached to their home country than to the new environment.[88]

The close links that are maintained between the emigrants to the United States and their places of origin create particular patterns among the Dominicans in the United States. These links also exert an influence on their old neighborhood or village. When an emigrant comes home, it is customary that he brings gifts to friends and relatives. He often strives after a pattern of behavior that demonstrates his success. As some peasants say: *regresan más cultos, más blancos*, they come back more cultivated, more white. The peasants generally contrast the feeling of hopelessness and poverty in their villages with the wealth and progress the migrants meet abroad. This tends to emphasize the already strong desire to migrate among the peasantry.

Certain villages in the Dominican Republic, especially in the Cibao, the district most rural migrants to the US come from, have their twin communities in the US. In 1970, 85 percent of the inhabitants in a village located southeast of Santiago had one or more family members living in the US.[89] In their regular visits to their relatives in the

Dominican Republic, the *Dominicanos ausentes* (absent Dominicans) bring with them all sorts of sophisticated goods (TV sets, radios, stereo sets, etc.). The possession of these appliances is a source of status for the families of the emigrants, a proof of the success of the migrants, and consequently an important incentive for others to emigrate.

According to a 1983 Central Bank estimate, remittances from the US-bound emigrants to the Dominican Republic amounted to an average of US$ 150 million per year. Remittances come mainly in the form of money orders. Investments in real estate are also significant. In 1985, 91 percent of the benefited families received an average of US$ 183 per month. It is estimated that about 55 percent of the families receiving remittances are not engaged in any remunerated working activity.[90] In 1982, around one-fifth of the households in the city of Santiago benefited from remittances either in the form of money-orders or consumption goods. It is calculated that around 34 percent of the families in this city get some type of financial aid from relatives living abroad.[91]

There is no doubt that migration abroad has had a positive impact on the welfare of both migrants and their relatives at home.

The Economic Effects of Migration

For the country as a whole, migration abroad has contributed to alleviate the problem of unemployment and the scarcity of foreign exchange. However, migration abroad has also had detrimental effects in the source country. The selective character of migration implies that the country tends to be deprived of its most qualified manpower and even if these workers were unemployed, it cannot be argued that their social marginal product in the source country is zero. In the absence of the possibility of obtaining higher wages abroad, a medical doctor, for example, may be forced to seek employment in the hinterland where his services are in high demand.[92]

The outflow of peasants and its direct and indirect effects on the supply of total agricultural labor and agricultural production has been analyzed by Keith Griffin,[93] who argues that the negative effects of the migration of peasants to higher paid jobs abroad have been exaggerated. Accordingly, he rules out the allegations that the positive effects of migration, i.e., the remittances to the source country, tend to be offset by the fact that: a) remittances may turn some agricultural producers into consumers and this tends to decrease the domestic supply of food and agricultural exports, and b) the increase of purchasing power among recipients, in a situation of inelastic supply conditions, results in inflationary pressures.[94]

Griffin argues that under the assumption that there is surplus labor in agriculture, migration will reduce the available labor force but will have no effect on the labor inputs used in agriculture and he states that:

> Emigration rises the welfare both of the migrant and of those left behind who otherwise would have had to provide him with subsistence. Unemployment or surplus labour decline marginally while output remains unchanged.[95]

If the migrants are fully employed, and there is no surplus labor, agricultural output declines by an amount equivalent to the marginal product of labor. In this case, both the income of the migrants and the income of the remaining members of the family rise. The amount by which the combined income of the migrant and his remaining family increases depends on the difference between the wage income actually received abroad (w) and the marginal product of labor in agriculture (m). The division of this income increase (w - m) between the migrants and their family dependants at home depends on the value of remittances (r) and the annual consumption of the peasant before migration (c):

1. w - m = rise in total income
2. w - c - r = rise in the migrant's income
3. c - m + r = rise in the extended family's income

If w > m, the welfare of both migrants and relatives at home will rise. Even in the case where r = 0, as long as c > m, migration will have a positive effect on the income of relatives.[96] The direct and indirect positive effects of migration can be summarized as follows:[97]

i) Higher income for the migrants abroad. ii) Higher income for the migrants' dependants, due to remittances. iii) The reduction in labor inputs due to migration will be associated, *ceteris paribus*, with a rise in the amount of land (and fixed capital) per employed person and this will lead to an increase in the average and marginal productivity of labor. iv) The relative scarcity of labor and the higher output per man-day resulting from migration will tend to increase wages in agriculture. v) Remittances are likely to increase capital formation in the sector. vi) Increased agricultural wages may increase the share of labor in total agricultural income at the expense of profits and rents and this in turn will result in a more equal distribution of income in the sector.

Regarding the negative effects resulting from the selectivity of migration, Griffin argues that the drain of human capital, i.e., the loss of the more talented and skilled population, may have a negative effect on the welfare of those left behind, but this is a short-run effect since this gap will not remain unfilled for a long time.

In the Dominican Republic, the negative effects of rural migration have been largely emphasized. It has been argued that, when the head of family is absent from his farm, his wife and children generally subsist on the money he sends from the US. The emigrant's family turn into dependants and agricultural production decreases. A common view among rural emigrants is that they have to support the family they left behind, and that it is a disgrace if their family have to work the land in their absence. It is further argued that the money the emigrants send and the investments they make increase the unequal distribution of income in the countryside.[98]

To a certain extent, the above argument is true. Most of the Dominican rural migrants to the US are middle-holders which constitute the better-off portion of the peasant population. After migration, their land which was previously used to cultivate food crops, using a large input of labor, is generally turned into pasture, thus decreasing the demand for labor and food production in the sector.

This may, however, be a short-run effect. Remittances increase the possibility of investments in the sector and labor demand is likely to increase. The distribution of income in the sector is likely to become more unequal since it is the already better-off peasants that migrate. This tendency may be offset by the wage increase that may result from outward migration and higher investments due to remittances. However, in the Dominican case, the effects of outward migration in agriculture tend to be offset by the presence of Haitian immigrant workers. Thus, a wage increase in agriculture as a result of outward migration is not likely to take place.

Conclusions

Rural-urban migration has put tremendous pressure on the urban labor market, as well as on the physical urban environment. As a result, unemployment and underemployment in the urban areas have been increasing. At the same time, the majority of the urban population is concentrated in slum areas or impoverished settlements.

The industrialization policies pursued in the country in the early 1950s and 1960s, constituted a major attraction factor for the peasants to migrate to the cities. Although the newly created industries generated employment opportunities, these were largely insufficient to absorb the huge amount of workers who, with the expectation of obtaining higher incomes and better living conditions, migrated into the cities. Throughout the 1960s and 1970s, urban unemployment was above the 20 percent level. A major factor obstructing the creation of employment was the industrial structure generated by the industrialization policies pursued by the government. Due to different government measures, capital was priced below its opportunity cost and as a result, most industries tended to use highly capital intensive production methods.

Unable to find employment in the urban formal or industrial sector, many workers have turned to the informal sector. The informal sector is characterized by small-scale, low productivity operations, with easy entrance and low, flexible wages. This contrasts with the formal sector where wages are generally above the institutionally determined minimum. The importance of the informal sector has been steadily growing. It is in this sector that most of the migrants manage to gain a livelihood in the cities. Others may face unemployment. Nevertheless, most migrants seem to be satisfied with their decision to migrate. It was argued that the income-maximization objective is only one of the components of the expected value of migration. Other important factors, such as risk aversion, the opportunity of social advancement, etc., also enter the prospective migrant's calculations. Many of the self-employed workers in the urban informal sector have higher current incomes, better life time prospects and greater access to a range of social services than many hard working peasants in the countryside.

Rural-urban migration is likely to continue not only as long as the urban-rural wage differential exists, but also, and maybe more important, as long as most social services, such as education, health, enforcement of minimum-wage legislation, etc. are confined to urban areas, while the rural areas continue to be neglected.

Until the present time, migration abroad has represented an attractive alternative for many Dominican workers. Migration abroad has tended to alleviate the pressure on employment demand and it has represented an important source of foreign exchange. As in the case of internal migration, the migration of Dominicans abroad has been highly selective. It is the better educated and more enterprising individuals that tend to leave. This fact tends to be emphasized as one of the negative effects of migration. However, this is likely to be a short-run effect, since this gap will not remain unfilled for a long time. One of the positive effects of migration is the remittances that the migrants send back to the country and the possible increase in investments that they may generate.

The decision of the Dominican peasants to migrate either to the cities or abroad is based on an individual desire to improve their own welfare and that of their families, either directly through increases in income (by obtaining better paid jobs), or indirectly by having access to better educational and health facilities. In this sense, the gains from migration abroad are very similar to those implied in rural-urban migration within the country. Net benefits from international migration are, of course, much higher, partly because of the better possibilities of welfare gains abroad, but also because the different diseconomies generated by domestic rural-urban migration - urban slums, pressure on urban labor market, etc. - can be avoided. However, both international and domestic migration arise because of differences in earnings, living and working conditions, and possibilities of advancement that exist within a country and/or between countries.

Throughout this work, emphasis has been placed on the existence of these differences between rural and urban areas within the Dominican Republic. Thus, there is no doubt that if the Dominican peasants migrate it is because they are unsatisfied with the conditions that prevail in the countryside. Likewise, migration to the US is a reflection of the obvious differences that exist between the living conditions in this country, compared with those that prevail in the Dominican Republic.

In the present chapter we argued that an urban solution to the problem of rural-urban migration is likely to worsen the situation. A policy that intends to create more urban jobs, without simultaneously striving to improve living and working conditions in rural areas will undoubtedly attract more migrants and subsequently increase urban unemployment, slums and other inconveniences related to unplanned urban growth.

However, in the absence of adequate measures to change the situation of poverty and neglect experienced by the Dominican peasantry, migration might be a second-best solution, at least for the migrants themselves.

Notes

1. See Table 2.1.
2. Butterworth and Chance (1981), pp. vii and 29-30.
3. Ibid., p. vii.
4. See Table 2.1.
5. United Nations (1980), quoted by Gugler (1982), p. 173.
6. See Table 2.1.
7. Duarte (1980), pp. 190 and 188.
8. See ONAPLAN (1983:4), p. 13 and Duarte (1980), p. 252.
9. OIT (1975), p. 84.
10. For a discussion on the selectivity of migration in Latin America, see Butterworth and Chance (1981), pp. 52-59.
11. Ramírez (1980), pp. 56 and 63.
12. ONAPLAN (1981:1), p. 15.
13. Butterworth and Chance (1981), p. 147.

14. According to a IEPD study, 65 percent of the population in Santo Domingo lives in "barrios con hacinamiento," congested neighborhoods, occupying 18 percent of the total area of the city. However, not all congested neighborhoods can be considered to be "barrios marginados," we have therefore excluded 7 neighborhoods which are mainly populated by lower middle-class families. (See IEPD (1984), p. 8, Table 3.)

15. US AID (1981), p. 114.

16. Ross (1982), p. 30.

17. IEPD (1984), p. 7.

18. ONAPLAN (1983:2), pp. 423-25. This survey included a sample of 1,036 families mainly located in *barrios* of Santo Domingo and Santiago (ibid., p. 423). The average income of these families is very low in relation with the average incomes of urban residents, but not when compared to the situation in the rural areas. In 1983, the legally established minimum wage for agricultural day laborers was 5 pesos per day (i.e., approximately DR$ 130 per month) but, as we have seen, in this sector wages are, as a rule, far below the established minimum. Furthermore, the average income of some *minifundistas* is generally lower than that of the land-less workers (see Chapter 2). It is symptomatic that an inquiry carried out in 1981 in some *barrios* of Santo Domingo, showed that 87.6 percent of the head of families owned land in the countryside. Of these, 56 percent owned more than 80 *tareas* (Duarte (1981), Table 2).

19. These plastic bags are then sold in the two large market places of the city where they are used by the retailers. The recollection of used plastic mugs is also common. The mugs are washed and resold to ambulatory sellers of drinks. The list of different activities carried out by slum children could be much larger. (Cf. Duarte (1979).) It is amazing to observe the ingeniousness of these kids, most of them aged 5 to 12 years, in order to make a living many of them hang around the shopping centers and offer different services, such as watching your car or carrying your bags.

20. Cf. Cassá (1983), pp. 128-142 and 167-171.

21. Bosch (1979), p. 248.

22. Cf. Dominican Blue Book 1920 (1976). See also Bosch (1979), p. 257.

23. Traditionally, Dominicans consumed sea salt provided by small producers. A very rich, but highly underutilized salt mine existed in the country and this was promptly seized by Trujillo, who forced the congress to pass a law forbidding the extraction of salt from sea water since this practice was said to damage the coastline. (See Bosch (1979), pp. 253-54.)

24. See Cassá (1982), pp. 287 and 304.

25. For a discussion of the industrialization strategies pursued in underdeveloped countries see Little, Scitovsky and Scott (1970).

26. See World Bank (1978:1), Tables 5.29 and 531, pp. 355 and 357.

27. See ONAPLAN (1968).

28. For a detailed exposition of Law 299, see OIT (1975), pp. 156-57. For a discussion of the rationale for the Dominican industrialization policies, see Vedovato (1986), Chapter 6.

29. United Nations (1982), p. 301.

30. Sugar prices rose from an index of 16 in 1969 to 146 in 1974. During the same period the price of cocoa doubled and the price of coffee increased by two-thirds. (See IMF (1982), p. 171.)

31. OIT (1975), p. 168. In 1975, 17 percent of total government expenditure in construction was allocated to different urbanization work such as streets, promenades, avenues and beautifying works. Another 17 percent was invested in housing. About 70 percent of the urbanization works and 80 percent of the housing was allocated to Santo Domingo. (See World Bank (1978:1), Table 5.18, p. 330.)

32. World Bank (1985), p. v. GDP growth rates for the periods 1984-86 and 1987-90 were estimated to 1.6 and 3.5, respectively (ibid., Table 1.1, p. 6).

33. CODECO (1983), p. 5.

34. ONAPLAN (1983:2), p. 57.

35. OIT (1975), p. 161.

36. Ibid., p. 107.

37. OIT (1975), pp. 154 and 158.

38. World Bank (1978:2), p. 12.

39. CEDOPEX (1979), p. 38.

40. Index calculated from ONAPLAN (1983:2), p. 55. In 1988, total employment in the duty-free industrial zones amounted to 85,468 workers (FED (1989)).

41. See OIT (1975), p. 104.

42. Calculated from Dauhajre (1984), Table 5, p. 43.

43. World Bank (1985), p. 21. In 1987, the deficit of public enterprises amounted to 3,562.3 million pesos (Dauhajre (1989), Table 1, p. 72).

44. The informal sector in most underdeveloped countries is characterized by ease of entry, small-scale and labor-intensive operations, where technology is adapted and skills are acquired outside of the formal school system and operate in highly competitive labor and product markets. By contrast, the modern (formal) sector generally uses imported capital-intensive technology and presents barriers to entry (House (1984), p. 279).

45. Secretariado Técnico de la Presidencia (1983), p. 3.

46. OIT (1975), p. 105. The diversity of activities encountered in the informal sector of Nairobi, has led House to conclude that the simple dichotomy of the urban economy of underdeveloped countries into formal and informal sectors is largely inadequate. Accordingly, House suggests that the informal sector should be categorized into at least two subsectors: an "intermediate sector," which appears as a reservoir of dynamic entrepreneurs, and the "community of the poor," which contains a large body of residual and underemployed labor (House (1984), p. 298).

47. See Duarte (1980), p. 371. A more recent survey estimated that throughout the country there are 398,750 persons (19% of total employment) working in the micro-enterprise sector (US AID (1989), p. 14).

48. ONAPLAN (1981:2), p. 25.

49. Ibid., p. 23.

50. See Table 2.7.

51. Duarte (1980), p. 299. There seems to exist a tendency towards a formalization of some informal sector activities, in the sense that many of the self-employed persons in this sector present a relative job stability. Similar findings are reported on Bangkok's and Nairobi's informal sectors. In 1974, nearly 60 percent of the self-employed in the former had been in the same occupation for at least 5 years (Teilhet-Waldorf and Waldorf (1983), p. 594). In 1977, over 40 percent of the enterprises in Nairobi's informal sector were at least 5 years old (House (1984), p. 282). On the basis of his findings House concludes: "For the vast majority of the heads of these enterprises, operating informally has become a way of life, whether by circumstance or design, and not merely a means of subsisting in the urban sector job queue" (ibid.).

52. ONAPLAN (1981:1), p. 23.

53. Secretariado Técnico de la Presidencia (1983), pp. 3-4.

54. See Harris and Todaro (1970) and Todaro (1969).

55. Todaro (1981), p. 239.

56. Ibid., p. 241.

57. See Stark and Levhari (1982), pp. 190-96.

58. Butterworth and Chance (1981), p. 39.

59. See ONAPLAN (1983:4), p. 13.

60. See Butterworth and Chance (1981), pp. 41-43.

61. Cf. Lipton (1977), pp. 231-32.

62. Ramírez (1980), p. 151.

63. Ibid., p. 156.

64. Ibid., p. 151.

65. Ross (1982), p. 30.

66. The Dominican labor code presents large deficiencies, among other things, it practically ignores agricultural workers. (See OIT (1975), p. 215.) Furthermore, the provisions of the labor code relating to the protection of wages does not include those enterprises employing ten workers or less (Plant (1987), p. 116). It should be pointed out, however, that the Dominican labor movement is week and has been highly repressed. In 1961, the number of registered unions was only 42. It slowly increased during the period 1961-77, reaching 581 in 1977. Due to the relative increase in democracy during the PRD regimes (1978-86), the number of registered unions increased to 1,462 in 1985 (Espinal (1987), Table 3, p. 174).

67. For a discussion on the relevance of these factors among migrants to the city of Popayán in Colombia, see Butterworth and Chance (1981), pp. 47-48.

68. See ONAPLAN (1983:2), p. 426. Many of the urban poor acquire these durable goods on a credit basis. Credit facilities are easily available in the cities. Most establishments sell these goods on credit, without any initial outlay, but charging high interest rates. Very often the buyer is unable to fulfill the payment agreement and loses both the acquired good and the money paid. In some cases these items are purchased as a kind of security to be used in order to pawn and raise cash in times of crises.

69. Ramírez (1980), p. 151.

70. Duarte (1980), p. 343.

71. ONAPLAN (1981:1), p. 48.

72. See Harris and Todaro (1970), p. 127-28.

73. The assumption that migration ceases when the expected income differential equals zero is purely arbitrary. It is possible to assume as an equilibrium condition $W_A = \alpha W_U$, where α can take any positive value. (See ibid., p. 91, note 2.)

74. Ramírez (1980), pp. 152-53.

75. Ibid., pp. 156-57.

76. Todaro (1981), p. 242.

77. Ugalde et al. (1978), p. 1.

78. Ibid.

79. Bray (1983), p. 4.

80. Grasmuck (1981), p. 1.

81. Bray (1983), p. 4. In 1986, the number of Dominicans residing illegally in the US was estimated to be 250,000 (Báez E. and D'Oleo R. (1986), p. 34).

82. Bray (1983), p. 4.

83. Canelo (1983), pp. 215-16.

84. Ugalde et al. (1978), p. 9.

85. Kidd (1968), pp. 165-69.

86. Ugalde et al. (1978), p. 13.

87. Ibid., p. 12. In 1982, 69 percent of the return migrants in Santiago had lived in the US for less than 5 years, 20 percent lived in that country 5 to 15 years and 11 percent 15 to 20 years (Grasmuck (1984), p. 35).

88. Del Castillo (1981), pp. 157-59.

89. Hendricks (1978), p. 59.

90. Báez E. and D'Oleo R. (1986), p. 43-45. Based on an inquiry carried out in 1985, these authors estimated that remittances amounted to an average of US$ 229 million per year. The importance of remittances for the Dominican economy becomes evident if we consider that in 1984, foreign exchange earnings from sugar exports only amounted to US$ 288 million (ibid.).

91. Grasmuck (1984), p. 17.

92. See Bhagwati and Rodríguez (1976), p. 98.

93. Griffin (1976:2).

94. Ibid., pp. 81-82.

95. Ibid., p. 83.

96. This may not be possible in the case where the peasants' production is close to subsistence level and cash income and market facilities are inadequate (ibid., note 11, p. 95).

97. Ibid., pp. 86-88.

98. See Pessar (1982).

11

Concluding Remarks

In the present study, a diversity of topics has been discussed. Our point of departure was an analysis of the employment problem in the Dominican Republic. After scrutinizing the available statistics on this subject, we concluded that unemployment and underemployment figures hardly revealed the real dimension of the problem. The concepts of unemployment and underemployment are very difficult to define and measure adequately in countries such as the Dominican Republic where only a small fraction of the labor force is engaged in wage and salary employment, while the great majority of workers are occupied in low productivity agriculture and services. In the first part of the study we came to the conclusion that a more adequate way of analyzing the employment problem in the Dominican Republic is to put the emphasis on low productivity and poverty.

In the Dominican Republic most people work. Irrespective of age, men, women and children, all work long hours to earn a meager income. Very few can afford to be unemployed. In this sense, unemployment is not the major problem. The problem is poverty. This redefinition of the employment problem has important policy implications. Firstly, it implies that in an employment strategy, the main emphasis should not be put on the unemployed but on the working poor. Secondly, it means that the aim of such a strategy should not simply be to create jobs but to raise productivity in either existing jobs or in the new jobs that are to be created. (We will come back to this below.)

The poverty issue is central to this study. An attempt has been made to discover the circumstances in which poverty arises and to identify the different mechanisms that maintain it. We emphasized that the levels of poverty and low productivity that afflict the majority of Dominican workers are mainly the result of a development strategy where modernization, urbanization and industrialization has been given pride of place without much consideration taken to the country's resource endowment and development possibilities. This strategy mainly benefited the urban industrial sector, while the agricultural sector, particularly the peasant sector was highly penalized , if not totally neglected. Thus, we argued that the problems of unemployment and poverty afflicting the Dominican workers have their roots in the different policies that have affected the performance of the agricultural (rural) sector. Poverty and unemployment are mainly the result of a land policy that has concentrated the best lands in a few hands, a credit policy that mainly benefits the large producer, a pricing policy that tends to discourage agricultural production, a labor policy that encourages labor imports, etc.

The above factors have all been dealt with at length in the present study. We showed that contrary to what is generally believed, the poverty of the peasantry cannot be blamed on the intermediaries marketing agricultural products, or on usurious money lenders. These activities are carried out under fairly competitive conditions. The intervention of the state in the marketing system through INESPRE has not shown any sign of handling the marketing more efficiently than the existing traditional system. There is no sign of INESPRE being able to perform marketing activities at a lower cost to the economy. On the contrary, INESPRE has proved itself to be incapable of providing the different services offered by traditional intermediaries and, above all, INESPRE's price policy has mainly benefited the urban consumers by procuring cheap food staples, without much consideration to the negative effect of such a policy on the income of the rural producers.

We indicated that a major cause of rural poverty is the limited access that the peasants have to productive land and credit resources. In the Dominican Republic both land and credit resources are highly unequally distributed. The fact that different producers face different sets of relative prices has exerted a negative influence on the land use pattern, the introduction of modern technology, the demand for rural labor and the level of production. The large producers are mainly dedicated to cattle breeding and sugar cane production. As land is relatively cheap for these producers, they have tended to produce a land-intensive output such as tending cattle on natural pastures. Livestock production offers the lowest demand for labor in the agricultural sector. On the other hand, the sugar plantations require large amounts of labor, among the highest in agriculture. However, the plantations have traditionally depended on imported Haitian workers.

The policy of cheap credit implemented by the government has mainly benefited the large producers. Through a rationing mechanism, credit has tended to be allocated to the least risky borrowers. The large producers can use land as collateral and thus minimize the risk of lending.

The peasants, for whom land is relatively expensive, on the other hand, have tended to cultivate labor-intensive crops. Since most peasants are unable to obtain credit from official credit sources, they have to turn to informal sources where interest rates are relatively higher. This precludes the increase of productive investment and the introduction of improved techniques. In the absence of alternative rural employment, the increasing rural labor force has been concentrated in the peasant sector. Labor force growth, in combination with traditional cultivation methods, has put great pressure on the land. The peasants have been forced to intensify production on marginal lands and to open up fields on the mountain slopes. This process, in combination with increased demand for charcoal, has set in motion a deforestation and erosion process which seriously threatens the ecological balance of the island. As a result of erosion, the land base of the peasantry has been shrinking and the peasants have been facing lower productivity and incomes.

The tendency for peasant incomes to fall has been reinforced by the fact that the government, through its price stabilization policy, has mainly been concerned with the stabilization of prices at consumer and production levels, without paying much attention to income stabilization in rural areas. At the same time, the government, by means of taxation and exchange policies, has systematically extracted resources from agriculture. Agricultural exports have been heavily taxed and until 1985, the peso was overvalued and agricultural imports were heavily subsidized. The outcome has been stagnant agricultural production and falling rural income. For a significant number of peasants, the escape from this situation has been migration.

During the last decades, the Dominican Republic has been experiencing an unprecedented mass migration of peasants into the cities. This migration has taken place in spite of the high levels of urban unemployment. We have argued that a major factor behind this migration has been the deteriorating living conditions prevailing in the rural areas. Yet, while analyzing the migration process, the urban factors attracting rural migrants are as important as the factors pushing them from the countryside. The peasants would not take the decision to migrate if there were no significant gains from the move. Among the factors attracting the peasants into the cities are the higher wages paid in industrial and governmental sectors. The average income of an urban family is twice as high as those of a rural family. In addition, better access to public utilities such as education, health, electricity, amenities etc., which are more readily available in urban areas will also exert an influence on the decision to migrate.

The industrialization policies implemented by the government have proved to be successful in attracting workers from the rural areas but not when it comes to providing sufficient employment for the growing urban labor force. The industrial sector has been highly protected. Most industries have tended to use capital-intensive technologies and an installed production capacity which is out of proportion with the size of the market. This has resulted in an underutilization of installed capacity and a reduced demand for labor. The failure of industry to increase employment has been partly compensated by increased government employment. Especially during the PRD administrations (1978-86), the public sector acted as a sponge to absorb part of the redundant urban labor. Government employment policy was inspired by political interests rather than by specific economic goals. Nevertheless, the largest increase in urban employment took place in the informal sector. It is in this sector that the majority of the rural migrants manage to make a living. Workers there face lower productivity and incomes than workers in the industry or government sectors, but their situation is still significantly better than that of the rural workers.

Migration may have entailed significant gains for the rural migrants, but for the country as a whole, it has created a large range of problems. In the urban areas, it has put great pressures on the labor market and created considerable social disequilibrium in the urban environment. The slums have been growing at an accelerated rate and the cities have proved to be incapable of providing adequate shelter and public services for the growing population. In the rural areas, migration may have lessened the pressure on the land and reduced the employment problem. However, the role assigned to migration as a factor reducing the imbalances between rural and urban areas has proved to be a myth. In spite of the massive outflow of workers from the agricultural sector, there has been no sign of a rise of the marginal productivity of labor for those who remain in agriculture. At the same time, despite the high rates of urban unemployment, the wage differentials between agriculture and non-agricultural activities are still maintained. Migration has tended to increase the marginalization of the rural areas. It is the younger, healthier, better educated, enterprising and risk-taking individuals that have left for the cities. In this sense, the selective character of the migration process has tended to devoid the rural areas of an important part of its valuable human capital stock. This has further increased the marginalization of agriculture and the polarization between rural and urban areas.

Migration abroad has also been highly selective. But, unlike internal migration, the outflow of workers to foreign countries has alleviated the pressure on employment at the same time as it has led to an important inflow of foreign exchange. Actually, remittances from "absent Dominicans" and the newly created tourist industry constitute the major sources of foreign exchange for the country.

The concentration of a large population in the cities implies that the political clientele in the urban areas is more important than the one in the countryside. It is easier for the urban poor to make their voice heard and exercise political pressure on the government than for the rural population. The pressure for lower food prices and an increased supply of urban public utilities can no longer be met with indifference by politicians who want to attract urban votes. This makes it difficult for the government to reduce the urban bias that for centuries has penalized the rural inhabitants.

However, even if the government's freedom of maneuver is limited, either because of political pressures or because of its ties to different interest groups, it has become evident that an urban solution to the problems of unemployment and poverty is largely inadequate. On the one hand, providing cheap food to the urban poor may temporarily reduce social unrest in the slums, but at the same time, such a policy implies lower producer prices and lower rural incomes. Subsequently, the peasants are discouraged from staying on the land, migration increases, agricultural production decreases and food imports increase. On the other hand, creating more urban job opportunities and better access to urban public utilities will lead to a further polarization between urban and rural areas, which in turn provides a further stimulus to the migration process.

If urban unemployment and poverty are to be reduced, a more adequate policy measure would be to reduce the rural-urban drift by attacking the rural problems. As long as urban wages and incomes rise more rapidly than average rural incomes, migration will continue in spite of rising urban unemployment. If the migration flow is to be reduced, it is necessary to address the different problems that have given rise to the prevailing imbalances between rural and urban areas. To this end, it is important to modify policies that have turned the terms of trade against agriculture, to reduce taxes on agricultural exports, to eliminate tariff protection on industrial inputs and consumer goods, etc. But, above all, what is needed is the implementation of an integrated rural development program where due consideration is given to policies that will counteract the push out of rural areas and encourage workers to remain in the countryside. To this end, it is necessary to increase employment opportunities in rural areas and to increase the delivery of public services and amenities there.

The obstacles to such a development strategy have been dealt with at length in the present study. We have emphasized the important role that inappropriate policies, market imperfections and systematic

342

neglect of the peasants have played in the malfunctioning of the Dominican economy. It has become evident that the removal of certain market imperfections and the modification of some policies may not increase efficiency and welfare as long as other imperfections and policies remain unchanged. Getting prices right is but one of the important ingredients needed in order to increase agricultural efficiency. However this would be of limited effect as long as other important obstacles to increased rural welfare prevail.

The present work does not pretend to provide concrete solutions to the wide range of different factors constraining development in the Dominican Republic. The number of problems is so large and their interrelations so complex that detailed policy recommendations for possible solutions fall outside the scope of this study. Nevertheless, it is evident on the basis of our analysis that in order to tackle the problems of poverty and unemployment that harass the Dominican population, urgent measures must be taken to change the path of development. However, the resources needed to undertake such measures are, at present, not readily available. The Dominican Republic is facing one of the major economic crises in its history. Therefore, efforts should be concentrated on identifying priority areas which have the largest impact on redirecting the path of development.

The role of the agricultural sector is clearly of crucial importance. Even in the case that the future of the Dominican economy lies in the development of a strong industrial sector and/or the development of the tourism industry, it is unrealistic to think that such a goal will be reached without the support of an agricultural sector which could produce enough food for the increasing population and generate a surplus to improve welfare in the rural areas and enlarge the market for industrial production. However, in order to increase agricultural production, rural employment and incomes, two key issues should be given priority: a more realistic and efficient labor and land-use policy, as well as increased attention to the needs of the rural population and increased participation of the peasantry in the decision making process.

Labor and Land Use Policy

It has become evident for both international and Dominican observers that a sound agricultural sector could be one of the driving forces in Dominican development.[1] The country has ample natural and human resources which may be used to develop a dynamic agriculture. With good management and adequate policies, the country could increase production to a level where the food supply for the growing population is secured and agro-exports are further developed.

Throughout the 1970s and 1980s, agricultural production has been stagnant. A major factor behind this stagnation has been the implementation of policies that increased the burden on producers while providing subsidies for consumers. During these two decades, agriculture subsidized consumption and production in other sectors of the economy. The government taxed agriculture directly through taxes on traditional exports and indirectly through a dual foreign exchange policy. With the unification of the exchange rate in 1985, both agricultural inputs and outputs were moved into the parallel market. However, the government imposed a 36 percent tax on traditional exports. As a result, the cost of inputs was raised to a rate of 3 pesos to 1 dollar while output was priced at 2 pesos to 1 dollar. This measure further discouraged production of traditional export crops.[2]

Domestic tax and price policies in combination with a depressed international market has plunged the sugar industry, the country's main agricultural activity, into a crisis from which it may be very difficult to recover. Low prices have compelled one of the two private sugar producers to close down two of his three sugar mills. More recently, in 1986 and 1987, the state owned CEA closed two of its mills and plantations.[3] Both private and state owned sugar producers are facing large deficits.[4] On top of increased taxes and low international prices, sugar producers have been compelled to subsidize domestic consumption of both sugar and molasses. At the same time, the fiscal crisis has forced the authorities to use CEA resources to subsidize electricity and other activities.[5]

The policies towards the food sector were implemented to keep prices low for urban consumers. This end was achieved by means of direct subsidies, price controls, selected export prohibitions and imports at the official exchange rate, i.e., using an overvalued peso. The Price Stabilization Institute (INESPRE) acquired monopoly control over the marketing of rice and worked actively to set ceiling prices for numerous agricultural products. Furthermore, INESPRE imports of cheap agricultural products were facilitated through access to cheap foreign exchange and subsidized foreign loans. At the same time, in order to support its operating losses, INESPRE received large government subsidies. These policies constituted a strong disincentive for agricultural producers, depressed agricultural production and made the country highly dependent on food imports. These measures also had a negative effect on income distribution. It was the small producers that were mainly affected. Since most food crops are labor-intensive and produced on small farms, the discouragement of food crop production thus tended to depress rural employment and incomes.

The policy changes brought about through negotiations with the IMF in the mid-1980s have removed many of the price disincentives that have penalized agricultural production. The unification of the exchange rate in 1985 put an end to foreign exchange subsidies. The export surcharge has also been eliminated. Loan subsidies have been reduced due to the end of Commodity Credit Corporation (CCC) borrowings. Imports through the US PL (Public Law) 480, which provide subsidized food loans, have been transferred from INESPRE to the Technical Secretariat's Office. Likewise, INESPRE's monopoly on rice marketing has been transferred to the Agricultural Bank. Through these measures, INESPRE's activities have been significantly reduced.[6]

Although recent policy changes have been significant, there is no guarantee that they will be maintained for a long time.[7] Moreover, the changes will be of little effect as long as the land use policy is not radically changed as well.

The Dominican government ought to initiate a program to encourage an efficient use of land resources of which soil conservation practices must be an integrated part. Alternative use should be found for some of the lands presently occupied by sugar cane. This crop has become increasingly unprofitable and its prospects on the world market are very discouraging. Furthermore, the continued dependence of sugar production on Haitian labor makes that industry very vulnerable. The political changes that have taken place in Haiti since 1985 have introduced considerable insecurity concerning the labor supply for this troubled industry. During the last three years (1985-88), the *zafra* has mainly been carried out by "resident" Haitians. Since the majority of Haitians residing in the Dominican Republic have an illegal status, the sugar producers in collaboration with Dominican authorities have chased them down and forced them to work on the plantations. Since the old agreements with the Duvalier regime were nullified through the escape of Jean-Claude Duvalier in 1986, the Dominican government no longer pays large sums to the Haitian authorities in order to secure labor for the yearly *zafra*. This has created a situation where any Haitian citizen living in the Dominican Republic runs the risk of being forced to work in the sugar fields. This frees the Dominican state and the private sugar producers from the costs involved in the previous arrangements for obtaining Haitian labor. The wages paid for cutting sugar are so low that the Haitians prefer to work in other activities even if they have to pay in order to be employed.[8]

The method used to recruit Haitians to work in the sugar fields has attracted the attention of the international community. The living and working conditions endured by Haitians in the Dominican Republic have been described as a form of slavery. This is very unfortunate, especially for a country which, as is the case with the Dominican

Republic, is trying to conduct an aggressive tourism campaign abroad. The inhuman treatment of Haitian workers must be put to an end, even if that means closing down the already unprofitable sugar industry.

The closing down of sugar mills has already started. However, it was a private company that started this process rather than the state owned CEA which runs the less efficient mills. In this sense, the recent efforts to diversify out of sugar has been characterized as "occurring backwards, closing some of the most efficient mills first while leaving some of the most inefficient in operation."[9]

The closing down of the most unprofitable mills may bring productive lands into better use, but there is no guarantee that rural wages, and the working and living conditions of the workers will be improved through such measures. Producers will probably continue to prefer cheap Haitian labor. If the latter retain their status as illegal immigrants, they will probably be subject to the same treatment as they received from the sugar producers. This means that, as long as the influx of Haitian workers continues, and as long as the Haitians residing in the Dominican Republic continue to have an illegal status, the problems of low wages, rural poverty and rural-urban migration will continue to affect Dominican agriculture.

This implies that if the problem of rural poverty is going to be curbed in the Dominican Republic, a close bilateral collaboration dealing with development issues common to both Haiti and the Dominican Republic has to be established. As long as Haiti continues to be the poorest country in the western hemisphere, migration will continue to be an option to starvation for a considerable number of Haitians. In the face of the restrictive immigration policies of its wealthiest neighbors, (the US and Canada), the Dominican Republic will continue to be the last resort for desperate Haitian rural migrants even if that implies their submission to conditions resembling that of slavery.

A better alternative to keeping alive a bankrupt sugar industry would probably be to incorporate some of the CEA land in the agrarian reform program. As we have seen, there are a considerable number of peasant families in need of productive land. Settling these families on CEA land and on the many other private lands which are underutilized on *latifundios* would imply increased production of food, increased rural employment and incomes. However, before new land can be incorporated into the agrarian reform, the goals and functioning mechanisms of this program ought to be redefined. It seems that the least that the Dominican Agrarian Institute (IAD) is in need of is land. Literally speaking, the IAD constitutes the largest *latifundista* in the country. Its land resources are largely underutilized. The institute has neither the financial means nor the administrative capacity to put all the land it controls into production.

The majority of the IAD settlements are inefficient and, in the case they have shown increased production, they have done so as a result of large subsidies. The main factor behind the poor performance of the settlements has been the paternalistic way in which the program has been carried out. The peasants were to contribute their labor without any real participation in the program, while the IAD owned the land and was in charge of administering the settlements. This has meant a large drain on IAD resources. Unable to sustain such a trend, some IAD representatives have suggested that the Dominican state should encourage the participation of the private sector (which apparently disposes of larger financial resources than the state) in the support of agrarian reform settlements since financial difficulties clearly prevent it from carrying out an efficient agrarian reform on its own. Accordingly, the administrative role of IAD would be taken over by private urban investors who have the means that IAD lack to put its land into efficient production. Or, as an IAD director has put it, the private sector invests and the state "contributes with the usufruct of the land and the *parceleros* [settlers]."[10]

This view reflects, deliberately or not, a perception of the settlers as a sort of state property. The Dominican land reform is considered to be a failure in the sense that its explicit goals of social justice, decreased rural inequalities, increased agricultural production and increased rural employment and incomes have not been fully achieved. However, if one of the implicit goals of this reform was to reinforce state control of the rural areas and to contain the threats to the social order presented by rural protests, then a great deal has been achieved. Such has been one of the major outcomes of agrarian reform attempts in most of Latin America:

> The sources and effects of reforms differed throughout the region, of course, but a consistent outcome in all countries was the increased influence of the state on economic and political conditions in rural areas. In large part, then, a major beneficiary of agrarian reform initiatives was the state itself.[11]

The agrarian reform program has not had a commitment to changing the fate of the rural poor. In order to do so, the program should not be limited to a mere distribution of land. Other means such as credit, education and extension works must be delivered as well. Furthermore, the state should determine the market price of the land it controls and sell it to the beneficiaries on a long-term payment basis. This view has been expressed by the peasants themselves[12] who have traditionally shown a certain reluctance to work collectively on state owned land. Peasants farming on an individual basis could then sell or purchase land freely. To prevent a reaccumulation of large land properties, different measures can be implemented.[13]

A redefinition of the land tenure and land use policy should not only include redistribution of land but also aim to increase output and employment on existing farms. The pressure on the *minifundios* should be lowered by stimulating the creation of labor-intensive rural industries and the provision of services such as supervised credit, health, education, housing and safe water. These measures could improve the welfare of the rural population more readily than mere land redistribution.[14]

On the state and private owned *latifundios* which the government have been unable or unwilling to include in the agrarian reform program, a more intensive and efficient use of land could be attained by levying a substantial land tax based on the productive capacity of the land. Although land is one of the country's most scarce resources, there are practically no urban or rural land taxes in the Dominican Republic.[15]

It has become evident that an agrarian reform which is solely limited to the redistribution of land does not offer an adequate solution to rural poverty. An efficient land reform program should include a wide range of measures directed towards an improvement of the living conditions of the peasantry. In order to achieve this objective, the peasants must be given a more active role in the implementation of such a program and increased participation in the decision making process.

The Neglect of the Peasantry

We have seen that in nearly all respects, the rural population is much worse off than their urban counterparts. This state of affairs is mainly the outcome of a constant neglect of the peasant population by the governing urban elite. The latter have largely ignored the fate of the peasants. The rural population has traditionally been considered mainly as a source of taxation and cheap labor.

This is not a new situation. The Dominican peasantry has always been without representation in the political sphere. Its voice has never been properly heard. The peasants have, however, not remained passive, but whenever they have protested they have been suppressed by the authorities, often with violence.

The welfare of the peasantry has never been taken into consideration whenever the state has intervened to modernize agriculture. The introduction of large-scale agriculture at the turn of the century which abolished the traditional land tenure and land use pattern, sealed the fate of the Dominican peasantry:

> Important to an understanding of the rural poor - who make up as much as 90 percent of the rural population of Latin America - is the fact that their condition and fate are inextricably linked to the expansion of large-scale capitalist agriculture. They are not isolated, backward, or "traditional" members of society who have simply been left behind in the process of development; they do not have to be forced, trained, or cajoled into "modernity" by government programs. The growth in their unemployment, underemployment, landlessness, wage dependence, subsistence orientation, and migration is a direct result of developments in the modern capitalist sector and of state policies, and as such cannot be understood or remedied without reference to these changes. Nevertheless, in the wake of these changes, the most significant of which have been imposed from without, these peasants have not remained passive. Instead, they have adopted a variety of strategies to ensure family subsistence in the face of deteriorating conditions.[16]

For the Dominican peasantry, the strategy has been to work their small pieces of land to the utmost, to engage in small-scale trade, to become wage laborers or to migrate to the cities or abroad. The survival strategy adopted by the Dominican peasantry has created two major problems which any government concerned with the future of the country must deal with seriously: the increasing deterioration of land resources caused by deforestation and soil erosion and the problem of rural-urban migration.

Many of the problems that afflict the Dominican countryside tend to be blamed on the peasants themselves. Already during the nineteenth century, Dominican authors made complaints about the laziness and lack of initiative that they considered to be dominant characteristics of the Dominican peasants. Explanations were sought along racial lines about a supposed inferiority inherited from their African ancestry. Others stated that the shortcomings of the peasants were due to the tropical environment in general, or inadequate diet and education.[17] Propositions for improvements often stressed the benefits that could be reaped from the importation of Caucasian European farmers.[18] Such vulgar opinions are nowadays not expressed openly, at least not to the same extent as before. However people still talk about the lack of initiative shown by the peasants in seeking to change their situation themselves. The Dominican sociologist, Frank Marino Hernández, recently pointed to the lack of education and sense of hopelessness that prevail among many peasants: "In reality we have *campesinos* [peasants] but we do not have enough *agricultores* [agriculturalists]."[19]

In order to make his point clear he told a little story:

I bought a little plot of 50.5 tareas. Instead of going to the Sheraton to do gymnastics with my friends, because I do not like the odor of men, I wanted to sweat while planting fruits. And what happened? In the surroundings of my plot, no campesino plants anything whatsoever. I told myself, with malice aforethought, well, if I distribute oranges, good mangos and good avocados, at least they will not steal from me or covet the fruits I would plant since in this way the neighbors will also have them; ... so I told a gentleman called Barahona, who lived in front of my doorstep, look, Baraho, would you like to plant some orange trees that I will give you, they are grafted, they are the good ones. He said: - "Well, if you fix the holes ..." Then I told him: - "Well, let us go on with it, I will help you." This was in November 1981; I have still neither fixed the holes for Baraho nor has he planted the oranges. The same is true of all the plots around my place. On my plot, I have now eaten oranges over the two years that have passed now in November; not many, but I have eaten oranges, and the plots around mine continue to be uncultivated.[20]

After telling his tale, the storyteller goes on to ask what will happen if land is distributed to people like Barahona, people who "do not know how to plant, who do not have any interest in planting, who are waiting that something will fall down from heaven, or that someone will hire them as day-laborers."[21]

What Hernández is aiming at, is the fact that a state of apathy reigns among many of the rural inhabitants. He rightly acknowledges that the Dominican peasants have not been educated to be *agricultores* and points to the detrimental state of rural education. This is true. The Dominican peasants have been devoid not only of education but also of most social services. Still, they have shown a strong will to survive in spite of the different obstacles that they have confronted. They continue to be the producers of most of the food staples in the country. This strong will is slowly being eroded by the continuous setbacks experienced by the peasants. As a fellow peasant expresses it: "What is the use? Why struggle when the benefits of the struggle are so meager and insecure? Why break your back for nothing? What difference can a few oranges make in my hopeless situation?" Barahona has probably seen the car and shaven face of his Sunday-farmer neighbor and pondered on the fact that it is wholly impossible for him to gain only a fragment of his wealth. Living as a neighbor to abundance is maybe not a stimulus. It may also mean a constant confrontation with your own inferiority and hopeless situation.

The feelings of apathy and hopelessness which today prevail among many of the rural inhabitants are not an intrinsic characteristic of peasants. They are mainly the result of a set of policies that bring about a systematic neglect of the peasants and a disincentive to work the land.

Notes

1. See World Bank (1987), p. 55 and Forum (1984).

2. World Bank (1987), p. 57.

3. Murphy (1988), p. 4.

4. The estimated deficits of the two private companies in 1985 amounted to DR$ 5 - 20 million while the State Sugar Council (CEA) had an operating deficit (before transfer) of about RD$ 100 million (World Bank (1987), p. 57).

5. Ibid., pp. 57 and 62.

6. Ibid., p. 61.

7. In June 1987, the government reintroduced exchange control. The growing government deficit has been covered by the Central Bank. By mid-1987, annual inflation had already soared to 35 percent (from 9.8 percent at the end of 1986) (*Latin American Economic Report* (1987), p. 12). By the end of 1988, inflation was estimated to be 60 percent (FED (1988)). Traditional exports continued to be penalized through the exchange rate policy. In mid-1988, export earnings were received at the current official exchange rate of RD$ 5.14 = US$ 1.00 while the open market rate was RD$ 8.00 = US$ 1.00 (Murphy (1988), pp. 10-11). At the end of 1988, the Central Bank took control over the foreign exchange market and the exchange rate was unified.

8. A recent report on the situation of the Haitian workers in the Dominican Republic is given by Torres (1988), pp. 28-47.

9. World Bank (1987), p. 64.

10. De Ovín Filpo (1985), p. 108.

11. Grindle (1986), p. 8.

12. See for example the peasant leader Américo Jiménez's contribution to the debate on agrarian reform in Forum (1985), pp. 84-85. He suggests payment terms of 30 or 40 years (ibid.).

13. The reaccumulation of large tracts can, for example, be prevented by limiting sales to buyers not already owning more than a given amount of land (World Bank (1987), note 12, p. 69).

14. Such an effort is being implemented by the *Plan Sierra*, a very promising rural development program where the peasants themselves are actively participating. The project aims at improving farm income and rural living conditions. It provides credit for crops and introduces production methods that reduce soil erosion. Reforestation includes the plantation of timber, fruit trees and coffee. *Plan Sierra* is the only Dominican program which both directly contributes to an improvement of the peasants lives and deals with the problems of deforestation and erosion at a local level. The program has been in operation since 1979, and in spite of its relative success it has not been

extended to other regions of the country. (For a firsthand description of this program see Lang (1988), pp. 1-39.)

15. The creation of a progressive land tax was suggested by the World Bank mission in 1978. (See World Bank (1978:1), p. 18 and 76.) More recently, an IAD director expressed: "Let me say something even if I take the risk of being dismissed tomorrow. This is one of the few countries in the world where land taxes are not paid. If we introduced a land tax based on productivity ... we would have more millions than the reform requires ... If we some day get a sufficiently serious government that brought the money extracted from the countryside back to the countryside, then we would not need any money either from international funds, nor from other domestic funds." (De Ovín Filpo, cited in Forum (1985), p. 113.)

16. Grindle (1986), p. 7.

17. For a critical exposition of such ideas see Cassá (1976) and Franco (1981).

18. See SEA (1924), p. 13.

19. Forum (1984), p. 65.

20. Ibid., pp. 64-65.

21. Ibid., p. 65.

Bibliography

Acosta, M. (1981). "Azúcar e inmigración," in: Corten et al. (1981).

Adams, D. W. (1978). "Mobilizing Household Savings through Rural Financial Markets." *Economic Development and Cultural Change*, vol. 26.

_____ . (1984). "Are the Arguments for Cheap Agricultural Credit Sound?" in: Adams et al. (1984).

Adams, D. W., Graham, D. H. and Von Pischke, J. D. (eds.) (1984). *Undermining Rural Development with Cheap Credit*. Boulder, Colorado.

Ahluwalia, M. S. (1979). "Income Inequality: Some Dimensions of the Problem," in: Chenery et al. (1979).

"Ahora" (1977). *Revista Ahora*, no. 700, April. Santo Domingo.

_____ . (1981). *Revista Ahora*, no. 938. Santo Domingo.

_____ . (1986). *Revista Ahora*, no. 1094, May. Santo Domingo.

Alcántara Z., E. (1981). "Estudio acerca de la reforma agraria en la República Dominicana en el período 1972-78." *Mimeo*, UNPHU (Universidad Nacional Pedro Henriquez Ureña). Santo Domingo.

Alemán, J. L. (1982). *27 ensayos de economía y sociedad dominicana*. Santiago de los Caballeros.

Alemany, W., Alvarez, A. and Feria, R. (1981). "La expansión del capitalismo en el período 1966-1978. (El papel de la industria)." *CERESD 11*. Santo Domingo.

Allen, F. (1985). "The Activities and Operations of the Institute for Price Stabilization of the Dominican Republic." *Mimeo*, Tufts University. Medford, Massachusetts.

"Amigo del Hogar" (1986). *Revista Amigo del Hogar*, no. 470, March. Santo Domingo.

Anti-Slavery Society for the Protection of Human Rights (1979). "Migrant Workers in the Dominican Republic." Report for 1979 to the United Nations Working Group of Experts on Slavery, in: United Nations (1979).

Arndt, H. W. and Sundrum, R. M. (1980). "Employment, Unemployment and Under-Employment." *Bulletin of Indonesian Economic Studies*, 16 (3), November.

Arndt, H. W. (1987). *Economic Development. The History of an Idea*. Chicago.

Anschel, K. R. and Wiegand, K. B. (1983). "Market Failure Among Small Scale Farmers: The Causes and Implications." *Mimeo*, University of Kentucky, Department of Agricultural Economics.

Báez E., F. (1978). *Azúcar y Dependencia en la República Dominicana*. Santo Domingo.

354

Báez E., F. and D'Oleo R., F. (1986). *La emigración de dominicanos a Estados Unidos: determinantes socio-económicos y consequencias.* Santo Domingo.
Balaguer, J. (1947). *La realidad dominicana.* Buenos Aires.
_____ . (1983). *La isla al revés.* Santo Domingo.
Banco Agrícola (1983). *Boletín Estadístico 1982.* Santo Domingo.
Banco Central (1985). *Boletín Mensual,* no. 1, January. Santo Domingo.
Bardhan, P. K. (1978). "On Measuring Rural Unemployment." *Journal of Development Studies,* vol. 14, pp. 342-352.
Baud, M. (1984). "La gente del tabaco. Villa González en el siglo veinte." *Ciencia y Sociedad,* vol. IX, no. 1, January-April. Santo Domingo.
_____ . (1986). "Transformación capitalista y regionalización en la República Dominicana, 1875-1920." *Investigación y Ciencia,* no. 1, January-April. Santo Domingo.
_____ . (1987). "The Struggle for Autonomy. Peasant Resistance to Capitalism in the Dominican Republic, 1870-1924," in: Cross and Human (1988).
Barraclough, S. and Domike, A. L. (1966). "Agrarian Structure in Latin American Countries." *Land Economics,* vol. 42.
Barraclough, S. (1970). "Agrarian Reform Programs for the Dominican Republic." USAID. Santo Domingo.
Bell, I. (1981). *The Dominican Republic.* Boulder, Colorado.
Berry, A. and Sabot, R. H. (1984). "Unemployment and Economic Development." *Economic Development and Cultural Change,* vol. 33, no. 1, pp. 99-116.
Bhagwati, J. N. (ed.) (1976). *The Brain Drain and Taxation, II: Theory and Empirical Analysis.* Amsterdam.
Bhagwati, J. N. (1983). *Essays in International Economic Theory. Vol. 1: The Theory of Commercial Policy.* Cambridge, Mass. and London.
Bhagwati, J. N., Jones, R. W., Mundell, R. A. and Vanek, J. (eds.) (1971). *Trade, Balance of Payments, and Growth. Papers in International Economics in Honour of Charles P. Kindleberger.* Amsterdam.
Bhagwati, J. N. and Rodríguez, C. (1976). "Welfare-Theoretical Analysis of the Brain Drain," in: Bhagwati (1976).
Bhagwati, J. N. and Srinivasan, T. N. (1971). "The Theory of Wage Differentials: Production Response and Factor Price Equalization," in: Bhagwati (1983).
_____ . (1983). *Lectures on International Trade.* Cambridge, Mass. and London.
Black, J. K. (1986). *The Dominican Republic. Politics and Development in an Unsovereign State.* Boston.
Boin, J. and Serulle, R. J. (1979). *El proceso de desarrollo del capitalismo en la República Dominicana, (1844-1930).* Santo Domingo.
Bonó, P. F. (1980:1). "Apuntes sobre las clases trabajadoras dominicanas," in: Rodríguez Demorizi (1980).
_____ . (1980:2). "Cuestiones sociales y agrícolas," in: Rodríguez Demorizi (1980).
_____ . (1980:3). "Opiniones de un Dominicano," in: Rodríguez Demorizi (1980).
_____ . (1980:4). "Apuntes para los cuatro ministerios de la República," in: Rodríguez Demorizi (1980).

Bosch, J. (1979). *Composición social Dominicana. Historia e interpretación.* Santo Domingo.

_____. (1985). *La fortuna de Trujillo.* Santo Domingo.

Boserup, E. (1965). *The Conditions of Agricultural Growth. The Economics of Agrarian Change under Population Pressure.* London.

Bouman, F. J. A. (1977). "Indigenous Savings and Credit Societies in the Third World. A Message." *Savings and Development,* no. 1.

Bouman, F. J. A. (1984). "Informal Savings and Credit Arrangements in Developing Countries: Observations from Sri Lanka," in: Adams et al. (1984).

Bray, D. (1983). "La agricultura de exportación, la formación de clases y mano de obra excedente: El caso de la migración interna e internacional en la República Dominicana." *Mimeo,* Center of Latin American Studies, University of Florida. Gainesville.

Bruton, H. J. (1978). "Unemployment Problems and Policies in Less Developed Countries." *American Economic Review,* vol. 68, no. 2.

Butterworth, D. and Chance, J. K. (1981). *Latin American Urbanization.* New York.

Byres, T. J. (1979). "Of Neo-Populist Pipe-Dreams: Daedalus in the Third World and the Myth of Urban Bias." *Journal of Peasant Studies,* vol. 6, no. 2, pp. 210-44.

Cabrera, O. (1984). "Mercados financieros rurales: aspectos económicos." *Mimeo,* UCMM (Universidad Católica Madre y Maestra). Santiago de los Caballeros.

Calder, B. J. (1984). *The Impact of Intervention: The Dominican Republic during the U.S. Occupation of 1916-1924.* Austin, Texas.

Candler, J. (1842). *Brief Notice of Hayti with its Conditions, Resources and Prospects.* London.

Canelo, F. (1982). *Dónde, porqué, de qué, cómo viven los Dominicanos en el extranjero? Un informe sociológico sobre la migración Dominicana, 1961-1982.* Santo Domingo.

Casanovas, C. (1983). "La población y su relación con los recursos naturales." Paper presented at the seminar "Población y Sociedad." Santo Domingo.

Cassá, R. (1974). *Los Taínos de la Española.* Santo Domingo.

_____. (1976). "El racismo en la ideología de la clase dominante dominicana." *Ciencia,* vol. III, no. 1, January-March.

_____. (1977). *Historia social y económica de la República Dominicana. Tomo I.* Santo Domingo.

_____. (1982). *Capitalismo y dictadura.* Santo Domingo.

_____. (1983). *Historia social y económica de la República Dominicana. Tomo II.* Santo Domingo.

_____. (1986). *Los doce años: contrarevolución y desarrollismo. Tomo I.* Santo Domingo.

Castor, S. (1983). *Migración y relaciones internacionales (el caso haitiano-dominicano).* Mexico, D.F.

Ceara H., M. (1989). "La economía Dominicana: crisis y reestructuración 1968-1988." *Mimeo.* Santo Domingo.

CEDOPEX (Centro de Promoción de Exportaciones) (1979). *Estudio de actualización de la oferta exportable industrial de la República Dominicana. Documento No. I.* Santo Domingo.

Chenery, H., Ahluwalia, M. S., Bell, C. L. G., Duloy, J. H. and Jolly, R. (1979). *Redistribution with Growth.* Washington, D. C.

Clausner, M. D. (1970). "Rural Santo Domingo: Settled, Unsettled and Resettled." Ph.D. thesis, Temple University. Philadelphia.

CODECO (Colegio Dominicano de Economístas) (1983). "Posición del CODECO sobre la ley de incentivo y protección industrial y el proyecto de ley 18 que la modifica." *Mimeo.* Santo Domingo.

Consejo Nacional de Agricultura (1984). "El financiamiento agropecuario: el déficit de la oferta y alternativas viables." *Mimeo.* Consejo Nacional de Agricultura - Unidad de Estudios Agropecuarios. Santo Domingo.

_____ . (1989). *Compendio de estudios sobre políticas agropecuarias en República Dominicana 1985-1988. Tomo I y II.* Santo Domingo.

Cook, S. and Borah, W. (1971). *Essays in Population History: Mexico and the Caribbean. Vol. I.* Berkeley.

Cordero, W. and Puig, M. (1975). *Tendencias de la economía cafetalera dominicana, 1955-1972.* Santo Domingo.

Corten, A. (1970). "La migration des travailleurs haïtiens vers les centrales sucriéres dominicaines." *Cultures et Développement,* vol. 2.

Corten, A., Vilas, C. Ma., Acosta, M. and Duarte, I. (1981). *Azúcar y política en la República Dominicana.* Santo Domingo.

Crassweller, R. D. (1966). *Trujillo, The Life and Times of a Caribbean Dictator.* New York.

Cross, M. and Human, G. (1988), (forthcoming). *Labor in the Caribbean: From Emancipation to Independence.* London.

Crouch, L. A. (1981). "The Development of Capitalism in Dominican Agriculture." Ph.D. thesis, University of California. Berkeley.

Cruz Brache, J. A. (1975). "Pesos y medidas folkloricos de la República Dominicana." *Revista Dominicana de Folklore,* no. 1. Santo Domingo.

Cuello H., J. I. (1985). *Documentos del conflicto dominico-haitiano de 1937.* Santo Domingo.

Cuevas, C. E. and Poyo, J. (1986). *Costos de operación y economías de escala en el Banco Agrícola de la República Dominicana.* Santo Domingo.

Cuevas J., J. C. (1981). "La reforma agraria y niveles de vida. Estudio de caso Proyecto 149 Haras Nacionales, Villa Mella." *Mimeo,* UNPHU (Universidad Nacional Pedro Henriquez Ureña). Santo Domingo.

Currie, L. (1979). "Is There an Urban Bias? Critique of Michael Lipton's Why Poor People Stay Poor." *Journal of Economic Studies,* vol. 6, no. 1, pp. 87-105.

Dauhajre, A. hijo (1984). "República Dominicana: 18 años de política económica 1966-1983." *Mimeo,* UCMM (Universidad Católica Madre y Maestra). Santo Domingo.

_____ . (1989). "El estado dominicano como empresario. Costos y beneficios de las empresas públicas," in: PNUD - PUCMM (1989).

Dechamps, E. (1907). *La República Dominicana: directorio y guía general.* Barcelona.

Deive, C. E. (1977). "El 'san' dominicano nació en Africa." *Ahora*, no. 716, August. Santo Domingo.

_____. (1978). *El Indio, el negro, y la vida tradicional dominicana.* Santo Domingo.

_____. (1979). *Vodú y mágia en Santo Domingo.* Santo Domingo.

_____. (1980). *La esclavitud del negro en Santo Domingo (1492-1844). Tomo II.* Santo Domingo.

De Janvry, A. (1981). *The Agrarian Question and Reformism in Latin America.* Baltimore, Maryland.

De la Mota, M. (1980). "Palma Sola: 1962." *Boletín del Museo del Hombre Dominicano*, no. 14. Santo Domingo.

Del Castillo, J. (1979). "Las emigraciones y su aporte a la cultura dominicana. Finales del siglo XIX y principios del XX." *EME EME*, no. 45, vol. VIII, November-December. Santiago de los Caballeros.

_____. (1981). *Ensayos de sociología dominicana.* Santo Domingo.

_____. (1982). "Azúcar & braceros: historia de un problema." *EME EME*, no. 58, vol. X, January-February. Santiago de los Caballeros.

Del Rosario, G. (1982). "Empleo y distribución de ingreso en la República Dominicana." *Revista de Estudios Económicos*, vol. I, no. 2, July-December. Santo Domingo.

Del Rosario, G. and Gámez, S. (1987). *Estructura impositiva y bienestar social en la República Dominicana 1976-1984.* Santo Domingo.

De Moya Espinal, F. A. (1980). "Algunos aspectos sobre mano de obra en la República Dominicana," in: ONAPLAN, (1980).

De Ovín Filpo, M. (1985). "Estrategias administrativas para la reforma agraria," in: Forum (1985).

Díaz Santana, A. (1976). "The Role of Haitian Braceros in Dominican Sugar Production." *Latin American Perspectives*, vol. 3.

Diederich, B. and Burt, A. (1972). *Papa Doc: Haiti and its Dictator.* Harmondsworth.

Dominican Blue Book 1920 (1976). Santo Domingo.

Dore Cabral, C. (1979). *Problemas de la estructura agraria dominicana.* Santo Domingo.

_____. (1982). "Posibilidades y límites de la reforma agraria en la República Dominicana," in: Forum (1982).

Duarte, I. (1979). "La fuerza de trabajo infantil en Santo Domingo." *Estudios Sociales*, no. 46, April-May-June. Santo Domingo.

_____. (1980). *Capitalismo y superpoblación en Santo Domingo.* Santo Domingo.

_____. (1981). "Patrones característicos de la fuerza de trabajo migratoria en la República Dominicana." *Mimeo*, (UASD) Universidad Autónoma de Santo Domingo. Santo Domingo.

Economía Dominicana (1976). *Economía Dominicana 1975.* Academia de Ciencias de la República Dominicana. Comisión de Economía. Santo Domingo.

Edouard, B. (1969). "Les migrations de travailleurs," in: Secrétairerie d'Etat des Affairs Sociales, *Actes du IIème Congrès National du Travail.* Port-au-Prince.

Espinal, R. (1987). *Autoritarismo y democracia en la política dominicana.* San José.

Eusebio Pol, N. (1980). "Las asociaciones campesinas dominicanas y el caso de San Juan de la Maguana." *Mimeo,* UNPHU (Universidad Nacional Pedro Henriquez Ureña). Santo Domingo.

FAO (Food and Agriculture Organization of the United Nations) (1975). *Production Yearbook,* vol. 36. Rome.

_____. (1985). *Production Yearbook,* vol. 38. Rome.

FED (Fundación Economía y Desarrollo) (1988). "Sabado Económico," no. 53, in: *Listín Diario,* Nov. 5, 1988.

_____. (1989). "Estudio sobre zonas francas." *Mimeo.* Santo Domingo.

Feder, E. (1971). *The Rape of the Peasantry. Latin America's Landholding System.* Garden City, New York.

Fei, J. C. H. and Ranis, G. (1964). *Development of the Labor Surplus Economy: Theory and Policy.* Homewood.

Ferman, L. A., Kornbluh, J. L. and Haber, A. (eds.) (1968). *Poverty in America: A Book of Readings.* Ann Arbor, University of Michigan.

Ferrán, F. I. (1976). *Tabaco y sociedad. La organización del poder en el mercado de tabaco dominicano.* Santo Domingo.

Fisher, I. (1930). *The Theory of Interest.* New York.

Forum (1982). *Los problemas del sector rural en la República Dominicana. Forum no. 3.* Santo Domingo.

_____. (1984). *Población y pobreza en la República Dominicana. Forum no. 12.* Santo Domingo.

_____. (1985). *Presente y futuro de la reforma agraria en la República Dominicana. Forum no. 15.* Santo Domingo.

Fraginals, M. M., Moya Pons, F. and Stanley, E. (eds.) (1985). *Slavery and Free Labor in the Spanish Speaking Caribbean.* Baltimore.

Franco, F. J. (1967). *República Dominicana. Clases, crisis y comandos.* Santo Domingo.

_____. (1981). *Historia de las ideas políticas en la República Dominicana.* Santo Domingo.

Frank, A. G. (1967). "The Development of Underdevelopment." *Catalyst,* 1967.

Galbraith, K. (1979). *The Nature of Mass Poverty.* Harmondsworth, Middlesex.

Galíndez, J. de (1962). *La era de Trujillo.* Buenos Aires.

García, J. M. (1983). *La matanza de los haitianos. Genocidio de Trujillo, 1937.* Santo Domingo.

Gardiner, C. H. (1979). *La política de inmigración del dictador Trujillo.* Santo Domingo.

Garrido Puello, E. O. (1981). *El Sur en la historia, las ciencias y la literatura.* Santo Domingo.

Gingras, J-P. O. (1967). *Duvalier, Caribbean Cyclone. The History of Haiti and Its Present Government.* New York.

Godfrey, E. M. (1967). "Measuring the Removable Surplus of Agricultural Labour in Low-income Economies." *Journal of Economic Studies,* vol. 2, no. 1, pp. 50-72.

González, M. F. (1985). "Desiderio Arias y el caudillismo." *Estudios Sociales,* no. 61, July-September. Santo Domingo.

González-Vega, C. (1982). "Las políticas de tasas de interés y la asignación del crédito agropecuario por las instituciones financieras de desarrollo de América Latina." *Mimeo*, paper presented at the Seminario de Alto Nivel Sobre Mercados Financieros Rurales, October. Santo Domingo.

_____. (1984). "Credit-Rationing Behavior of Agricultural Lenders: the Iron Law of Interest-Rate Restrictions," in: Adams et al. (1984).

Graber, E. S. (1978). "Strategy, Policies and Programs for Economic Growth and Social Progress in the Dominican Republic: With Reference to Rural Development." Ph.D. thesis, Iowa State University. Iowa.

Grassman, S. and Lundberg, E. (ed.) (1981). *The World Economic Order: Past and Prospects*. London.

Grasmuck, S. (1981). "Fuerza de trabajo dominicana en EU y fuerza de trabajo haitiana en R.D." *Mimeo*. Santo Domingo.

_____. (1982). "The Impact of Emigration on National Development: Three Sending Communities in the Dominican Republic." *International Migration Review XVI*, no. 2.

_____. (1984). "Las consecuencias de la emigración urbana para el desarrollo nacional: el caso de Santiago." *Mimeo*, paper presented at "Seminario sobre la inmigración Dominicana en los Estados Unidos", April. Santo Domingo.

Griffin, K. (1969). *Underdevelopment in Spanish America*. London.

_____. (1974). *The Political Economy of Agrarian Change. An Essay on the Green Revolution*. London.

_____. (1976:1). *Land Concentration and Rural Poverty*. London.

_____. (1976:2). "On the Emigration of the Peasantry." *World Development*, vol. 4.

Grindle, M. S. (1986). *State and Countryside. Development Policy and Agrarian Politics in Latin America*. Baltimore, Maryland.

Gudeman, S. (1972). "The Compadrazgo as a Reflection of the Natural and Spiritual Person," in: *Proceedings of the Royal Anthropological Institute of Great Britain and Ireland for 1971*. London.

Gugler, J. (1982). "Overurbanization Reconsidered." *Economic Development and Cultural Change*, vol. 31, no. 1, pp. 173-189, October.

Haiti Información. Organo del Comité Democrático Haitiano, no. 13, Sept. 1979, no. 18, Feb. 1980, no. 23, Oct. 1980. Mexico, D.F.

Harris, J. R. and Todaro, M. P. (1970). "Migration, Unemployment and Development: A two-sector analysis." *American Economic Review*, vol. 60, pp. 126-140.

Harris, M. (1975). *Culture, People, Nature: An Introduction to General Anthropology*. Second edition. New York.

Hazard, S. (1873). *Santo Domingo, Past and Present. With a Glance at Hayti*. New York.

Heinl, R. D. Jr. and Heinl, N. G. (1978). *Written in Blood: The Story of the Haitian People 1492-1971*. Boston.

Henderson, J. M. and Quandt, R. E. (1971). *Microeconomic Theory: A Mathematical Treatment*. New York.

Hendricks, G. (1978). *Los dominicanos ausentes: un pueblo en transición*. Santo Domingo.

Henige, D. (1978). "On the Contact Population of Hispaniola: History as Higher Mathematics." *Hispanic American Historical Review* 52 (2).

Herberg, H. and Kemp, M. C. (1971). "Factor Market Distortions, the Shape of the Locus of Competitive Outputs, and the Relation between Product Prices and Equilibrium Outputs," in: Bhagwati et al. (1971).

_____ . (1980). "In Defence of Some 'Paradoxes' of Trade Theory." *American Economic Review*, vol. 70.

Herberg, H., Kemp, M. C. and Magee, S. P. (1971). "Factor Market Distortions, the Reversal of Relative Factor Intensities, and the Relation between Product Prices and Equilibrium Outputs." *Economic Record*, vol. 70.

Heredia y Mieses, J. F. de (1955). "Informe presentado al muy ilustrísimo ayuntamiento de Santo Domingo, capital de la Isla Española," in: Rodríguez Demorizi (1955).

Hernández, F. M. (1973). *La inmigración haitiana*. Santo Domingo.

Hicks, A. C. (1946). *Blood in the Streets: The Life and Rule of Trujillo*. New York.

Hobsbawm, E. J. (1967). "Peasants and Rural Migrants in Politics," in: Veliz (1967).

_____ . (1972). *Bandits*. Bungay, Suffolk.

Hoetink, H. (1971). *El pueblo dominicano: 1850-1900. Apuntes para su sociología histórica*. Santiago de los Caballeros.

Horowitz, M. M. (ed.) (1971). *Peoples and Cultures of the Caribbean*. Garden City, New York.

House, W. J. (1984). "Nairobi's Informal Sector: Dynamic Entrepreneurs or Surplus Labor?" *Economic Development and Cultural Change*, vol. 32, pp. 277-302.

"Hoy" (1986). 24 January and 22 February. Santo Domingo.

IAD (Instituto Agrario Dominicano) (1981:1). *Estudio de la realidad campesina y sus alternativas de desarrollo*. Santo Domingo.

_____ . (1981:2). *Compendio de las leyes agrarias*. Santo Domingo.

_____ . (1983:1). *Boletín Informativo Anual*, vol. 8. Santo Domingo.

_____ . (1983:2). "Situación actual y perspectivas de la reforma agraria en la República Dominicana." *Mimeo*, Informe a Conferencia Mundial sobre Desarrollo Rural, Roma 1983. Santo Domingo.

IEPD (Instituto de Estudio de Población y Desarrollo) (1983:1). *Boletín no. 2*, July-October. Santo Domingo.

_____ . (1983:2). *Boletín no. 4*, March-April-May. Santo Domingo.

_____ . (1983:3). *Población y mano de obra en la República Dominicana: perspectivas de la fuerza de trabajo y el empleo en el período 1980-1990*. Santo Domingo.

_____ . (1984). *Boletín no. 6*, January-April. Santo Domingo.

_____ . (1985). *Boletín no. 9*, January-March. Santo Domingo.

_____ . (1988). *Boletín no. 21*, January-March. Santo Domingo.

Illy, H. F. (1983). "Social Control instead of Social Change; the Administration of Land Reform in the Dominican Republic," in: Illy (ed.) (1983).

Illy, H. F. (ed.) (1983). *Politics, Public Administration and Rural Development in the Caribbean*. Munich.

IMF (International Monetary Fund) (1982). *International Financial Statistics Yearbook*. Washington, D.C.

INESPRE (Instituto de Estabilización de Precios) (1984). *Boletín Estadístico 1983*. Santo Domingo.

Informe de la Comisión de Investigación de los E.U.A. en Santo Domingo en 1871 (1960). Santo Domingo.

Institut Haïtien de Statistique (1976). Département des Finances et des Affaires Economiques. *L'économie haïtienne, son évolution récente*. Port-au-Prince.

International Bank for Reconstruction and Development (1976). *Current Economic Position and Prospects of Haiti. Volume II: Statistical Appendix*. Washington, D.C.

ISA (Instituto Superior de Agricultura) (1979). Centro de Investigaciones Económicas y Alimenticias. "Desarrollo del capitalismo en el campo dominicano. Política agraria, pobreza rural y crecimiento agrícola." Versión preliminar, *Mimeo*. Santiago de los Caballeros.

Isa, M. (1985). "Las presas no han cumplido su cometido en materia de riego." *Hoy*, 21 November. Santo Domingo.

Jiménes Grullón, J. I. (1943). *El contrasentido de una política*. La Habana.

_____ . (1965). *La República Dominicana. Una ficción*. Mérida, Venezuela.

Johnson, H. G. (1966). "Factor Market Distortions and the Shape of the Transformation Curve. "*Econometrica*, vol. 34.

Jolly, R., de Kadt, E., Singer, H. and Wilson, F. (eds.) (1973). *Third World Employment: Problems and Strategy*. Harmondsworth.

Jones, R. W. (1971). "The Structure of Simple General Equilibrium Models." *Journal of Political Economy*, vol. 73.

Kahn, R. (1976). "Unemployment as seen by the Keynesians," in: Worswick (1976).

Keynes, J. M. (1973). *The General Theory of Employment, Interest and Money*. Cambridge.

Kidd, C. V. (1968). "Migration of Highly Educated Personnel from Latin America to the U.S." *Report of the Commission on Western Hemisphere Immigration*. U.S. Government Printing Office, Washington, D.C.

Knight, M. H. (1928). *The Americans in Santo Domingo*. New York.

Krishna, R. (1973). "Unemployment in India." *Economic and Political Weekly*, March 3.

Ladman, J. R. and Adams, D. W. (1978). "The Rural Poor and the Recent Performance of Formal Rural Financial Markets in the Dominican Republic." *Canadian Journal of Agricultural Economics*, no. 1, pp. 43-50.

Ladman, J. R. and Liz, R. (1988). "Small-Farmer Credit vía Agroindustry: The Case of the Dominican Republic." *Mimeo*, Department of Agricultural Economics and Rural Sociology, Ohio State University.

LaGra, J. (1983). "Developing Marketing Systems in the Dominican Republic," in: Illy (ed.) (1983).

Laguerre, M. S., (1976). "Le sangue haïtien: un système de crédit rotatoire." *Mimeo*, Institut Interaméricain des Sciences Agricoles (IICA). Port-au-Prince.

Landsberger, H. A. (ed.) (1969). *Latin American Peasant Movements*. Ithaca, New York.

Landsberger, H. A. (1974:1). "Peasant Unrest: Themes and Variations," in: Landsberger (1974:2).

Landsberger, H. A. (ed.) (1974:2). *Rural Protest: Peasant Movements and Social Change.* London.

Lang, J. (1988). *Inside Development in Latin America: A Report from the Dominican Republic, Colombia, and Brazil.* North Carolina.

Latin American Economic Report (1987). 31 August, 1987.

Lemoine, M. (1983). *Azúcar amargo - hay esclavos en el Caribe.* Santo Domingo.

Lewis, A. W. (1954). "Economic Development with Unlimited Supply of Labor." *Manchester School of Economic and Social Studies,* vol. 22.

_____ . (1955). *The Theory of Economic Growth.* London.

_____ . (1958). "Unlimited Labour: Further Notes." *Manchester School.* vol. 32.

_____ . (1972). "Four Steps to Full Employment." Presidential Address to the Board of Governors of the Caribbean Development Bank, April. Reprinted in Meier (1976).

Lewis, O. (1966). *La Vida: A Puerto Rican Family in the Culture of Poverty.* San Juan and New York.

_____ . (1968). "The Culture of Poverty," in: Ferman et al. (1968).

Linares, M. (1984). "Modelo econométrico de la economía cafetalera dominicana." *Mimeo,* UCMM (Universidad Católica Madre y Maestra). Santo Domingo.

_____ . (1985). "Un exámen del nuevo sistema de distribución de cuotas de exportación de café." *Mimeo,* Santo Domingo.

Lipton, M. (1977). *Why Poor People Stay Poor.* London.

Little, I. (1982). *Economic Development: Theory, Policy, and International Relations.* New York.

Little, I., Scitovsky, T. and Scott, M. (1970). *Industry and Trade in Some Developing Countries.* London.

Lluberes, N. A. (1977). "Tabaco y Catalanes en Santo Domingo durante el siglo XVIII." *EME EME,* vol. V, January-February, pp. 13-26. Santiago de los Caballeros.

_____ . (1983). "El enclave azucarero, 1902-1930." *Revista del Museo Nacional de Historia y Geografía,* no. 2. Santo Domingo.

Lundahl, M. (1979). *Peasants and Poverty: A Study of Haiti.* London.

_____ . (1981). "Teorins plats inom utvecklingsekonomin." *Ekonomisk Debatt,* no. 8.

_____ . (1982). "A Note on Haitian Migration to Cuba, 1890-1934." *Cuban Studies,* vol. 12.

_____ . (1983). *The Haitian Economy: Man, Land and Markets.* London.

_____ . (1984). "Jord och fattigdom i Latin Amerika." *Ekonomisk Debatt,* no. 8, pp. 523-30.

Lundahl, M. and Lundius, J. (1987). "Olivorio - Peasant God: Folk Religion, Economy and Society in the Dominican Republic." *Mimeo,* Department of Economics and Department of History of Religions, University of Lund. Lund.

Lundahl, M. and Vargas, R. (1983). "Haitian Migration to the Dominican Republic," in: Lundahl (1983). A Spanish version was published in *EME-EME*, vol. 12, no. 68, September-October. Santiago de los Caballeros.

Lundahl, M. and Vedovato, C. (1988:1). "The State and Economic Development in Haiti and the Dominican Republic." *Mimeo*, Department of Economics, University of Lund. Lund.

Lundahl, M. and Vedovato, C. (1988:2). "The Structure of Land Ownership in Haiti and the Dominican Republic - Causes and Consequences," in: Mörner and Svensson (1989).

Machado Báez, M. A. (1955). *La dominicanización fronteriza*. Ciudad Trujillo.

Madruga, M. J. (1986). *Azúcar y haitianos en la República Dominicana*. Santo Domingo.

Magee, S. P. (1973). "Factor Market Distortions, Production and Trade: A Survey." *Oxford Economic Papers*, N.S., vol. 25.

_____. (1976). *International Trade and Distortions in Factor Markets*. New York.

Mañón, M. (1985). *Cambio de mandos*. Santo Domingo.

Marchetti, P. E. (1971). "El poder del intermediario-usurero en comunidades minifundistas y las cooperativas campesinas de San José de Ocoa." *Estudios Sociales*, no. 15, July-August-September. Santo Domingo.

Maríñez, P. A. (1984). *Resistencia campesina, imperialismo y reforma agraria (1899-1978)*. Santo Domingo.

Martin, J. B. (1975). *El destino dominicano: La crisis dominicana desde la caída de Trujillo hasta la guerra civil*. Barcelona.

Marx, K. (1977:1). *The Capital*. Moscow.

_____. (1977:2). "The Eighteenth Brumaire of Louis Bonaparte," in: Marx and Engels (1977).

_____. (1977:3). "The Class Struggles in France," in: Marx and Engels (1977).

Marx, K. and Engels, F. (1977). *Selected Works, Vol. I*. Moscow.

Meier, G. M. (ed.) (1976). *Leading Issues in Economic Development*. Third edition. New York.

Miller, W. (1968)."Focal Concerns of Lower Class Culture," in: Ferman et al. (1968).

Miller, R. L. (1982). *Intermediate Microeconomics: Theory, Issues, Applications*. Second edition. New York.

Millspaugh, A. C. (1931). *Haiti under American Control 1915-1930*. Boston.

Mörner, M. and Svensson, T. (eds.) (1989). *Third World Rural Societies in Transition: The Challenge of Regional History*. London.

Moya Pons, F. (1972). *La dominación haitiana 1822-1844*. Santiago de los Caballeros.

_____. (1980). *Manual de historia dominicana*. Barcelona.

_____. (1985). "The Land Question in Haiti and Santo Domingo: The Sociopolitical Context of the Transition from Slavery to Free Labor, 1801-1843," in: Fraginals et al. (1985).

_____. (1986). *Despues de Colón: Trabajo, sociedad y política en la economía del oro*. Madrid.

Moya Pons, F. et al. (1986). *El Batey: Estudio socioeconómico de los bateyes del Consejo Estatal del Azúcar*. Santo Domingo.

Munguía, G. A. (1975). "Transitional Stage in the Agricultural Sector: The Case of the Dominican Republic." Ph.D. thesis, Fordham University. New York.

Murphy, M. F. (1988). "Dominican Responses to the Contemporary World Sugar Crisis. "*Mimeo*, Museo del Hombre Dominicano. Santo Domingo.

Murray, G. F. (1974). "Selected Aspects of the Internal Marketing System of the Dominican Republic. "*Mimeo*, IICA. Santo Domingo.

Muto, P. (1976). "The Illusory Promise: The Dominican Republic and the Process of Economic Development, 1900-1930." Ph.D. thesis, University of Washington.

Myrdal, G. (1971). *Asian Drama*. Abridged edition. New York.

_____ . (1981). "Need for Reforms in Underdeveloped Countries," in: Grassman and Lundberg (1981).

Neary, J. P. (1978). "Dynamic Stability and the Theory of Factor-Market Distortions." *American Economic Review*, vol. 70.

_____ . (1980). "This Side of Paradox, or, in Defence of the Correspondence Principle: A Reply to Herberg and Kemp." *American Economic Review*, vol. 70.

Norvell, D. G. and Billingsley, R. V. (1971). "Traditional Markets and Marketers in the Cibao Valley of the Dominican Republic," in: Horowitz, (1971).

Norvell, D. G. and Wehrly, J. S. (1969). "A Rotating Credit Association in the Dominican Republic." *Caribbean Studies*, vol. 9, no. 1, April.

Nugent, J. B. and Yotopoulos, P. A. (1979). "What has Orthodox Development Economics Learned from Recent Experience?" *World Development*, vol. 7, pp. 541-54.

OIT (Oficina Internacional del Trabajo) (1975). *Generación de empleo productivo y crecimiento económico, el caso de la República Dominicana*. Geneva.

ONAPLAN (Oficina Nacional de Planificación) (1968). *Plataforma para el desarrollo económico y social de la República Dominicana (1968-1985)*. Santo Domingo.

_____ . (1980). *Hacia una política de empleo en la República Dominicana*. Santo Domingo.

_____ . (1981:1). *La situación del empleo en Santo Domingo y Santiago en Noviembre 1979*. Santo Domingo.

_____ . (1981:2). *Participación de la mano de obra haitiana en el mercado laboral: los casos de la caña y el café*. Santo Domingo.

_____ . (1982). *La situación del empleo en la zona urbana en Junio de 1980*. Santo Domingo.

_____ . (1983:1). *Estudio de base del sector agropecuario y forestal*. Santo Domingo.

_____ . (1983:2). *La situación de la infancia en la República Dominicana*. Santo Domingo.

_____ . (1983:3). *Estudio del sector salud-nutrición-fármacos*. Santo Domingo.

_____ . (1983:4). *El proceso de urbanización en la República Dominicana*. Santo Domingo.

_____ . (1984). "Primer Informe de la encuesta national de mano de obra rural, Octubre 1980," in: Secretariado Técnico (1984:2).

ONE (Oficina Nacional de Estadísticas) (1966). *IV censo nacional de población 1960*. Santo Domingo.

_____. (1971). *V censo nacional de población y vivienda 1970*. Santo Domingo.

_____. (1982:1). *VI censo nacional de población y vivienda 1981*. Santo Domingo.

_____. (1982:2). *República Dominicana en cifras*. Santo Domingo.

_____. (1983). *República Dominicana en cifras*. Santo Domingo.

Palmer, E. C. (1976). "Land Use and Landscape Change along the Dominican-Haitian Border." Ph.D. thesis, University of Florida. Gainesville.

Peña Batlle, M. A. (1954). *Política de Trujillo*. Ciudad Trujillo.

Pérez Minaya, R. (1985). "El ordenamiento del sistema cambiario: una propuesta." *Hoy*, 23 May.

Pessar, P. (1982). "The Role of Households in International Migration: The Case of US-bound Migrants from the Dominican Republic." *International Migration Review*, 16:2.

Peynado, F. J. (1909). *Por la inmigración*. Santo Domingo.

_____. (1919). "Deslinde, mensura y partición de terrenos." *Revista Jurídica*, no. 4. Santo Domingo.

Pierre-Charles, G. (1965). *La economía haitiana y su vía de desarrollo*. México, D.F.

_____. (1969). *Haiti: radiografía de una dictadura - Haití bajo el régimen del doctor Duvalier*. México, D.F.

Plant, R. (1987). *Sugar and Modern Slavery: A Tale of Two Countries*. London and New Jersey.

PNUD - PUCMM (Programa de las Naciones Unidas para el Desarrollo - Pontificia Universidad Católica Madre y Maestra) (1989). *Primera conferencia nacional sobre privatización y desregulación*. Santo Domingo.

Poyo, J. (1986). *Los bancos agropecuarios y la captación de depósitos*. Santo Domingo.

Price-Mars, J. (1953). *La République d'Haïti et la République Dominicaine: Les aspects divers d'un problème d'histoire, de géographie et éthnologie*. Port-au-Prince.

Primer censo nacional de la República Dominicana 1920 (1923). Santo Domingo.

Quezada S., N. A. (1981). "Endogenous Agricultural Prices and Trade Policy in the Dominican Republic." Ph.D. thesis, Purdue University.

Ramírez E., C. E. (1984). "Mercados financieros rurales: aspectos sociales." *Mimeo*, UCMM (Universidad Católica Madre y Maestra). Santiago de los Caballeros.

Ramírez, N. M. (1980). *Encuesta de migración a Santo Domingo y Santiago. Informe general*. Santo Domingo.

Rao, C. H. and Joshi, P. C. (eds.) (1979). *Reflections on Economic Development and Social Change*. New Delhi.

Redfield, R. (1955). *The Little Community*. Chicago.

Rivera, T. (1986). *Relación de los bienes e inversiones de Rafael Leonidas Trujillo Molina, esposa e hijos al día 5 de Julio de 1961*. Santo Domingo.

Rodríguez Demorizi, E. (ed.) (1955). *Invasiones haitianas de 1801, 1805 y 1822*. Ciudad Trujillo.

_____. (ed.) (1980). *Papeles de Pedro F. Bonó*. Barcelona.

Rodríguez Demorizi, E. (1982). *Seudónimos dominicanos*. Segunda edición. Santo Domingo.

Rodríguez, F. (1987). *Campesinos sin tierra*. Santo Domingo.

Rodríguez N., P. (1984). "La economía agraria, la pobreza y la población en la República Dominicana," in: Forum (1984).

Romain, J-B. (1959). *Quelques moeurs et coutumes des paysans haïtiens*. Port-au-Prince.

Rotberg, R. I. with Clague, C. K. (1971). *Haiti: The Politics of Squalor*. Boston.

Ross, L. (1982). "Evaluación del bienestar familiar: comparaciones especiales con respecto a Santo Domingo." *Revista de Estudios Económicos*, vol. I, no. 2, July-December. Santo Domingo.

Rostow, W. W. (1960). *The Stages of Economic Growth: A Non-communist Manifesto*. Cambridge.

Rybczynski, T. M. (1955). "Factor Endowment and Relative Commodity Prices." *Economica*, vol. 22.

Samuelson, P. A. (1979). *Foundations of Economic Analysis*. New York.

Sánchez de Bonilla, F. (1973). "Los problemas de los negros en la industria azucarera." *Mimeo*, Coloquio sobre la presencia de Africa en las Antillas y el Caribe. Santo Domingo.

Santos, B. (1980). "Una experiencia de desarrollo rural en las montañas de la República Dominicana." *Mimeo*, paper presented at a seminar in Turrialba, Costa Rica.

Schoenrich, O. (1977). *Santo Domingo, un país con futuro*. Santo Domingo.

Schultz, T. W. (1964). *Transforming Traditional Agriculture*. New Haven.

SEA (Secretaría de Estado de Agricultura) (1924). *Memoria de la Secretaría de Estado de Agricultura e Inmigración, Año 1923*. Santo Domingo.

_____. (1976). *Diagnóstico y estrategia del desarrollo agropecuario 1976-1986*. Santo Domingo.

_____. (1977). *Aspectos del empleo rural en la República Dominicana*. Santo Domingo.

_____. (1981:1). *Plan Operativo 1981*. Santo Domingo.

_____. (1981:2). *Plan Operativo, 1982*. Santo Domingo.

_____. (1981:3). *Estudio sobre uso de crédito en la República Dominicana 1978*. Santo Domingo.

_____. (1983). *El Cacaotalero*, no. 8 y 9, July-December.

_____. (1984:1). "El sistema de comercialización del cacao en República Dominicana." *Mimeo*. Santo Domingo.

_____. (1984:2). *El Cacaotalero*, no. 12, July-December. Santo Domingo.

_____. (1986). *Encuesta nacional sobre el uso de créditos agrícolas y pecuarios*. Santo Domingo.

SEA-IICA (Secretaría de Estado de Agricultura - Instituto Interamericano de Ciencias Agrícolas) (1977). *Diagnóstico del sistema de mercadeo agrícola en República Dominicana*. Santo Domingo.

_____. (1984). "Estudio de factibilidad de un proyecto para el fortalecimiento del sistema de mercadeo tradicional en la República Dominicana." Documento No. 5, *Mimeo*. Santo Domingo.

Secretariado Técnico de la Presidencia (1983). *Boletín no. 4*, July. Santo Domingo.

_____ . (1984:1). *Boletín no. 11*, February. Santo Domingo.

_____ . (1984:2). *Boletín no. 15*, June, and *Boletín no. 16*, July-September. Santo Domingo.

Seers, D. (1977). " 'Urban Bias' - Seers Versus Lipton" (IDS Discussion Paper 116), Institute of Development Studies, Brighton.

Segal, A. L. (1975:1). "Haiti," in: Segal (1975:2).

Segal, A. L. (ed.) (1975:2). *Population Policies in the Caribbean*. Lexington, Mass.

Seguino, S. (1987). "Report on the Impact of the Coffee Tax Reduction of 1984-1985." *Mimeo*, USAID. Port-au-Prince.

Sen, A. (1975). *Employment, Technology and Development*. Oxford.

_____ . (1981). *Poverty and Famines: An Essay on Entitlement and Deprivation*. New York.

SESPAS (Secretaría de Estado de Salud Pública y Asistencia Social) (1982). *Salud pública: cuatro años de Gobierno (1978-1982)*. Santo Domingo.

Shanin, T. (ed.) (1971). *Peasants and Peasant Societies*. Harmondsworth.

Sharpe, K. E. (1977). *Peasant Politics: Struggle in a Dominican Village*. Baltimore, Maryland.

Södersten, B. (1964). *A Study of Economic Growth and International Trade*. Stockholm.

Spitzer, D. C. (1972). "A Contemporary Political and Socio-Economic History of Haiti and the Dominican Republic." Ph.D. thesis, University of Michigan.

Squire, L. (1981). *Employment Policy in Developing Countries: A Survey of Issues and Evidence*. London.

Standing, G. (1981). *Labour Force Participation and Development*. Second edition. Geneva.

Stark, O. and Levhari, D. (1982). "On Migration and Risk in LDCs." *Economic Development and Cultural Change*, vol. 31, no. 1, October, pp. 191-196.

Streeten, P. P. (1970). "A Critique of Concepts of Employment and Underemployment," in: Jolly et al. (1973).

Taylor, C. L. and Hudson, M. C. (1972). *World Handbook of Political and Social Indicators*. Second edition. London.

Teilhet-Waldorf, S. and Waldorf, W. H.(1983). "Earnings of Self-Employed in an Informal Sector: A Case Study of Bangkok." *Economic Development and Cultural Change*, vol. 31, pp. 587-607.

Thomas, H. (1971). *Cuba: The Pursuit of Freedom*. New York.

Todaro, M. P. (1969). "A Model of Labor Migration and Urban Unemployment in Less Developed Countries." *American Economic Review*, no. 59, pp. 138-148.

_____ . (1981). *Economic Development in the Third World*. Second edition. New York.

Torres, M. (1988). "Haitianos, el otro infierno." *El País Semanal*, no. 583, 12 June, 1988.

Tun Wai, U. (1956). "Interest Rates in the Organized Money Markets of Underdeveloped Countries." *IMF Staff Papers*, vol. 5.

_____ . (1957). "Interest Rates Outside the Organized Money Markets of Underdeveloped Countries." *IMF Staff Papers,* vol. 6.

Turnham, D. (1971). *The Employment Problem in Less Developed Countries.* Paris.

Ugalde, A., Bean, F. and Cardenas, G. (1978). "International Migration from the Dominican Republic: Preliminary Findings from a National Survey." *Mimeo,* University of Texas. Austin.

"Ultima Hora" (1986). 10 February. Santo Domingo.

United Nations (1979). United Nations Economic and Social Council. Commission on Human Rights. Sub-Commission on Prevention of Discrimination and Protection of Minorities. "Question of Slavery and the Slave Trade in All Their Practices and Manifestations, including the Slavery-like Practices of Apartheid and Colonialism: Report of the Working Group on Slavery on its Fifth Session." *Mimeo,* New York.

_____ . (1980). "Patterns of Urban and Rural Population Growth." *Population Studies 68,* p. 24. United Nations, Department of International Economic and Social Affairs. New York.

_____ . (1982). *Yearbook of National Accounts 1980,* vol. 2. New York.

USAID (1981). *La República Dominicana: perfil ambiental del país. Un estudio de campo.* Santo Domingo.

_____ . (1989), "Microempresas in the Dominican Republic." *Mimeo.* Santo Domingo.

Vargas G., R. (1981). "Unemployment, Underemployment and Labor Imports in the Dominican Republic: A Sketch of Some Problems." *Ibero-Americana,* vol. 10.

_____ . (1987). "Marketing Agricultural Products in the Dominican Republic - Competition or Exploitation?" *Minor Field Studies Series,* no. 3, Department of Economics, University of Lund.

Vedovato, C. (1986). *Politics, Foreign Trade and Economic Development: A Study of the Dominican Republic.* London.

Vega, W. (1977). "El regimen laboral y de tierras en la primera República." *EME EME,* no. 30, May-June. Santiago de los Caballeros.

Veliz, C. (ed.) (1967). *The Politics of Conformity in Latin America.* Oxford.

Veloz Maggiolo, M. (1977). *Sobre cultura dominicana ... y otras culturas.* Santo Domingo.

Veras, R. A. (1981). "Legalidad e ilegalidad de los inmigrantes haitianos en R.D." *Ahora,* no. 943. Santo Domingo.

_____ . (1982). "El tráfico de braceros; forma de enriquecimiento oficial." *Ahora,* no. 945, 1982. Santo Domingo.

_____ . (1983). *Inmigración-haitianos-esclavitud.* Santo Domingo.

_____ . (1985). *Migración caribeña y un capítulo haitiano.* Santo Domingo.

Vincent, S. (1938). *Efforts et résultats.* Port-au-Prince.

Wallace, A. F. C. (1956). "Revitalization Movements." *American Anthropologist,* LVIII.

Weber, M. (1963). *The Sociology of Religion.* Boston.

Webster, C. C. and Wilson, P. N. (1966). *Agriculture in the Tropics.* London.

Welles, S. (1975). *La viña de Naboth: La República Dominicana 1844-1924. Tomo I y II.* Santo Domingo.

Wharton, C. R. Jr. (1962). "Marketing, Merchandizing and Moneylending: A Note on Middleman Monopsony in Malaya." *Malayan Economic Review*, vol. 7.

Wiarda, H. (1968). *Dictatorship and Development*. Gainesville.

Wingfield, R. (1966). "Haiti. A Case Study of an Underdeveloped Area." Ph.D. thesis, Louisiana State University. Baton Rouge.

Wipfler, W. L. (1978). "Power, Influence and Impotence: The Church as a Socio-Political Factor in the Dominican Republic." Ph.D. thesis, Union Theological Seminary. New York.

Wolf, E. (1966). *Peasants*. New Jersey.

World Bank (1978:1). *Dominican Republic, Its Main Economic Development Problems*. Washington, D.C.

_____ . (1978:2). *Economic Memorandum on the Dominican Republic*. Washington, D.C.

_____ . (1985). *Dominican Republic, Economic Prospects and Policies to Review Growth*. Washington, D.C.

_____ . (1986). *World Development Report, 1986*. Washington, D.C.

_____ . (1987). *Dominican Republic: An Agenda for Reform*. Washington, D.C.

World Council of Churches, Migration Secretariat (1980). *"Sold Like Cattle," Haitian Workers in the Dominican Republic.*. Geneva.

Worswick, G. D. N. (ed.) (1976). *The Concept and Measurement of Involuntary Unemployment*. London.

Yotopoulos, P. A. and Nugent, J. B. (1976). *Economic Development. Empirical Investigations*. New York.

Zuvekas, C. Jr. (1978). "Land Tenure, Income, and Employment in Rural Haiti: A Survey." *Mimeo*, USAID. Washington, D.C.

Series in Political Economy
and Economic Development in Latin America

Series Editor

Andrew Zimbalist

Smith College

Through country case studies and regional analyses this series will contribute to a deeper understanding of development issues in Latin America. Shifting political environments, increasing economic interdependence, and the difficulties with regard to debt, foreign investment, and trade policy demand novel conceptualizations of development strategies and potentials for the region. Individual volumes in this series will explore the deficiencies in conventional formulations of the Latin American development experience by examining new evidence and material. Topics will include, among others, women and development in Latin America; the impact of IMF interventions; the effects of redemocratization on development; Cubanology and Cuban political economy; Nicaraguan political economy; and individual case studies on development and debt policy in various countries in the region.

Index

373

Venezuela: Dominican
    immigration to 325
venta a la flor 199
ventas populares 144, 145
ventorillos 121, 122, 316
Ventura, Plinio 111n
veterinary sciences 109n
Vicini Burgos, Juan B. 162
villas miserias 307
Villa González 5, 9, 179n
voodoo 230, 231

wages: 16, 48n; average in rural
    areas 44; in cane-cutting 45,
    233, 234; in coffee-picking 46;
    constant real in the modern
    sector 60-61; differentials 46,
    50n; fixed 38; and labor
    shortage 45-46; and the
    presence of Haitian workers
    22; minimum 16, 48n, 76n,
    245n, 314, 319, 321, 323, 324,
    331, 333n; in the informal
    sector 331, 316-317; according

to regions 34; rural 22, 237,
    248, 264-265; within the sugar
    sector 216, 219, 227, 228, 233-
    234, 344; and work within the
    agricultural sector 46
Wessin y Wessin, Elias 232
Wharton, Clifton 135
Wingfield, Roland 228
Wolf, Eric 105n
wood-cutting: 85, 86, 87, 90, 156,
    266-267, 269-271, 290n; in
    order to clear fields 6, 7, 271;
    efforts to limit 269
work: defined 60-61
workers: categories of
    Dominican 36-37, 39;
    domestic 38; low productive
    61; migration affecting
    qualified 328
World Bank 29, 32, 142, 143, 201

zafra: 45, 52, 218, 221, 223, 224,
    225, 226, 233, 238, 242n, 344;
    dominicanization of 238, 242n
Zuvekas, Clarence 233